GLOBALIZATION AND NEW INTERNATIONAL PUBLIC WORKS AGREEMENTS IN DEVELOPING COUNTRIES

To my mother's soul,
To my father
To Rania, Youssef and Ahmed Ismail

Globalization and New International Public Works Agreements in Developing Countries

An Analytical Perspective

JUDGE DR MOHAMED A.M. ISMAIL
LLB, LLM, PhD, FCI Arb
Vice-President of the Egyptian Conseil d'Etat

Routledge
Taylor & Francis Group
LONDON AND NEW YORK

First published 2011 by Ashgate Publishing

Published 2016 by Routledge
2 Park Square, Milton Park, Abingdon, Oxfordshire OX14 4RN
711 Third Avenue, New York, NY 10017, USA

First issued in paperback 2016

Routledge is an imprint of the Taylor & Francis Group, an informa business

British Library Cataloguing in Publication Data
Ismail, Mohamed A.M.
Globalization and new international public works agreements
in developing countries : an analytical perspective.
1. Public works--Law and legislation--Developing
countries.
I. Title
344.1'2406-dc22

Library of Congress Cataloging-in-Publication Data
Ismail, Mohamed A.M.
Globalization and new international public works agreements in developing countries : an analytical perspective / by Mohamed A.M. Ismail.
p. cm.
Includes bibliographical references and index.
ISBN 978-1-4094-2796-4 (hbk)
1. Public contracts. 2. Government purchasing--Law and legislation. 3. Contracts (International law)
4. Arbitration and award, International. 5. Public contracts--Developing countries. I. Title.
K884.I83 2011
346.02'3--dc23

2011032861

ISBN 13: 978-1-138-25511-1 (pbk)
ISBN 13:978-1-4094-2796-4 (hbk)

Contents

List of Figures and Table

Figures

Table

About the Author

Dr Mohamed A.M. Ismail is a Vice President of the Egyptian State Council (*Conseil d'Etat*), Judge at the Court of Appeal (Contracts Circuit), Fellow of the Chartered Institute of Arbitrators (UK), Visiting Professor and PhD examiner in the Egyptian universities in International State Contracts and Arbitration, particularly on infrastructure projects, Lecturer at the Cairo Regional Centre of International Commercial Arbitration (CRCICA) and Arbitrator in International Construction Contracts disputes, particularly International Public Works Agreements. Dr Ismail was formerly a Senior Legal Advisor of HE the Egyptian Minister of Petroleum and represented the Egyptian government in state international business transactions in the oil and gas industry, especially in the United Kingdom with law firms such as Shearman Sterling, the international counsel to the Egyptian government. He was a Senior Legal Advisor of HE to the Egyptian Minister of Trade and Industry and formerly a Senior Legal Advisor of the Investment Sector in Egypt and represented the Egyptian government at the United Nations Conference on Trade and Development (UNCTAD), Geneva, for the Bilateral Investment Treaties (BITs) negotiations when developing states were involved.

Foreword

I have been honored to be invited to write a foreword to the latest book by Dr Mohammed A.M. Ismail. As Editor-in-Chief of *The International Construction Law Review* I had the advantage of having had a preview of his thoughts on "Globalization" and its impact on International Public Works Contracts, since we had been able to publish some of his papers. Now he has written a book on the subject. As readers will discover, the work is both bold in its concept and stimulating in its application. Dr Ismail writes from the point of view of someone who has a wide conspectus of legal, economic and cultural life both within and outside Egypt. That country is a good spring board to consider "Globalization" since, perhaps more than any other, it stands at what might be described as the junction between influences from Europe and the West, where concepts from the French Napoleonic code have been fused with indigenous norms by a catalyst of multi-faceted legal and cultural factors. Like many countries in similar positions Egypt therefore is in itself a striking instance of the effects of globalization, both cultural and legal. Since Dr Ismail examines "Globalization" as it applies in developing countries, it is sensible to start with Egypt which has grappled with it. However readers will also find helpful references to many other jurisdictions as the work is by no means confined to Egypt, but extends westwards along the North African littoral and eastwards as far as Oman.

Although law serves and reflects society Dr Ismail's study is not confined to legal influences but draws on a wide range of cultural and economic factors in order to discuss the direction in which the law may be heading. As Dr Ismail percipiently says:

> Globalization includes the flow of capital and many other tangible concepts plus intangible values, such as culture. Among these is legal culture. Legal culture has flowed from Anglo-American jurisdictions to civil law legal systems. Moreover, globalization has considerably influenced Egyptian legislature and judicial decisions taken by the Egyptian State Council (Conseil d'État) and the General Assembly for Legal Opinion and Legislation; the legal nature of the administrative contract, *le contract administratif*, has drastically changed.

So Dr Ismail's study begins with an overview of cultural and legal globalization before descending to consider its most interesting applications, for example, in Chapter 4 the effect of the concept of "public private partnership" in developing countries and in particular in France and Egypt. But the book also intriguingly reminds the reader of areas in which, in some countries, globalization has yet to make a significant impact, e.g. in certain techniques for dispute resolution. Dr Ismail's discussions may enable one to assess whether in certain areas a cautious approach is required to some elements of "Globalization". Some Western techniques for dispute resolution are overly formalistic or institutional in nature and ill suited for countries, especially in the Middle East where tradition and culture calls for every avenue of discussion, negotiation, assistance from outsiders to be fully exhausted, before embarking upon formal proceedings, including arbitration. There is, however, a real tension generated by the expectations fostered by the competition that leads to an International Public Works Agreement and the practice for domestic projects, whether in the public or private sector.

The book is ostensibly about International Public Works Agreements. Dr Ismail takes as given that "a contract cannot be described as a Public Works Agreement unless the object of the contract is real estate". However readers will discover that Dr Ismail's discussion is limited to such contracts as his exploration of the principles shows that they must be equally applicable to contracts for systems, such as wireless telecommunications, as they are to contracts in the classic public works form. For example, a recurring theme of the work is an investigation of the extent to which the French concept of the administrative contract is still, to use common parlance, "fit for purpose": how far can it be applied in today's world where contracts are no longer domestic. Dr Ismail pertinently recalls that, traditionally, the French approach was that a contract only was international if it related to a transaction beyond the national economic interest. Latterly however, the approach has been to look at the contractual arrangements and its substance to determine whether or not the contract is an international business transaction, i.e. if its conclusion or implementation or the status of the parties, whatever their nationality or domicile or the substance are connected to one or more jurisdictions or legal systems.

The work finishes with some helpful and also, in places, provocative conclusions which pull together the strands running through the work. Dr Ismail's introduction sets the scene:

> The legal globalization phenomenon is a fundamental factor behind the flow of the Anglo-American jurisdictions to Arab civil law jurisdictions in terms of International Public Works Agreements. Its new legal nature due to the new contractual clauses, new types of agreement, new legislative steps to maintain financial equilibrium and new trends taken by the judiciary in Arab countries to protect foreign investors is a direct effect of legal globalization. A direct result is that dispute settlement in the domain of International Public Works Agreements and state contracts considerably changed, regarding the fact that new mechanisms have appeared in the last two decades, particularly arbitration.

There is much of great interest in this book. Readers may not agree with everything that Dr Ismail has written but, thanks to him, they now have a wealth of material on which to base and to justify any disagreement. It is a work which I warmly commend.

Humphrey Lloyd
London,
July 2011

Preface

Cultural globalization nowadays plays a significant role in the flow of Anglo-American legal culture to Arab Middle Eastern civil law jurisdictions. The growth of construction and industrial projects in International Public Works Agreements has been considerable in recent decades in developing countries generally and in Arab Middle Eastern states in particular. In the light of economic developments in the Arab Middle East, International Public Works Agreements are increasingly playing a fundamental role in the infrastructure sector in the region. Current economic reforms in various Arab countries, following the change of political and economic ideologies from socialist to more market-led economies, particularly in North African states, was the motivation for countries such as Egypt, which changed the Egyptian Constitution in 2007, to open doors for Inward Foreign Direct Investment (IFDI) to the country.

Nevertheless, amendments to the constitution have not adopted a certain economic or political ideology to ensure that the electoral process – whether parliamentary or presidential – shall impose the proposed ideology chosen by the nation. This ideology will be changed from one decade to another according to the economic situation. The ideology adopted before the 2008 economic crises is certainly different from the one that is being adopted after the crises. It is worth mentioning that this flexibility, which currently is codified in the constitutional amendments, is reflecting a huge growth in Egyptian infrastructure and the influence of this trend in the North African states of Tunisia, Algeria and Morocco. These countries are codifying new legislation for the BOT (Build, Operate, Transfer), BOOT (Build, Own, Operate, Transfer) and PPP (Public Private Partnership) transactions and arbitration. Furthermore, some other countries, like Lebanon, Syria and Jordan, have made considerable steps in infrastructure developments through the International Public Works Agreements and codifying arbitration legislation as the main mechanism in dispute settlements between developing states and foreign investors in the international sphere. The Gulf States institutionalized the infrastructure industry decades ago through huge Engineering, Procurement, Construction (EPC) site agreements, various types of International Public Works Agreements such as BOO (Build, Own, Operate), BOT (Build, Own, Transfer) and BOOT (Build, Own, Operate, Transfer) and the modernization, liberalization and internationalization of arbitration legislation. These modifications in all Arab civil law legal systems were adopted in accordance with international instruments such as the United Nations Commission on International Trade Law (UNCITRAL) Model Law, which influenced all Arab legislation, and the Washington Convention (ICSID Convention) of 1965, as well as the 1958 New York Convention.

This study focuses on the international construction contracts, state contracts and arbitration in Arab Middle Eastern and North African countries, as most Arab jurisdictions were considerably influenced by the Egyptian legal system. Comparison with the French legal system will be made when appropriate, particularly on state contracts and arbitration. This book scrutinizes the French arbitration legislation as amended in January 2011 as the most recent legislative tool worldwide. It has long been clear that French legislation, as the leading civil law jurisdiction, supersedes party autonomy. The subject matter of this book deals with the new legal nature of states' infrastructure agreements. The legal term for these agreements in civil law jurisdictions is "International Public Works Agreements."

Where appropriate, it is of fundamental importance to refer to some Latin American jurisdictions, particularly Brazil and Argentina. The Latin American jurisdictions have valuable experience in terms of PPP legislation and dispute settlement in the infrastructure industry.

Appendices show the most recent trends worldwide and the most recent international instruments in the arbitration world in both theory and practice.

A fundamental question arises about cultural and legal globalization and the new legal nature of International Public Works Agreements in the light of new contractual clauses that are not known in the domain of *Le Contrat Administratif* theory in Arab civil law legal systems. New types of International Public Works Agreements such as BOT, BOOT and PPPs began to appear as a result of the impact of the new legal nature of the contract as new mechanisms in dispute settlement developed in Arab Middle Eastern countries. New means of dispute settlement in *Le Contrat Administratif* in civil law jurisdiction in the last two decades, particularly arbitration, are the direct result of cultural and legal globalization.

The book focuses on these issues in detail, with special reference to Arab arbitration legislation that was influenced directly by the UNCITRAL Model Law and the Egyptian Arbitration Act, as well as the Egyptian Civil Code and State Procurement Laws that were introduced decades ago.

The academic basis of the work is an extensive discussion of the new contractual clauses and new types of infrastructure projects. New arbitration legislation that began to appear in the Arab Middle Eastern developing countries was a direct effect of legal globalization. The book examines the Alternative Dispute Resolution (ADR) and other dispute settlement mechanisms that have a special significance in this context, particularly arbitration in Arab countries following the Egyptian legal system in terms of doctrine, legislation and litigation, with reference to the leading role of the Cairo Regional Centre of International Commercial Arbitration (CRCICA) in the region. The book examines the international standard forms of contracts and international instruments in terms of institutionalization of international commercial arbitration in a multicultural legal context. This monograph further explores the contractual characteristics of the International Public Works Agreements and their new forms in Arab Middle East countries.

Finally, international practices and national laws of developed and developing countries are assessed, providing conclusions and recommendations for the future.

Acknowledgments

This book started as views and thoughts in a few pages of the *International Construction Law Review*, and in some of my publications in the Middle East region in *International Construction Contracts Arbitration: State Contracts*. Despite the fact that these publications were preliminary perspectives compared to the theme and the contents of this book, they were significantly important as a start. I was most fortune to have His Honor Humphrey Lloyd QC, formerly judge at the Technology and Construction Court, the High Court of Justice and a former visiting professor at the Centre of Commercial Law Studies (CCLS), Queen Mary, University of London, supervising my previous work as editor-in-chief of the *International Construction Law Review*, as his constructive comments were of fundamental assistance to me in writing this book. I would like also to express my appreciation to the co-editor-in-chief Mr Douglas Jones. I would especially like to express my gratitude to Professor Chris Bovis, Professor of Law at the University of Hull and the editor-in-chief of the *European Public Private Partnership Law Review*, Berlin, Germany, for his valuable advice, comments and provocative discussions for a proposal of a table of contents for this book. Many thanks to His Excellency Judge M. Amin El Mahdi, former President of the Egyptian *Conseil d'Etat*, a distinguished arbitrator in The International Centre for Settlement of Investment Disputes (ICSID), The International Chamber of Commerce (ICC) and the Middle East region and formerly an international judge at The Hague International Criminal Tribunal for the former Yugoslavia for his considerable advice and remarkable discussions during the past years, which positively influenced my work in this book. Special thanks and sincere gratitude go to Ashgate's publisher for Law and Legal Studies, Alison Kirk, to whom I address my deep appreciation for her continual support, help, fruitful cooperation and constructive coordination. I strongly believe that without her continual and faithful meetings and discussions, this book would not have appeared. I would especially like to express my appreciation to Sarah Horsley for her cooperation and successful coordination, Jude Chillman and all of Ashgate's staff, particularly Adam Guppy and the editing staff who participated in this work.

I wish to express my appreciation to the following for their support in helping me to complete this project: the UNCITRAL staff in Vienna, Austria; the ICSID staff at the World Bank, Washington, DC; Vale Columbia Center on Sustainable International Investment, Columbia Law School; The Earth Institute, Columbia University, New York, particularly Professor Karl Sauvant, executive director; the staff of the Institute of Advanced Legal Studies (IALS), University of London, United Kingdom. I am grateful to the book *Comparative International Commercial Arbitration* by Professors Julian D.M. Lew QC, Lukas A. Mistelis and Stefan M. Kröll, published by Kluwer Law International, as the leading authority in arbitration law and practice worldwide. This book was a main source to enrich my thoughts and imagination in the art and science of International Commercial Arbitration during the writing process. My gratitude goes to the ICLR editorial board and the staff of the publisher, Informa. Many thanks, in particular, go to Catherine Lauder for her fruitful cooperation and faithful help during the last two years.

Last and most important, my sincere thanks and deep emotions go to my wife, Rania Adel Koura, LLM, USA, to whom I owe much for her warm support and endless feelings; to her goes my everlasting gratitude.

List of Abbreviations

AAA	American Arbitration Association
AC	Law Reports, House of Lords (Appeal Cases)
ADR	Alternative Dispute Resolution
All ER	All England Law Reports
Arbitration	The Journal of the Chartered Institute of Arbitrators
BITs	Bilateral Investment Treaties
BOO	Build, Own, Operate
BOOT	Build, Own, Operate, Transfer
BOT	Build, Own, Transfer
CA	Court of Appeal of England and Wales
CRCICA	The Cairo Regional Centre for International Commercial Arbitration
CIA	The Chartered Institute of Arbitrators
CIF	Cost, Insurance and Freight
Con LR	Construction Law Reports
EC	European Community
EPC	Engineering, Procurement, Construction
EPPPL	*European Public Private Partnership Law Review*
EU	European Union
FAA	United States Federal Arbitration Act
FDI	Foreign Direct Investment
FIDIC	*Fédération Internationale des Ingenieurs-Conseils*
FOB	Free on Board
GAFTA	Green and Feed Trade Association
HL	The House of Lords
IBA Rules	IBA Rules on the Taking of Evidence as Amended 2010
ICC	The International Chamber of Commerce
ICDR	The International Centre for Dispute Resolution
ICLR	*The International Construction Law Review*
ICSID	The International Centre for Settlement of Investment Disputes
IFDI	Inward of Foreign Direct Investment; Inflow of Foreign Direct Investment
LCIA	The London Court of International Commercial Arbitration
LMAA	London Maritime Arbitration Association
MITs	Multilateral Investment Treaties
Model Law	UNCITRAL Model Law on International Commercial Arbitration (adopted in June 1985 and amended in 2006)
New York Convention	The 1958 New York Convention on the Recognition and Enforcement of Foreign Arbitral Awards
OECD	Organization for Economic Co-operation and Development
PC	Privy Council
PCA	Permanent Court of Arbitration (The Hague)

PIL	The Swiss Private International Law
PPP	Public Private Partnership
RCADI	*Recueil des Cours de l'Academie de Droit International de la Haye*
Rev Arb	*Revue de l'arbitrage*
SCC	The Stockholm Chamber of Commerce Arbitration Institute
SIAC	Singapore International Arbitration Center.
State Council	*Conseil d'Etat*
UNCITRAL RULES	UNCITRAL Arbitration Rules as Amended 2010
UNCITRAL	The United Nations Commission on International Trade Law
UNCTAD	United Nations Conference on Trade and Development
UNIDEROIT	International Institute for the Unification of Private Law
Washington Convention	Washington Convention on the Settlement of the Investment Disputes between States and Nationals of Other States, 1965
WIPO	World Intellectual Property Organization

Chapter 1
Cultural and Legal Globalization: Social and Legal Phenomena

Cultural Globalization Phenomenon

Cultural globalization is a cultural socioeconomic phenomenon. The first element that was influenced by globalization was culture. Cultural interaction is the main outcome of the flow of ideas and values into developing countries. Culture represents a set of practices, values, beliefs and customs acquired by individuals as members of a distinctive society and resulting from interaction among people.[1]

Culture has reacted to globalization in two contrasting ways:

1. Acceptance of a new global culture.
2. Rejection of a total loss of cultural identity as each distinctive group of people strengthens localization.[2]

In fact, globalization, according to many authors, has two faces. As is stated above, with respect to the economic dimension of globalization, Stiglitz[3] refers to the understanding of globalization in some parts of the world:

> The current process of globalization is generating unbalanced outcomes, both between and within countries. Wealth is being created, but too many countries and people are not sharing its benefits. They also have little or no voice in shaping the process. Seen through the eyes of the vast majority of women and men, globalization has not met their simple and legitimate aspiration for decent jobs and a better future for their children. ... Even in the economically successful countries, some workers and communities have been adversely affected by globalization. Meanwhile, the revolution in global communications heightens awareness of these disparities. ... [T]hese global imbalances are morally unacceptable and politically unsustainable.

It is true that "Those who are discontented with economic globalization generally do not object to the greater access to global markets or to the spread of global knowledge, which allows the developing world to take advantage of the discoveries and innovation made in developed countries."[4]

It is argued that globalization is a debate with two different views, Universalism versus Territorialism, or Globalization versus Globaphobia. However, from the economic perspective of globalization, economists used to refer to "international economic integration" when discussing the growth of overseas transactions. Today, they refer to "globalization," which has become the

---

1 Stiglitz 2004. See also Stiglitz 2007; Snowdon 2007; Abdel-Wahab 2005, Vol. 8: 306.
2 Abdel-Wahab 2005: 364.
3 Stiglitz 2007.
4 Stiglitz 2007.

popular term. For example, in his article "The Globalization of Markets," published in the *Harvard Business Review*, May–June 1983, Theodore Levitt stated that a powerful force drives the world toward a converging commonality; that force is technology, and the direct result emanating from that is a new commercial reality.[5]

Culture is a very complex entity that in the age of globalization is seen to be torn between two powerful forces: "a centrifugal force" and "a centripetal force." The latter force works to facilitate cultural homogenization and the formation of a true global society that has dissolved all differences, while the "centrifugal force," under the influence of national movements and the fear of loss of identity, mitigates the impact of globalization by preserving local identities.[6]

In modern and civilized systems it is common to find high degrees of differentiation.

As society expands and increases in complexity, the degree of social and cultural differentiation develops to the point that, even for members of the same society, the only commonality is their humanity.[7]

It has been argued that cultural globalization is a form of cultural imperialism, as it tends to associate cultural cosmopolitanism with Westernization or Americanization. Yet the process of cultural interaction and globalization does not mean, in its true sense, that the world should be dominated by a single logic or culture. The process is one that aims to achieve mutual respect and trust and to search for common interests, values and principles. It is not a one-way process, but rather, a two-way interaction.

The Clash of Civilizations: Is It Real or Is It Co-ordinated?

In his famous thesis, Samuel Huntington pointed out that the world is far from being dominated by a single logic. He added that the great divisions where humans are concerned are cultural, rather than ideological or economic. The clash of civilizations will dominate global politics.[8]

Huntington divides the world into eight civilizations that are in potential conflict. These include Western, Confucian, Japanese, Islamic, Hindu, Slavic Orthodox, Latin American and African. He predicts that conflict and clash will occur among these civilizations in general and between the West and the Islamic–Confucian axis in particular.

Huntington's arguments are based on several reasons that are believed to have caused the clash:[9]

- Differences between civilizations are basic.
- Increases in cultural interaction raise the level of awareness of the differences among civilizations.
- Social change and economic modernization are weakening the status of the state as a provider of identity.
- Cultural characteristics and differences are less easily compromised and resolved than political and economic ones.
- Successful economic regionalism may reinforce civilization's consciousness.[10]

5 Snowdon 2007.

6 See Abdel-Wahab 2005: 364.

7 Abdel-Wahab, referring to Durkheim's opinion cited in Featherstone 1990.

8 Huntington 1996. Henry Kissinger described *The Clash of Civilisations* as "one of the most important books to have emerged since the end of the Cold War."

9 See Huntington 1996: 25.

10 Abdel-Wahab 2005: 367.

Huntington concluded that:[11]

> The futures of both peace and civilization depend upon understanding and cooperation among the political, spiritual and intellectual leaders of the world's major civilizations. In the clash of civilizations Europe and America will hang together or hang separately. In the greater clash, the global 'real clash', between civilization and barbarism the world's great civilizations with their rich accomplishment in religion, art, literature, philosophy, science, technology, morality and compassion will also hang together or hang separately. In the emerging era, a clash of civilizations is the greatest threat to world peace and an international order based on civilization is the surest safeguard against world war.

Criticism of Huntington's Thesis

Many scholars have criticized Huntington's views. Criticism arises because it is known that culture is a sharp-edged entity that is nowadays rationalized.

There are differences in civilizations and cultures, but to what extent? Are there no commonalities? Huntington argues that these different civilizations have to learn to co-exist with each other.

In fact, there are many similarities among civilizations as a result of the increased interaction among cultures.[12] Nowadays, globalization plays a significant role in enhancing comprehension between varied and diversified civilizations. This transnational cultural phenomenon will create coordination rather than political conflict.

Also, similarities and commonalities are increasing, but these are narrowing the constant gap of existing differences. It should be noted that the reason behind the two world wars of the twentieth century was not a consequence of the clash of civilizations.[13] At the outbreak of the First World War and again at the outbreak of the Second World War, globalization was not yet recognized. Today, the situation is totally different: globalization is currently enhancing the world atmosphere and is familiar to people from a diversity of civilizations.

Universalism Versus Territorialism (the Two Faces of Globalization)

The first modern protest against globalization took place in Seattle in December 1999; this was supposed to be the start of a new round of trade negotiations leading to further liberalization. Farmers in developing countries found that their jobs were threatened by the highly subsidized crops from the United States and Europe. Opposition to globalization came not only from developing states but also from developed countries. These protesters "did not accept the argument that, economically at least globalization would ultimately make everybody better off."[14]

The International Labour Organization and the World Commission on the Social Dimensions of Globalization, which was established in 2001, surveyed 73 countries on all continents except South Asia. In the United States and the European Union, the unemployment rate increased between

11 See Huntington 1996: 321.

12 Abdel-Wahab 2005: 367.

13 Ismail 2010b: 49.

14 Stiglitz 2007: 7.

1990 and 2002. The commission also found that 59 per cent of the world's people were living in countries with growing inequality, and only 5 per cent lived in countries with declining inequality. In brief, globalization may have helped some countries to increase their gross domestic product (GDP; the total sum of the goods and services produced, usually in one year), but it did not help most of the people in these countries.[15] It is worth mentioning that there are many forms of a market economy. The American model differs from the Japanese model and from the European social model. It is argued in developed countries that globalization has been used to advance the "Anglo-American liberal model." Moreover, wages in the United States have been stagnant for more than a quarter of a century, and incomes are as high as they can be partly because Americans work far longer than their European counterparts. In the developing world, there is strong resentment that globalization has been used to advance a version of market economics reflecting corporate interests that are to be found in huge parts of the developed world.[16]

It is doubtless that development progresses from levels of subsistence agriculture toward light manufacturing and urbanization and then to high-tech services. More than half the world not only has a foothold on the development ladder but it is actually climbing it. This ascension is evident in rising personal incomes and the acquisition of goods such as cell phones, television sets and scooters. Progress can also be monitored through rising life expectancy, falling infant mortality rates, rising educational attainment and increasing access to water.[17]

It is of fundamental importance to realize why a vast gap exists between rich and poor today. It is appropriate to return to the very recent period of human history when this divide emerged. The past two centuries constitute a unique era in economic history, a period referred to as growth by Jeffrey Sachs, an eminent modern economist.[18] In conclusion, all regions such as Western Europe, Eastern Europe, the former USSR, the United States and Canada, Latin America, Japan, Asia and Africa, were poor in 1820. However, economic progress has been universal, and today's rich regions have experienced by far the greatest economic progress.[19]

There are three goals of development strategy that are shared globally. First, it is recommended that development strategy be developed and adopted on a global scale, and that sustainable technologies allow us to combine a high level of prosperity with lower environmental impacts. Second, stabilization of global populations is appropriate, particularly populations in the poorest countries, in order to combine economic prosperity with environmental sustainability. Third, it is the duty of the developed world to help the poorest countries to escape from the poverty trap. These three goals – environmental sustainability, population stabilization and ending extreme poverty – are the essence of the promises of the new millennium.[20]

It is true that the latter goals are not only the essence of the new millennium but also the essence of globalization. Protesters of globalization should note that mutual cooperation between developed countries and developing states may directly lead to a global consensus of understanding among various civilizations to mitigate cultural controversies and poverty. In light of the new technology that substantially changed life in recent decades and improved ordinary citizens' lifestyles in both developed and developing countries, a fundamental factor of a globalized and harmonized world emerges.

---

15 Stiglitz 2007: 8.
16 Stiglitz 2007: 91–100.
17 Sachs 2005: 19.
18 Sachs 2005: 27.
19 Sachs 2005: 29.
20 Sachs 2008: 31–2.

Legal Globalization Phenomenon

Law is a social science that performs an important role as an essential mechanism fulfilling the requirements of all human societies. On the one hand, law reflects and represents the mirror image of a society, determines its common interests and reflects its cultural traditions.[21] On the other hand, globalization has had its influence on various human societies, breaching cultural barriers through the flow of commodities, capital, people and intangibles such as culture and values from one country to another.

Information technology developments during the last two decades have facilitated the globalization process and intensified cultural interaction, especially legal cultural interaction among legal institutions in the entire world. Rigid and traditional legal patterns and traditions began to accept modifications and enhancements. Some of those patterns began to deteriorate while others created a new legal system with new characteristics as a result of cooperation among legal cultures.[22] Despite globalization movements and the flow of a new legal culture to the legal systems of developing countries, as well as to their socioeconomic structure and social traditions, the author strongly believes that some areas can still preserve their original national identity. The latter concept applies to most developing countries, particularly in the areas of family law and in social traditions in Middle Eastern societies, as well as in other developing countries. Religious beliefs and social customs practised in these countries are not influenced by cultural globalization in the socio-legal domain. Regardless of minor religious and social controversy among nationals in developing countries in areas of family law, conservative legal social cultures in Middle Eastern societies impose the same traditions and customs on the domain of human family relations.

On the other hand, legal matters that are considerably influenced by legal cultural globalization, such as the Administrative Contract Theory (*Le Contrat Administratif*), maintain some of their basic features. It is true that penalties and sanctions stipulated in the Administrative Contract Theory have not changed to date in civil law jurisdictions, even with the existence of new trends aimed at the modernization and internationalization of the traditional Theory of Administrative Contracts.

Accordingly, it can be said that the rigid patterns of administrative contracts, as well as their substance and exorbitant features, have significantly changed over the last decades in civil legal culture, especially where infrastructure agreements with foreign private entities are concerned. These new legal patterns such as the introduction of International Public Works Agreements; Build, Operate, Transfer (BOT) – Build, Own, Operate and Transfer (BOOT) – and Public Private Partnership (PPP) transactions posed the start of a new era in Egyptian legal culture – one with unique, liberal mechanisms and stipulations.

Legal cultural globalization has had its influence on legislation, litigation and the contractual regime of the administrative contract (in developed countries such as France and in developing countries such as Brazil, Egypt and Tunisia). For instance in 2004, France issued Decree No. 559, which has changed to a great extent the legal nature of the administrative contract (*Le Contrat Administratif*), and Brazil promulgated new PPP legislation. The latter legislation was enacted mainly to increase the inflow of foreign direct investments (IFDI) in the infrastructure sector. The Arbitration Act No. 27 of 1994 in Egypt and the PPP new legislation that is currently promulgated by the Egyptian Parliament by Law No. 67 of 2010 are the direct result of legal globalization. The situation in Tunisia is markedly progressing in the area of infrastructure projects through PPPs

21 Stiglitz 2004, 2007; Snowdon 2007.

22 Ismail 2010b: 54.

and the exploitation of natural resources such as oil and gas with cooperation from European Mediterranean countries across the Mediterranean Sea. It is of fundamental importance to refer to Latin American states, which have new legislative policies toward encouraging foreign direct investment (FDI) in the infrastructure sector.[23]

Despite the above-mentioned facts, states still maintain their roles as the employers, regulators and supervisors of these new types of contracts, although nowadays these roles are limited. In developed civil law jurisdictions, and especially in France as a leading civil law country, the state (*L'Administration*) still maintains its role to a great extent. It supervises the PPP contract as an administrative contract and still has the authority to exercise its unilateral powers through penalties (e.g., penalty for delay and unilateral termination of the contract – *La Résiliation Administrative*).

Despite some states' controversial attitudes toward the private sector and the trend toward the encouragement of FDI in the infrastructure sector, the latter trend is expected to open doors to the private sector to participate positively in economic life. The private sector has to increase its role in building, financing systems and operating infrastructure projects related to public utilities in developing states. This approach is particularly relevant to some Middle Eastern and North African states that have been the victims of socialist ideologies and state interference in various economic activities in recent decades.

The expansion of the private sector's role in Egypt is codified by the constitutional amendments in 2007 that reject socialism and Marxism. These ideologies were adopted by the 1971 constitution. The new constitutional modifications, nevertheless, adopted no specific ideology; they provided the opportunity for presidential and parliamentary elections to determine the necessary political and economic ideology to be followed during each presidential or parliamentary term. This flexible trend is a direct result of cultural globalization and the influence of a free market economy policy on the national socioeconomic culture.

In conclusion, as the eminent economist Adam Smith pointed out, the role of the state is confined to basic and fundamental functions.

Cultural Globalization and the New Public Economic Law

Cultural globalization has influenced social life and economy and has considerably affected legal cultures of civil law. State international business transactions and the traditional Administrative Contract Theory were subject to the flow of liberal and global perspectives. The state in its transactions is not in an equal bargaining power with other private entities. Hence, administrative contracts include exorbitant clauses, such as the right of the administrative authority to amend or terminate a contract unilaterally. Further, the state may also unilaterally impose certain penalties upon the other contracting party. These may include a penalty for delay (liquidated damages in common law jurisdictions) and rescission of the contract (*La Résiliation Administrative*) as well as the forfeiture of deposits (performance bonds). The impact of legal cultural globalization is significant in the development of the domain of international administrative contracts, especially International Public Works Agreements. New clauses have appeared in these contracts, including stabilization and arbitration clauses. The contractual regime has undergone various changes,

23 FDI has significantly increased in Latin America, particularly before the economic crises of 2008, in Brazil and most Latin American developing states in infrastructure projects and after promulgation of the 2004 PPP Brazilian Act. For details, see: Monteira De Barros 2009, Part 2: 180–81.

especially with respect to the new types of International Public Works Agreements concerning infrastructure projects, such as BOOT contracts and PPP agreements. The main target of these new contractual mechanisms aims to finance, build and operate infrastructure projects (public utilities) in developing countries.

Legislation has appreciably developed in the area of PPPs and in the granting of concessions for infrastructure projects and public utilities. In developed jurisdictions, France issued Decree No. 559 (2004) for regulating PPPs in the French legal system. The French *Conseil d'Etat* rejected cases in order to annul the PPP decree as it is legal and not violating the *Principe de Légalité* and affirmed the legality of PPP transactions in the country.[24] In Latin American countries, there was a considerable trend to promote PPPs and grant concessions through legislation and to encourage IFDI, particularly in Brazil and Argentina. The PPP legislation of Brazil of 2004 is the consequence of developments and enhancement of investment policies in the country.

Regarding North African states, it is worth mentioning that Egypt promulgated Laws Nos. 100 of 1996, 229 of 1996, 3 of 1997 and 22 of 1998 amending old existing legislation such as Law No. 129 of 1947 granting concessions for public utilities and Law No. 61 of 1958 granting concessions related to the exploitation of natural resources and public utilities. Four new laws pertain to the electricity sector, the roads sector, specialized ports, civil aviation and airports. The latter laws are a real revolution in administrative contracts and state international administrative transactions. Further, Lebanon and Tunisia have made significant progress in the growth of new PPP infrastructure transactions.[25]

State Procurement Laws in Egypt were enhancements and modifications to the law concerning contract price. New amendments grant the administration the authority to review contract prices every three months. The administration can exercise this power in cooperation with the contractor, pursuant to certain stipulations and parameters stated in Law No. 191 of 2008,[26] amending State Procurement law in Egypt.

It is also true that the Arbitration Act 1994 and its amendments by Law No. 9 (1997) created some considerable changes to the Administrative Contract Theory, especially contracts concluded by and between the state and foreign private entities. The same situation exists in most Arab jurisdictions such as the Jordanian Arbitration Act 2001, Tunisian Arbitration Act 1993, Omani Arbitration Act 1997 and other arbitration rules incorporated in Codes of Civil and Commercial Procedures in Lebanon, the United Arab Emirates and Qatar.

Liquidated damages have new trends under State Procurement Law No. 89 of 1998 in Egypt, as well as in litigations by State Council (*Le Conseil d'Etat*) courts, even though they are of a punitive nature under the penalty for delay clause.

In conclusion, cultural and legal globalization has influenced civil law legal culture in Arab countries, especially concerning international administrative transactions and contracts entered into by and between the state and foreign private entities. Public utility projects and International Public Works Agreements (infrastructure projects) attract special emphasis. The entire legal regime of legislation, litigation and contractual regime was influenced by these transnational phenomena. Where state international transactions were concerned, a set of new rules and international customs has emerged from common law jurisdictions to the legal culture in developing states and created a new branch of public law in these countries. This branch of law is the Public Economic Law and

---

24 Ismail 2010c.

25 Hanafi and El Dardiry 2010: 432–47.

26 Ismail 2010a.

is a result of the new changes in PPPs, granting concessions, state procurement law amendments, liquidated damages, equity and new arbitration legislation.

This branch of law was well known in France but has only recently begun in Egypt, a developing country. Lately, few academic studies[27] in Egyptian doctrine have begun to focus on this new branch, which is considered to be of fundamental importance for administration and foreign private entities.

27 Ismail 2010c.

Chapter 2
Definition of International Public Works Agreements

Definition and Characteristics

In view of the global changes in civil law legal culture, International Public Works Agreements are many and varied. Changes in International Public Works Agreements impose significant forms and mechanisms on normal types of contracts. Despite the latter changes, jurisdictions indicate that traditional International Public Works Agreements still maintain some basic features. These features have not changed to date despite the influence of cultural and legal globalization on state international business transactions. It is appropriate at this stage to refer to the definition in accordance with comparative law.

The goal of the International Public Works Agreements is to fulfil public interests "*Utilité Générale.*" This was settled a long time ago in French doctrine and jurisprudence[1] and in most Middle Eastern civil law legal systems.[2] In identifying these contracts it is appropriate to discuss the main features of the contracts in the comparative doctrine.

Object of Public Works Agreements Must Be Real Estate

A contract cannot be described as a Public Works Agreement unless the object of the contract is real estate. In Middle Eastern countries, a contract is usual for the building of a barrage, a dam, a bridge, an airport, an underground railway, or other kind of construction. French and Egyptian jurisprudence as well as Syrian Civil Code[3] require assurance that public works are genuine.[4]

Purpose Must Be for Public Interest

Public Works Agreements concern real estate that is owned by a public entity. If the real estate belongs to a private entity, a construction contract is not considered a Public Works Agreement and consequently is not an administrative contract. However, this concept has been changed by the French *Tribunal des Conflits*, which considers the transaction a Public Works Agreement if it is

1 De Laubadère, Venezia et Gaudement 1995, Tome II: 436; De Laubadère, Moderne et Delvolvé 1983–1984: Tome 1. Chabanol et Jouquelet 1994, Tome 1: 15; Dufau 1988: 58; Chapus, 1995: 484; Brard 1994: Ch.1, p. 147; Auby et Bon 1995: 188. In French jurisprudence, see: TRIB-Confl. 2 Mai 1988, *Caisse D'Assurance Mutuelle du Bâtiment*, Rec. LEBON,1088; TRIB-Confl. 11 Octobre 1993, *Société Central Siderurgique Richemount*.

2 In Arab civil law jurisdictions, see: El Tamawy 1991: 125; El Sharkawy 1995: 106; Amin 1992: 174; Helmy Fahmy n.d.: 111; El Hassan 1997: 7.

3 Syrian Civil Code, Articles (612–20).

4 De Laubadère, Venezia et Gaudement 1995, Tome II: 435; Sabiani 1995: 18; in the Egyptian Conseil d'Etat: Legal Opinion on 28 May 1950, p. 868; Administrative Appeal Court, Case 284 05 Judicial Year (8), 104, 23 December 1956.

implemented by a public juristic entity for real estate belonging to a private entity when its purpose is in the public interest.[5]

Public interest disclosure is fundamental in identifying a contract as a Public Works Agreement as the French *Conseil d'Etat* maintains that, as such, it is not a public utility but a contract that is aimed at public interests.

In most cases, public works and public interests are two interrelated concepts. In socialist jurisdictions in the last decades, building houses for citizens was a public works process.

Public Interest is Independent of the Financial Interest of the Administration

An administration's financial interest is not considered as public interest and stipulates that works are public works. French jurisprudence decided the latter principle and added that if administration was aimed at many purposes and one of those interests is financial, it is not important to consider financial interest a justification to identifying construction works as public works. The crucial point is the motive behind the transaction, resolved by and between the administration and the private entity. If the transaction is aimed at achieving public interest, it is a Public Works Agreement. Further, French jurisprudence elaborated public works interest to include all logistics related to public works, excluding equipment and including all related services such as consultant agreements with consultancy firms.[6]

Performance Must Be for the Account of a Public Juristic Entity

If the contract is concluded by and between a public juristic entity and a private entity, even if the real estate is owned by a private entity, it is sufficient in matching public works for the contract, if the public juristic entity is party to the contract. Works may be carried out in the interests of the public juristic entity. In the latter scenario, the project must be under direct supervision by the public juristic entity, or the project asset shall be transferred to the public entity after a certain period of time.[7]

International Elements

The existence of international elements in International Public Works Agreements is important in terms of consequences, such as being applicable to transactions and dispute settlement mechanisms. The concept of *Le Contrat Administratif* does not recognize, in civil jurisdictions, the application of foreign substantive law, particularly in domestic Public Works Agreements.[8] However, in International Public Works Agreements and in the light of legal globalization, developing states tend to accept the application of foreign law to International Public Works Agreements on very rare occasions. The existence of an international element hereby justifies the latter scenario. Large transactions involving foreign private entities try to increase IFDIs, which are fundamental factors in enabling developing states to accept the application of foreign substantive law rather than their national laws to International Public Works Agreements.

5 Tribunal de Conflits, 24 Octobre 1942; Sirey 1945, see El Tamawy 1991: 125.

6 El Tamawy 1991: 129.

7 De Laubadère, Venezia et Gaudement 1995, Tome II: 439; Auby et Bon 1995: 192; Chapus 1995: 482; Chabanol et Jouquelet 1994: 17; Dufau 1988: 65.

8 Ismail 2003b: 33.

Economic Criterion

For international contracts, the economic criterion can be discharged through the transnational ebb and flow of goods. The French *Court de Cassation*, held on 2 April 1934, maintained that a contract is international if it is related to a transaction beyond the national economic interest. On 27 April 1964, the same court held that it is more appropriate to scrutinize the contractual arrangement and its substance to determine whether the transaction is an international business transaction.[9] French doctrine and jurisprudence recognize the concept of the transaction that is generally related to international trade law. This has more flexible criteria.[10]

Legal Criterion

A contract can be an international transaction if it is connected to one or more jurisdictions or legal systems. As Batiffol pointed out, the contract is an international transaction if its conclusion or implementation or status of the parties, whatever their nationality or domicile, or its substance, are connected to one or more jurisdictions or legal systems. In Arab Middle Eastern doctrine, a contract is considered international if it contains an international element.[11]

A question raised by the doctrine was that the criteria stipulated by Batiffol related to various factors of law and/or facts – where parties' nationality or their domiciles are legal factors that have particular dimensions related to facts. Conversely, the place of conclusion and place of implementation are two factors related to facts but, at the same time, have various legal implications. Another question arises: Is the list stipulated by Batiffol an exhaustive list, or is it an example of the legal elements that can be connected to more than one jurisdiction or legal system?[12]

Batiffol's list cannot be considered exhaustive, but by way of analogy, various facts related to law and/or facts can be added to justify the internationalization of a transaction. It is hereby confirmed that the existence of an international element is crucial to identify Public Works Agreements as an international business transaction. This is a direct result of cultural and legal globalization. Consequently, the application of foreign substantive law seems to be acceptable on rare occasions in civil law jurisdictions by some developing states. It is clear that the existence of a foreign private entity as an international element to the contract has significant change (*Le Contrat Administratif*) for concepts in legal culture.

Complex Long-term Agreements

One of the main characteristics of the International Public Works Agreement is that it is a complex long-term agreement. When developing states enter into an agreement with a private foreign entity for the implementation of an infrastructure project, the contract duration is for some years. This contract includes several undertakings for many contracting parties. Further, it includes undertakings between a public juristic entity and a main contractor on the one hand, and other

9 Ismail 2003b: 34.

10 Loquin 1977: 106–14; Fouchard 1970: 74.

11 Batiffol 1968: 564. In Arab doctrine, see Riad 1988: 245; El Sharkawi 1992.

12 Kassis 1993: 24.

commitments that are to be undertaken by the main contractor and subcontractors on the other. Lending banks and insurers are also involved.

In most Middle Eastern civil law jurisdictions, the main contractor assigns his or her financial rights to the lending financial institutions.[13] Contractual relations in International Public Works Agreements are complex. Dynamic relations are implicated, not static, since all parties are interacting in several interrelated transactions.

As the contract may be a long-term agreement, an efficient dispute settlement mechanism should be in place. A mechanism for stabilization of prices during the contract's duration is fundamental. Prices of reinforcement iron, cement, wood and some services such as electricity are unpredictable, particularly in developing countries. These prices are constantly changing because of inflation and the depreciation of local currencies. Moreover, costs related to change of legislation such as taxes and tariffs need a mechanism to compensate the foreign contractor promptly in case of cost increases.

Definition

An International Public Works Agreement in developing states can be defined as "a contractual agreement between the administration and a foreign private entity for the implementation of works related to real estate for the account of public juristic entity and for the purpose of public interests, in a particular period of time and for a certain price."[14]

This definition reflects the existence of an international element in an agreement related to infrastructure projects. This element has its significance in the transaction.

Differentiation

Supply Agreements

Supply agreements have considerable importance as they are an integral part of the construction process in most cases. In civil law administrative doctrine, public works, concessions and supply agreements in the domestic or in the international sphere are called "the Nominated Administrative Contracts." Accordingly, supply agreement was defined by the Egyptian *Conseil d'Etat* decisions as "an agreement between a public juristic entity and a private entity by which the private entity undertakes to supply movables to the public entity that are necessary to the management and operation of the public utilities for a certain lump sum."[15]

The subject matter of the supply agreement is the delivery of goods and movables, and it is subject to the Egyptian *Conseil d'Etat* judicial jurisdiction as it is an administrative contract pursuant to Egyptian State Procurement Law No. 89 (1998) and arises in most Arabic jurisdictions.

A supply agreement is a sale-of-goods contract that is necessary to the public utility; a Public Works Agreement is a construction contract as outlined in the above explanation.[16]

---

13 For example, pursuant to Articles (303–5) of the Egyptian Civil Law, "Assignment."

14 Kadiki 1979: 68–72.

15 Appeal Administrative Court, Egyptian Conseil D'Etat, 16/12/1956, Case No. 1609 of Judicial Year 10; Appeal Administrative Court, 17/3/1957, Case No. 1827 of Judicial Year 10.

16 El Sanhoury 1989; El Sharkawy 1995: 200.

Contractual undertakings differ from supply agreements to public works and from supply agreements to concessions.

Public Works Agreements and Concessions

Concession agreements in civil law jurisdictions are similar to Public Works Agreements and are the oldest type of administrative contracts. A concessionaire undertakes services for public utilities for a certain tariff to be paid by end-users (the public), which is the contract price. Doctrines in French and Arab Middle Eastern jurisdictions define the concession agreement traditionally as a contract by which the concessionaire (a private entity) undertakes for the administration the operation and management of a public utility under private sector responsibility and assumes the risk for a tariff paid by an end-user.[17] Modifications of the latter definition by French doctrine impose modernization to the concept of exploitation of public utility. The tariff that is to be collected by the private sector as a latter tariff is determined according to the financial success of public utility operations and exploitation.[18]

The Egyptian Civil Code, as Arab Middle Eastern civil legislation[19] based on Napoleonic Codes, stipulates in Article (668) that a concession for public utilities is an agreement aiming at the management and operation of a public utility. The concession usually has economic dimensions. This contract is made by and between the administration and a private entity for the operation of the public utility for a specific period of time. The Administrative Appeal Court defined the concession for public utilities as an administrative contract that has special jurisdiction, and its main purpose is the management of the public utility. The basic feature is that the concessionaire assumes risks and bears costs of the project. The contract price is the tariff to be collected by the end-user – "the public." The court confirmed that the main purpose of contractual mechanisms in the concession agreement is to maintain the application of the fundamental principle in *Conseil d'Etat* jurisprudence in France and civil law jurisdictions. This principle is the continuity and regularity of public utilities (*Déroulement des Services Publics avec Régularité et Continuité*).[20]

Concession agreements differ from the direct operation by the way public utilities were commonly allocated during socialist decades in Northern African countries. The management and operations of public utilities have taken liberalizing and modernizing steps toward a new era of public utilities and advanced services, offering new technologies that are friendly to the environment for end-users in developing countries.

Concessionary contractual obligations can be diversified. Administration has the right to supervise the construction and operation of public utilities. In traditional concessions, which do not include an international element, administration has the right to amend an agreement unilaterally, including its financial aspects (e.g., tariffs). This was done in most Arab Middle Eastern jurisdictions. The latter trend has currently, in the light of legal globalization, been rejected, particularly in transactions with an international element.

Accordingly, a concessionaire has rights, in the light of the concession agreement clauses, to ensure that the administration has to maintain financial equilibrium of the contractual process during performance regarding its power to amend the agreement unilaterally.[21]

17 De Laubadère, Moderne et Delvolvé 1983–1984, Tome 1: 2842–85; El Sharkawy 1995: 123.

18 De Laubadère, Moderne et Delvolvé 1983–1984, Tome 1: 2902–91; El Sharkawy 1995: 124; El Tamawy 1991: 108.

19 For instance, see Syrian Civil Code, Articles (634–9).

20 Appeal Administrative Court, case No. 146 of Judicial Year 8, 25/3/1956, 259.

21 Ismail 2003b: 48–49.

Conversely, rights and obligations of the Public Works Agreements differ from those of concessions.[22] This will be clarified in a later stage of this book.

Concessions for Natural Resource Exploitation

In most Arab countries, concessions for natural resource exploitation are subject to a constitutional stipulation that must be promulgated by legislation on a case-by-case situation (123) in the Egyptian Constitution, as amended (2007), stipulates that a concession for the exploitation of natural resources (e.g., oil and gas) must be through legislation promulgated by the Egyptian Parliament.[23] A public juristic entity cannot enter into an agreement with any other entity concerning an agreement for natural resources exploitation without legislation promulgated by the Egyptian Parliament. This situation is completely different from the International Public Works Agreements and concessions for public utilities.[24]

Legal Globalization and New Types of Contracts in Civil Law Legal Culture[25]

Traditional Turnkey Contracts

In large infrastructure projects, the International Public Works Agreements have the so-called turnkey contract (*Clé-en-Main*) as described in civil law countries.

The American expression *turnkey* appears to have emanated originally from the United States in the oil industry. In both civil law and common law jurisdictions, discussions on *Clé-en-Main* seem to share a similar attitude.[26]

The contractor undertakes the performance of all contractual obligations until the completion of all construction works (stipulated in a construction site agreement). In some cases, the contractor undertakes the supply of equipment in these types of contracts in fulfilling engineering, procurement and construction (EPC) contracts. The turnkey contract is the oldest type of infrastructure agreement in developing countries. Administration in developing states enters into a contract with a foreign private entity for the implementation of the entire works as stipulated in the agreement. Consequently, the main contractor enters into subcontracting

22 On rights and obligations in Public Works Agreements, generally in French doctrine, see: El Attar 1955: 122; Dufau 1988: 159; Kadiki 1979: 162. In Arab doctrine, see: El Sanhoury 1989; El Hassan 1997; El Sharkawy 1995; Ismail 2003b: 157.

23 In similar Arab constitutions, see: generally, Libyan Constitution, Kuwaiti Constitution, Sudan Constitution, Morocco Constitution, Syrian Constitution, Omani Constitution and Lebanese Constitution.

24 Ismail 2010d: 119.

25 This section deals with types of International Public Works Agreements. It is appropriate to refer to the difference with standard forms of contracts such as JCT, ICE, GC/Works/1 and FIDIC forms of contracts that are now widely dominant in the international construction industry. For more elaboration and analysis of the latter forms, see Uff 2009: 348–66, and particularly for FIDIC forms of contracts, see Bunni 2005. In civil law, countries where detailed legislation is usually to be found cover the rights of the parties to construction projects; meanwhile, in the UK and most common law jurisdictions, obligations, rights and liabilities of the parties are set out in detail in contracts. Standard forms of contracts are not found in most civil law countries in domestic public works agreements; conversely, in International Public Works Agreements it is likely that developing states in the Middle East region adopt FIDIC forms of contracts in many infrastructure projects. For detailed study of the JCT standard form, see Turner 1994.

26 Duncan Wallace 1986: 34.

agreements with various subcontractors to achieve final completion at the stipulated time. Some of those subcontractors are local contractors hired for the feasible implementation of works, and they are employed as they are technically capable of carrying out their contractual undertakings.

The main contractor in these types of contracts undertakes, among other tasks, the transfer of technology and technical assistance and gives a guarantee to provide quality works in an agreed time.[27]

BOT and BOOT Agreements and Various Legislations

BOT and BOOT are well-known techniques to grant a concession from administration to a concessionaire for the construction, financing, operation, management and maintenance of a facility for a certain period of time, as stipulated at the time of the agreement and without costs[28] to the administration.

International Public Works Concession is defined in civil law jurisdictions by De Laubadère as an agreement by which a public juristic entity designates a private entity for the construction of public works and the receipt of financial rewards by a certain tariff to be collected from end-users (the public).[29]

BOT/BOOT agreements are projects by which a private entity (either national or international) undertakes to construct a public utility, controls its management and operation during the contract period and then delegates it to the state. Some scholars define the BOT/BOOT process as a mechanism for financing infrastructure projects in the light of the above undertakings.[30] Both types of project have become more popular in the last decades in developing countries, where the private sector undertakes to finance infrastructure projects to reduce budget deficit, supplies advanced technologies and assigns the know-how of these technologies to developing states. Moreover, these agreements increase foreign currency flow owing to the increase of IFDI to developing countries, enhancing the quality of services offered to end-users and reducing unemployment rates as new projects create more job opportunities. The private sector undertakes contractual obligations in these types of projects for various sectors of society, such as railways, highways, energy, electricity, specialized ports, airports and civil aviation.

In socialist decades in Middle Eastern countries, particularly North African states, the private sector was not allowed to participate in infrastructure projects involving finance or in public utility projects. It is worth mentioning the case of Egypt, as a leading country in North Africa. At that stage, the situation was uncertain, pursuant to the Egyptian Constitution 1971 (before amendments in 2007). This constitution, before amendments, adopted Marxist and socialist ideologies.[31] Egypt began a promising program of economic reform by 1987 through adopting new policies to encourage and increase the role of the private sector in economic life, reduce the role of the public sector and state monopoly over major economic activities and increase the IFDI. In 1991, the Egyptian government promulgated Law No. 203 of 1991. This legislation concerned the liberalization of the public sector administration (state-owned companies) as

27 Chafiek n.d.: 34.

28 Bateson 1997; Westring 1997; Verveniotis 1994; Stein 1994.

29 De Laubadère, Moderne et Delvolvé 1983–1984, Tome 1: 309. The same definition was adopted in Arab doctrine by El Sharkawy 1995: 157.

30 In Arab Middle Eastern doctrine, see Gad Nassar 2002: 38; Sarie El Din 2001: 44; Sarie El Din 2002: 3.

31 El Sharkawy 1993: 106.

a preliminary step toward total privatization. The latter legislation, after promulgation by the Egyptian Parliament, faced opposition by the socialist and associated movements in the country. The legislation was subject to an appeal of unconstitutionality before the Egyptian Supreme Constitutional Court. The Supreme Constitutional Court is a mechanism for judicial review of constitutionality of legislation and is widely publicized by the Egyptian Parliament for its compatibility and consistency with the Constitution. In one of the leading judgments, which positively affected the economic reform process, the court affirmed the private sector's role as a genuine participant in economic life, as well as the parallel role of state-owned entities, particularly in infrastructure and public utilities. The Supreme Constitutional Court of Egypt held that this legislation is in coordination with the Egyptian Constitution of 1971. In the light of this vision, the privatization process achieved its economic goal because of the legitimate and legal regime adopted by the Egyptian government, which was approved as a constitutional legal framework.[32]

Types of Private Sector Participation

Private sector participation in infrastructure projects has various characteristics. There are management and operation agreements, lease agreements, service agreements, concession agreements, financing, construction, operations, personal agreements and privatization agreements. Projects carried out through BOT or BOOT commence with parallel arrangements such as an invitation to tender pursuant to state procurement laws of developing states and feasibility studies. Feasibility studies have, among other dimensions, environmentally friendly technologies which are of fundamental importance to developing states in adopting certain precautions necessary for climate-change effects. This is necessary to raise the level of awareness of climate-change challenges for these states. The next step is to select contractors from various bidders. This is subject to state procurement legislation in developing countries, particularly in Arab Middle Eastern and North African countries that adopted the same legislative policy of the Egyptian State Procurement Law. The latter legislation and executive regulations adopt the same concepts as have French legislation, and as have previous and current administrative regulations (*Le Cahier des Clauses Administratives Générales*).

The following steps[33] concern the formulation of the Project Company. This is usually a joint stock company pursuant to company laws in Middle Eastern Arab and North African countries. Concession or licensing agreements are known for financing agreements and arrangements with lenders. Construction site agreements, equipment supply, operation and insurance contracts are crucial to the process. The public works are carried out by the contractor until final completion and the public utility is ready for commercial exploitation. Works should be technically accepted by the administration according to tender stipulations.

The public utility is now at the development stage by the foreign investor. This will last for the life of the agreement. At the end of the contract, the foreign contractor has to transfer the assets of the property to the state. Equipment and technology must be in good condition both quantitatively and qualitatively in order to satisfy the end-user of the public utility services. Moreover, assets must be free from mortgages or any such rights to third parties.

---

32 The Egyptian Supreme Constitutional Court, Constitutional Case No. 7 of Judicial Year No.16, session 1/2/1997.

33 For details of these steps in Arab Middle Eastern doctrine and practice, see Sarie El Din 2001: 67.

Is BOOT Agreement a Public Works or a Concession Agreement?

Many questions have arisen in relation to the legal nature of the BOOT agreement. Some Arab commentators recommend that if the contract price is paid by the administration, the contract is not a concession for public works in civil law jurisdictions; rather, it is a traditional Public Works Agreement.[34] If the contract price is paid by the foreign contractor or by lending banks or international financial institutions, it is still an International Public Works Agreement. The legal nature of the contract justifies the latter option and aims at the construction of an infrastructure project or public utility and the operation of the public utility for a certain price, whether it is to be paid by the administration or a tariff to be paid by the end-user. In BOOT agreements, operations are in line with the construction of works, so the contractor can collect the costs that financed the projects. In all scenarios, the goal of the administration is running the public utility regularly and continuously: *Déroulement des Services Publics avec Régularité et Continuité.*[35]

The vision adopted by Andre de Laubadère[36] is that the Public Works Concession is an agreement by which a private entity undertakes the execution of works until final completion and financial costs from tariffs have been honored by end-users. The account of the public juristic entity is criticized, as the contract is a type of International Public Works Agreement. If contractors collect the contract price from end-users, they are only agents for the state to collect the above-mentioned tariffs and deliver payments to themselves instead of the state delivering payment to them. This legal mechanism is subject to agency contract stipulations in civil codes in Arab Middle Eastern jurisdictions (e.g., in the Egyptian Civil Code Articles (699–717). It can also be interpreted through assignment (Articles (303–305) of the Egyptian Civil Code and Articles (303–314) of the Syrian Civil Code).

It is appropriate to refer to the differences between BOOT and traditional concession agreements in Arab Middle Eastern countries. Projects' assets are owned by the private sector during the contract's duration. The private sector finances, designs, constructs, operates and maintains the public utility. This concept does not exist in traditional concessions, as the state still owns the project during the duration of the contract. Traditional concessions are administrative contracts by nature in Arab Middle Eastern doctrine and legislation;[37] meanwhile, most Arab doctrines[38] recommend that BOOT agreements are civil or commercial transactions. A BOOT agreement, generally, does not include exorbitant clauses and does not refer to any exceptional legal regime.

BOOT Characteristics

A BOOT agreement is a complex, long-term agreement, a type of International Public Works Agreement. It has similar, but not identical, contractual arrangements and agreements that conform to an International Public Works Agreement. It maintains the highest of dynamic contractual relationships with the main contractor, subcontractors, lenders, insurers, operation companies and others. This is a turnkey contract, and the main contractor assumes risks and is liable for defective work or technology and all related works on behalf of subcontractors. Further, the extent to which risk can be passed through to the construction contractor may depend on market parameters and nature, as well as the role of the construction contractor in the project. The process, which involves

34 El Sharkawi 1992: 109.

35 Egyptian Appeal Administrative Court, case No. 146 of Judicial Year 8, 25/3/1956, 259.

36 De Laubadère, Moderne et Delvolvé 1983–1984, Tome 1: 309.

37 Syrian Civil Code, Articles (634–9).

38 Sarie El Din 2001: 30, 22.

placing on the contractor as much construction risk as possible by the project company under the concession agreement, is commonly referred to as "back-to-backing."[39]

The quasi-arbitral role of the engineer, previously in the *Fédération Internationale Des Ingenieurs-Conseils* (FIDIC) form of contracts, is said to have deteriorated.[40] Contractors may be obliged to offer an unconditioned (on demand) Performance Bond.[41]

It is now appropriate to refer in summary to the legal regime governing BOOT transactions in the Egyptian legal system. BOOT transactions are of fundamental importance to understanding the current situation of International Public Works Agreements and PPPs in the Middle East.

Traditional Concession Agreements and BOOT Transactions

The legal regime governing the grant of concessions in public utilities is governed by the Concession Law for Public Utility No. 129 of 1947 and the Concession Law for the Exploitation for Natural Resources No. 61 of 1958. The latter law is concerned with granting concessions in exploration and exploitation of oil, gas and natural resources pursuant to (123) of the Egyptian Constitution. Both laws were promulgated more than half a century ago. In fact, dynamic contractual relationships need rapid changes and modifications rather than static ones. However, Egyptian legislators have realized that these old laws are not applicable to BOOT transactions and that they contradict the character of BOOT. BOOT transactions are not suitable under administrative contracts, nor are they compatible with the administrative contract *(Le Contrat Administratif)*. Accordingly, by the late 1990s, the Egyptian Parliament promulgated four new laws in the field of granting public utility concessions through BOOT agreements. These are laws No. 100 of 1996, No. 229 of 1996, No. 3 of 1997 and No. 22 of 1998, concerning the granting of BOOT concessions in electricity, public roads and highways, airports and civil aviation and specialized ports.

The new legislation included various modifications and enhancements to the existing legal regime, governing the grant of concessions in public utilities. The concession period has increased from 30 years in the previous two laws to 99 years (as a cap) in the four laws. The state plays a limited role in the contractual process; it is the technical and financial supervisors who have control over the entire process. It cannot unilaterally amend service prices offered by the concessionaire, as is the case in traditional concessional legislation. Service prices to end-users are subject to contractual clauses, as is the consent of the foreign contractor, rather than regulatory clauses that can be amended unilaterally by the state.[42] State intervention in the contractual process in BOOT agreements is very limited compared with the old regime in traditional concession agreements as concluded by and between the state and domestic contractors. The aim of current legislation is to satisfy the economic expectations of foreign contractors at the time of tendering and preparing technical and financial feasibility studies, especially as these are long-term agreements which, from the contractor's perspective, necessitates the maintenance of financial equilibrium during the span of the contract, which may last for many decades. Some of the fundamental legislative policies behind the promulgation of the current four laws aim at encouraging private foreign entities to enter into international infrastructure project tenders announced by the Egyptian government. Moreover, the aim of the policies in encouraging major foreign entities in the sector is to generate further FDI, as Egypt is a developing country that started intensive infrastructure developments

39 Scriven and Pritchard 1999: 161.

40 Nicklish 1990: 322; Bunni 1997: 155. See also Bunni 2005.

41 For more elaboration in practice, see Jarvin, Derains and Arnaldez 1994: Case No. 3790.

42 For the regulatory clauses that can be unilaterally amended by the state in Arab doctrine, see El Sharkawy 2003: 65.

more than three decades ago. It is worth mentioning that there is an essential need to promulgate new legislation for BOOT transactions for all sectors in the country, as well as detailed executive regulations that are compatible with each sector's needs.

Finally, Law No. 22 of 1998 concerning specialized ports included both procedural and substantive rules. Procedural rules concerning contractor selection are both competitive and transparent. The most substantive adjustment, as is stated above, is the increase or ceiling of the BOOT concession duration not to exceed 99 years. These developments were important in the Egyptian legal system, as the old Concession Law (which is applicable to other infrastructure sectors) stipulates a cap for concessions not to exceed 30 years (Law No. 129 of 1947).

Despite partial developments in Egyptian legislation in BOOT transactions, a complete set of legislative and regulatory rules is still needed. Partial legislation concerns some sectors, as is stated above; meanwhile, other sectors require a new legislative policy which needs to be adopted.

Legal Framework of International Public Works Agreements

Legislative Rules

International Public Works Agreements are subject to state procurement laws in civil law jurisdictions, particularly in Middle Eastern developing states. A clear example is the Egyptian Public Procurement Law No. 89 of 1998 and its Executive Regulations. State Procurement Law includes all procedural rules and some substantive rules of an administrative contract. All civil codes of Arab Middle Eastern states are based on Napoleonic Codes and were influenced by Egyptian legislation. International Public Works Agreements are governed by Article (648) and the following articles of the Egyptian Civil Code in case of lack of any stipulations in the State Procurement Law, as this legislation embodies few substantive rules (e.g., *La Résiliation Administrative*, Forfeiture of Performance Bond, and so forth). Meanwhile, all substantive rules are included in the civil law code.

It is worth mentioning that international treaties that developing states have ratified are an integral part of the internal legal system of the latter states. Most constitutions of developing states stipulate that international treaties, after ratification from parliamentary states, are valid legislation in the internal legal system (e.g., Article (151) of the Egyptian Constitution).

Executive Regulations and "Le Cahier des Clauses Administratives Générales"

French legislation issued *Le Cahier des Clauses Administratives Générales Applicable aux Marchés Publics de Travaux (CCAG)* on 21 January 1976 and the current version in 2009.

Doctrine identified that these clauses by their legal nature were of a contractual character for the contractor and of a regulatory character for the administration.[43] Moreover, there are certain results to be concluded from these clauses:

First, it is fundamental to refer to these clauses in the Public Works Agreement in order for them to be part of the contract, so that the administration and the contractor can count on them. Second, if the contracting parties referred to a particular "*Cahier des Clauses*" at the time the agreement was made, these clauses are applicable to the contract, even if they were amended later. These clauses are of a contractual nature.

43 De Laubadère, Venezia et Gaudement 1995, Tome II: 468–9.

These clauses include technical rules related to Public Works Agreements such as construction works or maintenance and other agreements.

Contract and Appendices

The contract is the document by which parties agree to undertake their contractual obligations. The contract and appendices include all contractual arrangements and steps from the invitation to bid and all contractual processes until final completion, maintenance and guarantees. A crucial question arises as to whether the contract clauses in civil law jurisdictions supersede the State Procurement legislation and Executive Regulations. Do the latter rules (as they are legislative and regulatory) supersede party autonomy expressed in the contract? The answer is that autonomy partly supersedes legislative and regulatory rules to the extent that the contractual clauses are not contrary to mandatory rules and public policy.[44]

FIDIC form of contracts (1999) adopted the same vision as Article (1/5), which stipulated the relevance of document priority to the contract clauses, to acceptance letters, answer of letter to bid, private conditions, general conditions, specifications, drawings and any documents constituting an integral part of the agreement.

Administrative Jurisprudence

Since the rules of Administrative Law and Administrative Contract Theory are not codified in most civil law jurisdictions, the Egyptian court (*Conseil d'Etat*) has played an important part in codifying these rules since 1946, the date when the *Conseil d'Etat* was established. There are some legislative and regulatory rules concerning administrative contracts in Egypt, particularly the rules and executive regulations of State Procurement Law, but the Egyptian *Conseil d'Etat* had to codify various substantive and procedural rules decades ago. This shows the critical role that administrative jurisprudence has in civil law jurisdictions. Substantive theories such as *hardship* and *Le Fait du Prince dans les Contrats Administratifs* in administrative contracts were created by *Conseil d'Etat* judgments following the French *Conseil d'Etat*.[45]

Despite the leading role of jurisprudence in civil law jurisdictions, the rules established by the Supreme Administrative Court in Egypt or by the General Assembly for Legal Opinion (*Fatwa*) and Legislation or by courts in Arab Middle Eastern jurisdictions are not mandatory. Courts in these states are not obliged to follow these decisions when resolving disputes.

International Customs and International Arbitral Awards

International arbitral awards are of considerable importance in constituting the legal framework of International Public Works Agreements. The International Chamber of Commerce (ICC), the International Centre for Settlement of Investment Disputes (ICSID), the London Court of International Commercial Arbitration (LCIA) and the Cairo Regional Centre for International Commercial Arbitration (CRCICA) are some of the main arbitral institutions worldwide. Arbitral awards issued under the umbrella of any of those arbitral institutions are distinguished sources

44 The Egyptian *Conseil d'Etat*, the General Assembly for Legal Opinion (*Fatwa*) and Legislation, Legal Opinion No. 100, 20/3/1985, file No. 47/2/350, 294.

45 De Laubadère Venezia et Gaudement 1995, Tome II: 469. In Arab Doctrine see Badawi 1994: 98; Raslan 1994: 61; Kamel Leila 1969: 109; Elbana 1992: 83; El Hassan 1997: 23.

of the legal regime of the International Public Works Agreements. Moreover, standard forms of contracts such as the FIDIC form of contracts – which was drafted by the *Fédération Internationale des Ingenieurs-Conseils* play an important role in drafting agreements between developing states and foreign private entities.

However, international arbitral awards and standard forms of contracts do not encompass compulsory or obligatory rules that should be followed by developing states.

Doctrine

Doctrine in civil law jurisdictions, particularly in Arab Middle Eastern states, has important implications for parliaments that act as legislator, as well as for states that administer rules and draft agreements for public works in a domestic and international capacity. Doctrine underlines judicial precedents and jurisprudence decisions and can criticize policies and legislation. Since administrative law is not codified in Egypt, *Le Conseil d'Etat* analyzes doctrine decisions and comments in view of the theoretical and practical reality of jurisprudence decisions and their impact on infrastructure. Doctrine has several dimensions in the spheres of legal, economic and international investment law. These scrutinize international community requirements and international organizations such as the Organisation for Economic Co-operation and Development (OECD) and the United Nations Conference on Trade and Development (UNCTAD), and adopt new policies in the light of an organization's reports, profiles and directives.

Chapter 3
Legal Nature of International Public Works Agreements[1]

Domestic Public Works Agreements

In the domestic domain, traditional Public Works Agreements have the rights to administrative contracts (*Le Contrat Administratif*). This chapter examines traditional administrative contract theory (*Le Contrat Administratif*) and discusses the new contractual regime of the International Public Works Agreements, particularly the new clauses to the contract in the light of cultural and legal globalization. The latter clauses impose a new legal nature for International Public Works Agreements that directly affect this transaction to a great extent.

"*Le Contrat Administratif*" in Civil Law Legal Systems[2]

It is appropriate to refer to the characteristics and stipulations of "*Le Contrat Administratif*" in civil law legal systems since it seems unique in state contracts comparative law. The theoretical and conceptual values of *Le Contrat Administratif* existed in French doctrine and jurisprudence decades ago.

Le Contrat Administratif in France and Egypt

The notion of "*Le Contrat Administratif*" or "administrative contract" is unique in civil law legal systems. The contract must be concluded by and between a public juristic entity on the one hand and a private entity on the other. It must be for the benefit of one or more of the public utilities, and it must include excessive clauses. French and Egyptian doctrine and *Le Conseil d'Etat* in civil law legal culture recognize it as *Les Clauses Exorbitantes.*[3]

---

1 © Informa UK Limited. This chapter first appeared in *The International Construction Law Review* in [2010] 27, 3, 363–74 and is reproduced by kind permission of the publishers and editors.

2 In English law there is no such formal distinction between public (administrative) and private contracts. The ordinary law of contracts applies equally to all persons and institutions whether they are in the public or private sectors. However, in substance, it may on occasions be important to distinguish the two sectors where public bodies are subject to rules that are not applicable to private sector; see: Samuel 2010.

3 See the leading authority on administrative contracts in civil law legal culture decades ago: De Laubadère, Moderne et Delvolvé 1983, Tome 1: 150, 211 *et seq.*; Richer 1995: 80; in Egypt: El Tamawy 1991: 88 Badawi 1994: 54; El Sharkawy 2003: 14; Supreme Administrative Court, case No. 559, session, 24/2/1968; case No. 2184, session, 21/2/1987; and case No. 3128, session 24/1/1995; The General Assembly for Legal Opinion *(Fatwa)* and Legislation, Legal Opinion No. 403, session 21/3/1990, dated 11/4/1990.

One of the fundamental principles that govern state contracts, in theory and practice, is the principle of *Principe du Déroulement des Utilitiés Publiques avec Regularité et Continuité*, which means that public utilities must be run regularly and uninterruptedly. Decades ago, the latter principle largely influenced judicial precedents in France and Egypt as it is established in civil law legal systems.[4]

Public Juristic Entity Must Be Party to a Contract

As state contracts are one of the means whereby states (the administration) run public utilities, it is well known in administrative law that the administration can run the state regularly through state contracts or administrative decrees (*Actes Unilatérales*).[5] Hence, the state must be party to the contract through one of its public juristic entities (e.g., ministries, public corporations or governorates). A public juristic entity may constitute territorial, industrial and/or commercial corporations. Thus, the state is represented in the contractual relationship through its public juristic entities.

As De Laubadère points out,[6] this principle stipulates that a public juristic entity must be party to the administrative contract. It is *Le Critère Organique* that represents the administrative contract, and it is fundamental for the contract to have this clause.

If the contract is concluded between more than two parties, it is sufficient that one person to the contract is a public juristic entity.[7]

If the contract is concluded between private persons, it is a private contact unless this private person is representing a public juristic entity.[8] If so, the contract is deemed to be an administrative contract.[9]

A logical perspective implies that administrative contract rules govern public authorities' activities. Consequently, contracts concluded between concessionaire and end-users in concession agreements are not administrative contracts. A contract between a concessionaire and the government (a public juristic entity) is an administrative contract. Another example is the doctrine of contracts between contractors and subcontractors. The latter contracts are civil contracts.[10] However, jurisprudence and doctrine in France and Egypt provide for objective stipulations in order to classify the contract as administrative.

Contracts Should Run One of the Public Utilities

Principe du Déroulement des Utilitiés Publiques avec Regularité et Continuité is a fundamental principle in French and Egyptian doctrine and jurisprudence. It is one of the main features of the administrative contracts that are provided for the benefit of public utilities that are managed

4 De Laubadère, Moderne et Delvolvé 1983–1984, Tome II, 706; Richer 1995: 86; El Tamawy 1991: 124. Badawi 1994: 142–84; Supreme Administrative Court, 28/12/1963, Judicial Year 9, 324, referred to in Badawi 1994: 145. See also: Appeal Administrative Court, 2/6/1957, Judicial Year 11, 494.

5 In analyzing distinctions between state contracts and "*Les Actes Unilatérales*" in French doctrine, see: De Laubadère, Moderne et Delvolvé 1983–1984, Tome 1: 3, 55 *et seq*., and in old French doctrine for this traditional concept: Duguit 1927, Tome 1: 367; Ferrari 1975: 215 *et seq*.; for further elaboration, see: Moderne 1975: 505 *et seq*. In Arab doctrine see the leading authority, El Tamawy 1966.

6 De Laubadère, Moderne et Delvolvé. Tome 1. 1983–1984: 163.

7 De Laubadère, Moderne and Delvolvé Tome 1. 1983–1984: 164.

8 De Laubadère, Moderne and Delvolvé Tome 1. 1983–1984: 168.

9 Badawi 1994: 59.

10 Badawi 1994: 59.

by public juristic entities.[11] Although the principle is fundamental, the definition of "public utility" is a matter of debate. However, in view of long-settled jurisprudence doctrines, public utility may concern any activity that cannot be exercised by the private sector and has to be exercised, organized and supervised by the administration. This interpretation is too broad to consider contracts made by economic public juristic entities as administrative contracts.[12]

The administrative contract in civil law jurisdictions is one of the fundamental means of organizing public utilities. This contract is not regarded as a source of obligation to the contracting parties as a case in civil law transactions. It is rather the main tool that maintains regular and sustained organization and management of public utilities. Pursuant to the *Conseil d'Etat*'s historical judgment of February 8, 1918, the Egyptian doctrine[13] made reference to the remarks of Corneille – the *Commissaire d'Etat* – that if the contract is designed to run one of the public utilities, the state, unlike private entities, does not have an equal bargaining power with private entities. The state does not seek to attain personal interests, as individuals may resort to, rather, its target rests with achieving public interest for the benefit of end-users and generally its citizens.

In socialist times, the Supreme Administrative Court in Egypt held that:

> The source of the administration's privileges is not only derived from the administrative contract clauses but is also attributed to the nature of public utilities and how the contracts are connected to public utilities with the necessity that the public utility is running regularly and uninterruptedly. The administration is exercising these privileges in administrative contracts, even if it is not stipulated at the latter contracts.[14]

Le Principe du Déroulement des Utilitiés Publiques avec Régularité et Continuité is a leading principle in French and Egyptian jurisprudence and doctrine, and there are significant results in this respect that elucidate the unilateral and unlimited powers exercised by the state. From the individual's perspective, this principle is in interpreting the hardship *L'imprivision, Le Fait du Prince dans le Contrat Administratif* theories, and contractual equilibrium concepts.

In addition to the above-mentioned principle, the rule of changing and amending public utilities from time to time explains the authorities' unilateral dedication to the administration and to amending the contracting party's obligations *vis-à-vis* the state without the former's consent.[15]

Excessive Clauses (Les Clauses Exorbitantes)

As the two contracting parties herein do not have an equal bargaining power, it is mandatory that a state contract, "the administrative contract," should include excessive clauses. Therefore, such a

11 It is well known in the civil law legal culture that public juristic entities upon running public utilities are representing people and receive their power from people, as public utilities are the property of the nation. To scrutinize this view in the Egyptian and Arab legal systems, see The General Assembly for Legal Opinion (*Fatwa*) and Legislation, Legal Opinion No. (8), Dated 4/1/1997, session 18/12/1996, file No. (68/3/1932).

12 De Laubadère, Moderne et Delvolvé. Tome 1. 1983–1984: 60; Richer 1995: 41; Badawi 1994: 62; and the leading authority in Arab doctrine, El Tamawy 1991: 429–32.

13 El Tamawy 1991: 429.

14 The Supreme Administrative Court in Egypt, session 19/12/1981, case 194, Judicial Year 24; see also: session 17/6/1972, Judicial Year 17 and El Tamawy 1991: 430.

15 The Supreme Administrative Court, session 30/6/1957, case 983 of Judicial Year 7; session 20/4/1957, Judicial Year 2; El Tamawy 1991: 422–3.

contract may include a penalty delay clause that implies liquidated damages (*Pénalité de Retard*), forfeiture of performance bond or administration's right to rescind the contract unilaterally (*La Résiliation Administrative*).

The state can, to a great extent, exercise unlimited powers in administrative contracts, enabling it unilaterally to amend, terminate or rescind contracts (*Le Contrat Administratif*). The administrative contract either includes these excessive clauses that can be exercised unilaterally by the state or it can refer to certain administrative sets of rules (e.g., *Le Cahier des Clauses Administratives Générales*) in France, or to the State Procurement Law in Egypt promulgated by Law No. 89 of 1998 and its executive regulations issued by Decree No. 1367 of 1998 of the Ministry of Finance.

It is essential to adopt public law mechanisms that are *Les Clauses Exorbitantes*. The latter can be scrutinized from the substance of their contract and contractual clauses. These clauses confirm the parties' intentions to adopt public law stipulations. The above-mentioned public stipulations fall short of recognizing the administrative nature of the contract. More than a century ago, the French *Conseil d'Etat* had taken into account, and, in particular, in the *Terrier* case in 1903,[16] a reservation that was of paramount importance at the time when it decided that the contract must include excessive clauses in order to be considered as administrative.[17] In the latter case, this judgment distinguished between public administration (*gestion publique*) and private administration (*gestion privée*). In the latter case, public utilities may be subject to private and civil law rules; meanwhile, public law rules are applicable to the cases where public utilities operate through public administration mechanisms. Decisions of *Le Conseil d'Etat* and *Les Tribunaux des Conflits* maintained this vision for decades until present times.[18]

Conclusion

Administrative contracts have advantages and rights because of the manner in which public utilities are administered and the regularity and continuity these contracts impose to public utilities. This special nature was imposed pursuant to the constitutional stipulations in both the Egyptian and French legal systems. Consequently, administrative contract stipulations were adopted by the *Conseil d'Etat* in both countries, as explained, to satisfy administrative needs and to maintain the regular operation of public utilities.

16 For more details and comments about this leading case, see: Badawi 1994: 76–8.

17 See: comments on this historical case, Badawi 1994: 76–7.

18 *Département de Maine-et-Loire*. c.e. 11 Nov. 1910, D.P. 1912.3.128; R.P. 777; S*oc. des Granits Porphyroïdes des Vosges*, c.e. 31 juillet 1912, R.p. 909; D.P. 916.3.35, *conclusions Léon Blum*. For further elaboration, see: Badawi 1994: 779; and in French doctrine and jurisprudence, see: as this stipulation is described "*Les Critères Jurisprudentiels*," Richer 1995: 779–80; De Laubadère, Moderne et Delvolvé. Tome 1. 1983–1984: 211–29; *Conseil d'Etat* 14 Mai 1943, *Commune de Joiville-le-Pont*, Rec. 123; T.C. 12 janvier 1987, *Ville d'Eaubonne, D.* 1987, 205, concl. Massot; C.E 26 janvier 1951, *Société anonyme minière*, Rec. 49; Civ. 1, 9 octobre 1991, *Ville de la Ferté-Saint-Aubin, Quot*. Jur. 26 mars 1992. 5; and for more details see: Richer 1995: 78. The Supreme Administrative Court in Egypt, session 1, 3/5/1961, case No. 62 and another case: session 19/11/1983 case no. 3390, Judicial Year 27; the General Assembly for Legal Opinion and Legislation dated 11/4/1990, Legal Opinion No. 403, session 31/3/1990. Conversely, when the contract is not adopting public law mechanism and its excessive nature, it is a civil law transaction; see: The Supreme Administrative Court 18/2/1989, case no. 2644 Judicial Year 30 and case no. 1194, Judicial Year 33. It is worth mentioning the leading authority El Tamawy 1991: 86–97.

The New Legal Nature of International Public Works Agreements

Introduction

The contractual regime of International Public Works Agreements in developing countries[19] has been significantly influenced by cultural globalization. Globalization, in addition to the flow of commodities, includes capital and many other tangible concepts,[20] plus intangible values, such as culture. Among these is legal culture. Legal culture has flowed from Anglo-American jurisdictions to civil law legal systems. Some scholars have addressed the fact that culture has a sharp edge that has been mitigated by globalization.[21] As was pointed out in previous opinions,[22] globalization has considerably influenced Egyptian legislators and judicial decisions taken by the Egyptian State Council (*Conseil d'Etat*) courts and the General Assembly for Legal Opinion and Legislation; the legal nature of administrative contracts (*Le Contrat Administratif*) has drastically changed. Currently, the state cannot exercise the same excessive powers it once did over foreign contractors. In France[23] and Egypt,[24] the state can, to a great extent, exercise unlimited powers in administrative contracts enabling it unilaterally to amend, terminate or rescind (*La Résiliation Administrative*) a contract or impose penalties, such as forfeiture of performance bonds and penalties for delay, which differ from liquidated damages.[25]

The new legal nature is scrutinized in four parts. First, it discusses stabilization clauses as a mechanism to compensate the contractor against price fluctuations, in particular, those related to new legislation and regulations; second, it discusses the judicial stipulation prohibiting the principle of termination of performance (*Exception non Adimpleti Contractus*), which is a well-known principle in commercial and civil transactions (Article (161) of the Egyptian Civil Code); third, it analyzes the arbitration clause and its effect on new legal nature; and fourth, its effect on infrastructure projects under PPP agreements.

Stabilization Clauses in International Public Works Agreements

A stabilization clause (*Les Clauses des Stabilisations*) can be defined as a contractual stipulation that prohibits the state, without making an adjustment to the price, from changing the legal regime so as to affect contractual and financial equilibrium, for instance a change in legislation that increases taxes or customs duties during the performance of a long-term agreement. Stabilization clauses exempt contractors from the financial consequences that follow the application of new legislation or regulations.[26]

19 © Informa UK Limited. This part of this chapter to the end was published by the *International Construction Law Review*, [2010] 27, 3, July, 363–74.

20 Stiglitz 2007: 3–5.

21 See Mohamed S. Abdel-Wahab, 2006: 367.

22 Ismail 2009: 506; Ismail 2010a: 92.

23 See the leading authority on administrative contracts in the civil law legal culture decades ago: De Laubadère, Moderne and Delvolvé, 1983–1984, Tome I: 210 *et seq.*; see also Tome II; Richer 1995: 85 *et seq.*

24 In Arab doctrine, see El Tamawy 1991:,53.

25 See Stiglitz 2007: 3–5.

26 On French doctrine, see El Younsi 1994, Tome II: 242 *et seq.*

A well-known example[27] occurs when the state enters into a contract for the construction of an oil pipeline but, during its execution, it changes its economic strategy and promulgates new legislation that causes damage to the contractor. From the state's perspective, the amendment, which is made in the interests of the public, could not be considered as nationalization merely due to the economic and financial effect on the contractor. The stabilization clause is a legal mechanism to avoid these effects. The *Pyramids* case was a good example of such a change of political and economic strategy.[28] International Public Works Agreements in Egypt in the 1980s, such as for the Esnaa Barrage on the Nile in the south of Egypt, included stabilization clauses. They are common today. Egypt is one of the countries that recognized stabilization clauses. However, this trend has considerably increased in the last two decades. The stabilization clause includes compensating the contractor for changes of taxes and social insurance (for thousands of employees) and governmental prices (at the time) for cement, reinforcement, gas and electricity. The contractor will be compensated by a separate invoice within 60 days of submitting proper documents proving damages.[29] The legal justification is to maintain a kind of immunity for foreign contractors.[30]

In a recent example, the liquefied natural gas (LNG) construction site agreement between an Egyptian LNG company whose shareholders included two state-owned companies, the Egyptian General Petroleum Corporation (EGPC) and Egyptian Gas Holding Company (E Gas), and a leading American construction company for the engineering, design, construction, installation, commissioning and testing of an LNG plant to be located in Idku near Alexandria, included a clause for stabilizing the contract price in favour of the contractor. It is of fundamental importance to distinguish between legislative or legal actions that aim to achieve public interest and other legislative actions that violate contractual obligations. In the former case, the state bears no responsibility. In the latter scenario, the state is accused of bad faith in the use of its legislative power (*Détournement de Pouvoir Législatif*). It is of fundamental importance to scrutinize the state's intention, which is a very sensitive issue.[31]

In oil and gas agreements, the mechanism to compensate the contractor differs from that in International Public Works Agreements. As the Egyptian Constitution stipulates in (123), granting concessions for exploiting natural resources (oil and gas) must be by legislation, on a case-by-case basis, and not pursuant to legislation (for example, an administrative decree from the cabinet, pursuant to the applicable laws). In the light of such cases, the stabilization clauses must be in the legislation that granted the concession. This rule is well known in public law doctrine in France and Egypt (*Principe du Parallelisme des Formes*).[32] Legislation cannot be amended by another mechanism such as an administrative decree or any other legal mechanism.[33] In many cases in the last decade, the Egyptian government established private companies (private juristic entities), pursuant to Company Law No. 159 of 1981 and Investment Law No. 8 of 1997, to enter into international infrastructure and oil and gas agreements and to avoid the application of state procurement law.

27 Lalive 1983, Tome II: 58.

28 For details of the *Pyramids* case, see Jarvin and Derains 1990: 124–38.

29 Ismail 2003a: 107–8.

30 Leboulanger 1985: 94.

31 Leboulanger 1985: 96 *et seq.*

32 Badawi 2007: 112.

33 E.g., concessions promulgated by Law No. 70 of 2006, Law No. 88 of 2007, Law No. 90 of 2007 and Law No. 147 of 2009.

Principle of Termination of Performance *(Exception non Adimpleti Contractus)*

The General Principle in the Egyptian Civil Code

The Egyptian Civil Code stipulates pursuant to Article (161) that "in contracts that are obligatory for both parties, if mutual obligations are due, it is optional for any of the contracting parties to terminate performance if the other party has not performed its obligation." In Egypt, the doctrine affirms that this principle is an application of the general rules of contract[34] in civil law. The basis of this concept in civil and commercial transactions is that, where two mutual obligations are due at the same time and reciprocity in executing obligations is not sufficient, the obligations are also conditional on each other. In civil construction contracts concluded by and between private entities, it is an obligation by the employer to deliver the construction site to the contractor without any obstacles that might prevent performance. That obligation is a precondition to performance by the contractor. Moreover, the obligation to pay the contractor is a precondition to the contractor continuing performance. Consequently, if the employer stops paying, the contractor has the right to terminate performance until payment is received from the employer. It can be argued[35] that this concept is a self-defence mechanism in favour of contractors to get their rights promptly instead of starting litigation or arbitral proceedings to claim payments as such measures that would take a long time and incur heavy costs.[36] In case of termination, the contract is still valid and is not rescinded. It is a form of suspension of mutual obligations until the party in default resumes its part.[37]

The Administrative Contracts Principle in the State Council (Conseil d'Etat) Decisions

This administrative contracts principle was rejected decades ago by the Egyptian State Council. In one of the leading cases concerning a contract concluded by and between a public juristic entity and a private company for the maintenance of elevators, the Administrative Appeal Court, after consolidation of the procedure of the two cases, dismissed the contractor's claims and held that the contractor was obliged to pay a penalty for delay as it was in breach of its contractual obligations.[38]

After the case was referred to the Supreme Administrative Court, that court held that:

> it is not permitted for the contracting company to terminate works at any stage of the contract performance, even if the public juristic entity is in breach of its obligations to make payments to the contractor. This contract is related to the management and operation of one of the public utilities.[39]

Public utility is the main concern of the administration. In a recent case, the Supreme Administrative Court held that:

---

34 Abdel Baki, Abdel Fatah, 1984: 667.

35 Said 2006: 16.

36 Ismail 2010d: 277–8.

37 Termination of performance, as is mentioned above, is a totally different concept from "set off" in the Egyptian legal system. "Set off" is a cause or mechanism by which the financial obligation is totally paid and the obligation settled (Article (362) of the Egyptian Civil Code).

38 Supreme Administrative Court, Case No. 2606, 24 April 1990, Judicial Year 31. See also Supreme Administrative Court Case No. 3177, 12 May 1998, Judicial Year 41.

39 Ibid.

> All contracts must be performed *bona fide* whether the contracts are concluded between private entities or between the state and private entities. Accordingly, if the state delays delivery of the construction site to contractor, the contractor does not have the right to claim not performing his contractual obligations. The contractor cannot argue that the state terminated or delayed in any of its contractual obligations. The principle of terminating contractual obligations by the contractor is not permitted in any circumstances under administrative contracts as they have their unique characteristics in addition to the fact that they are connected to public utilities which must run regularly and in a disciplinary manner. The contractor only has the right to claim compensation.[40]

The General Assembly for Legal Opinion and Legislation upheld all legal opinions that the principle of termination of the contractual obligation is not permitted in administrative contracts.[41]

New Trends in the State Council Decisions

Cultural and legal globalization has to some extent influenced the Egyptian State Council decisions in rejecting the principle in some exceptional cases, in which the Supreme Administrative Court has held that:[42]

> the breach of contractual obligations by the administration and terminating contractors' payments is a considerable reason for termination of performance by the contractor. As the project financing by the state in Public Works Agreements is the fundamental element in executing works, there is an essential obligation upon the administration to deliver to the contractor his payments promptly, otherwise, it will be impossible for him to continue to perform his contractual obligations. The well established principle in administrative contracts in the *Conseil d'Etat* decisions and in the Egyptian administrative doctrine, rejecting granting the right to the contractor to terminate or suspend performance upon getting his payments from the state, is not applicable in this case before the court. It could be applicable in suspending some contractual obligations by the state but not one of the fundamental contractual obligations such as payments. The obligation to pay the contractor is a fundamental obligation, by which the contract cannot continue without payments on due date, especially if it is a great sum that substantially affects performance. The contract must be executed by the administration in a *bona fide* manner. Moreover, the administration delayed in delivering designs for the contractor in the preliminary stages of the contractual process.

The court accepted that the contractor could suspend performance until such time as payments were made by the state. A clear example of violating such substantial obligations is not paying large sums to the contractor without any reason where the absence of such payment would substantially affect performance.

In another leading decision, also in 1997, the Supreme Administrative Court held that:

---

40 Supreme Administrative Court, Case No. 6337, 16 March 2004, Judicial Year 46; see also Supreme Administrative Court, Case No. 834, 18 October 2005, Judicial Year 46; and Supreme Administrative Court, Case No. 9689, 17 January 2006, Judicial Year 49.

41 For example, General Assembly for Legal Opinion and Legislation, No. 453, 8 June 1995, session 31; May 1995, file 32/2/2545; and see also No. 137, 20 February 2008, session 15 March 2008, file No. 32/2/3808.

42 Supreme Administrative Court, Case No. 4483, 6 May 1997, Judicial Year 41.

> Project financing by the administration is the crucial factor that directly affects performance by the contractor. Suspending or terminating administrations' obligation for payments shall affect contractor's credit-worthiness and performance of the contractual obligations to execute works until final completion. The court found that the fundamental principle of rejecting contractor's right to suspend works is not applicable in the current case before the court. Suspending works by the contractor is a legal right as he did not get paid. The latter is a default by the contracting public juristic entity.[43]

The General Assembly for Legal Opinion and Legislation has held the same views (but in rare decisions) and has granted the contractor the right to suspend performance in case of delay in obtaining payments from the administration.[44]

The decisions were a real revolution in the basic and fundamental principle of rejecting principles of termination of performance. Despite the fact that they were in 1997 and that other decisions rejecting the principle were in 2004, this marks a new trend in State Council decisions since the end of the last decade. It is a new era of modernization of the traditional concepts of the administrative contract. The latter enhancements are as a direct result of globalization and liberalization of the traditional theory of the administrative contract (*Le Contrat Administratif*). In 2004,[45] the Supreme Administrative Court stated:

> the basic and fundamental principle in implementing administrative contracts is that the contractor cannot stop or terminate performance in contracts with the state, concerning public utilities, but there are exceptions to this principle when there is a serious violation by the administration (a violation of substantial obligation) in order that the contractor can continue performance, there is no reason to affirm the old principle. In some cases when the administration did not submit drawings to the contractor or terminated his payments as it is the source which enables contractor to finance the public works project, especially when it is a large sum of money, it is the right of the contractor to suspend or terminate performance until the administration fulfils its contractual obligations. However, the administration cannot impose penalty for delay upon the contractor because the latter's fault was a result of the administration's default in one of its substantial obligations.

This controversial new view is a direct result of cultural and legal globalization.

There is, however, an essential need for a legislative reform to add an extension of time to the contract duration if the state delays a contractor's payments, and to avoid payment of liquidated damages.

Conclusion

In conclusion, despite the fact that the State Council decisions have begun a new era, in a few cases more than a decade ago, in trying to apply the principle in favour of the contractor, the decisions do not have a specific judicial methodology. In order to achieve fairness in the contractual relationship and to maintain equal bargaining power for the contracting parties, we submit that

43 Supreme Administrative Court, Cases Nos. 4697 and 4717, 24 June 1997, Judicial Year 39; see Said 2006: 89–90. See also recent cases, e.g., Case No. 291, 14 March 2000, Judicial Year 43.

44 E.g., General Assembly for Legal Opinion, opinion No. 541, 8 July 1993, session 16 May 1993; *The General Principles of the General Assembly*, Judicial Years, 47 and 48 (1999).

45 Supreme Administrative Court, Case No. 10572, 30 November 2004, Judicial Year 47; see also, e.g., No. 291, session 14 March 2000, Judicial Year 43.

the principle should be applied in the domain of the administrative contracts and it will maintain contractual equilibrium, as the contractor usually has project financing from lending banks and assigns payments to the lenders. If the state suspended the payments the contractor would pay more interest during a longer period of time. The latter scenario would violate the financial expectations and feasibility studies made for tendering purposes.

Arbitration Clause and the Theory of New Legal Nature

Introduction

Cultural Globalization is currently playing a significant role in enhancing rigid patterns in certain areas of administrative law and dispute resolution mechanisms in state contracts, *Le Contrat Administratif*, in particular arbitration. The substance and excessive features of these contracts and dispute mechanisms, excluding arbitration from state contracts disputes, have considerably changed in the last two decades in the Egyptian legal culture. The Egyptian parliament promulgated a new legislation for arbitration in 1994 and adopted international standards to maintain the arbitration process, liberalization and internationalization.

A considerable debate arose in Egypt, before the promulgation of the new Arbitration Act No. 27 of 1994, about arbitration in state administrative contracts.

In 1989 and 1993, before the new legislation, the General Assembly for Legal Opinion (*Fatwa*) and Legislation of the Egyptian State Council (*Conseil d'Etat*) had a unique perspective that permitted arbitration in state contracts; meanwhile, the Supreme Administrative Court rejected arbitration in state contracts. The Arbitration Act was promulgated in 1994. Despite the fact that Article (1) of Act No. 27 of 1994 allowed arbitration in state contracts, the General Assembly, in a legal opinion issued on 18 December 1996, rejected arbitration in state contracts. In 1997, Amendment No. 9 to the Arbitration Act allowed arbitration in state contracts. The latter amendment stipulated the consent of the minister concerned, who cannot delegate this power to any other public juristic entity.

The influence of cultural globalization is clear on the legislative policy behind amendments, despite the criticism to the provision stipulating the consent of the minister concerned. It is appropriate to analyze these legislative trends and the current changes in the Egyptian legal culture.

Nowadays, a crucial question has arisen: Has the Egyptian *Conseil d'Etat* adopted a new judicial policy, influenced by cultural globalization, and has it achieved tangible results in assisting the arbitral process?

It is suggested that scrutinization of the legislation concerning arbitration is fundamental, in order to answer various questions arising about the extent by which legislation and litigation were influenced by cultural and legal globalization movements.

Egyptian Legislation

Conseil d'Etat decisions before the Arbitration Act No. 27 of 1994 are of great significance to research.

On 17 May 1989,[46] the General Assembly of the *Conseil d'Etat* allowed arbitration in state contracts in an administrative contract concluded between the Ministry of Housing and the

46 The General Assembly for Legal Opinion and Legislation, No. [missing], session 17/5/1989, dated [missing] file (54/1/265).

Architect Group (a consultancy firm). The contract contained an arbitration clause for dispute settlement.

The General Assembly pointed out that arbitration is allowed in administrative contracts as it is not contrary to the objective nature of administrative contracts.[47] The General Assembly elaborated that Article (10) of the *Conseil d'Etat* Law No. 47 of 1972 was promulgated, not to prohibit arbitration in administrative contracts, but to draw the line between the *Conseil d'Etat* administrative court jurisdictions and civil court jurisdictions. This was a unique approach by that time.

Contrary to this approach, the *Conseil d'Etat* courts rejected arbitration in the administrative contract. On 9 December 1990, the Administrative Appeal[48] Court rejected arbitration in administrative contracts. Nowadays, scrutinization of these judicial precedents is of less significance than analyzing the Arbitration Act, its amendments and State Council court precedents in the last decade after promulgation of the Arbitration Act in 1994.

Arbitration Act No. 27 of 1994

This legislation was promulgated on 18 April 1994 and was scheduled to enter into effect as of 19 May 1994.

> Article (1) of the above-mentioned legislation stipulates that without violation to the valid international treaties applicable in Egypt, provisions of the law shall be applicable to any arbitration held between parties from public juristic entities or private entities regardless of the legal relation to the dispute and whether the arbitration is held in Egypt or such is an international commercial arbitration held outside Egypt and the parties thereto have chosen said law as the applicable law.
>
> Omani and Jordanian Arbitration Act have similar provisions.[49]

From the above legislation, it can be concluded that arbitration in state contracts is permitted. Despite this fact, on 18 December 1996, the General Assembly for Legal Opinion and Legislation in the *Conseil d'Etat*, in one of its leading decisions,[50] rejected arbitration in state administrative contracts. The General Assembly found that it is more appropriate to focus on the legal nature of administrative contracts and its compatibility with arbitration, rather than the *Conseil d'Etat* jurisdictional perspective and the concept of depriving *Conseil d'Etat* courts from exercising their constitutional rights granted to them pursuant to Article (172) of the Egyptian Constitution for judicial review and litigation on state contracts. The General Assembly elaborated that Article (1) of the Arbitration Act is not a confirmed provision; it is a general clause, and, in terms of interpretation, general clauses are not affirmative in their nature. The General Assembly concluded

47 For example, the objective nature of the administrative contracts rejects the application of foreign substantive law by arbitrators to the administrative contract as it is a state contract concerning public utilities or the exploitation of natural resources. For more analysis and elaboration on "*Le Contrat Administratif*" concept in civil law legal systems, see: De Laubadère, Moderne and Delvolvé 1983–1984, Tome 1: 210 *et seq.*; and Richer 1995: 85 *et seq.* In Egypt, see the leading authority: El Tamawy 1991: 53; and Badawi 1994: 5–109.

48 Case No. 5837, session 9/12/1990, Judicial Year 44, unpublished.

49 Omani Arbitration Act, Article (1) and Jordanian Arbitration Act of 2001, Article (3).

50 Legal opinion No. 160, session 18/12/1996, dated 22/2/1997, file 45/1/339.

that public juristic entities are delegated the power from people to run and manage public utilities. As the public juristic entities were delegated this power, they cannot delegate it to arbitrators. The General Assembly confirmed the fundamental judicial principle, in the *Conseil d'Etat* decisions, which stipulate that the delegated entity cannot delegate power to any other public juristic entity. Private foreign entities insist upon an arbitration clause as a dispute settlement mechanism; consequently this leads to the internationalization of *Le Contract Administratif* and the increase of IFDI.

In another case before the *Conseil d'Etat* courts (the Administrative Appeal Court), the claimant, the General Corporation for the National Cultural Centre (The Opera House) started litigation proceedings against the defendant, an agency company, seeking a sum of £E2,768,000 Egyptian pounds (EGP) as compensation for the breach of contract between the claimant and defendant. The contract stated that the defendant shall contract with The Spanish Flamenco Team to perform its bullfighting shows in El Shams Club in Egypt from 20 November 1997 until 26 November 1997.

The defendant was in breach of its contractual obligations, which caused damages to the Egyptian Opera House. The court held[51] that despite the existence of an arbitration clause, the breach of contract by the defendant was beyond its reasonable control because of the rejection of the Minister of Agriculture and the General Veterinary Authority to grant permission to allow Spanish bulls to enter the country. The rejection was based on a religious opinion of *Dar El Efta* (the General Assembly for Religious Opinion) prohibiting bullfighting. Even if these objections were waived after the effective date of the contract, this was a duty upon the claimant as a public juristic entity to obtain these permissions pursuant to Article (2) of the contract, stipulating that the public juristic entity shall obtain these permissions.

The court applied the general principles of the contract law stipulated under the Egyptian Civil Code and denied contractual liability; accordingly, the case was dismissed.

In conclusion, the *Conseil d'Etat* courts have not been greatly influenced by the flow of cultural and legal globalization in the application of the provisions of the Arbitration Act. Although the administrative courts have violated the *competence-competence* principle,[52] it is clear that an arbitral award (as is explained above) has adopted a liberal perspective. It is presumed an act of bad faith by the administration if it breached its obligations and did not obtain a ministerial consent on the arbitration clause. Conversely, the *Conseil d'Etat* courts adopted reasonable findings in some other cases and applied civil law principles to protect private entities from the administration upon exercising its excessive power, even if there is an arbitration clause.[53] It is true that the *Conseil d'Etat* courts, at this stage, are obliged to apply the legislative stipulation to obtain the ministerial consent. On the other hand, the above-mentioned arbitral award has adopted a more fair and liberal approach in interpreting Article (1) of the Egyptian Arbitration Act.

The arbitration clause nowadays is one of the most fundamental pillars in changing the International Public Works Agreements legal nature as it is a condition precedent by the foreign investor before entering into the contractual process.

---

51 The Appeal Administrative Court, Case No. 11498, session 23/4/2006, Legal Year 53, unpublished.

52 *Competence/Competence* Principle stipulated in Article (22) of the Egyptian Arbitration Act and also in the English Arbitration Act (1996) that the arbitral tribunal shall decide its jurisdiction itself at any dispute before the tribunal.

53 See Ismail 2010d: 363.

Conclusions: Significance of the Arbitration Clause to Foreign Investors (Arbitration versus. State Courts)

The Arbitration Clause in the past decades has been one of the fundamental clauses in infrastructure agreements, whether International Public Works Agreements, BOOT Agreements (including various types of these transactions such as BOT, BOO and others) or currently PPPs. In natural resource concessions (oil and gas), the arbitration clause is promulgated by legislation issued by the Egyptian Parliament that approves the concept of arbitration as an effective mechanism for the resolution of disputes arising, as a result of globalization and of the promulgation of the Arbitration Act No. 27 of 1994, Omani Arbitration Act of 1997, Jordanian Arbitration Act of 2001 and Tunisian Arbitration Act of 1993. The main concerns of foreign investors are the arbitration and applicable law (substantive law) clauses as the two clauses representing fast, effective and fair alternative means of dispute resolution from the perspective of investors. During precontractual negotiations with the state, it is of great importance from the investors' perspective to procure agreement that the state maintains access to arbitration, if needed, through an arbitration clause. It is true that foreign investors will be in a better situation if they are protected by a Bilateral Investment Treaty (BIT) which, if it is ratified by the Parliament, is part of the internal legislation pursuant to Article 151 of the Egyptian Constitution and most Arab Middle Eastern States.[54]

It is worth mentioning that the State Procurement Law No. 89 of 1998 stipulates in Article (42) that arbitration is an effective mechanism for dispute settlement by the state and contracting entities, whether domestic or international. Further steps are needed, by the Egyptian *Conseil d'Etat* as well as jurisprudence in Arab states, to adopt new enhancements and modifications to assist arbitration as a process toward internationalization, decentralization and liberalization of arbitration in Egypt. This will appear soon as a tangible result of cultural and legal globalization.

It is strongly recommended that mediation be viewed by developing countries as an effective and fast resolution to avoid costs and unpredictable findings. In certain cases, arbitration confounds party expectations by achieving final and binding results unpredictable by any of the disputing parties. Unpredictable findings vary from one arbitral tribunal to another according to various interpretations that, in some cases, differ from one legal cultural perspective to another. The same question of law in different jurisdictions has different interpretations. Legal interpretation is a dynamic, although rather static, methodology that differs from time to time, from one jurisdiction to another and from economic welfare to economic crisis situations. Meanwhile, in engineering, for instance, it is unlikely to find different views in measuring dimensions of a dam or a building that is always the same in various cultures and decades.

Public Private Partnership (PPP) Agreements

Public private partnership agreements (PPP) are beginning to be used in state transactions in Egypt. This mechanism interests legal scholars despite rare references to Arab doctrine. The system is well known in the United Kingdom and elsewhere. PPP is of great significance to developing countries as it primarily procures financing to avoid or reduce public debt by promises of construction and operation of infrastructure projects.

54 For the same concept, see: the Libyan constitution, the Lebanese Constitution, the Kuwaiti Constitution, the Omani Constitution, the Sudan Constitution, the Syrian Constitution.

The French legal system considers agreements as administrative contracts[55] but allows intervention by the administration unilaterally to amend, terminate or rescind the contract (*La Résiliation Administrative*). The French legal system acknowledges the administrative nature of PPP transactions. It is, nowadays, one of the main features of public economic law in France.[56] Simultaneously, France adopted similar policies and contractual mechanisms.

In France, PPP transactions were permitted by Decree 559/2004. The French Constitutional Council (*Conseil Constitutionnel*) has approved all the legislation concerning PPP agreements. Moreover, the French State Council (*Conseil d'Etat*) has rejected all cases related to the Decree of 2004 and has affirmed its legality.[57]

Conclusions

The legal globalization phenomenon is a result of the flow of Anglo-American legal culture into civil law culture. In his famous thesis,[58] Samuel Huntington pointed out the potential clash of civilizations after dividing the world into eight cultures. He argued that the world is far from being dominated by a single logic. He also added that the great division among human kind would be cultural rather than ideological or economic, as differences in civilizations are basic.

Huntington elaborated that cultural characteristics and differences are less easily compromised and resolved than political and economic ones.[59]

It is strongly recommended that this is an advanced step toward the integration of civil law legal culture into Anglo-American global legal culture. Thus, there is currently a trend toward internationalization of administrative contract stipulations and excessive clauses.[60]

55 The French *Conseil d'Etat* on 29 October 2004 rejected and dismissed all cases relating to the annulations of the 17 June 2004 decree regulating PPP transactions. This means that the French legal and judicial systems accept PPPs in principle. For further information, see: www.conseil-etat.fr(file://I:/conseildEtatPPPArret.htm. Cases Nos. 269814, 271119, 271357, 271362. See also on the administrative nature of PPP agreements, Ragab 2007: 181–3.

56 Ragab 2007: 2.

57 Ragab 2007: 22–3; Ismail 2010d: 179; and visit: www.conseil-etat.fr/cde/media/document//annexes1/col-16122008.pdf (*Article sur la fiscalité des PPP, les nouvelles fiscales*, 1er Décembre 2008).

58 Huntington 1996. Henry Kissinger described this book as "one of the most important books to have emerged since the end of the Cold War."

59 For an analysis of Huntington's views, see Abdel-Wahab 2006: 367.

60 Ismail 2009: 506; Ismail: 2010a: 92.

Chapter 4
PPPs in Developing Countries

Introduction: New Type of Contract as a Direct Result of Globalization

PPP transactions are one of the new types and mechanisms of partnerships between the public and private sectors in developing countries, by which the private sector can create, fund and finance infrastructure projects in developing countries.[1] PPPs create new opportunities for delivering public services in the twenty-first century:

> The term 'public services' refers to services which are offered to the general public or highlights that a service has been assigned a specific role in the public interest, or refers to the ownership or status of the entity providing the service. In the latter situation, public service fuses with the concept of public sector which covers the state and its public bodies which are covered by public law and undertakings controlled by public authorities.[2]

The main characteristics of PPPs mechanisms are the financing methods and the risk allocation in such agreements between the public and the private sector. It is of fundamental importance to refer to the compatibility of the PPPs with the principles of competition, transparency, accountability and equality, which are the main concerns of the various jurisdictions, as the governments' basic principles.[3]

Developing states expect to benefit from the know-how, experience and resources of the private sectors to facilitate the timely and cost-effective procurement of works and services. Further, governments seek to ensure better contract management through fair incentives for the developers, to avoid shortterm significant capital expenditure and, therefore, procure a larger number of projects, to limit the government's debt and to pass a substantial part of the project risk to the private sector. Their main objectives are to create a market-friendly regulatory environment, establish the administrative basis necessary to coordinate this development and clarify the procurement process for PPPs.[4]

In the United Kingdom, PPPs, including Private Finance Initiative (PFIs) schemes,[5] are currently responsible for around 24 per cent of public investment in most of the key infrastructure areas. Most European Union states including Ireland, Sweden, Finland, Germany, Greece, Italy, The Netherlands, Portugal and Spain have developed legal and policy frameworks to deliver PPP projects.[6] Moreover, in Latin American states, Mexico and Chile started a new era of public private partnerships to promote private-sector participation in public-investment projects to reduce budget deficit. In Mexico, PPPs were used in the 1980s to finance highways and, in the mid1990s, the

---

1 See: Donnelly 2007; Auby et Bon 1995: 218; De Laubadère, Venezia et Gaudement 1995, Tome II: 462; El Attar 1955: 11.

2 Bovis 2010.

3 Bovis 2010; Ismail 2003b.

4 See: http://www.mof.gov.eg (accessed 31 July 2011).

5 Bovis 2006: 454–61.

6 See: Bovis 2010: 4; See also: Uff 2009: 370.

energy sector. Chile has a wellestablished PPP program for the development of transport, airports, prisons and irrigation.[7] In recent decades, Brazil, as will be explained later, adopted a significant legislative policy to maintain Inward Foreign Direct Investments (IFDI).[8]

Developing states' legislation aims to regulate most private financing in these countries, encouraging Inward Foreign Direct Investments while also enforcing institutional framework reforms in the same direction. It also sets out the number of elements in respect of risk allocation. Its aim is for the eventual standardization of all related processes combined with public administration responsiveness and effectiveness.

A PPP usually takes the form of a contract between a private sector entity and the government that calls for the private sponsor to deliver a desired service (in economic and social infrastructure or other area) and assume the associated risk in exchange for the right to earn an adequate return. The government may currently be providing the service, or it may be a new service that would benefit developing states and their economies, but which is not currently provided. Risk allocation is at the heart of how PPPs are structured.[9] PPPs allow better risk allocation as they are procured as services, not assets. Unlike conventional procurement, the focus is on output, not input. Under conventional procurement, a public sector institution prepares detailed specifications that describe the work to be delivered. The work is then put out to tender in order to get the most competitive price. Once the contract is awarded, the government of a developing state closely supervises the work carried out by the successful partner in order to ensure complete and successful compliance with the specifications. Thus, governments take responsibility for the design and planning of the project, all statutory requirements (e.g., environmental, town planning) and any additional costs that may arise due to unforeseen circumstances or elements that were omitted from the tender. Meanwhile, the contractor is responsible for the construction of the work in accordance with the tender documentation and is only responsible for matters covered in the tender documentation or those which could reasonably have been unforeseen from the tender documents. The governments in this scenario take full responsibility for all work relating to the delivery of the service. The latter scenario is based on input specifications.[10]

It is appropriate, at this stage, to refer to the drawbacks of the traditional tendering[11] system by which the state, in civil law jurisdictions, imposes penalties and exercises exorbitant clauses upon foreign private entities and poor contractual performances, as a result of overbudget completion and, in most cases, delayed performance. The latter is a direct result of the low price competition during the competitive tendering process. State procurement legislation (traditional public procurement), particularly in Egypt, refers to the principle of the lowest price in tendering to preserve public funds and reduce budget deficit. The award criteria for certain specifications laid down in the documents, and the most economically advantageous tender, is the target of the administration, as the tender must be finetuned at the request of the contracting authority. Consequently, a poor specification in performing contractual undertakings in infrastructure projects and low quality services offered by public utilities to endusers in concessions, are one of the main features of the State International Public Works Agreements and traditional concession agreements for infrastructure projects.[12]

When assessing a project through public private partnerships, the key element is the definition for procurement of a desired function through output specifications. Governments define the

7 Bovis 2010: 5.

8 Bovis 2010: 5.

9 See: http://www.mof.gov.eg (accessed 31 July 2011).

10 See: http://www.mof.gov.eg (accessed 31 July 2011).

11 In Public Procurement Law from the international dimension, generally see: Reich 1999.

12 Bovis 2010. See also www: mof.gov.eg (accessed 31 July 2011).

No Investment Risk			Investment Risk		
Works and Services Contracts	Management and Maintenance Contracts	Operations and Maintenance Concessions	Build Operate and Transfer	Concessions	Full Privatization

Low ⟶ High

Figure 4.1 Full Spectrum of Private Sector Participation in Service Delivery[13]

service that is required. These output specifications are then calculated in a financial model to allow comparability between the two forms of procurement – public and private. If the PPP option is preferred, the government leaves certain stages of the designs of the work necessary to deliver that service to the partner that will be selected through a bidding process. The preferred approach is to ensure that projects are driven substantially by the private party and thereby ensure greater value for money for the government.

Public Private Partnerships fall into broad categories:

Financially self-standing concessions These comprise toll roads and river crossings where the traffic volumes and toll charges are sufficient to finance the investments and ongoing services and support. They also apply to water treatment and supply, sewerage and wastewater, waste collection and management and transport services. For such concessions, it is essential that user charges be regulated but set at economic levels to pay for the investment required as well as ongoing services.

Hybrid Public Private Partnerships These cover areas of service where user charges are made but for political and/or social reasons in developing states, they are maintained at levels that are insufficient to sustain the required outlay of capital and operational expenses. In these cases, user charges have to be supplemented by public juristic entities.

Private Finance Initiatives (PFI-type) This category has seen the largest growth, particularly in the United Kingdom[14] and is applicable to all those sectors where no user charge is possible or politically acceptable. For public (i.e. state-run) services, schools, hospitals and health centres and, for governmental use, courts, prisons and police and fire stations are clear examples of this scenario (see Figure 4.1).[15]

Public Private Partnership

Developing countries' current experience shows that potential PPP projects should conform to some characteristics. The investment required, in particular for pilot projects, should exceed a

13 See: http://www.mof.gov.eg (accessed 31 July 2010).

14 Bovis 2006: 454–77. See also for PPPs in various jurisdictions: Hanafi and El Dardiry 2010: 432–47; Ismail 2010c: 54–67. In Eastern Europe, see: International Centre for Public Enterprises in Developing Countries 1981; and generally see: Akitoby, Hemming and Schwartz 2007; Khoo 2001; in Sri Lanka, see: A.D.V. de S. Indraratna 2006; in Ghana, see: Germain 2005; Harper 2000; OECD Reports, see: Bird 2000, Burdon 2000, Eberlei 2000; Fiszbein and Lowden 1999.

15 See: http://www.mof.gov.eg (accessed 31 July 2010); Bovis 2006: 454.

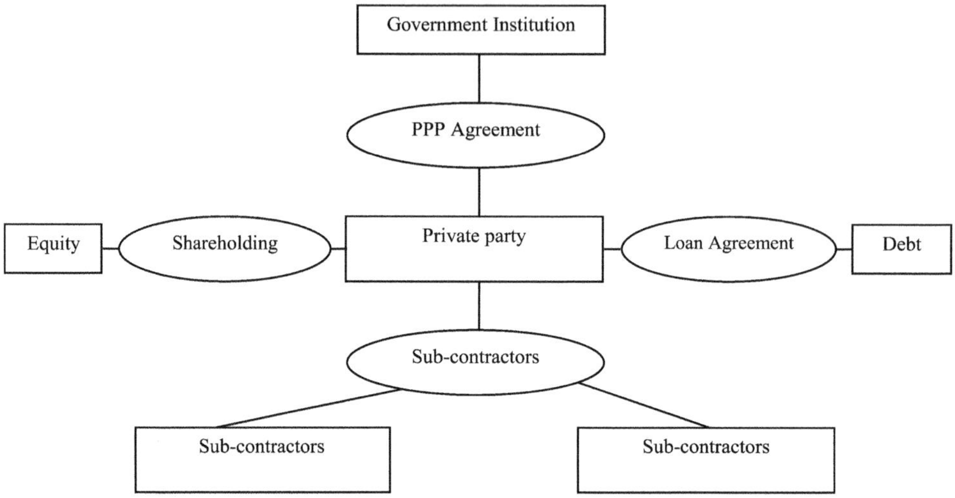

Figure 4.2 Typical Structure of a Project Financed Based on PPP[16]

certain amount of money that varies, due to currency exchange rates, from one country to another. This is because the complexity and expenses involved in launching such projects, using proper public procurement procedures, are only justified for projects of a larger scale. The assets and services required should be those that the private sector is capable of supplying, and there should be an actual or potential competitive market for such supply. The public juristic entity proposing a PPP should be able to specify in output or outcome terms the scope and scale of its needs for the life of the project. Furthermore, the project proposal should be justified by a detailed analysis of needs and arguments for the suitability of the PPP approach. It is essential that the latter analysis receives the formal approval of senior governmental or political authorities before a PPP project be put out to formal tender. Such approvals and consents differ from one country to another. This is due to the legal framework, whether legislative or regulatory, and the policies adopted in each particular jurisdiction.

Why the PPP Route Is Proposed

Governments tend to use PPP techniques when they decide how the project could be addressed under traditional procurement and then they consider the expectations and justifications for choosing a PPP route (Figure 4.2). Consideration for proposing PPPs include:

- Previous experience of any similar projects under conventional procurement;
- Analysis of quantifiable and unquantifiable costs and benefits of possible solutions to the investment needs;
- The level of investment required at the outset and how it is likely to be funded under a PPP;
- The required performance standards and how these will address the projects' objectives and how they will be measured;
- The flexibility required of both assets and services over time;

16 See: http://www.mof.gov.eg (accessed 31 July 2010).

- Whether any technology which will have to be deployed is subject to rapid change or in restricted supply;
- Whether any user charges are to be levied and if so how they will be set and collected.;
- The proposed term of the PPP contract and the relative advantages/disadvantages of shorter or longer terms;
- The reasons to believe that there will be a good competitive response to a PPP approach.[17]

The proposal for a PPP project is to be considered if it is broadly affordable and appears to offer value for money, which can be addressed during the dialogue phase by exploring reallocation of the risks between the parties.

Value for Money

To ensure that benefits of PPPs are realized, a "value-for-money" test is important in PPP schemes that involve the public sector paying a fee or tariff for the provision of services. In most countries with developed PPP programs, the public sector establishes a public sector comparator (PSC) before deciding to launch a project as a PPP. The PSC is an estimate of what the project would cost the public sector were it to be realized on the conventional basis of International Public Works Agreements being tendered using public sector finance.

> Since the public sector typically borrows at rates lower than those available to the private sector for any project to be approved as a PPP project, there must be a significant transfer of risk which the private sector can manage better than public juristic entities. The ability to better manage risk will be reflected by lower costs including a lower cost of capital for risk adjusted calculations.
>
> All relevant capital and life cycle costs must be included in the PSC in order to determine whether the PPP demonstrates real value for money.[18]

The notion of Value for Money (VFM) is crucial for any type of PPP as a method of procurement of public works and services. PPP contracting is different from conventional public procurement in that it is value-based, not pricebased. The terminology used in the European Union Directives on Public Procurement is the most economically advantageous. VFM expresses the clear relationship between the cost and the quality, reliability, quantity and flexibility of those services. It is substantially determined in the qualitative and quantitative manners of the service.

PPP contracting addresses this pattern of project failure by basing contracts on certain key principles:

- Governments specify their needs in terms of output, performance levels and standards during the extended term of the contract.
- The partner provides the full technical package of input (design, construction, operational method, etc.), which meets the output and accepts the inherent technical and commercial risks.
- The partner finances the necessary investments and therefore has "capital at risk."
- The partner only receives payments when the project enters its operational phase after construction, and those payments are spread evenly throughout the contract period.

17 See: http://www.mof.gov.eg (accessed 31 July 2010).

18 See: http://www.mof.gov.eg (accessed 31 July 2010).

- If performance levels or standards fall short of what is specified, payments are reduced to compensate the authority for shortfall.

The effect is that the public authority achieves the output and quality of service it stipulates during the long term, within pricing parameters known and settled at the contract date.

VFM is not the sole economic hurdle for project investment, whether by conventional or PPP procurement. A proposed project must also be affordable. Even if affordability and VFM are clearly distinguishable concepts, there is a critical interdependency. First, each is calculated from the same basic assumptions as to scope, scale, costs and risks of the projects. Second, no public authority should enter procurement for a PPP project if its business case analysis indicates that even a VFM PPP offer, coupled with the costs and risks retained by the government, would be unaffordable.

The key to successful PPP contracting is the fair allocation of project risk and the financial consequences of risk between the public and private sector partners. There are many categories of risk that can affect the successful outcome of the project. Some of the most common are:

- timing and availability of planning and licensing consent
- unforeseen ground conditions
- proper design and engineering
- cost and time overruns during construction
- compliance with technical standards
- user contributions
- cost of services during operational phase
- increased cost due to change of legislation
- inflation
- availability and cost of insurance
- technology change
- industrial action

The purpose of the PPP contract is to allocate project risks between the government and the PPP partner. The government should achieve the best value when each is responsible for those risks it can best manage and/or mitigate.

States, either in their own capacity or through delegated monopolies and publicly controlled enterprises, engage in market activities in order to provide and deliver public services. Privatization, by which public assets and public service operations can be completely transferred to the private sector, on grounds of market efficiency and competition as well as quality of service considerations, differ from public private partnerships. Privatization, in its substance, is a permanent transfer of ownership. In the process of public private partnership, the public sector could receive VFM in the delivery of public services. To sum up, the concept of VFM in its substance means the effectiveness and efficiency of the public service, product or process comparing the input cost to the value of the output and the qualitative and quantitative judgment on the manner in which the resources involved had been utilized and managed.[19]

PPPs seek to transfer risk from the public sector to the private sector. Significant risk transfer from the public to the private sector is necessary to express a VFM partnership. The risk transfer on financing cost and pricing are crucial in understanding how risk is treated within public private

19 Bovis 2010: 2–3.

Table 4.1 Example of Risk Matrix

Risk Area	**Risk Transfer and Allocation**			**Comments**
	Client	***Shared***	***Partner***	
Scheme layout and design	✔			Client
Planning/Approvals				
Outline planning	✔			
Detailed planning		✔		
Building regulations		✔		
Construction:				
Scope change	✔			
Cost/time overruns		✔		
Unforeseen ground conditions		✔		
Latent defects		✔		
Impact on adjacent properties		✔		
Compliance with environmental Regulations		✔		
Compliance with technical Specifications		✔		
Insurance		✔		Except civil unrest
Force majeure		✔		
Demand risk	✔			
Operations and maintenance				
Service levels and quality			✔	
Availability			✔	
Security			✔	
Legislative change				
General – capital cost			✔	
General – service delivery			✔	
Foreseeable specific			✔	
Unforeseeable community				
Homes specific	✔			
Unforeseeable PPP specific	✔			
Financial				Divergence from general index
Taxation			✔	
Interest Rates		✔	✔	
Inflation				
Other				If assets to return to authority at
Technology			✔	nil cost at end of contract
Obsolescence			✔	
Industrial Action				
Consortium Bankruptcy			✔	
Residual value	✔			

partnership.[20] It is argued that the public sector can generally spread risk across taxpayers; the usual argument is that this gives the public sector an advantage over the private sector in terms of managing risk. On the other hand, the private sector can spread risk across financial markets. It is concluded that project risk is lower in the private sector. Risk transfer from the public sector to the private sector has considerable influence on whether a PPP is a more efficient and costeffective

20 Bovis 2010: 6.

alternative to public investment. Conversely, in traditional public tendering, risk allocation is driven from the private sector to the public sector, as is stated above. As in public private partnerships, the private sector provides financing that is specialized financing differing from both public finance and corporate finance. Thus, the pivotal characteristics are that the private sector partner is expected to play a strategic role in financing and delivering the infrastructure project or the public service by providing designs, implementation, construction, completion, management and operation and maintenance. Distribution of risks between public sector and private sector should lead to a certain result that the private sector will assume substantial risks (Table 4.1).

In conclusion, the Public Private Partnerships, as a concept of public sector management, have currently changed the method of assessing delivery of infrastructure projects and of public services both in qualitative and quantitative manners. The private sector assumes a direct responsibility in offering public services as part of contractual obligations *vis-à-vis* the public sector. The phenomenon of Public Private Partnerships represents an attempt at the modernization and liberalization of the delivery of public services through the private sector as an investor and financier of public services.[21]

The Internationalization of PPPs and *Le Contrat Administratif* Constraints

Introduction

The nature of an administrative contract has a special significance in civil law legal systems, especially in France and Egypt. It has its special characteristics and nature through its exorbitant clauses, as the state and contracting parties do not have equal bargaining powers. However, in private law (civil and commercial) transactions, contracting parties have the same power, which leads to an equal and balanced contractual relationship.

PPPs nowadays constitute an underlying tool in the domain of the states' international business transactions as in the concession agreements. Currently, significant enhancements and modifications are introduced to the concession agreement mechanisms. However, there is the crucial question: How can civil law legal systems, in the light of *Le Contrat Administratif* traditional theory, stride toward harmonizing the internationalization of PPPs and *Le Contrat Administratif* constraints?

The following part of this chapter discusses concession agreements in civil law legal systems, particularly in Egypt, and the effect of legal globalization on concessions, PPPs in the comparative legal culture and in Egypt; and there follows a summary of conclusions.

The Legal Nature of PPP Contracts in Civil Law Legal Systems

As has been stated earlier in this book, the administrative contract has a unique nature. Accordingly, if a contract is entered into between a developing state and a private foreign entity in the form of a Public Private Partnership agreement in the light of the State Procurement Law and its Executive Regulations, it is an administrative contract. Consequently, PPP agreements that were, for instance, made in Egypt before the promulgation of the new PPP legislation were administrative contracts. A clear example is the New Cairo Wastewater Treatment Plant project that was made pursuant to the Egyptian State Procurement Law and its Executive Regulations. Today, it is a matter of debate

21 Bovis 2010: 14.

as to the legal nature of these transactions in the light of the new legislation currently promulgated by the Egyptian Parliament.

Concession Agreements in Civil Law Legal Systems: France and Egypt

An Overview

A concession agreement (*Concession des Services Publics*) is one of the most noted administrative contracts in France and Egypt as well as in countries that are not adopting socialist ideologies.

A concession agreement can be defined as an agreement by which the concessionaire, a private entity, may, as per the contract and under the concessionaire's responsibility, run an economic public utility. Running and exploiting the latter will be for a certain fee refunded by end-users. It shall be obligatory for the concessionaire to become subject to the principal rules governing the management of public utilities. Furthermore, the private entity shall be subject to the concession agreement stipulations that are included by the administration. The Administrative Court of Appeal, in one of its leading cases, held that the concessionaire was obliged, by virtue of the contract stipulations and mandatory rules developed by the administration, to provide public service to endusers. The state shall permit the concessionaire to operate the project for a certain period of time and to gain profit to the extent permissible by state conditions. This concession has a special nature, pursuant to the above-mentioned terms, in the course of aiming at running public utilities. Therefore, a concession agreement, as apprehended in doctrine and jurisprudence, contains contractual clauses (*clauses contractuelles*) and regulatory clauses (*clauses règlementaires*). The contractual clauses source stands for the agreement between the contracting parties but is not extended to cover the quality of service that is offered to endusers. The regulatory clauses can be unilaterally amended by the state at any time depending on public utility needs; they usually describe the quality of services rendered to endusers.[22]

The concession agreement in civil law legal culture establishes a regulatory framework that imposes, on the concessionaire, certain stipulations and dedicates to that person the rights gained from public administration mechanisms (*gestion publique*). The latter concept of regulatory framework constitutes a fundamental principle that governs the running and exploiting of public utilities. Consequently, the contractual framework does not prohibit the administration from issuing any regulations, unilaterally, within the context of the abovementioned regulatory framework that, in some cases, is related to contract price.[23]

The legislative framework governing public utility concessions in Egypt is subject to Legislation Nos. 129 of 1947 and 61 of 1958. These laws were subject to partial legislative amendments in

---

22 The Appeal Administrative Court 27/1/1957, Cases Nos. 485 and 1367 of Judicial Year 7. In Egyptian doctrine, see: El Tamawy 1991: 108–24; same meaning, S. Badawi 1994: 115–29. In French doctrine, see: Richer 1995: 354 *et seq*. In Egyptian jurisprudence, see: the Supreme Administrative Court, session 17/1/1970, Case No. 440, Judicial Year 11 and session 30/12/1977, Case No. 110 of Judicial Year 23. In French jurisprudence, the distinction between concession public utilities and concession public works is clear: C.E 10 Avril 1970, Beau et Lagarde, Rec.243; C.E. 6 Mai 1991, Syndicat Intercommunal du Bocage, A.J.D.A. 1991, 717; C.E. 26 Septembre 1994, Commune de Labenne, D.A. 1994, No. 588. For more elaboration, see: Richer 1995: 360.

23 In Egyptian jurisprudence, the General Assembly for Legal Opinion and Legislation, session 4/2/1956, Legal Opinion No.92 and Legal Opinion No. 414, session 4/11/1954.

some sectors of infrastructure in Egypt. In Syria, the Civil Code includes Articles (634) to (639) as the main legislative framework governing concessions.

However, there are entirely new trends, modifications and enhancements in connection with this traditional legal framework as a result of legal globalization.

Legal Globalization and the New Contractual Regime of Concession Agreements in Egypt

The new contractual regime of concession agreements in Egypt has been significantly influenced by cultural globalization.[24] Globalization includes the flow of capital and many other tangible concepts plus intangible values, such as culture. Among these is legal culture. Legal culture has flowed from Anglo-American jurisdictions to civil law legal systems. Moreover, globalization has considerably influenced Egyptian legislator and judicial decisions taken by the Egyptian State Council (*Conseil d'Etat*) and the General Assembly for Legal Opinion and Legislation; the legal nature of the administrative contract (*Le Contrat Administrative*) has drastically changed.[25]

This transnational, cultural and socioeconomic phenomenon is a co-ordination among cultures rather than potential conflicts. Integration among various cultures rather than potential conflicts is increasing in many aspects, including, inter alia, legal globalization. It has been noted that the flow of Anglo-American legal culture has considerably influenced the legal and economic atmosphere, particularly in the fields of international business transactions, transactions between developing states, foreign private entities and dispute settlement mechanisms, especially arbitration. This is an advanced step toward the integration of civil law legal culture into Anglo-American global legal culture. Therefore, a trend toward internationalization of administrative contract stipulations and exorbitant clauses is in place. It is argued that rigid and traditional legal patterns and traditions began to accept modifications and enhancements. Some of these patterns are deteriorating while others have created a new legal system with new characteristics in the wake of the merge of legal cultures.

Penalties and sanctions stated in the administrative contract theory have not changed to date, even with the existence of new trends aimed at the liberalization, modernization and internationalization of the traditional theory of administrative contracts.

Accordingly, it can be said that the rigid patterns of administrative contracts, their substance and exorbitant features have significantly changed during the last two decades as far as Egyptian legal culture is concerned, with special emphasis on infrastructure agreements with foreign private entities. These new legal patterns such as the introduction of International Public Works Agreements, BOT/BOOT/BOO agreements and PPP transactions have started a new era in Egyptian legal culture, one with unique and liberal mechanisms and stipulations.[26] Legal globalization has had its influence on legislation, litigation and the contractual regime of administrative contracts.

Notwithstanding the above facts, the state still maintains its role as the employer, regulator and supervisor of these new types of contracts although, nowadays, this role appears to be very limited. It is, however, expected to open doors to the private sector to participate positively in economic life and increase Inward Foreign Direct Investment (IFDI) through financing and

24 For PPPs in various jurisdictions, see: note 13.

25 See: Ismail 2009: 506; Colaiuta 2010: 268; Ismail 2010a: 92; Ismail 2010b: 363; see: also in French doctrine: Leboulonger 1985; and in Arab doctrine, Mohamed A.M. Ismail 2010d; and Ragab 2007.

26 Ismail 2010c: 54–67.

operating infrastructure projects related to public utilities, as well as exploiting natural resources, in particular oil and gas agreements.

The growing role of the private sector is codified upon the legislation prior to 2007 as well as the new constitutional amendments of 2007 in Egypt, which reject socialism and Marxism. The latter ideologies were adopted by the 1971 Constitution. The new constitutional modifications, nevertheless, adopt no specific ideology, giving latitude to presidential and parliamentary elections to determine the necessary ideological political and economic policy to be followed during each presidential or parliamentary term.

This new approach is the direct result of cultural globalization and the influence of the free market economy policy on the national socioeconomic structure. Despite the current economic crises, a free market economy policy will be maintained by developed and developing states to keep in place the prevailing socioeconomic strategy worldwide with more precautions to enhance the state's role as supervisor, regulator and employer. The role of the state will be limited to its basic and fundamental functions, as was indicated by eminent economist Adam Smith.

It is argued that it is a debate between two different menus, Universalism versus Territorialism or Globalization versus Globaphobia. However, from the economic dimension of globalization, economists would previously refer to "international economic integration" when discussing the growth of overseas transactions; however, nowadays they refer to "globalization," which is the popular term now commonly used.[27]

It has been argued that cultural globalization is a form of cultural imperialism. The aim of the process is, in fact, to achieve mutual respect and trust and to search for common interests, values and principles. It is not a one-way process but rather a two-way interaction. It is neither Westernization nor Americanization but actually a cultural interaction and mutual understanding among various cultures.[28] It is a key player in stepping up and promoting understanding among diverse civilizations. In fact, it is a phenomenon that will create co-ordination among nations rather than cause potential conflicts, as has been pointed out by some eminent scholars.[29]

New Partial Legislative Reforms

The existing legal framework concerning the granting of concession agreements was promulgated by the Egyptian legislator more than five decades ago.

Legislation has significantly developed with regard to granting concessions to infrastructure projects and public utilities. Laws Nos. 100 of 1996, 229 of 1996, 3 of 1997 and 22 of 1998 amended long-standing legislation such as Laws No. 129 of 1947 in respect of granting concessions relating to exploitation of natural resources and public utilities.

The four new laws cover the electricity sector, road sectors, specialized ports and civil aviation and airports, virtually marking a new advanced trend as far as administrative contracts and state international administrative transactions are concerned.

At this stage, it is appropriate to refer briefly to the legal regime governing BOOT transactions as part of the Egyptian legal system, in view of its critical importance in understanding the current situation of PPPs and the proposed modifications and enhancements to the related legal

27 Snowdon 2007. See also: Abdel-Wahab, 2006: 306; and Stiglitz 2004.

28 Abdel-Wahab 2006: 364.

29 Huntington 1996. Also see: Ismail 2010c: 54–67.

regime. As has been pointed out previously, the legal regime controlling the concession-granting process for public utilities is governed by Laws Nos. 129 of 1947 and 61 of 1958. The latter is concerned with granting concessions in the area of exploiting and exploring oil, gas and natural resources pursuant to Article (123) of the Egyptian Constitution. Both laws were promulgated more than half a century ago. In fact, dynamic contractual relationships needed rapid changes and modifications rather than static ones. Accordingly, the Egyptian legislature realized that such outdated legislation was not applicable to BOOT transactions because of its contradiction that BOOT transactions are not finetuning either with administrative contracts or with their nature. Therefore, the Egyptian Parliament promulgated the abovementioned four new laws in the late 1990s for granting public utility concessions by virtue of BOOT agreements. These four are Laws Nos. 100 of 1996, 229 of 1996, 3 of 1997 and 22 of 1998, granting BOOT concessions for the sectors of electricity, public roads and highways, airports and civil aviation and specialized ports, respectively.

The new legislation includes various modifications and enhancements to the previous legal regime governing concession-granting in the field of public utilities. The concession-granting period has been extended from 30 years under the previous two laws to 99 years (as a cap) under the four new laws. In addition, the state now plays a limited role in the contractual process; it is merely the technical and financial supervisor of the entire process. It cannot unilaterally amend service prices offered by the concessionaire as was the case in the traditional concession legislation. Service pricing for endusers is subject to contractual clauses as well as to the consent of the foreign contractor rather than to a regulatory clause that could be amended unilaterally by the state.[30] State intervention in the contractual process in terms of BOOT agreements is very limited compared to the old regime in the traditional concession agreements concluded by and between the state and domestic contractors. The aim of current legislation is to meet economic expectations of foreign contractors at the time of tendering and also in the course of preparing technical and financial feasibility studies, especially given the fact that this is a longterm agreement that renders it necessary, from the contractor's perspective, that a financial equilibrium be maintained during the span of the contract, which may last for decades.[31] Some of the fundamental legislative policies behind the promulgation of the current four laws aim to encourage private foreign entities to enter into international infrastructure project tenders announced by the Egyptian government. Moreover, these policies further aim to encourage major foreign entities in the sector to generate more FDI, as Egypt is a developing country that had intensively embarked on infrastructure developments a few decades ago. There is an essential need to promulgate new legislation for good transactions for all sectors in the country as well as detailed executive regulations that are compatible with each sector's needs.[32]

PPPs in Comparative Legal Culture

PPPs in the International and Comparative Sphere: Defining PPPs (Legal Comparative Perspective)

PPPs can be defined in the international arena:

---

30 For the regulatory clauses that can unilaterally be amended by the state in the Arab doctrine, see: El Sharkawy 2003: 65.

31 Ismail 2010c: 62.

32 Ismail 2010c: 64.

> PPPs are concession type arrangements where public projects are completed with private financing. The private company awarded the PPP contract will build and operate a public facility that would otherwise be operated by the government. Concessionaires are granted certain rights by the public partner, usually including the right to charge users of the services or infrastructure a price in exchange for use; however, concessionaires are also subject to increased governmental regulations on their services, usually including price and operation regulations.[33]

In another definition:

> A PPP is a contract between the government and a private entity where the entity assumes a greater role in the planning, financing, design, construction, operation and maintenance of the public infrastructure project as compared to the traditional procurement contract. All PPPs transfer risks to private entities.[34]

PPP technique can be used for infrastructure projects such as toll roads, bridges, museums, hospitals, prisons, ports and public transportation (i.e., underground or overground railway).

On an international level, a comprehensive legal framework for PPPs, with contract administration issues taken into account, has yet to be developed. The UNCITRAL model legislation provisions[35] on privately financed infrastructure projects cover award procedures for PPPs in depth, but provide minor guidance on how to terminate a concession contract or what happens when a termination occurs. If the contracting authority wishes to terminate the PPP contract, it may do so for compelling reasons of public interest but would meanwhile be subject to payment of compensation to the concessionaire, the terms of which would be agreed in the concession contract. The proposed UNCITRAL rules hardly imply how disputes should be settled, exclusively focusing on settlement of disputes likely to arise between the contracting authority and the concessionaire through the dispute settlement mechanisms agreed by the parties to the concession contract. Contract termination and dispute settlements are left to the discretion of contracting parties in the course of drafting the agreement, with little guidance regarding problems that may arise in respect of current and future viable PPP arrangements.

In Norway, Australia, New Zealand and Germany, funding delays and shortages have caused states to turn to the private sector to fund the building of infrastructure projects. Moreover, the private sector has more experience, efficiency and costeffectiveness with regard to traditional government-run infrastructure techniques and operations.[36]

The situation in Brazil is unprecedented. Brazil became the leading recipient of Foreign Direct Investments in Latin America in 2007, followed by Mexico and Chile. While global foreign investment flows declined in 2008 and 2009, developing countries are likely to be less affected by the current financial crises. Brazil, during the 1990s, had sustained a lack of capacity of the government to invest. It followed an ideological agenda, chiefly targeting efficiency and innovation. Currently, however, Brazil enacts comprehensive concession and public procurement laws governing PPPs.[37] as it is nowadays facing the challenge of attracting private investment in infrastructure, which it is essential to keep up and proceed with its development, both in profitable

33 Southard 2010: 2.

34 Cook 2008: 28.

35 United Nations Commission on International Trade Law. Online at: http://www.uncitral.org/pdf/english/texts/procurem/pfip/model/annex1-e.pdf. See also: appendices to this book.

36 Southard 2010: 3.

37 Monteira De Barros 2009: 180–81.

infrastructure facilities such as electricity, transport (roads, airports, underground railways and seaports) and in areas that require government expenditure, to repay the sponsors, such as roads that do not have a high enough demand, hospitals, irrigation, schools and prisons.[38]

The globalization wave of business activities that characterized the 1980s occurred mostly within the world of the industrialized countries. One indicator is the share of developing countries in the overall FDI, which is an important indicator of globalization.[39]

Brazilian PPP law enacted on 30 December 2004 adopted new policies to attract private investments for infrastructure projects. Among these policies were: the Design, Build, Finance, Operate and Transfer Scheme (DBFOT); the remuneration of concessionaire via cash payments given by the public sector partner in addition to revenues drawn, in some cases, from the endusers of the infrastructure facility; the contract duration ranged from 5 to 35 years with permission to indicate in the contract that the consideration owed by the government to the private sector be based on the fulfilment of performance standards regarding the facility.[40]

Further assurance to party autonomy was made through the 11.079/04 Act to the effect that the contract's sole objective was to execute a public project.[41] Disputes can be settled on the basis of arbitration,[42] an automatic price restatement in reference to an inflation index or parametric formula or provision of guarantees by international financing entities or non-state-owned institutions.[43]

The Brazilian legal system distinguishes between administrative and sponsored concessions. The first difference relates to the enduser. In administrative concessions, the user, directly or indirectly, is the administration. In sponsored concessions, on the other hand, the user is the community. The use of administrative concessions to explore public services has always been an important theme of discussion. The second difference between the PPPs' modalities in Brazil resides in the remuneration charged to the investor. In administrative concessions, the private partner will be compensated only by government payments, whereas in sponsored concessions, the investor will also receive users' charges.[44]

In the Brazilian legal system, administrative concessions differ from general building contracts. In the latter agreements, the administration contracts with a private entity to implement a project, whereas in an administrative concession, the contractual object is to provide a service to the administration even if the implementation of a project is involved. Further, the 11.079/04 Act prohibits the use of PPPs when contracts are under R$20 million (Brazilian reals), the service will continue for less than five years or the contract's sole objective is to supply handworks or goods or to execute a public project.

Pursuant to Brazilian PPP law, there were several PPPs at state or municipal levels, while at federal level, an irrigation project and a project for the improvement of an airport were under way. At state and municipal levels, six PPP contracts have been executed, namely an underground railway line in Sao Paulo, sewage treatment by the State of Bahia, Paiva Beach urban access,

38 For education and a comparative perspective between private education and public policy in Latin America, see: Villa and Duarte 2005: 95–130. On the situation in Argentina, see: Morduchowicz 2001; in Chile, see: Peirano and Vargas 2005: 67–91; and Wolff 2005: 247.

39 Meyer-Stamer 1997: 66–7.

40 Monteira de Barros 2009: 182.

41 Barral and Haas 2007: 41.

42 Arbitration must be held in Brazil and in the Portuguese language.

43 Monteira de Barros 2009: 183.

44 Barral and Haas 2007. For more reading, see also: Maim Green and McGrath Beaumont 2006.

highway MG 50, sewage treatment by the Municipality of Rio Claro in 2007 and sewage treatment launched by the Municipality of Rio das Ostras in 2007.[45]

In fact, at federal level, the bureaucratic and lengthy period of consultation and preparation prior to the launch of the public tendering process, which takes an average of two years, is one of the factors contributing to minimal opportunities at the federal level for PPP growth.

One may refer to technology, competitiveness and radical policy change, the experience of which in Brazil as in other Latin American countries has been remarkable. The Nova República, for the first time, established the Ministry of Research and Technology (MCT). In the 1987 fiscal year, the Ministry successfully increased its fund to roughly US$750 million, which was twice the amount it received in 1984. Technology transfer has considerably developed during the last three decades due to the advanced policies adopted by the Brazilian government.[46]

In Europe, particularly in The Netherlands, due to the success of the 300 kilometer per hour (km/hr) Thalys train services running on the BKA high speed rail network linking Paris, Brussels, Cologne and Amsterdam, North European governments are looking into other ways of improving the quality and profile of rail routes in the region.[47]

Many projects were of great significance to the railway sector in Europe. High-speed rail displayed its debut in Europe via the Train *à* Grande Vitesse (TGV) in France in 1982. Since then, other nations have begun to simulate this technology: Italy developed the Pendolino, Spain has the AVE, Germany the ICE, Sweden the X2000, while the United Kingdom, France and Belgium benefit from the Eurostar.

In South Korea, two huge project consultancy contracts valued at a total of $2.84 billion, to be completed, have been awarded to a UK-based company in order to provide assistance with the design and construction of two new road crossings connecting the islands of Geoje, in the South, near Busan, and Incheon, in the North, near Seoul, to the mainland.

The first project (Incheon) consists of a huge bridge, built as a PPP concession. Through this project, a UK company became the first foreign investor to lead an important PPP project in South Korea. The cost to complete the project by October 2009 was estimated at $1.24 billion. The second project (the Geoje), awarded to a UK-based company, comprised two cablestay bridges at an estimated cost of $1.6 billion, to be completed by December 2010.[48]

In France, PPPs were approved as a part of the legal system by virtue of Decree No. 559 of 2004, issued on 17 June 2004 and affirmed by the French *Conseil* Judgment on 29 October 2004.[49] However, the financial crises increased the cost of funding, rendering it more difficult to finance infrastructure projects.

PPPs include various legal instruments whereby a private party is responsible for the definition, conception, completion and execution of a public infrastructure project. In France this includes, in particular, partnership contracts (*Contrats de Partenariat*) and delegations of public services (*Délégations de Services Publics*), particularly concessions. However, a legal fact states that partnership contracts and concessions are subject to different legal regimes in France. PPP mechanisms stipulate that the public authority, "the administration," remunerates a private party through periodic payments. Concessions are an old instrument under French law,

45 Monteira de Barros 2009: 184.

46 Meyer-Stamer 1997: 66–7.

47 Privatization International Ltd. (UK), Land Marl PPP for The Netherlands. Online. *LexisNexis*, 1.

48 WWP – Report on Engineering Construct & Plant Operations in the Developing World. Online. *LexisNexis* (September 2005).

49 See: Ismail 2010c: 506;, and C.E Case Nos. 271362, 271357, 271119, 269814. For more details, visit: www.conseil-etat-fr/jurispd/index-ac.

whereby the private party is remunerated by user fees and taxes and thus substantially assumes exploitation risks.[50]

France, in order to boost PPP financing and mitigate financial risks of crises, started a new era of project guarantee policy to cover significant parts of project financing. Project guarantee is one of two main measures aimed at boosting the PPP market in France. The second is a €8 billion co-financing envelope of funds.

The *Mission d'Appui à la réalisation des contracts de Partenariat* (MAPP), the French task force for PPPs, is affiliated with the Ministry of the Economy. The Guarantee Committee, composed of members from the Budget, Treasury, Legal Affairs and the MAPPP, recommends projects to the Minister of Economy that will benefit from the guarantee, and the minister decides on the matter.

In March 2010, the Ministry of the Economy approved the project guarantee for four projects, two partnership contracts and two concessions. The partnership contracts are set for a tram-train on the French island of La Réunion and a high-speed rail project: *Bretagne, Pays de la Loire*. This will cover up to 80 per cent of the construction risk, whereas the post-construction phase will be covered by the Dailly mechanism,[51] guaranteeing that the lenders will benefit from regularly available payments made by the state. The proposed amount of the project guarantee is slightly above €1 billion, and the guarantee could have a potential life of 30 years, covering half of the concession's demand risk. The impact that the project guarantee has on pricing is also difficult to assess, given that no project has been closed to date.

For targeted mitigation of the impact of the financial crises, the French government adopted an expanded stimulus package (*Plan de Reliance*) at the beginning of 2009. The plan was particularly geared to support investments in public infrastructure and comprises a state guarantee for PPP (the project guarantee), which the French Ministry of the Economy can award under certain terms pursuant to Article (6) of the Law Amending the French Finance Law (*Loi de Finance Rectificative*) on 4 February 2009 (the LFR 2009).

The measure is showing some positive effects, despite the fact that none of the projects benefitting from the guarantee has so far been closed; it is, therefore, still premature to measure its precise adequacy. Up to 80 per cent of the loan or securities financing the project can be subject to project guarantee. The issuer of securities can be either a signatory on the PPP contract or the bank financing the project.[52]

In order to benefit from the project guarantee, the criteria are to have a solid technical and economic plan, balanced risk-sharing between public and private parties during the construction and execution of the project, a balanced contractual scheme particularly considering clauses related to early contract termination and, finally, balance among financial players of the projects which the state is guaranteeing.

Even in Middle Eastern and Northern African countries, PPPs are being promoted to undertake infrastructure projects. For example, in the energy sector, the administration in Tunisia has been keen on electricity investors. One of the administration's priorities is the planned energy integration with Europe and fellow Maghreb countries. The Ministry of Industry, together with the head of the *Entreprise Tunisienne d'Activités Pétrolières* (ETAP), which is in charge of the petroleum

50 Zatezalo-Falator 2010.

51 Zatezalo-Falator 2010: 5 "A Dailly mechanism is an assignment of receivables whereby a creditor transfers the benefit of certain receivables directly to its banks. In case of French Partnership contracts, the public authority granting the contract can in advance decide to accept the transfer of the benefit of a portion of these payments to the lenders, under certain conditions provided for in the contract." See also Zatezalo-Falator 2010: 1–3 (the same article, with further elaboration).

52 Zatezalo-Falator 2010: 2.

sector as well as the state's partnership with foreign and local operators, signed many agreements with foreign and local companies. One example is the Trans-Tunisian Pipeline Co. (TTPC), part of ETAP and STEG, the *Société Tunisienne de l'Electricité et du Gas*, which manages the system of gas pipelines in the country. The administration has been involved in the spread of PPPs. The Carthage Power Co. (CPC), which operates a 471 MW power plant at Rades on the Bay of Tunis, is another major example of PPP in Tunisia.[53]

Despite the fact that the government in Tunisia is demonstrating its intent to involve foreign investors increasingly in the local economy, a tendency toward protectionism still characterizes the relationship between state entities and the private sector.[54]

Considering the increased use and popularity of PPP arrangements worldwide, it is surprising to find that no specific legal framework is in place to govern their operation. There has been no consensus, in the United States or in any other nation, on what aspects of public procurement law should apply to PPPs. Traditionally, the public procurement law focuses on buying and award procedures. European Community procurement laws only govern the award procedure and contain no guidance concerning contract administration.[55]

It is recommended that PPP contracts must advance the purposes of traditional procurement laws because administering the contract, after the award, is of much greater importance. The traditional contract theory is not adequately developed to anticipate problems that may arise upon agreement by public and private partners to give up a certain amount of a project's contract to each other.[56]

It is worth mentioning that the United States lacks not only a comprehensive legal framework to authorize contracts and guide PPPs but also experience, compared to European experience, which is more than ten years ahead of the United States' system.[57]

The European Union is also lacking a legal framework for the administration of PPPs. European community leaders have to decide whether or not their directives covering procurement apply to PPPs with the European Commission, conceding that the rules governing PPPs are insufficient, unclear, and differ from one member state to another.

The EU Public Procurement Directives address only contract awards and do not contain any law governing performance of public contracts; PPP success depends mainly on contract performance.[58]

In French and Egyptian legal systems, the concept of *Le Contrat Administratif* is still prevailing where the state entertains its exorbitant powers during the execution of the contract.

Government price setting is often required to ensure private partners do not charge abusive monopolistic rates for their services. It is fundamental to encourage private partners to keep their operating costs down, and this requires putting in place special measures to help the government make sure that investment in new infrastructure is reasonable and prudent.

The infrastructure concession to private companies is not a recent innovation; the Suez and Panama Canals, centuries ago, were carried out initially as private concessions.

In Latin American and Third World countries, private parties are the first to invest and develop electric, water and transportation infrastructure in exchange for licences and concessions from the central government.[59]

53 Chelbi 2010: 2.
54 Chelbi 2010: 2.
55 Southard 2010: 3–4.
56 Southard 2010: 4.
57 Southard 2010: 4.
58 Southard 2010: 4.
59 Cook 2008: 2.

The Egyptian Legislature and PPPs

An Overview: What are PPPs in Egypt?

The Egyptian government announced a national program for public private partnership in infrastructure projects. The program aims at encouraging private financing for public utilities in Egypt. In 2006, the Egyptian government adopted a new longterm policy of pursuing partnerships with the private sector to expand and increase the country's infrastructure investments. Hence, the Egyptian government established the PPP Central Unit (PPPCU) within the Ministry of Finance.

As announced by the Ministry of Investment in the third quarter of 2008/2009, the economic growth rate decreased to 4.1 per cent in the second quarter of the same year compared to 7.7 per cent recorded during the same period of the previous fiscal year (2007/2008). The state budget deficit has decreased from approximately EGP 45 billion (9.5 per cent) in February to July of FY 2007/2008 to EGP 38.4 billion (6.9 per cent) in FY 2007/2008. The aim of the Egyptian government was to reduce the deficit to 3 per cent by 2011.[60] The Egyptian government is seeking to set a national policy to generate funds and increase existing private sector participation in infrastructure projects in the country.

The climate change phenomenon is a global challenge threatening the planet. The effects of this phenomenon, some of which are higher temperatures, greater climate variations, rising sea levels and high incidences of extreme weather conditions, i.e., heat waves, storms, and floods, are nowadays being monitored. Longerterm estimates, up to 2050, show that global reduction of CO_2 emissions would be necessary. The four major polluting sectors are energy, transportation, building and industry. The types of technology appropriate for climate mitigation are energysufficiency improvements from production to end use – solar, wind, fusion geothermal biomass and clean fossil technologies, including Carbon Capture and Storage (CCS), energy from waste, hydrogen production from non-fossil energy sources, and fuel cells. Generally, the governments of developing countries are looking for international business models in the field of infrastructure developments to generate funding, provide technology and mitigate climate change in the polluting sectors. PPPs can be feasible mechanisms to achieve this goal. The target of climate change mitigation is to reach a low carbon economy through the application of environmentally friendly technology. PPPs are a mechanism that can be used to mobilize the necessary resources in an effective way to reach this goal and to share the risk between the governments of developing countries and private foreign entities as contractors in these transactions. Environmentally friendly technologies can enable the reduction of carbon dioxide emissions arising from industrial sites. Indeed, public participation, as well as incentives provided by the governments of developing countries, will enhance CCS, as the private entities will receive sufficient incentives to develop these technologies. PPP contributions to mitigate the effects of climate change can be useful to countries using PPP models. Landfill, particularly in developing countries, leads to the avoidance of methane and CO_2 emission.[61]

---

60 Egyptian Ministry of Investment, Report on the Ministry of Investment Performance in the Fiscal Year 2007/2008, 12.

61 Methane is of special concern to global warming since the warming effect of methane in the atmosphere is 23 times stronger than that of CO_2. For details of the role of PPPs in mitigating climate change and increasing FDI, see: Hamilton 2009. For further elaboration, see: Sachs 2005: Chapter 4: 84–114. Also visit: http://www.globalwarmingart.com/wiki/Image:Mauna_Loa_Carbon_Dioxide_png.

The fundamental aspect of Egypt's PPP policy framework is the use of performance based contracts. Under these contracts, the private sector provides public services for the duration of the contract and is paid either by the public sector, the endusers, or a mix of both.[62]

Some commentators define PPPs as "innovative, long term contractual arrangements for developing infrastructure and providing public services by introducing public sector funds, expertise and motivation into areas that are normally the responsibility of the government."[63] This approach divides public infrastructure from "economic infrastructure" (i.e., transportation, water, sewage, electricity, etc.) and "social infrastructure" (i.e., schools, hospitals, prisons, and so forth).

The Ministry of Finance in Egypt defines PPP transactions as "a long term contractual relationship between the public sector and the private sector for the purpose of having the private sector deliver a project or service traditionally provided by the public sector."[64]

The project is mainly undertaken by a consortium of private firms, Special Purpose Vehicle (the SPV), capitalizing to expand, improve and operate a public service distribution network. The project company borrows significant longterm funds from commercial lenders. The lenders look primarily at the projected future revenue stream generated by the project, as well as the company's limited assets, to assess its ability to repay all loans. The host country government does not provide financial guarantees to lenders. The project structure is to Design, Finance, Build, Maintain and Transfer (DFBMT) the public utility for the host country.

It is appropriate at this stage to refer to a fundamental reality, namely, risksharing. Significant risks relating to the costs of designs and construction of assets, the cost of time overruns, market demand for the use of the assets, and service provided by the assets and the facility's operation and maintenance costs[65] are transferred from the public juristic entity to the contractor.

The PPP success factors are the PPP model and documentation that can be easily replicated (feasibility analysis, risk allocations, PPP contracts, and so forth). The deal flow considers quantity, which is of a sufficient scale to justify a PPP strategy, and quality, to determine which candidates are appropriate for a PPP. Projects must be clear and bankable. The project in the Egyptian model aims to create more opportunities to be able to attract new finances through the use of credit enhancements, needed to reduce sovereign risks. PPPs will not work unless the public sector understands its governance and oversight responsibilities from beginning to end.[66]

The Egyptian Ministry of Finance summarizes elements of legal and institutional frameworks for PPPs that are multisectoral, such as PPP legislation, PPP technical unit(s), PPP project development and preparation facilities, PPP guidelines and longterm service contracts and PPP procurement regulations, adopting the concept that the lowest bid is often not the best bid. Public credit enhancements are financial performance guarantees, as well as partial risk guarantees. A public sector risk management unit is available, as well as systematic PPP training and capacitybuilding, and PPP contract performance-monitoring capacity.[67]

It is left to the private sector to design, finance, build and operate the facility to meet these longterm specifications. The project company receives payments during the span of the PPP project (normally 20 to 30 years on average), pursuant to the conclusion of the agreement.

62 Egyptian Ministry of Finance 2009. Update on the National Program for Public Private Partnership, PPP Central Unit, June: 6. See: http://www.mof.gov.eg (accessed 31 July 2011).

63 Hamilton 2009: 3.

64 Egyptian Ministry of Finance 2009: 6.

65 See: Hamilton 2009: 4.

66 Egyptian Ministry of Finance 2009: 15.

67 Egyptian Ministry of Finance 2009: 15.

The agreement normally stipulates repayment of the financing costs to the investor during the period of the contract, preconditional upon fulfilling certain criteria and meeting the agreed specifications.[68]

From the Egyptian government's perspective, PPPs in Egypt provide a new source of investment capital for required infrastructure projects, reduce the Egyptian government's sovereign borrowings and associated risks and drive the creation of local longterm funding markets. Furthermore, PPPs create a new privatesector facility management market, expand the economy, stimulate job creation and increase the quality of public services provided to the Egyptian citizen. PPPs introduce the disciplines and efficiencies of privatesector management and methods to the provision of public services. The public sector can realize significant advantages in terms of cost, value and quality of the delivered services. Privatesector participation aims to, among other things, improve the quality of services provided to citizens, create job opportunities and stimulate investment as well as consumption, thus boosting growth and attracting FDI. Throughout a PPP project, the government maintains close control over the delivery of the specified level and standard of services. Where core social services are involved, such as teaching and medical care, the delivery of services to end-users (the public) will be rendered by publicsector professionals. PPPs, in turn, will open up opportunities for the domestic contracting and financing sectors, including smaller contractors who are expected to benefit considerably from the program.

Since 2004, the government has been giving effect to key structural reforms that prove to be delivering favourable results. To sustain Egypt's growth prospects of around 7–8 per cent in the future, the government needs to invest more in infrastructure. It is estimated that Egypt should allocate between 5.5 per cent and 7 per cent of its yearly GDP to cover its infrastructure needs (new investment and maintenance); this is equivalent to the sum of US$13 billion annually. The key challenge, therefore, is to bridge this financial gap by accelerating the mobilization of private capital. International experience shows that 10–30 per cent of infrastructure capital needs can be derived from the private sector through PPPs if appropriate and regulatory framework and other catalytic measures are established. It is estimated that Egypt can realistically target the mobilization of 10–13 per cent of its infrastructure needs through PPPs.[69]

The Egyptian government adopted an advanced policy to enhance the legal (legislative and regulatory) atmosphere in the PPP sector. The right environment for implementation is reached through the adoption and localization of international successful PPP models (such as in the UK, South Africa, India, and elsewhere). Provision for a supportive legislative environment now exists after the promulgation of the new legislative framework for PPP projects.

The Egyptian government aims to establish regulatory bodies for post-contract implementation.[70] The implementation strategy aims at placing clear PPP initiatives under the reformed macro fiscal agenda, establishing a PPP Central Unit in the Ministry of Finance, as well as satellite units in line ministries, and identifying projects with potential for PPPs, as part of the fiveyear strategic plan of line ministries. Moreover, after establishing a legislative framework (PPP legislation), developing a toolkit for the implementation of projects, arranging for credit enhancement mechanisms and stimulating the local banking sector, the strategy aims to offer longer tenders and competitive prices.[71]

---

68 Similarly, see: Hamilton 2009: 4.

69 W B Report, Options to Develop PPP Market Supply Side Institutions, July 2008, see: Egyptian Ministry of Finance 2009: 17.

70 Egyptian Ministry of Finance 2009: 18.

71 Egyptian Ministry of Finance 2009: 18

To date, the government of Egypt has achieved the award and closure of the New Cairo Waste Water Treatment Plant Project and has other pilot projects underway. Pilot projects have also been launched in the education, universities, hospitals and utility sectors.[72]

The public profile of PPPs in Egypt has been raised significantly, to the extent that Egypt is perceived to be one of the leaders in the PPP field in the Middle East and North Africa (MENA) region. Consequently, the PPP Central Unit won the PPP 2008 award from among all the Euro Mediterranean countries at the Second International Conference for Public Private Partnership held in Paris, France, on 29–30 October 2008.[73]

PPPs and the Current Economic Crisis

Financing for new PPPs will be primarily influenced by their assets. Private developers will be more selective, demanding higher quality and more "bankable" PPPs with clearer forms of public support and risksharing. In addition, infrastructure, as an asset, will be preferred by many investors as opposed to other types of investments.

Donors should be prepared to play an increased role in providing and facilitating financing for PPPs. Future PPPs in emerging markets will likely see an increase both in smallscale contracts (using local contractors) and in "PFI type" investments. Longterm fundamentals still remain, however, as the demand for infrastructure in emerging markets is large and growing. In the meantime, financial and implementation capacities of governments are inadequate.[74]

PPPs versus Concessions in Theory and Practice

As is stated above, PPP agreements are similar to concessions in some aspects and different in others. Nevertheless, both transactions aim to achieve continuity and regularity of public utilities (*La Continuité du Service Public*).

PPPs are similar to concessions[75] in their hybrid nature. In both types of contract, the contractual relationship consists of similar consequences: The two contracts contain, among other elements, the construction, operation, management and maintenance of public utilities. Concessions, under the Egyptian legal system, may include, among other elements, construction agreements and the abovementioned mechanisms in the contractual relationship. Moreover, both types of contracts will undergo public tenders and free competition (*La Libre Concurrence*) in the tendering proceedings; this permits the submission of more than just an offer to the contracting authority. The latter offer must be scrutinized from a technical and financial dimension in order to maintain regularity and continuity of public utilities and guarantee equality among endusers in accessing and benefiting from public services offered to them by the public utilities.

The Egyptian government, when it started the implementation of the BOOT system under its legal regime during the last decade of the twentieth century, announced many international public tenders, through that system, to construct and operate public utilities. It allowed private juristic entities, whether local or foreign, to enter into these tenders.

72 See: http://www.mof.gov.eg (accessed 31 July 2011).

73 Egyptian Ministry of Finance 2009: 26.

74 Egyptian Ministry of Finance 2009: 27.

75 Ismail 2010b: 106–10.

The procedural rules governing these tenders were set out to assure transparency and fairness in selecting the best offers compatible with the hybrid nature of these contracts, requiring advanced bidders in technical aspects. BOOT agreements are one of the most effective mechanisms for transferring advanced technology to developing countries. The direct result of regulating public utility agreements to transparency and fair competition rules is that these rules and acts by the administration are subject to the judicial review of the Egyptian State Council in order to maintain compliance with legislative provisions.[76]

This is the application of the legality principle (*Principe de Légalité)* in the Egyptian legal system, as the Egyptian Constitution affirmed the judicial review of the Egyptian State Council of all administrative decrees (Article (172) of the Egyptian Constitution). The administrative decree selecting a contractor for infrastructure public tenders is subject to judicial review by the State Council pursuant to the Egyptian Constitution, as stated above, under Law No. 47 of 1972.

PPPs and concessions substantially differ in one fundamental dimension, namely, that PPPs are mainly for financing public utilities, and operation is a result of the financing. Moreover, in concessions, the risk falls on the concessionaire who bears the risk during operation and management whereas, in PPP agreements, sharing risk has different concepts that come to light upon the negotiating and signing of the contract and before entering into the contractual relationship.

In the preliminary step before contracting, risksharing is made clear to both parties so that all technical and financial issues relating to the mechanism considered for transferring technology are duly clarified. In addition to project financing, as a main factor, contracting parties may predict various kinds of risk, whether financial or technical, which may affect the project.[77] These factors directly affect the contractual relationship and enable parties to divide risk factors threatening the contract before, during and after performance.

In addition, there are differences between concessions and PPPs in the Egyptian legal system relating to payments to the contractor on the PPP from the starting date of the operation and after constructing the public utility, on a regular basis. In concession agreements, payments to the concessionaire are subject to the achievement.

As PPP agreements were created by the early 1990s in the United Kingdom, followed by the French legal system, administrations were allowed to finance their infrastructure and public utility projects through private financing. It is true that the goal of the PPP agreement is, to a great extent, different from concession agreements in developing countries where there is an essential need for financing by private foreign entities.

Legal Framework of PPP Transactions in Egypt

Before promulgating the new Egyptian PPP Legislation No. 67 of 2010, all PPP transactions were subject to the State Procurement Law and its Executive Regulations. Undoubtedly, these transactions had an administrative nature as administrative contracts. However, there are some changes and modifications to the legal nature of the PPP transactions that aim mainly to encourage the private sector to participate in the infrastructure projects and to increase the Inward Foreign Direct Investment (IFDI).

76 The judicial review in this respect differs from the unconstitutional judicial review by the Supreme Constitutional Court (Article (175) of the Egyptian Constitution).

77 Ismail 2010b: 113.

PPP Current Legal Regime (Challenges of the New Legal Nature)

This legislative and regulatory framework of the State Procurement Law resembles the procedural structure of the rules governing the selection of the entity entering into contract with the state, in terms of financial and technical eligibility as well as creditworthiness. Moreover, the State Procurement Law contains some legislative stipulations relating to the termination of the contract unilaterally by the state or through litigation by a court judgment.

The penalty for terminating the contract is always accompanied by the forfeiture of the performance bond (Article (24) of the State Procurement Law and Article (84) of the Executive Regulations). The legislation also includes, among other penalties, the penalty for delay clause (Article (23) of the State Procurement Law and Article (83) of the Executive Regulations). Under the Egyptian legal system, being a civil law system, the clause has a punitive nature, contrary to the concept of liquidated damages in common law jurisdictions.[78]

Despite the latest changes in the Anglo-American legal culture in the field of liquidated damages,[79] the new State Procurement Law No. 89 of 1998 has adopted some new concepts that differ from those of the previous State Procurement Law Legislation No. 9 of 1983. In the 1998 legislation, the penalty for delay is not compulsorily deducted by the administration (by way of set-off) from the final certificate if the State Council Opinion Department has issued a legal opinion exempting the contractor from the penalty. In certain cases, where there is no damage to the state, the State Council can exercise its judicial power by a legal opinion to exempt the contractor. Conversely, the general principles in State Council court decisions are that the contactor has to pay damages to the state in cases where there is a delay, regardless of the practical reality and of the existence of damages to the state or not. Under the Egyptian legal system, damages are presumed to exist in case of delay regardless of the actual loss; this vision is, to some extent, still applicable. However, the situation underwent modifications and enhancements after the promulgation of the current legislation in 1998. Under the previous Law No. 9 of 1983 and until the application of the new legislation in mid1998, the situation was very different.[80] Moreover, the cap of the penalty was reduced in the 1998 legislation to a maximum of 10 per cent of the total contract value after a certain period of delay, whereas the cap of the previous law of 1983 was 15 per cent of the total value.

Various changes have been introduced by the State Council courts to the legal nature of the penalty interpretation of the State Procurement Law and the application of the latter legislation clauses to infrastructure agreements. Since the Administrative Law and administrative contract

78 In the Egyptian judicial system, see: Supreme Administrative Court, The Egyptian State Council (*Conseil d'Etat*), Case No. 4545, session dated 23/3/1999, Judicial Year 39. In English case law see: Dunlop Pneumatic Tyre Ltd v. New Garage Motors Company Ltd, HL (1915), AC, 79, and current changes in: Phillips Hong Kong v. Attorney General of Hong Kong, 61 BLR 41 (1993), M & Polymers Ltd v. IMERYS Mineral Ltd, (2008) 1, ALL ER, and Liberty Mercian Ltd vs. Dean & DYBALL Construction Limited (2009), BLR, 29.

79 In United States case law, see: W.P. Tinkham v. Ferdinand Satori, 44 Mo. App.659:1891 Mo. App Lexis 206; County of Mercer v. Stupp Bros Bridge Iron Company, 115, III App. 208, 1904 II App. Lexis 312 and The Pacific Hardware and Steel Company v. The United States, No. 31187-48 Ct. Cl 399:1913 US, Ct. Cl. Lexis 89. In recent cases, see new trends: Barrie School v. Andrew Patch, 401 Md. 497:933 A.2d 382:2007 Md. Lexis 643, and El Centro Mall.LLc v. Payless Shoe-Source Inc., 174 Cal. App.4th 58:2009 Cal. App. Lexis 806.

80 For an analytical perspective on the penalty for delay (liquidated damages in the Egyptian legal system), see: Ismail 2010c: 506–13.

principles in Egypt were not codified and since the Egyptian State Council has been playing a significant role in codifying these principles since 1946, State Council decisions were, to some extent, influenced by legal and cultural globalization of the Egyptian legal system. This has been especially the case as Egypt is a civil law country, which has been influenced considerably by the flow of Anglo-American legal globalization.

The current situation in PPP projects awarded by the state to contractors during the past years, is that these transactions are subject to State Procurement Law No. 89 of 1998 and its Executive Regulations; they follow the administrative nature on procedural aspects and consequently on substantive ones. Conversely, the draft PPP Law prepared by the National Democratic Party (the recent governing party in Egypt) and the Ministry of Finance, excluded PPP transactions from the scope of application of the State Procurement Law No. 89 of 1998, the Public Utilities Concession Legislation No. 129 of 1947 and Concession Law No. 61 of 1958. Through this mechanism and legislative stipulation, all PPP transactions must be subject to the new law, as the Egyptian Parliament has accepted this concept. Today, it is true that the Egyptian legislature shall, directly after the promulgation of the new legislation, promptly exclude PPP transactions from the scope of application of the Administrative Contracts Theory – but to what extent?

There are legal and economic justifications behind excluding PPP transactions from the scope of application of administrative contracts, as the Administrative Contract Theory *(Le Contrat Administratif)* has its own unique nature and stipulations. It is of fundamental importance, at this stage, to explain the administrative nature and the specific stipulations of the Administrative Contracts Theory and their implications on PPP transactions and International Administrative Contracts, which are necessary for the state's activities.

It is appropriate to refer to the situation in France where the French *Conseil d'Etat* has confirmed the legality of Order (*L'Ordonnance*) No. 559 of 2004, which does not contradict the French legislation. The order regulates and permits PPP transactions in the French legal system. The famous judgment issued by the French *Conseil d'Etat* on 29 October 2004[81] affirmed that this order is compatible with the French legal system and legislation. It rejected all cases aimed at revoking the decree that implies the legality of PPPs in France as an integrated part of the French legal system.

PPP New Legislation in Egypt

The Egyptian legislature promulgated the new PPPrelated legislation in summer 2010 by Law No. 67 of 2010. PPP transactions are subject to this legislation; before this legislation, they were subject to the State Procurement Law No. 89 of 1998 and its Executive Regulations issued by the Minister of Finance (Decree No. 1367 of 1998).

Despite that fact, projects concluded with the private sector were implemented under the State Procurement Law, which included its exorbitant stipulations. These clauses were obligatory to PPP transactions.

Pursuant to the State Procurement Law, PPP transactions concluded under this law had the administrative nature in procedural and substantive rules.

Egypt, for example, has 99.3 per cent electricity coverage, and power demand is rising by 7 per cent per annum. A new Egyptian electricity law setting out the framework for a liberalized power sector was debated in the Egyptian Parliament in 2009. The Egyptian Electric Utility and Consumer

81 The French State Council, Cases Nos. 269814, 271119, 271357, 271362 on 29/10/2004. For more details, please visit www.conseil-etat.fr.

Protection Regulatory Agency (Egyptera) enlisted the help of an independent consultant to bring the final draft of the legislation into line with EU best practices in this regard. The new electricity law allows the producers and consumers to enter into direct bilateral contracts for powertrading. However, the bilateral market will be the first competitive market to be established in conjunction with the move to free up the power sector. Cairo has encouraged private participation in power generation. Private companies will be able to generate power on a Build–Own–Operate (BOO) basis, provided that a bilateral agreement is concluded with an enduser. In this respect, the European Commission had prepared a report on the potential for private investment, and experts pointed out that Egyptera had been approached by developers seeking to invest in projects with a capacity of up to 3,000 MW. A World Bankfunded study had examined another avenue for introducing private participation in the Egyptian power sector, with the prospect of using PPPs in power generation and distribution or in the supply business but specifically for generation because of it being highly capital-intensive.[82]

A fully liberalized market is still a long way off in Egypt. If and when it does take shape, it will necessitate a re-evaluation of the status of independent power projects and independent water and power projects.[83]

Pursuant to the current Egyptian PPP legislation announced by the Egyptian Parliament in June 2010, the Egyptian legislature offered various incentives, both procedural and substantive, which to some extent have changed the legal nature of the PPP transactions to a hybrid nature rather than being pure administrative contracts as they were before the promulgation of the new law. This new conceptualization of the nature of the contract is one of the direct results of the legal globalization and the flow of the Anglo-American concepts to civil law developing states. Further, new legislation aims to encourage IFDI in infrastructure industry, public utilities and natural resources sectors.

The new legislation adopted the following strategic legal concepts:

1. The new PPP law includes procedural and substantives rules.
2. PPP contracts will not be subject to provisions of Law No. 129 of 1947 on public utility concessions, Law No. 61 of 1958 on concessions relating to the investment of natural resources and public utilities or on public tenders, and Law No. 89 of 1998 for State Procurement Law and any specific laws on granting concessions of public utilities (Article (1), Promulgation articles).
3. The law defines the private sector as an Egyptian or foreign juristic entity in which the Egyptian stateowned shareholding is less than 20 per cent or as a consortium between two or more Egyptian or foreign juristic persons in which the stateowned shareholding is less than 20 per cent.
4. The duration of the PPP contract shall not be less than five years and shall not exceed 30 years from the date of completion of the construction and equipment works or completion of the rehabilitation works, provided that the total value of the PPP contract is not less than £E100 million.[84] However, the cabinet, based on the recommendations of the Supreme Committee for Public Private Partnership Affairs, may agree to conclude a PPP contract for a time period exceeding 30 years, if so required in connection with public interests.
5. Any amendments to the PPP contract shall be exclusively limited to the scope agreed upon in the PPP contract and upon the approval of the Supreme Committee for Public Private

82 APS Review Downstream Trends, 2010: 1–2.

83 APS Review Downstream Trends, 2010: 2.

84 Around US$18 million at the time of writing this book.

Partnership Affairs, without prejudice to compensation rights of the project company or the administrative authority (as the case may be) in accordance with the conditions and rules stipulated in the PPP contract.[85]

6. No seizure, attachment or executive procedures shall be undertaken with regard to facilities, tools, machinery or equipment allocated for the implementation of a PPP contract, as well as for the operation or utilization of the project subject of the PPP contract.[86]
7. Codifying the PPP Central Unit (PPPCU) role was of fundamental importance to the Egyptian legislature; thus, the new promulgated law stipulated that the PPPCU shall be established at the Ministry of Finance. It shall be competent to provide technical, financial and legal expertise to the Supreme Committee for PPP Affairs and to the PPP satellite units at the administrative authorities.
8. The PPPCU shall establish an electronic report covering all PPP project documentation and shall also be competent to receive, investigate and provide advice *vis-à-vis* complaints of investors participating in PPP projects in preparation for submitting such complaints to the Supreme Committee for PPP Affairs.
9. The investor selection is subject to principles of publicity, transparency, free competition, equal opportunity and fairness, in accordance with the rules and procedures provided for in this law and its executive regulations. All published advertisements for bids and preparations for PPP competition shall be undertaken in coordination with the PPPCU in the manner prescribed in the Executive Regulations.
10. A qualified investor may stipulate that the competent entity of the Administrative Authority may not disclose any confidential data relating to its reservations or its economic or financial expectations. Moreover, dealing with qualified investors shall be in a manner that ensures equal opportunity and fairness.
11. Substantive rules provided in the newly promulgated legislation stipulate the product sale price or the service availability payment on which the project is based and the rules governing its determination and amendment, either by increase or decrease, as well as the method of adjusting it for inflation indexes and changes in interest rates, if required.
12. Substantive rules regulate the right of the Administrative Authority to amend the terms of project construction, equipment, maintenance, operation and utilization as well as other obligations of the project company, in addition to the basis and mechanisms of compensation for such amendments.
13. Upon the approval of the Supreme Committee for PPP Affairs, disputes resulting from the PPP contract may be resolved through arbitration or any other non-judicial means of dispute resolution pursuant to stipulations in the PPP contract.
14. Articles of PPP contracts or their supplementary agreements shall not be amended unless approved by the contracting parties (Article (37), without prejudice to Articles (7) and (8) of this law. The latter stipulates that any amendments will only be likely within the scope agreed in the PPP contract. Moreover, Article (8) stipulates that in case of the occurrence of unforeseen circumstances upon execution of the PPP contract, including amendments to laws or regulations that were enforceable at the time of execution of the PPP contract, it

85 This is contrary to the fundamental concept of the traditional concession contract by which the administration, unilaterally, can amend prices.

86 The Investment Law in Egypt No. 8 of 1997 has the same stipulations in encouraging investment companies as those established pursuant to this law.

may be agreed to amend the PPP contract in accordance with the terms and conditions set forth in the contract.

15. A petition committee shall be formed and chaired by the Minister of Finance, with the membership of two vice presidents of the *Conseil d'Etat* to be selected by its president and the head of the PPPCU, as well as a non-government expert to be selected by the committee chairman. The petition committee shall be competent to consider all petitions and complaints submitted by investors (whether local or foreign) during the procedure of tendering, entering into and executing PPP contracts (Article (39) of the PPP Law).

It is clear that the Egyptian legislature supersedes the party autonomy principle, and *Le Contrat Administratif* excessive clauses have deteriorated. This latter trend has significant impact on increasing IFDI in the infrastructure sector.

What Has Been Achieved to Date?

The Egyptian Ministry of Finance has achieved significant results in a shortterm planning period after the implementation of the new PPP policies in Egypt. In light of the abovementioned government strategy, current PPP projects can be summarized as follows:

The government has invited private sector participation to finance, construct and operate the New Cairo Wastewater Treatment plant with a total capacity of 250,000 m^3 per day to treat wastewater in the New Cairo City, Madinaty and the El Mostakbal areas. The agreement was made through the New Urban Communities Authority and the Ministry of Housing, Utilities and Urban Development on behalf of the Egyptian government. A second project is the financing, construction, operation and maintenance of the October 6 wastewater treatment plant with a capacity of 150,000 m^3 per day, in addition to the operation and maintenance of an existing plant with a capacity of 100,000 m^3 per day through the implementation of a PPP model transaction. The investor will be required to design, construct, finance, operate and maintain the plant and transfer the ownership back to the Ministry of Housing, Utilities and Urban Development at the end of the contract. A third leading project in the country is the construction of two new public university hospitals and a blood bank in Alexandria. The new university hospital PPP projects are key PPP pilot projects to which Alexandria University, with the assistance of the PPP Unit at the Ministry of Finance, has invited private sector participation. In a competitive bidding process, the private sector entity is expected to finance, design, construct, equip, furnish, maintain and operate the two hospitals and the blood bank. This will be given effect by means of a contract to be tendered in two lots whereby each of the qualified bidders is entitled to submit a bid for one or both lots, as follows:

Lot 1: Somouha Maternity University Hospital and a blood bank: a 200 bed hospital and a blood bank located in the same building with a separate entrance;

Lot 2: Mowassat Specialized University Hospital: a 224 bed hospital with centres of excellence (highly specialized services in neurosurgery and urology/nephrology, including kidney transplants).

The above projects were implemented under the guidance of the PPPCU in the Egyptian Ministry of Finance. Moreover, the transactions were tendered under State Procurement Law No. 89 of 1998. It is of fundamental importance to refer to the fact that forthcoming projects will be tendered under the new PPP law.

The pipeline projects can be summarized in the highways, seawater desalination plant, wastewater treatment plants, hospitals and schools.

In light of these facts, the Egyptian government, in participation with the Ministry of Finance, invited the private sector to participate in implementing a PPP model for contracts to finance, construct, furnish, operate and maintain the West Gulf of Suez Seawater Desalination Plant, North Sinai Seawater Desalination Plant, Nahia Wastewater Treatment Plant, Boulak and El Abassia General Hospitals, Hurgada Seawater Desalination Plant, Helwan Wastewater Treatment Plant, El Galala Quarry Road, Alex West Wastewater Treatment Plant and Rod El Farag Highway Project.[87] The above projects are expected to be tendered and awarded pursuant to the new PPP legislation.

There is no doubt that these various sector projects, whether pilot or pipeline, established during a short period of time are an assurance of the intention and willingness of the Egyptian government to adopt and promote the implementation of the PPP model of contract in many sectors of public utility in the field of social and economic infrastructure, as stated above.

Conclusions

There are various enhancements to the different legal systems that have been achieved in the field of PPP transactions as a result of legal globalization despite the concept of *Le Contrat Administratif*, its special nature and constraints. The current PPP legal framework in various countries, in particular France, Brazil, and Egypt, is a coherent step toward liberalization, modernization and internationalization of *Le Contrat Administratif*. In Arab Middle Eastern countries, particularly Syria and Lebanon, it is strongly recommended that developing countries adopt a similar legislative and regulatory mechanism to achieve the quick implementation of a new prospective policy expected to promote development in the infrastructure sector; incentives to foreign investors are needed. It is appropriate at this stage to refer to the fact that it is difficult to increase Inward Foreign Direct Investment due to the implications of the current financial crisis. However, it is up to developing states to promote the abovementioned legislative and regulatory framework to minimize state intervention, as the latter is subject to a degree of economic and legal liberalization of the administrative system; it is also due to the ideology adopted by the constitutional framework that governs state international business transactions and state contracts with private foreign entities in the international sphere. Moreover, IFDI in the infrastructure sector through PPPs will promote the transfer of technology from developed countries to developing states, create more job opportunities and train experienced personnel in advanced technologies with a view to increasing experienced labour in various sectors in developing countries. This process will increase the export of experienced staff with reasonable wages from developing states, particularly Egypt, to neighbouring countries. Furthermore, it will lead to a total enhancement of public utility operations and services provided to endusers.[88]

In mitigating the effects of financial crisis, as pointed out above, states must offer their best endeavours to achieve that goal with a view to encouraging private foreign entities to participate in the infrastructure sectors. The French system, as the leading civil law jurisdiction, achieved significant steps to mitigate the effects of financial crises in the domain of PPP transactions.

Mitigating the effect of climate change is one of the goals of PPP, as the technique has a significant role to play. The private sector provides financing and technology, as well as the sharing

87 For more details, visit: http://www.mof.gov.eg (accessed 31 July 2011).

88 Ismail 2010c: 67.

of risks; these are strategic elements in implementing advanced policies against the threat of climate change. It is strongly recommended that governments maintain certain policies that comply with the mitigation of climate change, particularly during the tendering process. These policies may include specifications, contract award criteria and payment stipulations to contractors. In the light of the latter policies, PPPs in both developed and developing states should play a considerable role in decreasing the risks of climate change.[89]

Today, in light of the newly promulgated law in Egypt, for instance, a PPP transaction is not a purely administrative contract; it has a hybrid nature, as it is neither a purely commercial transaction nor a purely administrative contract. This is evidenced by the new law provisions that dedicate the right of the foreign investor to enter with the administration into PPP agreements in view of the new PPP legislation, regardless of traditional procurement laws and regulations. Moreover, Traditional Concession laws are not applicable; consequently, the administration cannot unilaterally amend the contract or impose penalties to a great extent as stated above. This will be followed by new legislation to be promulgated in most Arab countries, particularly Syria and Lebanon.

In addition, the consent of a foreign private entity is required to amend financial contractual clauses, including prices, regardless of the regulatory clauses in traditional concessions. These clauses do not exist in PPPs, as the administration cannot unilaterally amend contract prices in PPPs. This will not violate the foreign contractor's economic expectations in a longterm agreement. State intervention shall be kept to a minimum, as party autonomy appears to a great extent and leads the contracting parties into more or less equal bargaining power. Developing civil law states are now playing the role of employer, legislator, regulator and supervisor of all public utility transactions. The extent of state intervention is subject to the degree of economic and legal liberalization of the administrative systems that are directly influenced by cultural and legal globalization. The constitutional framework plays a significant role reflecting the legal and economic ideologies, as the constitution is at the top of the legislative instruments in the Arab Middle Eastern and North African developing states. Constitutions describe the state role and show the degree of state intervention in all aspects of administrative and economic systems relating to public utility management and operations.

89 For details of the role of PPPs in mitigating climate change and increasing FDI see: Hamilton 2009: 63. For further elaboration, see: Sachs 2005. See also: http://www.globalwarmingart.com/wiki/image:Mauna_Loa_Carbon_Dioxide_png.

Chapter 5
Globalization and Enhancements to State Procurement Legislations in Terms of Contract Price (Egyptian Case Study)[1]

Introduction

The traditional theory of the administrative contract is nowadays facing many challenges and difficulties.

The change in raw materials prices in the Egyptian construction industry used to be, and still is, constant before and after the global economic crisis. The Egyptian Parliament is facing these changes by amending and modifying State Procurement Law provisions. Meanwhile, the Ministry of Finance is modifying its executive regulations. The main aim of these amendments is to promote contractual equilibrium between the employer (state administration) and the contractor, because public works contracts are complex and long-term agreements. To maintain stability of the contract price, the Egyptian legislator created certain mechanisms in 2005 and 2008 instead of the customary parameters of the traditional theory of the administrative contract. These mechanisms changed considerably some of the leading principles of administrative contract theory which have existed since the establishment of the Egyptian State Council (*Conseil d'Etat*) in 1946.

The traditional theory of the State Council, which is mainly found in the Supreme Administrative Court judgments and in the General Assembly for Legal Opinion (*Fatwa*), as well as the Legislation Department, had certain stipulations about the maintenance of stable contract prices during the contract, and until its final completion. The new amendments in the Egyptian legislation created new mechanisms to change contract prices on a regular basis.

This chapter has three parts: first, the traditional theory of administrative contracts and its leading stipulations to maintain price stability are set out; second, modifications and enhancements of Egyptian State Procurement Law and its executive regulations since 2005 are described; and, third, current changes to the Egyptian State Procurement Law introduced in 2008 and their significance as a result of globalization, and their impact on the administrative contract, are discussed.

The Traditional Theory of the Administrative Contract and Price Stability

General Principles

Decades ago, in administrative contract theory, the contract price in public works agreements was fixed as of the signing of the contract by and between the administration and the contractor. There was always a stipulation under pre-contractual documents (which form part of the contract) stating

1 © Informa UK Limited. This chapter first appeared in *The International Construction Law Review* [2010] 27, 1, ICLR, 92–103, and is reproduced by kind permission of the publisher and editors.

that the contractor shall not, under any circumstances, claim any changes in the contract price as a result of changes in materials prices or wages. However, in some cases, claims could be made for increases in the price of cement and reinforcement if an administrative decree had been issued by the Prime Minister allowing a price increase (or if a ministerial decree had been issued by the minister concerned), during the period of performance of the contract. The contractor had first to claim an increase in the prices and the employer had to agree to pay them.

The contractor can also claim additional payment pursuant to the hardship or (*Le Fait du Prince dans les Contrats Administratifs*) theories in proceedings before State Council courts or an arbitral tribunal.

In one of the leading cases, the Supreme Administrative Court stated that:[2]

> the clause stipulating the price in administrative contracts is a general principle in fixing the price between the administration and the contractor. Both parties can amend the clause once there is an intention to change the price.

Price fluctuation clauses are common, however, in international and domestic public works agreements. In energy agreements, however (oil and gas in particular) the Egyptian Constitution stipulates, in Article (123), that concessions are granted by legislation, not by an administrative decree pursuant to legislation. Thus, amending prices in contracts of exploitation of natural resources of the country must be by legislation (*Parallelism des Competences*).

When the administration intends to compensate the contractor, it can do so either by issuing a separate invoice in international public works agreements or by legislation in oil and gas agreements.[3] The General Assembly for Legal Opinion (*Fatwa*) and Legislation stated, in a recent dispute between the Roads and Bridges General Corporation and the Nile Public Company for Desert Roads, that:[4]

> Article 8 of the contract stipulates that performance shall be as follows:
>
> 1. Private conditions for this tender.
>
> 2. …
>
> 3. …
>
> 4. Reservations made by the company and approved by the corporation.

---

2 The Supreme Administrative Court, Case 1222, Judicial Year 12, 17 January 1970. See also The General Assembly for Legal Opinion (*Fatwa*) and Legislation, legal opinion No 336, session 21 February 1990, dated 31 March 1990, file No. 78/2/17; legal opinion No 384, session 19 December 1990, dated 25 May 1991, file No. 78/2/19; and legal opinion No 600, session 24 August 1994, dated 4 September 1994; file No 78/2/34.

3 See: Ismail 2003b: 106, stating that in the Egyptian legal system, the technique adopted in international public works agreements, as they enter into force at the effective date, is a separate invoice to compensate the contractor for price fluctuations as stipulated in the agreement (stabilization clause). This mechanism is to maintain contractual equilibrium. Meanwhile, in oil and gas concession agreements, as promulgated by legislation, the contract price can only be amended to compensate a contractor by legislation.

4 General Assembly for Legal Opinion (*Fatwa*) and Legislation, legal opinion No. 499 session 8 in October 2008, dated 26 October 2008; file No 78/2/87. See also previous opinion No 1040, session 3 November 1991 dated 28 November 1991; file No. 78/2/22.

The pre-contractual documents are part of the contract. Article (18) of the financial conditions of the tender stipulates:

> with the exception of an increase in the prices of cement, reinforcing iron and bitumen, the contractor does not have the right to claim any price increases in materials or wages even if there is an administrative decree stating the new prices.

It is common under the Egyptian legal system that these are the only elements for which the employer can pay the contractor as a result of any increase in price since the contract. This is conditional upon the issue of an administrative decree by the authority concerned during the contract and before the final completion admitting price increases. Prices of all other materials must be unchanged as they are part of the ingredients of the whole tender. The last condition is that the contractor must claim payments as a result of increased prices in his offer to the tender and the employer must approve the request.[5]

Article (23) of the financial conditions stipulates:

> The contractor shall not be allowed to increase the contract price as a result of any currency fluctuations, wage increases, raw materials increases or any other reason. A contractor shall maintain all precautions that procure regularity in performance with the fixed contract price agreed upon when contracting regardless of any changes or fluctuations in prices in the market.

Upon applying these clauses to facts, the General Assembly stated:

> In applying Article 18 on financial conditions, the contract price shall be fixed and shall not be subject to review or any increase except for the price of cement, reinforcing iron and bitumen. It is clear that the offer of the public company (offer of the contractor) did not include, in the previous conditions, any reservation about extra payments in case of any increase in the above-mentioned materials prices, even if performance is strenuous on the contractor. A contractor can claim his payments before any court to maintain financial equilibrium.

In interpreting and analyzing this legal opinion, which falls under the scope of application of the State Procurement Law No. 89 of 1998 (before its amendment in 2005), the contractor, as a general principle compatible with the traditional theory of the administrative contract, cannot claim any increase in the contract price related to the increase in raw materials prices, wages, currency fluctuations or depreciation except for certain cases. For such cases, the contractor must, within the limits of certain and strict stipulations, make a reservation in his offer at the time of tender and before contracting.

The General Assembly reflected any additional payments and referred, at the end, to the contractual equilibrium principles of hardships for which the contractor can claim additional payments before any court or by means of arbitration, if there is an arbitration agreement, pursuant to the Civil Code and the administrative contract principles in contractual equilibrium. The General Assembly stated that:

---

5 This legal approach is understood from the application of the State Procurement Law in the Egyptian legal system. Moreover, the author of this article was honored to participate in deliberations (before voting) for this legal opinion by the General Assembly Board. He had the opportunity to study the legal opinion file. Unlike court deliberations, these deliberations are not confidential before voting for a legal opinion (see: previous opinion No. 499, n. 3, above).

> It is up to the contractor to initiate the relevant litigation proceedings as it is the administrative court's jurisdiction pursuant to general principles in administrative contracts maintaining financial equilibrium.[6]

When analyzing this opinion, as there is a conservative trend to change contract price, the General Assembly, contrary to the legislative policy behind its role, refused to apply the well-known hardship theory in administrative contracts, as Article (147(2)) of the Egyptian Civil Code is applicable in this case. Article (147(2)) states:

> If any unexpected circumstances took place during the performance, which were not expected at the time of contracting, and as a result of such unexpected circumstances the agreed obligations were economically difficult to maintain during performance, the judge (or arbitrator) is entitled to maintain economic balance. Any agreement to the contrary shall be null and void.

The General Assembly refused to maintain contractual equilibrium in the contract leaving jurisdiction to the State Council courts or arbitration if there is an arbitration agreement. It is strongly recommended that the General Assembly must exercise its power conferred upon it by Article (66(d)) of the State Council Law No. 47 of 1972. The Assembly should define the legal opinion request as being a dispute between the administration and the contractor to issue an obligatory legal opinion to compensate the contractor.

In this case, even if the contract stipulates fixed prices, it can be amended pursuant to the hardship clause (Article 147(2)). The latter article is a mandatory rule under the Egyptian legal system; the agreement between parties cannot violate its application.

Exercising this power by the General Assembly will avoid long and costly litigation or arbitral proceedings.

The Administration Authority Amending the Contract Price Without the Consent of the Contractor

As is set out above, the contractor can claim additional payments before any court or by means of arbitration pursuant to the principles of hardship or *Fait du Prince* stated in civil and administrative contracts and that it is a mandatory rule under the Egyptian legal system where parties may not exclude the application of such principles and may not agree to the contrary.

The administration can change contract quantities and prices at any time without any legal or judicial action. Article (78) of the Executive Regulations (Minister of Finance Decree No. 1367 of 1998) stipulates that:

> The administration has the right to amend quantities of its contracts ± 25% for each item with the same conditions and price without dedicating any right to the contractor to claim for compensation.
>
> The administration has the right, in emergency cases, to exceed 25%. In the latter case, the contractor must agree if the percentage is more than 25%.

6 Ibid.

In all modifying contract cases, the approval of the contractor is obligatory on any percentage exceeding that mentioned above. "The contractor must still offer the lowest price in the tender compared with other contractors under the same circumstances."

The Egyptian regulator elaborated, stipulating that: "In public works agreements which, according to special technical assistance, need the execution of new items by the same contractor, the administration can issue a (special) direct order to the contractor. The price of the new items must be relevant to market prices."

It is clear that the administration has, to some extent, the right to amend a contract unilaterally without the consent of the contractor within the ceiling of ± 25 per cent; furthermore, in emergency cases, it can amend the contract to exceed 25 per cent for each item with the consent of the contractor.

Moreover, when contractors need special technical assistance; the administration can enter into agreement directly with the same contractor without starting new tender proceedings (special or direct order with the contractor's consent).

Despite the fact that in emergency cases the contractor's consent is required for quantities exceeding 25 per cent of each item, in public works agreements the same contractor may be required for specific technical assistance. It is stipulated, only in this case, that the administration must enter into the latter contract with prices relevant to market prices. As a matter of practical reality, the administration should, to avoid imposing liability upon its employees, enter into a new agreement to obtain additional quantities and relevant prices as mentioned. It is stipulated that the contractors ranking in the tender, among other contractors, still keep the lowest prices,[7] as it is understood from Article (78), in all the above-mentioned cases.

From an economic perspective, this means that inflation and international market changes, which cause changes in materials prices and currency depreciation, may affect the value of the contract as the new prices for new quantities do not compensate the contractor to the extent of maintaining contractual equilibrium. The contract price will remain static; meanwhile, changes in materials prices are rapid.

Modifications and Enhancements of the Egyptian State Procurement Law Since 2005

Significant changes in materials prices in the last few years led the Egyptian legislator to amend some of the fundamental concepts of the traditional theory of administrative contracts. This is a direct impact of globalization,[8] as it shows the integration of the Egyptian legal system into the

7 Executive Regulations stipulate that the contractor must keep to the lowest prices offered by him upon entering the tender, in comparison with other contractors. The contractor must keep this priority of lowest prices during performance. It is argued, from the author's perspective, that this stipulation violates contractual equilibrium as public works agreements are long-term agreements and there are always changes in the contract value during performance period. This cap on the lowest price priority will keep contract prices stable despite changes and increases in market prices. Moreover, there is great concern about illegality and unconstitutionality, as the cap on the priority to keep the lowest prices is stipulated by Executive Regulations (Administrative Decree), not by legislation.

8 Despite the fact that inflation is a domestic factor, changes in materials prices are not. However, the Egyptian legislator was influenced by globalization as the increase in materials prices and price fluctuations have been normal phenomena for decades. Since then, it was subject to judicial or arbitral review to apply contractual equilibrium theories. The Egyptian legislator, nowadays, applies Law No. 5 of 2005 and Law No. 191 of 2008 vesting in the administration the authority to exercise its power in contract price review on

global legal culture. Despite the fact that pressure in some cases is domestic, the reaction of the legislator was influenced by liberal and global perspectives. The current stipulation in the 2008 amendments is that the administration shall exercise the power to review prices every three months instead of entering into long litigation and arbitration proceedings.

The direct influence of globalization upon the legal concepts of civil law achieved tangible results in the domain of administrative contracts, despite the fact that these achievements are still minor. But, in certain cases, the administration can now review contract prices regularly instead of maintaining contractual equilibrium through litigation or arbitration, as the case may be.

Article (1) of Law No. 5 of 2005 which amends some articles of the State Procurement Law No. 89 of 1998 stipulates that

> Two new Articles shall be added to Law No. 89 of 1998 (Articles 22 (*bis*) and 22 (*bis* 1)).

as follows:

> Article 22 (*bis*): The administration shall make advance payments to the contractor in accordance with work progress and pursuant to the stipulations of the executive regulations during a two-month period from the date of offering the certificate which shall be subject to review. The administration shall further pay all approved certificates; otherwise, the administration shall be obliged to pay the contractor a compensation which is equivalent to the financial cost of the said approved certificate. The compensation shall cover the delay period according to the credit and discount rate specified by the Central Bank of Egypt.
>
> Article 22 (*bis* 1): Where the duration of a contract lasts for more than one year, the contracting authority shall, at the end of each year, amend the contract price in accordance with the increase or decrease in prices which has occurred after the stipulated date of technical selection of the contractor in tenders, or after the contracting date based on a direct order, pursuant to an equation to be determined by the contractor in his offer to tender and the agreement based thereon. The amendment in contract price shall be obligatory upon both parties.

The Minister of Finance issued Decree No. 219 of 2006 adding new articles to the executive regulations:

> … Second Article: A new Article (No. 55 (*bis*)) shall be added to the regulations as follows:
>
> For public works agreements lasting for a period of one year or more, there shall be an obligation of the contracting authority to amend the contract price at the end of every year in accordance with the increase or decrease in contract prices (*price fluctuations*) which have occurred after the stipulated date of technical selection of the contractor in tenders, or after the contracting date based on a direct order in accordance with certain parameters determined by the contractors in the

---

a regular basis instead of litigation or arbitration. It is appropriate to refer to the fact that the increase in the price for reinforcement iron was a direct result of the increase in the price of the ingredients involved in the industrial process in previous times. All industrial products are imported by factories in Egypt. Moreover, exporting cement to many countries with high prices, compared to prices in the domestic market, increased international demand and directly affected the price in the domestic market. There has been a significant increase in cement prices in the last few years.

> offer thereof to tender and the agreement based thereon. The amendment in contract price shall be obligatory upon both parties.

The Egyptian legislator created changes in price mechanisms in a conservative manner limited to the costs of materials and labour as those are the main factors affecting prices from the legislator's perspective.

Article (22 (*bis*)) applies to contracts that last for one year or more with certain stipulations. Pursuant to this article, price must be reviewed every year. Calculation of price fluctuations, whether increased or decreased, shall be done in accordance with certain stipulations as mentioned.

In the second section of this new article, there are some regulatory stipulations to pay additional payments to the contractor. Among those stipulations is a fundamental condition stating that payment must be made to or deducted from the contractor according to cost elements determined by the application of an equation stipulated by regulations. Such payments shall be made or deducted after one year from the date of opening of the technical offer, or tender or direct order.[9] A typical equation would be as follows:

Price fluctuation equations (formula):

$$T1 = A + K\,(H1/H) + K1\,(M1/M) + K2\,(L1/L) + K3\,(N1/N) + F = T1 - T$$

Compensation or deduction value = the value of works subject to amendment according to the offer of the contractor to tender X. The percentage of rise or deduction to be paid or deducted by the contractor after amendment (F).

Where:

T_1	Parameters of Items or Items after amendment
A	Parameter of stable cost elements not subject to amendment under all contract items
K, K_1, K_2, K_3	Parameters of cost (labour, raw material, etc.) subject to amendment by the offer of the contractor (which is a percentage to be determined by the contractor in his offer to tender for each of the components subject to amendment)
H, L, M, N	Price of cost elements subject to amendment when entering into contract (date of opening of technical envelops or direct order) according to the price bulletin issued by the Central Agency for Public Mobilization and Statistics or by any other neutral entity according to the substance of the contract
H_1, L_1, M_1, N_1	Price of cost elements subject to amendment according to the price bulletin issued by the Central Agency for Public Mobilization and Statistics or any other neutral entity according to the substance of the contract at the date of payment of amendments
T	Parameter of item before amendment from the offer of the contractor = one
F	Parentage of raise or deductions which should be paid to the contractor or deducted from him after amendment

9 To enter into a contract directly with a specific contractor without starting public tender proceedings among more than one contractor is contrary to the stipulation made by Article (1) of the State Procurement Law of 1998 stating that the general principle in state contracting is to select a contractor through an engagement in a public tender. In very exceptional cases, restricted to special conditions, the administration can select a contractor directly with a special (direct) order. These particular cases, stipulated under Articles (7) and (8) of the Procurement Law, are not subject to analogy.

In practice it is generally understood by the administration that its engineers and engineering consultancy firms apply such regulatory equations; lawyers and state council judges do not participate or interfere in this mathematical process, but they can ask for the assistance of experts at the Egyptian Ministry of Justice.

It is clear from the amendments introduced by Law No. 5 of 2005 and its Executive Regulations that fundamental legal principles and procedures shall be considered:

1. In his offer to engage in a public tender or in a contract in case of special orders, as the case may be, the contractor must determine special parameters, otherwise the administration cannot compensate him in case of any price increase.
2. It is stipulated that the new amendments introduced by Law No. 5 only apply to contracts which last for one year or more.
3. Price fluctuations which have occurred after the date of technical selection of a contractor in tenders[10] or after the date of a direct order shall be considered as of the stipulated date, in accordance with the legislative and regulatory amendments.
4. Calculations and compensations shall be made every year by the engineers of the administration as of the above-mentioned dates.

The above-mentioned rules shall not apply in two cases:

1. Contracts lasting for a period less than one year and delayed due to the fault of the contractor.
2. Quantities delayed in performance and final completion by the contractor after the first year of the opening of technical offers of the tender or the date of a direct order, as the case may be.

Current Changes to the Egyptian State Procurement Law 2008: Legislative Amendments

The latest enhancements and modifications of the State Procurement Law promulgated by the amending law No. 191 of 2008 are significant. Article (1) of Amendments to Law No. 89 of 1998 stipulated that:

> Instead of article 22 (*bis*) of law No. 89 of 1998, the following provision shall apply:
>
> Article 22 (*bis* 1): The Administration shall, for contracts lasting for a period of six months or more, amend the contract price after the elapse of every three months in accordance with the increase or decrease in prices which happened after the stipulated date of opening of technical offers of the tender, or of the contracting date, based on a direct order and in accordance with the equation determined by the contractor in the offer thereof and upon which the contract shall be based. The amendment shall be obligatory upon both parties.
>
> Any agreement contrary to the above-mentioned rules shall be null and void.

10 In public tenders, procedures under the State Procurement Law of 1998 determine the date for technical selection, after which another session is set for financial selection. The final selection of a contractor by the tender committee is subject to technical grades obtained and lowest prices in the financial offer.

It is true that the reaction of the Egyptian legislator, in the latter amendments, was faster than normal, as the increase of materials prices was rapid due to international market changes in that period. Matters usually take longer in the Egyptian Parliament: for instance, the previous State Procurement Law No. 9 of 1983 was annulled by the current law of 1998 after 16 years, despite many changes and various factors that needed rapid modification. In the 2008 amendments, globalization and the effect of international market prices directly affected the materials industry and prices in the Egyptian domestic market. Pressure upon the Egyptian Parliament from contractors and the Egyptian media to adopt global changes in the construction industry encouraged the Egyptian legislator to modify the price review provisions regularly.

The new amendments introduced by Law No. 191 of 2008 considered the following legal issues:

1. The current legislation shall be applicable to contracts lasting for a period of six months or more.
2. A price review shall be conducted every three-month period to maintain contractual equilibrium and to face rapid financial changes. However these price fluctuations occur after the stipulated date of opening technical offers of the tender, or of the contractor date in case of direct order, as the case may be.
3. The contractor must determine certain parameters in the offer to tender or in the direct order agreement.
4. The current amendments introduced in 2008 are mandatory rules.

Conclusion

In conclusion, contract price, generally, has become nowadays a dynamic process rather than a static process as in the past and in the light of the traditional theory of administrative contracts. The following observations are of fundamental importance.

It is suggested that review should be on a monthly basis in order to update the value of payments with the same contract price and to face the rapid change in raw materials prices. In the first month of performance, the first certificate equals £E100,000 (Egyptian pounds); meanwhile, the true value of the nineteenth or the twentieth certificate (assuming that each certificate equals £E100,000) is £E118,000. Despite the fact that inflation and currency depreciation are domestic factors, change in materials prices is a regular international phenomenon.

Moreover, the current global economic crisis has caused currency depreciation globally. It is argued that materials prices were decreasing; but there is no doubt that global recession and the deterioration of FDI flows to developing countries in 2009 significantly affected the construction industry. The deterioration in real estate prices is known worldwide to have taken place in many countries, including Egypt. The above-mentioned circumstances currently affect public works agreements (state contracts) on the one hand, and the private sector construction industry on the other.

Following this concept, it is clear that there is an essential need to update the value, not the price. Price will remain the same (i.e., the true value of the Egyptian pound in month zero equals £1, while it equals £0.78 in month 36).

In addition, depreciation of the currency in developing countries, inflation rate and increase in materials prices play a considerable role in determining the contract value during the progress of work. Some of these factors are related to internal market mechanisms while others are influenced by international market prices and their fluctuations. All these factors play a significant role in the industrial process and in the international demand for exported cement, which consequently affects prices of construction materials in the Egyptian market.

It is suggested that currency units at the time of contracting should equal the same units at the final completion date.

Having a clear contractual regime is of fundamental importance to achieve financial equilibrium and to avoid uncertainties and unpredictability.

This will lead to the right application of legal provisions and clear interpretation of the contract clauses and parties' intentions, upon contracting, to some extent to maintain a balanced relationship with the administration in the domain of the administrative contract.

Article (134) of the Egyptian Civil Code stipulates that:

> If the obligation was for a certain amount of money, a debtor is obliged to pay such obligation as it is stipulated under the contract, regardless of any currency fluctuations (any increase or decrease in the value thereof) at the stipulated time of payment. Such fluctuations have no effect to pay the agreed amount.

Article (147(2)) of the Egyptian Civil Code has already been set out above and it is argued that the theory of hardship in civil and administrative contracts is applicable to any agreement or contract, as it is a mandatory rule under the Egyptian legal system.[11] Parties, and especially the administration, cannot impose any obligation upon the contractor to avoid its application. This provision in the Civil Code, being a mandatory rule, supersedes Article (134) and its stipulations.

Moreover, the right interpretation of Article (134) is that payment of the agreed amount should be made regardless of currency fluctuations. The debtor should pay the money value which, from the economic perspective, is still the same currency units stipulated under the contract at the time of contracting. Both the economic dimension and legal interpretation are interrelated. Articles (134) and (147(2)) must be interpreted together. All legal provisions are interrelated in the Egyptian legal system in terms of interpretation; private clauses restrict the application of general clauses and mandatory rules supersede the others.

In conclusion, globalization affects materials prices as most of the industrial ingredients are imported from international markets. The global economic crises affected, to some extent, the construction industry in the Egyptian market, and FDI flows,[12] and, consequently, economic growth in the country, as well as the situation in the entire world.

Finally, the new amendments to the Procurement Law are also mandatory rules under the Egyptian legal system. Parties cannot avoid their application by way of agreement. This is a new mechanism of protection to the contractor which is fundamental, in the writer's opinion, to maintaining a good investment atmosphere in infrastructure projects in Egypt and to ensuring the flow of foreign direct investments in the construction sector into the country. Globalization,[13] as the main factor of integration into diversified legal cultures, is also the main factor for the considerable enhancement of the environment of the construction industry whether in private sector projects or

11 The General Assembly for Legal Opinion (Fatwa) and Legislation, legal opinion No 778; session 22 October 2003, dated 15 November 2003; file No 78/2/67.

12 See: Sauvant 2008. The author pointed out that FDI declined at least 20 per cent in 2008 and is expected to fall another 30 per cent or more in 2009. This is a difficult economic situation worldwide (visit: www.vcc.columbia.edu).

13 See also Abdel-Wahab 2005.

in public works agreements in the domain of administrative contracts. Globalization is significantly changing the fundamental principles in administrative contracts which began to deteriorate as a result of the new substantial changes, as well as the new concepts integrated in international public works agreements in both arbitration and litigation.

As is stated above, materials price fluctuations in Egypt depend mainly on the international market, as most of the ingredients for the industrial process are imported and as there is a worldwide international demand for Egyptian cement. The international dimension of the global economic crisis is also worth considering, together with some other domestic factors such as inflation. However, currency depreciation is subject to both domestic and global parameters in the light of the above-mentioned scenarios.

These new concepts and mechanisms were enacted in the current amendments to Law No. 89 of 1998, and they will be effective and valid legislative mechanisms in the legal regime of public works and infrastructure projects.

Chapter 6
Performance of the Contract and Parties' Obligations

Performance of the Contract

Similar to a civil contract, in terms of its main elements, an administrative contract is an offer tendered to fulfil contractual obligations and an acceptance thereof. This constitutes the parties' mutual consent, where the state or an administrative authority is one of the two parties. Such a contract has the same principles and rules as those governing a civil contract. The contract takes effect upon the effective date determined by the parties, whereby they undertake to fulfil their mutual obligations.

The principle of public interest prevalence is the most important principle governing the performance of administrative contracts. It establishes that the public interest should prevail over the private interest. The authority has superintendence power for the contract performance, and is consequently entitled to unilaterally amend clauses it deems necessary for the public interest.[1]

The administrative jurisprudence establishes that administrative contracts have a distinctive characteristic compared to civil contracts. The theory of public utility stipulates that the contract aims to manage utilities and that the public interest prevails over the private interest. In civil contracts, the interests of both parties are parallel and equal, whereas in administrative contracts, their interests are not equal due to the principle of the prevalence of public interest. Such a notion governs the relationships emerging from administrative contracts, where the administration has a superintendence power for the contract performance.[2] The administration has the right to amend or add clauses[3] it deems necessary for the public interest, without being challenged by the other party, which would base his or her argument upon the rule of *Pacta sunt Servanda* (that all agreements and stipulations in a contract must be observed).

As a consequence, the administration is always entitled to terminate a contract if it deems it necessary for the public interest; the other party may then be entitled to damages. On the other hand, in civil contracts, neither party is entitled, unilaterally, to rescind or terminate the contract.[4]

---

1 See: The Supreme Administrative Court, Judgments No. 1520-2 on 20/4/1957–2/97/1937, and No. 1520-2 on 20/4/1957–2/97/1937, mentioned in Egyptian Conseil D'Etat 1996: 305–307. See also: Judgment No. 954-12 on 11/4/1970–43/264 in Egyptian Conseil D'Etat 1996: 308. On performing contracts under the French doctrine in general, see, for example: De Laubadère, Moderne et Delvolvé 1983–1984, Tome 2: 9 *et seq*., Richer 1995: 200 *et seq*. In English common law, see the leading authority, Hugh Beale 2008: 765–7. In Arab jurisprudence, see, for example, for obligations under administrative contracts: El Tamawy 1991:,407 *et seq*.

2 Dufau 1988, Tome 1: 196 *et seq*.; Richer 1995: 77; De Laubadère, Moderne et Delvolvé 1983–1984, Tome 2: 447; F. Sabiani 1995: 142; De Laubadère, Venezia et Gaudement 1995, Tome 2: 482–3; Auby et Bon 1995: 238. See also: El Hassan 1997: 281; El Tamawy 1991: 454; see also: Article (77) of the Executive Regulations of Law No. 9 of 1983, Articles (2.5), (24), (25) and (38) of the CCAG, 1976, and also 2009 version.

3 El Tamawy 1991: 457; El Hassan 1997: 302 *et seq*.; see also: Auby et Bon 1995: 238; De Laubadère, Venezia et Gaudement 1995, tome II: 483; Sabiani 1995: 150 *et seq*.

4 The Supreme Administrative Court, Case No. 1520-2 (20/4/1957–2/97/937), see Egyptian Conseil D'Etat 1996: 305.

The contract performance is governed by the recognized principles in public law, as is the case in private law, and pursuant to Article (148) of the Civil Code.[5] Furthermore, the performance of administrative contracts is governed by the principle of good faith applied in civil contracts.[6] However, this matter should not prejudice the distinct characteristic of administrative contracts, in terms of the requirements of public utility and prevalence of the public interest over the private interest.[7]

Pacta sunt Servanda is the fundamental legal principle governing administrative contracts. Similar to civil contracts, international administrative contracts must be performed according to the good faith principle in construing such contracts.[8]

However, legislative stability and contract stability clauses restrict the aforementioned power exercised by the state, whereby a foreign contracting party shall not be subject to legislative changes which may affect financial equilibrium.

Moreover, pursuant to the stabilization clause, the administration has no power unilaterally to amend the financial clauses of the contract; nevertheless, it has the right to direct the works in accordance with the public interest that has prevalence over the private interest. The authority can use its competence granted by the legislative and statutory powers to impose penalties upon the foreign contracting party in case of breach of contractual obligations, by rescinding the contract, forfeiting the deposit, performing the contract on the contractor's account and charging fines for delay in execution. This provides the International Public Works Agreements a new legal nature different from that of the administrative contracts. This applies to all Arab Middle Eastern jurisdictions.

Breaches committed by the administration and the foreign contracting party must be equally explored, since the probability of both occurrences exists.

The contractor must perform the contract in specified dates according to the agreed-upon specifications; while the owner (the state) is obliged to deliver the site clear of all impediments, to prevent any procedure obstructing the course of execution and to effect payments due to the contractor in the specified dates.[9]

Breaches of mutual obligations can be identified by reference to judicial precedents. Breaches committed by the administration can take the following forms:

- delay in the delivery of the site in a reasonable time
- delay in the preparation of designs and drawings
- impediments to the performance of the contract
- third party's claim of ownership of the land on which the project is developed

5 The Supreme Administrative Court, Case No. 954-12 (11/4/1969–15/43/264), see Egyptian Conseil D'Etat 1996:, 306.

6 The Supreme Administrative Court, Case No. 1520-2 (20/4/1957–2/97/937), see Egyptian Conseil D'Etat 1996:, 307.

7 The Supreme Administrative Court, Case No. 954-12 (11/4/1970–15/43/264), see Egyptian Conseil D'Etat 1996:, 307.

8 In implementing local administrative contracts, see: the legal opinion of the General Assembly of Counsel and Jurisprudence No. 75 of 14/1/1988, session (19/12/1987) 41, (42/214/598).

9 With regard to details of the parties' obligations in public works agreements, see French jurisprudence: Jean Dufau 1988: 159 *et seq.*; Kadiki 1979:, Tome 1: 165–200; see Arab jurisprudence: El Hassan 1997, Section 1: 25–201; in the parties' obligations in administrative contracts in general, see: El Tamawy,1991: 436 *et seq.*; and for the parties' rights in the face of the administrative authority, see: El Tamawy 1991: 566.

- delay in effecting the advance payment and paying other invoices
- delay in taking over the works in a reasonable time

Breaches committed by the contractor can take the following forms:

- breach of obligation to the personal performance of the contract
- delay in fulfilling the obligations set forth by virtue of the contract
- discrepancies in the work performed in contravention with the contract's specifications

Parties' Obligations

Breaches of Obligation by the Administration

Delay in the delivery of the site in a reasonable time The first form of breach, subsequent to concluding the contract between the administration and the contractor, is the delay in delivering the site in a reasonable time for the works execution subject of the contract.

It is recognized in all types of contracts, administrative or civil, that a contractual breach is the failure to execute the contractual obligations by any party, regardless of the cause thereof. This breach can be intentional or an unintentional, neglectful act. It is also recognized that failure of the administration to execute its obligations to deliver the site to the contracting party, resulting in work suspension for unreasonable time, is a breach of obligations which entitles the contractor to compensation.[10]

The facts of a dispute that arose between the General Authority for Sanitation for Greater Cairo Region and the Cooperative Society for Development of the Pyramids Desert, conclude that the former commissioned the latter by virtue of a contract dated 31 January 1989 to execute a sanitation project for the total amount of EGP 989623.740 in accordance with the tender documents and annexed minutes of the meeting. The tender documents specified that the delay in issuing permits did not give rise to any financial obligations by the administration, and that the time for execution was ten months from the date of receiving such permits, provided that the administration facilitated the process of receiving such permits. The commissioning order signed by the respondent stipulated that the prices were to remain unchanged throughout the performance period. The claimant requested compensation for the administration's breach of contract and for the price increases due to delay in delivering the site. The court held that there is a contractual breach committed by the administration, which had the consequence of prolonging the contracting execution period.[11]

This problem does not tend to occur in the decisions awarded by the ICC and the reputable arbitration centres where developing states are involved in arbitration. However, it does occur – as was previously mentioned – in local public works agreements, where the Egyptian State Council has often addressed them in its judgments.

---

10 The Supreme Administrative Court, Case No. 862 for the Judicial Year No. 9, session 3/6/1967, *The Supreme Court's Collection in 15 Years*; and in English common law, see: Beale 2008: 767; Murdoch and Hughes 2000: 160; Pickavance 2007: 269–91; I.N. Duncan Wallace 1995: 568, 591.

11 The Administrative Appeal Court, Case No. 530 for the Judicial Year No. 46, session 19/2/1995, not published.

Delay in the preparation of the designs and drawings In local and International Public Works Agreements, the state has a clear obligation for the timely preparation of designs and drawings, in pursuance with the provisions of law. The administration is clearly liable, in the event of delaying the preparation of designs and drawings, and discrepancies leading to practical execution problems or infringement of building requirements in the area where the works are executed.[12]

The facts of a dispute submitted before the Appeal Administrative Court concluded that the Supreme Council of Youth and Sport had mandated the Arab Bureau for Design & Technical Consultation to offer a tender for the construction of Al-Talladega Camp in Oyoon Moussa, south of Suez City.

It was held that the contractor was right when he was unable to complete the work due to the objection of the military forces stationed in the related zone, claiming that the designs were in violation of the building requirements in that zone, which stipulated to build at 100 meters distance from the seashore, whereas the designs set out the location of the site under execution at only 40 meters from the seashore. The contractor claimed to rescind the contract on the grounds of failure of the administration to conform with the building requirements in the military zone where the site should be built.[13]

Hence, the contract imposes upon the administration the obligation for the timely preparation of designs and drawings in a correct manner, so as to avoid any consequential legal problems, which may disrupt the execution and completion of the project in due time.

Impediments to the performance The obligation of the administration includes, among other things, delivering the site clear of any impediments that may disrupt such execution. The resulting delay will be accompanied by price increases in steel, cement and other basic materials necessary for the execution of the contracting works, jeopardizing the financial equilibrium. Such on-site impediments during execution are deemed a breach by the administration in fulfilling its obligation.

The Administrative Courts stressed this point in different contexts. The works may need to be modified if the execution is in conflict with the building line, giving rise to the suspension of work until the necessary examination and modification are carried out on site. This will require time until the work is resumed, which will in turn cause delay in handing over the work.

The contracting party with the administration can request to add the time delay caused by the work suspension to the contract performance period and to increase the unit prices at certain rates to compensate for the damage occurred therefrom.

The Administrative Court recognized that, in such a case, work suspension was a breach committed by the administration and concluded that the contract must be rescinded in specific cases where the administration was in breach of its contractual obligations and warranted rights to compensation for the contracting party. Where impediments, such as sewage overflow or water pipes obstruction to the pavement work, disrupt the project execution and cause delay, the contracting party is entitled to compensation for any delay penalties unduly imposed by the administrative authority, and where it is ascertained that the breach was committed by the former. Consequently, the Administrative Court ruled for compensation to the contracting party.[14]

The court judgment, which has been long established by the Administrative Court jurisprudence, suggests that the administration's obligations include delivering the site clear of impediments that

12 Generally see: Ismail 2003b.

13 The Appeal Administrative Court, Contracts Circuit, Case No. 3213 of the Judicial Year 44, session 21/5/1995, not published.

14 The Appeal Administrative Court, Contracts Circuit, Case No. 4831 of the Judicial Year 45, session 11/6/1995, not published.

may disrupt or delay the execution of the work, in addition to the timely delivery of the site, and in case of delay, it must be within a reasonable range. In all cases, the administration is in breach of its obligation for failing to exercise due care and diligence in fulfilling its contractual obligations; hence, the contracting party can have recourse to the court for compensation, since the delay carries with it price increases in raw materials used for the execution of the works, in addition to an increase in labour wages, which in turn burden the state with substantial financial costs.

Hence, the state must exercise due diligence and care to fulfil its obligations of delivering the site clear of impediments that may disrupt performance, avoiding delay for an unreasonable amount time that will entail a waste of public funds due to the court judgments issued against the state to compensate for the aggravated material sustained by the contracting party.

Where the above examples suggest that there are material problems encountered by the contracting party that cause delay in performance, some other problems that have a political nature may be expected to bring termination of works due to political reasons.

The *Pyramids* case arbitration[15] concluded that Southern Pacific Properties Ltd. (SPP) started to perform a public works contract with the Arab Republic of Egypt for the construction of a resort in the vicinity of the Giza Pyramids.

The construction works commenced on 2 June 1977. An objection to this project raised by the People's Assembly began in 1978; however, the Ministers of Tourism and the Economy defended the project, and the People's Assembly formed an ad hoc committee of experts in March 1978 to submit a report in this regard. By the end of May 1978, the court issued some decisions whereby the project was cancelled. As a consequence, SPP claimed damages for breach of contractual obligations.

The tribunal's award included the following statement: "The amount of damages includes losses suffered by the creditor and profits of which he has been deprived, provided that they are normal results of the failure to perform the obligation or of delay in such performance."

The arbitral tribunal added: "The project was originally well received and all competent bodies and agencies willingly acted perfectly. The contractual schemes aimed at securing its completion. The new events occurred whereby public opinion strongly demanded cancellation of the project."

The tribunal inferred from the aforementioned preamble that the Egyptian government was in breach of contract; yet it was not convinced that such breach was committed in bad faith or due to gross negligence: "Whereas this background does not exclude a contractual breach by the government, it convinces us that the breach was neither fraudulent nor grossly negligent in the sense pointed out above."

The claimants assessed their claims based upon the following criteria.

a) invested capital
b) value of investments in May 1978
c) missed opportunities

The arbitral tribunal ruled for compensation for the amount of US$12.5 million with 5 per cent annual interest to be paid by the Arab Republic of Egypt, as from the date of filing the claim for arbitration at the ICC secretariat in Paris.

The Paris Court of Appeals annulled such award in its session held on 12 July 1984, on the grounds that pursuant to Article (1504) of the French Civil Procedure Code of 1981, an international arbitral award can be rejected in the case that it was issued in France. The grounds for such award

15 Award of 16 February 1983, No. 3493, see Jarvin and Derains 1990: 124

are prescribed in (1502) of the said law, which states that an arbitral award may be repealed in case of absence of an arbitration agreement, or in case such agreement was void or expired. The Egyptian government decided that it was not a party to the contract of December and was not bound by the arbitration clause stated therein.

The arbitral award issued by the ICC in Paris established an important principle: Where an administrative authority fails to fulfil a contractual obligation in an international public works contract for the performance of a major project, as is the case with local works, such breach – though not grave – results in an award for compensation for the injuries sustained by the contracting party.

Third party's claim of ownership of the land on which the project is developed The administration must ensure that the land on which the project is developed is not subject to any claim of ownership by a third party.

The administration may not allege that the claim of ownership of the land on which the project is developed by a third party is an external cause beyond its control since it has contractual obligations to deliver the site clear of any impediments, be it material or legal, in order to start the performance.[16]

This contractual breach committed by the administration is unrelated to an external cause or force majeure. Thus, an award for compensation must be issued against the administration for any consequential damages caused by the delay in performance, such as price increases.

The breach of obligation committed by the administration tends to occur less in International Public Works Agreements than in local public works agreements. Nevertheless, such breach in International Public Works Agreements results in grave consequences due to delay in execution and compensation for injuries committed by the state, such as the increase in raw material prices and manpower wages. This can constitute payment of substantial sums of money due to the nature of such contracts, which are priced by hundreds of millions in local or foreign currency. The state is then encumbered by unnecessary financial burdens and faced with squandering public money that could have been better used for the public interest.

Delay in effecting the advance payment and paying other invoices It is evident that the main obligation of the administration is to effect the advance payment by virtue of the contract and pay all contractors' payments, in consideration of the works performed by the contractor.

Public works agreements are commutative contracts[17] based on *do ut des*, where the state has payment obligation in consideration of the works performed. This is the most important contractual obligation, whereby the state has to pay a percentage of the total payment due to the contracting party, and then it has to pay the invoices throughout the progress of performance.

In the event that the administration delays or fails to effect such payment, it is then in breach of contractual obligations, without taking into consideration claims made by the administration of lack of financial resources at the time of paying such invoices, particularly that the contracting party has fulfilled its obligation and performed the commissioned works. As a consequence, the contract can be rescinded and compensation for the injuries sustained by the contracting party has to be provided.[18]

---

16 The Appeal Administrative Court, Contracts Circuit, Case No. 3414 of the Judicial Year 42, session 13/6/1993, not published.

17 El Sanhoury 1989 (Part 7, Vol. 1, *Contracts Related to the Works*): 8.

18 The Appeal Administrative Court, Contracts Circuit, Case No. 3213 of the Judicial Year 44, session 21/5/1995.

The Administrative Court compensates the contracting party for the material damages suffered due to the work suspension and delay in payments,[19] as it is a contractual obligation of the authority to pay for the work executed at the specified time. Cash liquidity enables the contractor to carry out the work satisfactorily and on time, and any lost gains due to being unable to perform the whole contract must be compensated by the authority.

It is clearly evident that the approach of the Egyptian State Council to these types of contracts highlights the importance of fulfilling the contractual obligation by the administration, where payment of the contract price constitutes a key element and a main obligation to be observed by the authority.

In this regard, it is considered that such delay in effecting the advance payment and paying due invoices is attributed to lack of controls in the state's administrative body to superintend and perform such contracts. Administrative contractual liability and corruption are two major reasons for this type of breach, leading to grave consequences encumbered upon the state to compensate the contracting parties for the injuries sustained, in consideration of the work performed. This matter can be avoided by having a well-managed and fully controlled administrative body that properly performs its contractual obligations, such as effecting advance payments and paying the contractors' payments on time.

Delay in taking over the works in a reasonable time One of the administration's contractual obligations is to take over the site in a reasonable time; otherwise, the contractor may suffer damage, such as receiving final payment in settlement of all financial dues, transferring the labour force and machineries to other sites and receiving the final deposit by virtue of the Executive Regulations of the State Procurement Law[20] in Egypt and other relevant laws and regulations in Arab countries.

Breaches of Obligations by the Contractor[21]

Breaches are typically expected to be committed by the contractor in International Public Works Agreements as the contractor has the obligation to perform in person the commissioned works in a timely manner and with due diligence.

Delay occurs when the contractor fails to perform the works according to the timeline specified in the contract, and omission takes place when the works are not executed in conformity with the contract specifications.

The first aspect of the contractor's breaches of contractual obligations is as follows:

Breach of the personal performance of the contract The contractor is obliged to perform the contract in person, as the state mandates the work performance to a specific contractor with essential merits in terms of international exposure as well as technical and financial competencies for the performance of similar projects.

Due to the personal consideration of these types of public works agreements, the administration opts to conclude a contract based upon special merits and personal credentials. This fact leaves the

19 The Appeal Administrative Court, Contracts Circuit, Case No. 3213 of the Judicial Year 44, session 21/5/1995.

20 See the Executive Regulations of the Law of Tender and Auctions No. 9 of 1983, repealed and issued by Decree No. 157 of 1983 of the Minister of Finance, Article (83/d), and the Executive Regulations of the new law issued by Decree No. 1367 of 1998 of the Minister of Finance, Article (89).

21 In Arab doctrine generally, see: Ismail 2003b; El Sanhoury 1989. In English common law, see: Beale 2008: 769–71; Duncan Wallace 1986: 472; Murdoch and Hughes 2000: 147–57.

contractor with the responsibility to assume the contractual obligations in person, which is called "the principle of personal performance of administrative contracts."[22]

The rationale behind such principle is public interest's requirements sought to be observed by the administration, through the execution of large projects needed for the country. This is an established principle by the jurisprudence[23] and the State Council judgment,[24] whereby the contractor's obligations, for the aforementioned reasons, are personal obligations to be fulfilled in person and may not be assigned or subcontracted to a third party.[25]

Contract assignment means that the contractor concludes a contract with a third party to take over the execution of the contractor's obligations and to acquire the rights established by such contract.[26] This concept frustrates the principle of the personal performance of public works agreements. Without the consent of the administration, such contract assignment is deemed a breach of the contractual obligations.

While this is a characteristic of administrative contracts, International Public Works Agreements are totally different, due to the complicated and composite nature of the projects related thereto. The performance of such contracts cannot be delivered by only one contractor. The main contractor may consider commissioning subcontractors to carry out the electrical, mechanical and other related works, which require the special expertise and know-how of specialist subcontractors.

Considering the significant scientific progress achieved in modern time and the sophisticated specialization in various walks of life, the performance of a large project requires the synergy of diverse businesses in different areas of specialization to achieve the related works in a perfect manner. For example, executing projects for the building of a barrage, an airport or an underground metro requires the concerted works of many companies, such as construction and building works, technically sophisticated electric works including modern and giant apparatuses and machines, sanitation works including plants of multiple purposes and sizes and numerous other works.

The administration may opt for one of two approaches: to conclude several contracts with different companies, which entails much time and effort to assume various responsibilities; or to conclude a contract with one major contractor that takes charge of the whole management and performance of the project, with the right to subcontract. As such, subcontracting is the ideal way to perform public works agreements due to economic and technical requirements, where subcontractors conclude contracts with the main contractors for the timely performance of the original contracts.[27]

The Administrative Court established the principle of prohibiting the assignment of a contract without the consent of the administration. Doing otherwise, even if there is no mention to this

22 For details of obligation of personal performance of the contract in public works agreements, see: El Tamawy 1991: 438 *et seq.*; El Hassan 1997: 28 *et seq.* See also: French jurisprudence, for example: Dufau 1988: 159 *et seq.*; De Laubadère, Moderne et Delvolvé 1983–1984, Tome 2: 9.

23 De Laubadère, Moderne et Delvolvé, Tome 2: 10.

24 The Appeal Administrative Court, 27/1/1957, Judicial Year 11, 174; The Supreme Administrative Court, 28/12/1963, Case No. 1109, Judicial Year 9, 324, and its Judgment of 30/6/1960, Judicial Year 40, 69.

25 El Hassan 1997: 29.

26 De Laubadère, Moderne et Delvolvé 1883–1984: 12; Dufau 1988: 159. An application of the opinion of the second committee of the Counsel Department in the State Council after reviewing some local major public works agreements, such as the construction of a new building for Al-Azhar at Darrassa (Committee Record No. 84/51, File No. 31/13/1323) on 3/11/1997, where it stated that the original recognised rule was that the contracting party should refrain from assigning the execution of its obligations, partly or wholly, to a third party, as they are personal obligations with the administration.

27 See: El Hassan 1997: 45–6.

effect in the contract or in the law, will create a problem with the Administrative Court as it deems the personal consideration of the contract performance indispensable.[28]

Article (76) of the Executive Regulations of the old State Procurement Law, promulgated by virtue of Law No. 9 of 1983, prohibits assigning a contract or waiving payments due to the contractor, with the exception of banks, as the legislator deems the bank's approval for such assignment sufficient, without detriment to the contractor's responsibility to perform the contract, and where acceptance to waive due payments should not prejudice the other rights owed to the authority.

A controversial point of jurisprudence arose regarding Article (76) of the Executive Regulations of the State Procurement Law: whether it permits the contract assignment with the rights and obligations established thereby, upon the Administration's consent, be it explicit or implicit, as pursuant to Article (303) of the Civil Code, such consent is a mere transfer of right.

In this respect, the rule specifies that the contracting party refrains from having a third party as a replacement for the performance of all contractual obligations, except with the prior consent of the administration.

The jurisprudence is of the opinion that assigning a contract is permissible provided that the authority gives explicit or implicit[29] consent thereto, and it is reasonable for the contracting party to seek assistance when required.

However, another opinion suggests that it is improper to assign a contract even if the administration gives explicit or implicit consent thereto, as the law stipulates unconditional prohibition of such assignment, with the exception of payments due to the contractor, provided that the assignee bank gives approval. The permission to waive payments due to the contractor, as a transfer of right recognized by the Civil Code, does not mean the permission to assign a contract in the sense specified in the jurisprudence: assignment of the contract content, including the contractual rights and obligations.[30]

It is true that the nature of International Public Works Agreements, with the obligations of the contractor toward the state regarding the various expertise necessary for the works performance, permits the assignment of parts of the contract, by way of subcontracting and with the consent of the administration that will not hesitate to accept such assignment where the public interest is not jeopardized.

In France, the *Cahier des Clauses Administratives Générales* (CCAG) does not include matters related to assignment of a contract; thus, the jurisprudence deems such assignment to be subject to the conventional rule stipulating the non-assignability of the contract without the consent of the authority.[31]

It is then recognized that if such assignment takes place without the consent of the administration, the contract is null and void. The subcontractor may not claim having a contract with the administration, as the main contractor remains solely responsible before the administration for the performance of the contract.[32]

---

28 See: the Appeal Administrative Court, *The Judgments Collection of 15 Years*, from 1946 to 1961, Part II, 1921, issued on 4/6/1991.

29 See also: El Tamawy 1991: 441–2; Helmy Fahmy 1993: 299.

30 Supporters of this opinion are: Fekry 1994: 68 and El Hassan 1997: 32.

31 El Hassan 1997: 33.

32 De Laubadère, Moderne et Delvolvé 1983–1984: 40–42; El Tamawy 1991: 443; Said Amin, Mohamed 1992: 65; see also: the Supreme Administrative Court, Judgment No. 1094-29 (25/6/1985–30/198/1350), in Egyptian Conseil D'Etat 1996: 722.

The penalty ensued from the breach of the personal performance of the contract is the nullification of such assignment made by the main contractor to the subcontractor without the consent of the administration.

Delay in fulfilling the obligations set forth by virtue of the contract The contractor must perform all the work set forth in the contract in the specified time, without laxity or delay; otherwise, the administration has the right to withdraw the work from the contractor. This particularly happens if the latter causes a delay upon which the administration sees it impossible to complete the work in the specified time or causes a work suspension for more than 15 days. This matter is established by the French State Council[33] and the legal opinion of the General Assembly of the Legal Opinion and Legislation.[34]

The execution of the work in the specified time intends to ensure systematic and consistent functioning of the public utility and serve the public interest, which is the ultimate goal for performing the project.[35]

The General Assembly was of the opinion that:

> Pursuant to Article 26 of the State Procurement Law promulgated by virtue of Law No. 9 of 1983, and with Article 35 of the Executive Regulations of the said Law, issued by virtue of the Ministerial Decree No. 157 of 1983, the law maker imposes upon the contractor the obligation to execute the works subject of the contract at a specified date, and grants right unto the administration, to give the contractor – if it deems this necessary for the public interest – an additional timeline to complete the execution, if this latter was lax in carrying out the works, provided that the administration imposes a penalty for the delay as specified by the Executive Regulations of Article 81, to be no more than 15% of the contract value.

It is a recognized principle that public contracts are subject to a fundamental legal principle that provides the performance of such contracts in accordance with the good faith duties. According to the State Council's typical judgment and opinion:

> such principle must be undisputedly observed in administrative contracts, even more than in civil contracts, due to the intrinsic relation of such contracts with the public interest. Even if the parties to the contract do not specify a date for the execution of the contractual obligation, this does not imply that such execution is not restricted with a timeline, where it should be performed in reasonable time as a matter of course and according to the nature and purpose of the contract.[36]

It is a fundamental principle that the contracting party, in performing administrative contracts, may not act with neglect in executing its obligations, even if the administration delays in fulfilling its corresponding obligations. Such principle may be ignored if the administration deems that failing to

---

33 C.E., 4 Oct. 1989, *Centre Hospitalier de Vitre Sommaire au Clement*, and Richer 1995 ; 439; C.E., 13 Mai 1987, *Société Wanner isofi isolation, Sommaire Clement*, and Richer 1995: 407; C.E., 28 Fev. 1986, *entreprise Blondet, Sommaire au Clement* and Richer 1986: 385.

34 Opinion No. 344 of 15/4/1984, Session (21/2/1983) 37 and 38/174/424 mentioned in the Principles of the Supreme Administrative Court and the General Assembly of the Counsel and Jurisprudence Departments, in Egyptian Conseil D'Etat 1996: 701.

35 See: El Hassan 1997: 79; see: Sabiani 1995: 147; Chabanol et Jouquelet 1994: 143 *et seq*. Dufau,1988: 167 *et seq*. In English jurisprudence, see: Hughes and Barber 1993: 219; Eggleston 1997.

36 Opinion No. 1007, Session (1/11/1992) 47, in Egyptian Conseil D'Etat 1996: 311.

fulfil its obligations prevented the contracting party from executing its obligations in the specified time. In such case, if the suspension period was unreasonable, due to lack of financial credit in consideration of the works executed, the authority may – upon resuming the works – review the contracting prices in light of the prevailing market prices. This is to keep the equilibrium of the contract economies and prevent unjust prevalence of the public interest over the private interest, to the extent that it would hamper the contracting party to perform its obligations. The Administrative Court concluded that such consideration was not in contravention with the public order since the rules of justice and good faith, which govern the performance of any contract, provide that the administration must not execute the contractual works at the same contracting prices if it was lax in fulfilling its corresponding obligations.

Administrative contracts differ from civil contracts due to the special nature of the former, which is related to the public utility's requirements intended to be fulfilled thereby, and the prevalence of the public interest of the private interest. Where the interests of both parties are equivalent and parallel in civil contracts, it is not the same in administrative contracts for the prevalence concept mentioned above, which establishes the principle for performing such contracts by the contracting party with the authority, where the former may not act with neglect in performing its obligations, even if the administration delays in fulfilling its obligations. As previously stated, such principle may be ignored if the administration deems that failing to fulfil its obligations prevented the contracting party from performing its obligations in the specified time. In such case, if the suspension period was unreasonable, due to lack of financial credit in consideration of the works executed, the authority may – upon resuming the works – review the contracting prices in light of the prevailing market prices, so as to keep the equilibrium of the contract economies and prevent unjust prevalence of the public interest over the private interest, to the extent that it would hamper the contracting party in executing its obligations. The Administrative Court concluded that such consideration was not in contravention with the public order, since the rules of justice and good faith, which govern the performance of any contract, provide that the administration must not perform the contractual works at the same contracting prices if it was lax in fulfilling its corresponding obligations.[37]

The principle adopted by the Administrative Court is that the general principle in administrative contracts rests on the fact that the parties' interests are not equal as the public interest has prevalence over the private interest. The contracting party must not be lax in performing its obligations despite the administration's laxity in fulfilling its corresponding obligations, except when the latter decides that this will prevent the contracting party from fulfilling its contractual obligations; in that case, the authority must review the contract prices in light of the market prices at the time of the actual performance of the remaining work. This is to maintain the contract's financial equilibrium and the interests of the contracting party, which may be undermined through the prevalence of the public interest.

Article (19/11) of the CCAG confirms the obligation to execute the work in the specified time without any delay. In the event that the contract does not specify a time for the execution of the work, the date of notifying the contractor of the contract deems to be the starting date of the execution period.

It is evident that such principle is more relevant in International Public Works Agreements, when the authority breaches a contractual obligation, such as a delay in effecting the advance payment or regular payments, which impedes the contracting party to fulfil its obligations on the specified date. In order to avoid unfairness in the execution of the work, the contracting prices must

37 Opinion No. 541, session (8/7/1993) 47, in Egyptian Conseil D'Etat 1996: 713.

not be maintained, and rather the price differences must be taken into account when resuming the performance.

Discrepancies in the work performed in contravention of the contract's specifications Where the contract makes the law of the parties, there is an equally applicable rule in civil, administrative and international contracts, whereby the party to an international public works contract must endeavour its best to fulfil its obligation in terms of the specifications set forth in the contract and its annexes. This is to ensure the realization of the purpose for performing the project subject of the contract, without prejudice to the systematic and consistent functioning of public utilities.[38]

Article (80) of the Executive Regulations of the State Procurement Law, promulgated by virtue of Law No. 89 of 1998, stipulates that the contractor is obliged to undertake personal inspection of the condition of the work and the necessary tests to ascertain the accuracy of the approved specifications and designs, assuming full responsibility of such drawings and designs as if they were produced by the contractor and consequently must notify the administration in a timely manner with the findings and remarks.

The Administrative Courts[39] and the ICC[40] judgments in Paris have confirmed the contractor's obligation to undertake the above-mentioned responsibilities.

Other Obligations Imposed Upon the Contractor

In pursuance of Article (61) of the Executive Regulations of Law No. 89 of 1998 of the State Procurement Law, the contractor must reside in the proximity of the work site to follow closely the work progress and receive instructions from the administration.[41]

In France, Article (2/22) of the CCAG stipulates the same obligation, provided that the contractor informs the administration of such residence within 15 days from the notification date of the contract acceptance.

Pursuant to Article (79) of the Executive Regulations of Law No. 89 of 1998 of the State Procurement Law[42] and Article (31/41) of the CCAG, the contractor is obliged to comply with the laws and regulations, to maintain security and order on site, to be present and to perform the administration's orders.[43] Reasons for the above obligations are the proper performance of the project in the specified time, so as ensure the regular functioning of the public utility.

Description of the Breach of Obligations in International Public Works Agreements

A question is raised regarding the legal nature of breach of obligations in International Public Works Agreements. At the outset, it is appropriate to confirm that the breach of obligations in such types of agreements is similar to the breach of obligations in contracts in general, giving rise to

38 With regard to such obligation, see: Dufau 1988: 169.

39 C.E., 1er Juin 1984, S.A. Ronzat et Fils, Sommaire au Clement, and Richer 1995: 236; C.E., 26 Sept. 1986, M. de Bary.

40 Jarvin, Derains and Arnaldez 1994:, 180, Case No. 52294, 22 Feb. 1988. With regard to ICC judgment in Paris, see also: Arnaldez, Derains 1990: 350, Case 5634, 1988.

41 See: Article (59) of the old law promulgated by virtue of Law No. 9 of 1983.

42 See: Article (77) of the old law promulgated by virtue of Law No. 9 of 1983.

43 See the other contractor's obligations: El Hassan,1997: 60 *et seq.*

contractual breach that is, whether in civil or administrative contracts, the failure of the duty bearer to fulfill the obligations stated in the contract.

It is recognized in all contracts, whether they are administrative or civil, that the contractual breach is the failure of the debtor to fulfil the obligations set forth in the contract, for whatsoever reason, and whether such failure is due to an intentional/neglectful act or not.

The failure of the debtor to fulfil the obligations under public works agreement is a contractual breach, which empowers the other contracting party to claim for compensation for the damage sustained.[44]

A contractual breach is the failure of the debtor to fulfil the obligations set forth in the contract. Where it is impossible for the debtor to fulfill the obligations in kind, that person is then liable to compensation for non-fulfillment, unless he or she can prove that it was due to an external reason beyond control, such as an unexpected incident, force majeure, omission of a third party or the debtor himself.[45]

The opinion of the Administrative Court is that a contractual breach is failure of the debtor to fulfil the obligations stipulated in the contract for whatsoever reason. Pursuant to Article (1) of Egyptian Law of Evidence No. 25 of 1968, the burden of proof that the creditor fulfilled personal obligations lies upon that individual while the debtor must provide proof of delivering such.[46]

Pursuant to Article (215) of the Civil Code, the debtor is responsible for compensating for failure to deliver obligations in kind, unless it is impracticable due to an external reason beyond control.[47] The same rule applies to all Arab legislation.

The General Assembly of the Legal Opinion and Legislation Departments determines that in a contract whereby one party undertakes the manufacturing of a product or the performance of a job, for a consideration to be given by the other party, the owner is obliged to provide the necessary materials and the contractor is fully responsible for any loss of such materials and is obliged to carry out the work avoiding all extreme handling of such, by using proper technical methods and exercising due care for the safekeeping of such materials. The contractor should also present a statement indicating the amount of materials utilized and the remainder to be returned to the owner. Upon completion, the contractor is obliged to hand over to the owner the required work duly executed by virtue of the contract. In the event of the contractor's failure to carry through such obligation, the owner is entitled, according to the general principles, to demand the fulfilment of such obligation in kind, even by compelling the contractor to do so, given that this was the original contract whereby the will of both parties constitutes a legally binding contract. Where the owner cannot secure rights prescribed by the contract, that person may be satisfied with compensation as an alternative without detrimental effect.[48]

The basis of the aforementioned conditions is that the general principle for fulfilling an obligation is the performance the work in kind; however, if such performance is impossible to be undertaken in kind, the owner may be satisfied with compensation as an alternative, so long as this is not prejudicing that person's interests.

---

44 The Supreme Administrative Court – Cases Nos. 1320, 1340 – 12 (15/2/1969)14/8/373), see: Egyptian Conseil D'Etat 1996: 313.

45 Opinion No. 1322 on 22/12/1988, session (30/11/1988) 43, file 44/35/102.

46 Opinion No. 548 on 31/5/1989, session (5/4/1989) 43, file 44/119/320.

47 Opinion No. 266 on 11/3/1990, session (21/2/1990) 43, file 44/237/668.

48 Opinion No. 2025 on 16/12/1992, session (6/12/1992) 47.

The Legal Nature of Breach of Obligations in Comparative Jurisprudence

In comparative jurisprudence, breach of any of the previously mentioned obligations constitutes a breach of contract, as determined by Egyptian law.

In states governed by the civil law system, a breach of contract is classified under the title of the effects of contractual obligations while in the states governed by the Anglo-Saxon system, the notion of breach is not so important in contractual obligations, though the general assumption is that such breach should not take place.[49]

In French jurisprudence, the burden of proof is laid on the injured party while the party with the undertaking to fulfil the obligation has to prove that there was an external cause hindering the execution of such.

49 Treitel 1988.

Chapter 7
Penalties in International Public Works Agreements

It is evident that the overarching principle characterizing administrative contracts in general, and public works agreements in particular, is that of the general power exercised by the administration. Administrative contracts contain clauses uncommon to private law contracts, of which the most important are those imposing penalties by the state upon the contracting party, in the event of breach of contractual obligations.

The main forms of penalties are contract rescission and deposit forfeiture, in addition to the withdrawal of work and the execution by the contractor. These penalties are explored in this chapter by describing the penalties, the consequences of imposing some financial burdens upon the foreign contracting party and the effect of the new legal nature exercised by the state in these types of contracts.

Contract Rescission and Deposit Forfeiture

Introduction

The most evident general power in International Public Works Agreements is the administration's power to rescind unilaterally the contract and to forfeit the deposit submitted by the contracting party.[1]

Since the conventional theory of administrative contracts grants the administration the right to amend the contract unilaterally, it is obvious that the administration can rescind the contract unilaterally. During a long period of time, this rule has been by and large implemented in administrative contracts.[2] In the event the contractor commits a gross breach during the contract performance, the administration can terminate the contract without resorting to court proceedings.[3]

The procedure of unilateral rescission of the contract differs from the common rescission in private law, whereby no party can decide unilaterally to rescind the contract and must seek a court judgment for such rescission.

In France, contract rescission is either a simple straightforward measure, or on the contractor's account and under the contractor's responsibility. By simple straightforward action, the administration rescinds the contract without encumbering the contractor with the results of concluding a new contract with a new contractor for performance of the work, the subject of the original contract, without prejudicing the rights of the administration to impose fines and claim for compensation.[4] French jurisprudence considers such rescission a public order determined

---

1 El Howeidy 1994. Ga'far 2000: 147; Richer 1995: 184 *et seq.*; Sabiani 1995: 187 *et seq.*; Clément et Richer 1989.

2 C.E. Ass. 2 février 1987, Société TV6, Rec. 29; C.E. 27 Juin 1986; Clément, Jacques et Richer and Daniel n.d. *Syndicat Intercommunal du Bassin Darcachon, inedit*: 394.

3 El Hassan 1997: 168.

4 De Laubadère, Moderne et Delvolé 1983–1984: 168.

by the interest of the state, without being explicitly included in the contract or in the tender documents.[5]

The contract may be rescinded on the contractor's account and under his responsibility, where the administration executes the work, the subject of the original contract, on the contractor's account, by commissioning another contractor. The above procedure is not part of the public order; hence, the administration cannot resort to it unless it is set forth in the contract or in the tender documents.[6]

Article (84) of the new Executive Regulation of the State Procurement Law, issued by virtue of Decree 1367 of 1988 by the Minister of Finance, states that where the contractor is in breach of any contractual clause or neglectful in fulfilling a contractual obligation and does not carry out remedies therein within 15 days from the date of receiving a notice to this effect, by a registered signed-for letter, the competent authority has the right to adopt either of the two procedures specified by the said Article, which are as follows:

> Procedure 1: Rescinding the contract, forfeiting the deposit due at the time of rescission and imposing penalties or obtaining damages for the injuries sustained by the administration.
> Procedure 2: Withdrawing the work from the contractor and performing such on the contractor's account.

Article (20) of the State Procurement Law repealed by Law No. 9 of 1983 states that the offeror of the accepted tender shall pay, within 10 days maximum starting from the next day of receiving a notice of the offer's acceptance by a registered signedfor letter, an amount to bring the provisional deposit up to 5 per cent of the contract value. The percentage differs in other types of contracts to be 10 per cent of the contract value. As regards contracts concluded with foreign parties, such deposit must be supplied within a maximum of 20 days, and the competent authority may extend the specified period for payment of the final deposit for a maximum of another ten days. The same Article also states that the final deposit is a security to ensure the contract performance. Article (18) of the said new law specifies the same provision.

Article (27) of the same law stipulates rescinding the contract and forfeiting the deposit in the following three cases:

> (a) use of fraud;
> (b) attempt to bribe a civil servant;
> (b) bankruptcy or insolvency of the contractor.

Article (28) grants the administration the right to rescind a contract upon a breach committed by the contracting party to any contractual clause.

---

5 De Laubadère, Moderne et Delvolé 1983–1984: 163; Auby et Bon 1995: 243. In Arab jurisprudence, see also: Abdel-Latif 1990: 153.

6 Auby et Bon 1995: 2. See also: the French State Council: C.E., 8 Nov. 1985, *Intreprise cerilou et communauté urbaine de Bordeaux*, Leb., 317, A.J.D.A., 20 Janvier 1986, 52. The French State Council decided that in pursuance of Article 35 of the CCAG on the power to rescind the contract, that cannot be applied prior to observing the rule of giving notice to the contracting party, where the rescinding procedures were in contravention with such Article, the appellant company cannot be requested to pay additional expenses for the delay in the works' execution. See also: C.E. 27 Juin 1986, *Syndicat Intercommunal du Bassen d'Archachon, inedit*, Clément, Jacques et Richer, Daniel n.d.: 394; C.E., 21 Mai 1982, *Société de Protection Intégrale du Bâtiment*, Leb., 183 *et seq.*; C.E., 28 Mars 1984, *Commune de Basse-en-Chandesse et Saint-Anstaise, inedit*, Clement, Jacques et Richer, *Daniel* n.d.: 535.

Article (76) of the Executive Regulations, governing the old Law No. 9 of 1983, permits the authority to rescind the contract upon a breach committed by the contracting party to any contractual clause. It also permits the authority to rescind the contract upon the demise of the contractor. Article (82) also permits the competent authority to rescind the contract where the contractor is in breach of any contractual clause or is neglectful in fulfilling an obligation, provided that he or she is notified by a registered signedfor letter and granted 15 days for remedial work.

Article (24) of the new law, promulgated by virtue of Law No. 89 of 1998, states that the contract shall be automatically rescinded in the two following cases:

(a) Upon establishing that the contracting party has directly or indirectly attempted, in person or by means of a third party, to bribe a civil servant working for an authority governed by the provisions of said law, or has secured the contract by means of bribery;
(b) Upon bankruptcy or insolvency of the contracting party; as such, that person is removed from Register (A) of the suppliers or contractors. The General Authority of Government Services shall be notified of such removal through the administrative department's bulletin.

Upon a submitted request, the contracting party whose name was struck off can be relisted in the register of suppliers or contractors, if the reason for removal is not validated, by virtue of a decision issued by the Prosecutor General that there was no criminal case filed against the contracting party, or that the decision should be kept on file or by virtue of a final court judgment to absolve the contracting party of such charge. The General Authority of Government Services must be notified of such decision for relisting through the administrative department's bulletin.

Article (25) of the said law stipulates that the administration may rescind or perform the contract on the contracting party's account if the latter is in breach of any contractual clause.

Such rescission or performance on the contracting party's account shall be effected by virtue of a decision issued by the competent authority; the contracting party shall be notified by a registered signedfor letter to the address mentioned in the contract.

Article (26) of the same law stipulates:

> In all cases of contract rescission, and in case of execution on the contracting party's account, the administration has the right to keep the final deposit, and deduct any fines and damages suffered by such from the outstanding payment due to the contracting party. In case of inadequate funds to cover such fines and damages, it may seek such deduction at any other administrative authority where the contracting party has outstanding payment, whatever these dues are for and without taking any judicial proceedings, and without detriment to its rights for compensation for any unpaid fines or damages through administrative procedures.

Such rescission or execution on the contracting party's account shall be effected by virtue of a decision issued by the competent authority, and the contracting party shall be notified by a registered signedfor letter to the address mentioned in the contract.

Article (26) of the same law stipulates:

> In all the cases of contract rescission, and in the case of execution on the contracting party's account, the administration has the right to keep the final deposit, and deduct any fines and damages suffered by such from the outstanding payment due to the contracting party. In case of inadequate funds to cover such fines and damages, it may seek such deduction at any other administrative

> authority where the contracting party has outstanding payment, whatever these dues are for and without taking any judicial proceedings, and without detriment to its rights for compensation for any unpaid fines or damages through administrative procedures. It is recognised that the cases mentioned therein include but are not limited to these examples, since the administration has an inherent right to rescind the contract if the contracting party is in breach of his contractual obligations, whereby necessitating such a harsh penalty.[7]

The French State Council requires certain conditions to impose the penalty of rescinding the contract, which is the gross breach and notification prior to such rescission.[8]

The *Cahier des Clauses Administratives Générales* (CCAG) specifies two models for contract rescission whereas Article (49/4) stipulates that rescinding the contract (upon breach by the contractor) may be a simple and straightforward measure or a rescission where the execution of the contract is on the contractor's account.[9]

The grounds for two such stipulations are that if the contracting party is in breach of a contractual obligation and has not undertaken any remedial work within 15 days from the date of receiving a notice by a registered signedfor letter to carry out such remedies, the administration has the right to rescind the contract, forfeit the final deposit due at the time of rescission and obtain all fines and damages for the injuries occurred. The final deposit specified by Article (18) of the new law is 5 per cent of the contract value. In contracts concluded with private foreign parties, the date to perform such remedies can be extended to 20 days, with a grace period of a maximum of ten days.

The Approach of the Egyptian[10] and French Judiciary on This Matter

Where the administration has the right to amend the contract unilaterally, it obviously has the right to rescind it unilaterally.[11] Such a rule has become common in administrative contracts.

The French State Council laid down the grounds for rescinding the contract in light of Article (35) of the CCAG regarding the power to rescind the contract. The Council established that such power cannot be enforced before ascertaining that the contracting party has not observed the notice given to carry out remedial works. If the rescinding procedures are in contravention with the CCAG, the company may not be requested to pay the additional expenses for the delay in performance.[12]

The Supreme Administrative Court in Egypt also laid down common rules for the administration to impose such penalty upon the contracting party. The court was of the opinion that while the administration had the power unilaterally to rescind the administrative contract and forfeit the deposit without resorting to court proceedings – being a privilege granted since the administration is in charge of the operation of public utilities associated with such administrative contract – it must

---

7 In rescinding the contract as a penalty imposed by the authority upon the contracting party, see: Richer 1995: 183 *et seq.*; Dufau,1988: 192; Sabiani 1995: 189; Kadiki 1868, Tome 1: 292; Auby et Bon 1995: 243. In Arab jurisprudence, see: El Tamawy 1991: 545; Abdel Badie 1993: 107; El Hassan 1997: 168.

8 In rescinding the contract as a penalty imposed by the authority upon the contracting party, see: El Tamawy, *supra*, note 7, 553; Richer 1995: 183 *et seq.*

9 For more details, see: El Tamawy 1991: 554 *et seq.*

10 Generally, see: Ismail 2003b.

11 C.E. 17 Mars 1864, *Paul Dupont*, D, 1864, 3, 87; C.E. 9 décembre 1927, Gargiula, Rec.1198, C.E. Ass.2 féevrier 1987, société TV6, Rec.29.

12 C.E. 8 Nov. 1985, Entreprise Ozitou, Clement et Richer 1989: 380; C.E. 27 juin 1986, syndicat intercommunal, Clément et Richer 1989: 394; C.E. 21 mai 1982, Société de protection, Clément et Richer 1989: 322; C.E. 28 Mars 1984, Commune de Basse, Clement et Richer 1989: 353.

be for public interest reasons; otherwise, the contracting party is entitled to claim compensation for the damage incurred by such illegal procedure, which is a contractual breach. The damage could be material or moral; the main issue is that it is based upon conclusive evidence brought forward by the claimant, so as to prevent unjustified enrichment on the administration's account. It should be taken into account that compensation for material damage comprises compensatory elements, being the loss suffered by the contracting party and financial damage.[13]

The fact is that the Supreme Administrative Court laid down the general principles for such an important judicial issue, where it empowered the administration with the right to rescind the administrative contract and forfeit the deposit without having recourse to the courts. This principle exists since the contract is related to a public utility, and the administration aims to ensure systematic and consistent functioning of such.

The Supreme Court allowed the contracting party to claim compensation for any injuries incurred by an illegal procedure that is deemed by the court a contractual breach.

It is established that the nature of the right endowed upon the administration to rescind the contract and confiscate the deposit requires the occurrence of a contractual breach by the contracting party. Previous imposition of penalties set forth in the contract does not prevent the administration from exercising this right since its nature necessarily requires a previous breach by the contracting party to an obligation prescribed in the contract concluded with the state.[14]

It is recognized that rescinding any given contract is subject to a general legal rule that the creditor who decides to rescind the contract is entitled to compensation for any damage caused by the debtor, if failure to fulfil an obligation was due to a neglectful or intentional breach, giving rise to an injury. This general rule is applied in rescinding administrative contracts as well as civil contracts; hence, the grounds for compensation are only based upon the general legal rules. Such compensation differs in nature and purpose from deposit forfeiture, which is a financial penalty provided by administrative customary rules in administrative contracts as they are related to the needs for an operational public utility and to precedence of the public interest over the private interest, which is contrary to the private nature of civil contracts. Due to this peculiar nature of administrative contracts, the authority enjoys many powers such as imposing financial penalties, including deposit forfeiture. In addition, the nature and purpose of the reason for confiscating the deposit on one hand and claiming compensation on the other are different. It is acceptable in the event of rescinding a contract to forfeit the deposit as well as claim compensation as this is not deemed a prohibited duplication in compensation, even if the administrative contract did not mention the right to compensation, as such right is part of the general legal principles.

It is established that combining deposit confiscation and compensation is conditional upon the fact that the administrative contract does not explicitly prohibit such measure and that the damage incurred still exists even after forfeiting the deposit; that is to say, the value of the damage exceeds the deposit amount. According to the general rules, if the deposit confiscation makes good such damage, then the compensation is not justifiable, unless otherwise agreed. It is quite evident that such reservations in the mentioned general rule require examining each individual case according to the terms and conditions related thereto and necessitate prudence in generalizing a case judgment *per se* upon all other similar cases.

To sum up, combining deposit confiscation with compensation claim is not prohibited, provided that it is not explicitly otherwise stated in the contract, and that the injury incurred is not yet fully

---

13 Judgment No. 4682 – 35 (26/4/1994) – Egyptian Conseil d'Etat 1996: 634.

14 Judgment No. 523 – 11 (9/2/1971) 16/20/130 – *M* – Egyptian Conseil d'Etat 1996: 633.

covered by forfeiting the deposit, or else there is no ground for compensation unless otherwise agreed upon in the administrative contract.[15]

Nevertheless, the administration has discretionary power unrelated to the judicial supervision to confiscate the deposit on the grounds of a contractual breach, so long as it is consistent with the legitimacy principle and does not represent an abuse of such power.[16]

Defining the final deposit and its purpose in state contracts, the Supreme Court held that it intends to be a guarantee for the administration against any breach that may be committed by the contracting party while observing the administrative contract's terms and conditions. The administration may not overlook the deposit as it ensures the systematic functioning of the public utility.

The Supreme Court added that such guarantees include collecting fines for delays, compensation and any payments owed by the contracting party since the deposit is a security for the performance of the administrative contract. It is inconceivable that in the case of a failure to perform the contract, such security exists unless the administration has the right to confiscate the deposit directly, without resorting to court proceedings, or there was no need in the first place to require a deposit with the tender. If the deposit is a guarantee endowed upon the administration, as a security for its interest and protection, it is logically inconceivable that such deposit is a limitation or an undermining of the rights of the administration or a constraint upon the administration preventing it from claiming for all injuries incurred while executing the administrative contract terms and conditions, especially if the deposit is not sufficient to make good all the injuries in a comprehensive and adequate manner. To decide otherwise would disrupt the implementation of the administrative contract's provisions as it is recognized that the administration has the right to impose penalties upon the contracting party who delays in fulfilling obligations in a timely manner. It is also recognized that the administration has the right to confiscate the deposit upon a breach of the contractual obligations without having to prove the occurrence of an injury, not because such proof is not originally a required element, but it is rather assumed to be existent in an administrative contract without the need to prove otherwise. The contracting party may not prove that the value of the injury suffered by the administration is less than the deposit amount; thus, it is inconceivable that the administration has no right to claim the contracting party in breach for damages equal to the value of injuries when they exceed the deposit amount. Undoubtedly, the administration rather has the right to claim that the contracting party should compensate for all true and actual injuries by covering the difference between the amount of the deposit and the damages to be paid. The deposit represents the minimum amount for compensation entitled to the administration; however, by no means does it represent the maximum amount for any possible damages.[17]

This principle rests on the idea that if forfeiting the deposit had made good the injury, there is no case to claim for compensation, whereas if the deposit amount was not sufficient to compensate for the injury, then there must be a judgment for adequate damages.[18] It is obvious that such principle applies to all administrative contracts, including public works agreements.

---

15 The Supreme Administrative Court – Judgment No. 1180 – 8 (27/11/1965) 11/7/51– Egyptian Conseil d'Etat 1996: 629.

16 The Supreme Administrative Court – Judgment No. 1127 – 5 (22/4/1961) 6/115/891 – Egyptian Conseil d'Etat 1996: 554; see also: El Tamawy 1991: 554 *et seq.*; Elbana 1984: 209; Fayyad 1974: 280.

17 The Supreme Administrative Court – Judgment No. 1289 – (3/1/1965) 10/4/313 – Egyptian Conseil d'Etat 1996: 556.

18 The Supreme Administrative Court, Judgment No.508 – 9 (18/11/1967) 13/5/93 – Egyptian Conseil d'Etat 1996: 557.

International Public Works Agreements are governed by the rules related to final deposit and contract rescission in case of breach of obligations by the contracting party. The reason is that such rules are not in conflict with the complex nature of these contracts, which keeps some privileges endowed upon the administration in International Public Works Agreements. Where these contracts contain some conditions changing them into international contracts, with the complex nature characterizing administrative contracts, such nature does not deny that they are still governed by the provisions of public law and comply with many substantive rules of the conventional theory of administrative contracts, including multilateral rescission of the contract, forfeiture of the deposit withdrawal of work and execution on the contractor's account, as will be explained in detail, so long as the contract does not contain stability clauses or does not include an assertion of its binding power.

The fact that the administration claims other types of compensation from the contracting party when it confiscates the deposit (which amount is less than the total deposit amount) is not based upon the consideration that the contract is valid and performed on the contracting party's account, although it has been previously rescinded; it is rather based upon the provisions of the general rules governing any contract, which stipulate that any breach leading to an injury must be remedied by the party committing such, with damages equal to the value of such injury. These provisions are absolutely not in contradiction with the notion of deposit in administrative contracts in general.[19]

Confiscating the deposit upon a breach of any obligation by the contracting party is not necessarily associated with rescinding the contract, as nothing can stop confiscating the deposit after the contract completion, for reasons such as lax, omissive, inappropriate or delayed performance or any other forms of contractual breach.[20]

The legal nature for forfeiting the deposit is effectively an agreed compensation estimated in the contract as the value of the deposit submitted by the omissive party. Stipulating that the deposit be confiscated in the event of terminating the contract is an agreed compensation governed by the general rules set forth in Article (234) of the Civil Code. The Egyptian State Council stresses the fact that the administration may confiscate only a part of the deposit if the contract was partially performed, so that it is proportionate with the unfulfilled obligations and the amount withheld from the deposit.[21]

Models of renowned international construction contracts do not contain these types of penalties imposed by the state upon the contracting party, as they are civil contract models, for example, the FIDIC. The contracting state only has to add conditions related to its rights to rescind the contract and forfeit the deposit or otherwise, to add that the law of the State Procurement Law and its Executive Regulations are an integral part of the contract.[22]

Withdrawal of Project and Performance on the Contractor's Expenses

In administrative contracts, the administration can impose other penalties upon the contractor, the most important of which is withdrawing the work and execution on the contractor's account and under his responsibility.

---

19 The Supreme Administrative Court – Judgment No. 1289 (8/2/1/1965) 1/34/313 – Egyptian Conseil d'Etat 1996: 560.

20 The Supreme Administrative Court – Judgment No. 1127 – 5 (22/4/1961) 6/5/891 Egyptian Conseil d'Etat 1996: 560.

21 Opinion No. 260 on 13/5/1955 in Session of 13/5/1955 – 10/40/67 – Egyptian Conseil d'Etat 1996: 566.

22 For examples of state contracts, see: *Esna Barrage Contract*, Metro Underground Contracts, and *Sahhara Ter'et Essalam* in Egypt.

The administration cannot exercise both rescission of the contract penalty together with withdrawal of the project. If the contract was unilaterally rescinded, the administration cannot impose withdrawal of project and performance of the contractor's expenses as the latter penalty is based on the contract existence. The administration cannot exercise performance on the contractor's expenses unless there is a base for this penalty. This legal base is the contract.

Withdrawing the work[23] is a penalty imposed by the administration upon the contractor who is in breach of any contractual obligation. The administration commissions another contractor for execution on the omissive contractor's account,[24] which is known to be a privilege used by the administration to execute the work in kind. Execution of the work is administered by the authority on the contractor's account and under his responsibility. The omissive party is to bear the price differences according to the rule of fulfilling the obligation in kind.[25]

This procedure does not stop charging the omissive party with delay penalties and administrative expenses, as a means to force that party to execute the contract and a penalty imposed by the administration in case of omission. In its decision, the administration is not bound by the principles of the Civil Code, so that it can take a rapid and flexible procedure in line with the requirement for systematic and consistent functioning of the public utility.[26] [27]

The Egyptian State Council has established that it is a recognized principle in both civil and administrative contracts to fulfil the obligations in kind. If the party entrusted with the execution refuses to carry out his obligations, the other party is entitled to force him to fulfil such obligations in kind and pay damages for the injury incurred by such breach. Whereas the execution in kind is carried out through the courts of law in civil transactions, it is administered through the administration on the contractor's account and under the contractor's responsibility. Purchases made on the omissive party's account, with the obligation to pay for the price difference as it may occur, are not a penalty imposed upon him but rather an application of the rule of fulfilling the contractual obligations in kind, where the administration personally administers such execution so as to ensure the systematic and consistent functioning of the public utility and to prevent disruption that may undermine the public interest. This is in line with the principle of giving precedence to the public interest over the private interest. In civil contracts, the interests of both parties are balanced and equal, whereas in administrative contracts, they are not equal, given the principle of precedence of the public interest over the private interest, which governs the relationships in administrative contracts.[28]

The State Council's General Assembly of the Departments of Counsel and Legislation established the same principles stated above.[29]

---

23 El Hassan 1997: 131.

24 Auby et Bon 1995: 244; Dufau 1988: 192; De Laubadère, Venezia et Gaudement 1995, Tome 2: 480. In Arab jurisprudence, see: El Tamawy 1991: 528; El Hassan 1997: 131; Fayyad 1974: 214.

25 The Supreme Administrative Court – Judgment No. 5843 – 26, 20/11/1982, 28/18/86 – Egyptian Conseil d'Etat 1996: 596.

26 The Supreme Administrative Court – Judgment 17/3/1962, 7/48/459 – Egyptian Conseil d'Etat 1996: 595.

27 With regard to the description of withdrawing the works and execution on the contractor's account as a right exercised by the authority, see: El Tamawy 1991: 533 and El Hassan 1997: 131.

28 The Supreme Administrative Court – Judgment No. 2013, 6, 16/12//1962, 7/14/102 – Egyptian Ministry of Finance 2009: 596.

29 The General Assembly of the Counsel and Legislation Departments, Opinion No. 626 of 17/6/1987, session, 17/6/1987, 41 and 42/166/469 Egyptian Ministry of Finance 2009: 597.

The administration has discretionary power to enforce execution in both local and international administrative contracts as a means to exercise pressure on the omissive party. Such power is intended to ensure systematic and consistent functioning of the public utility and is, therefore, not a penalty clause prescribed by virtue of the Civil Code. Moreover, like all other penalties in administrative contracts, this penalty is a measure that the administration has the power to take without resorting to judicial proceedings and without the occurrence of any injury to the public utility.[30]

If the international public works contract is an administrative contract with some of its exceptional clauses uncommon to private law contracts, the procedure for the withdrawal of the work and execution on the contractor's account is a measure taken by the administration to enforce the execution, based upon the contractual clauses, and is not thus an administrative decision.

In this respect, the General Assembly of the Legal Opinion and Legislation decided that:

> there must be a definition of the legal characterization of the aforementioned work's withdrawal and whether it is withdrawable/ cancellable decision or not; or whether it is a mere procedure taken by the administration based upon a clause in the contract concluded with the company; as such, the administration may cancel its decision if it deems it in the public interest.

There must be a differentiation, in this context, between two types of decisions issued by the administration regarding administrative contracts:

> First type: decisions issued by the administration during the preliminary contracting process and prior to concluding the contract, which are called separate administrative decisions, such as launching a public tender for the intended work, excluding a tenderer, or cancelling or awarding a tender to a certain person. Similar to all administrative decisions, such decision is final and governed by all provisions related to final administrative decisions, which may be challenged to be cancelled on the specified dates.

> Second type: decisions issued by the administration to enforce an administrative contract, based upon a contractual clause therein, such as withdrawing the work from the contracting party, forfeiting the deposit or rescinding the contract. Such decisions are not administrative decisions where the Administrative Court is the competent court to take cognizance of conflicts arisen, based on its jurisdiction to cancel final administrative decisions, but as it is the court with full jurisdiction in settling disputes arising from administrative contracts in accordance with Article (10) of the State Council Law.

On the above basis, the decision to withdraw the work from the company is not an administrative decision; rather, it is merely a measure taken by the General Authority for Roads based on a clause specified in the contract concluded with the company. Such measure does not terminate the contract, as it is a preliminary procedure followed by another one dealt with in Article (94) of the Executive Regulations of the State Procurement Law, whereby the administration is allowed to administer the work and launch a tender to execute the incomplete work or to conclude a contract with a well-known contractor in the related industry to complete the work.

---

30 The Supreme Administrative Court – Judgment No. 1181, 25/1/1994 – Egyptian Ministry of Finance 2009: 596.

In all the above cases, the original contract remains valid with the proviso that it is performed on the account and under the responsibility of the original party.[31]

In implementing the provisions of the Executive Regulations of the State Procurement Law, the Supreme Administrative Court determines the cases whereby the administration is entitled to withdraw the work from the contractor, as it states that "the Supreme Administrative Court's judgment considers that administrative contracts have a nature distinct from that of civil contracts, where they intend to achieve the public interest which precedes over the private interest of the contracting party."

The authority is entitled to administer in person the incomplete work on the contractor's account, or to relaunch a public tender for the performance of such work, wholly or partly, and to impose fine for delays.

The Supreme Administrative Court implemented these principles and decided in one of the leading cases that:

> upon an induction of the Executive Regulations of the state procurement law issued by virtue of Decree No. 542 of 1957 by the Minister of Finance [by which the awarded tender was governed], it is concluded that Article 93 therefrom states that 'The contractor must complete all commissioned works including any additional or amended works issued by a decree from the ministry, the authority or the military forces, in pursuance with the granted rights under the contract, in a comprehensive and proper manner leading to their timely handover. Where a delay occurs in completing and handing over the works on the specified dates, a fine shall be imposed for the delay period, with the exception of any delays that the ministry, the administration or the military forces deem to be caused by force majeure.

Article (94) of the Executive Regulations stipulates that:

> the director of administration or the military chief has the right to withdraw the work from the contractor in any of the following cases:
>
> a) If the contractor delays or appears to be slow in the commencement of the work, to the extent that the ministry, the administration, or the military forces deem such to be impracticable for the timely completion of the work.
>
> b) If the work is suspended for more than 15 days.
>
> c) If the contractor withdraws from or abandons the work.
>
> The work shall be withdrawn upon a written notice dispatched to the contractor by a registered signed for letter.

Article (78) of the same Executive Regulations stipulates that:

> the ministry, the administration or the military forces maintain the right to amend the contract, by exclusion or inclusion, within the range of 15% of the value of supply contracts and

31 Opinion No. 399 of 16/5/1960, session 4/5/1960, 14 and 15/94/188 – Egyptian Ministry of Finance 2009: 601.

> 25% of the value of public works agreements, where the contractor has no right to claim for any compensation therefor. Upon a decision issued by the deputy minister, the director of administration, or the military chief, the aforementioned ranges may be exceeded in emergency or exceptional cases, provided that it does not undermine the prioritization of the contractor's tender, that the budget allowance affords such excess, and that the contractor's approval is obtained.

It can thus be concluded that the contractor has a contractual and legal obligation toward the administration for the undertakings prescribed in the contract, as well as any additional works within the limits indicated and during the term(s) specified. Where the contractor delays such execution, a penalty is to be imposed with the proportions and under the conditions provided in the Executive Regulations unless such delay is caused by reasons beyond the contractor's means. Further, the work may be withdrawn from the contractor in several instances, such as delay in commencing the work while the site has been delivered clear of any impediments, slow progress of work with clear indication that the work will not be completed in the specified term, unjustifiable suspension of work for more than 15 days, withdrawal of the contractor from the site together with his equipment and machineries or total abandoning of the site. As such, the administration is entitled to issue a decision to withdraw the work from the contractor, provided that the latter is informed by a written notice dispatched with a registered signedfor letter, with no further action required.[32]

The Administrative Court established another principle recognizing that the criterion that justified the withdrawal of the work from the contractor due to delay in the performance required specifying the date for commencing the performance and the level of responsiveness to execute the works assigned to the contractor. A short delay in commencing the work without any indication of possible breach committed by the contractor could not justify the withdrawal of work.[33] In the event of performance on the contractor's account, the contractor should bear all price differences, administrative expenses and fine for delays.

Costs Borne by the Omissive Contractor in the Event of Executing the Work on the Contractor's Account

1) Price differences In the event of work in an international public works contract on the omissive contractor's account, the administration charges the latter with the difference between the prices applicable at the time of the original execution and the actual prices when the authority carries out such execution as the prices of raw material such as cement and steel are constantly increasing. In international large-scale infrastructure contracts, the quantities used for the execution are vast, giving rise to substantial price differences charged upon the contractor, in the event of committing a breach, and consequently executing the work on his account.

The Supreme Administrative Court has in many instances concluded such principle, stating that:

> In administrative contracts, it is established that the execution in kind is a means to exercise pressure upon the omissive contractor, and to ensure the systematic and consistent functioning of

32 The Supreme Administrative Court – Judgment No. 4393, 37, 8/2/1994 – Egyptian Ministry of Finance 2009: 606.

33 The Supreme Administrative Court – Judgment No. 1786, 30, 18/1/1986 – Egyptian Ministry of Finance 2009: 607.

> the public utility. As a consequence, the authority is endowed with a discretionary power to resort to such a measure, which is not a part of the penal provisions set forth in the Civil Code. Similar to any other penalties in administrative contracts, the authority can enforce such penalty without resorting to court proceedings, and without evidence of any injury occurred to the public utility. The appellant is then obliged to bear the price differences arisen by the execution of the contract on his account, the administrative expenses amounting to 5% of the contract value, and the fine for delays at 4% of such value.[34]

However, in case the administration delays execution of the work on the contractor's account for reasons within its control, during which the prices even rise slightly, it has to bear all the costs incurred therefrom, as the contractor may not be held responsible for such breach. The rationale behind this is that having executed the work on the contractor's account, the administration is obliged to observe the same contractual clauses and terms prescribed in the first tender, with the exception of prices, as it assumes the agent's role. The administration is to comply with Article (704) of the Civil Code, whereby it has to exercise in such agency the same due care exercised in its private works. In case the administration exceeds the terms of the tender for a period of 15 days, such delay cannot be attributed to the contractor as an increase in price.[35] This is an established principle with regard to price differences, which applies to International Public Works Agreements.

2) Administrative expenses The contractor bears the administrative expenses in case of executing the work on his account; however, the rule states that the administrative expenses are not charged upon the omissive party in case of execution on his account, unless the administration substantiates the occurrence of damage or injuries, leading to relaunching the tender, with the consequences of tender republication and formation of committees to open envelopes and select tenderers. The state would have been spared all such efforts and costs, had the contracting party been appropriately fulfilling its obligations. The administration is then entitled to such costs upon warranted reasons and at the percentage specified by the State Procurement Law.

The Supreme Administrative Court judgment establishes that administrative expenses are deemed a part of the penalties imposed by the administration, pursuant to the Executive Regulations of the State Procurement Law, which explicitly or implicitly govern administrative contracts. The assumption is that the contracting party recognizes the methods, means and clauses governing the contracts concluded with the administrative authority; hence, the contractor accepts such terms and conditions unless otherwise specified.

In its judgment, the Supreme Administrative Court further states that although such clause is set forth in supply contracts, it is applicable in public works agreements, as it discloses the administration's intent to determine the administrative expenses incurred while performing an administrative contract, where the contracting party fails to perform the contract, and has knowledge of and accepts the specified expenses.[36]

Under the Executive Regulations of the Procurement Law, whose applicability precedes that of the repealed Law No. 9 of 1983 of the State Procurement Law, the Supreme Administrative Court confirms that such expenses are legal compensation owed to the administration, in consideration of recommencing the process of tender launching. The percentage of these expenses has been

34 Judgment No. 1181, 33, 25/1/1994 – Egyptian Ministry of Finance 2009: 598.

35 Judgment No. 94 – 9, 11/12/1965 – *Forty Years Collection of Court Judgments*, 613.

36 The Supreme Administrative Court – Judgment No. 94 – 9, 11/12/1965 – Egyptian Ministry of Finance 2009: 588.

estimated at 5 per cent of the value of the work performed on the contractor's account, in pursuance of Article (105) of the Executive Regulations of the said law.

Article (25) of Law No. 89 of 1989 states that where a breach of any contractual obligations takes place, the administration has the right to rescind or perform the contract on the contractor's account.

The contract rescission or performance on the party's account is determined by virtue of a decision issued by the competent authority. The contracting party is notified by a registered signedfor letter at the address set forth in the contract. This indicates that the authority can take these two measures without a court judgment.

Article (75) of the Executive Regulations issued by virtue of Decree No. 1367 of 1998 of the Minister of Finance confirmed the same argument.

The administration has the right to retain all or parts of the temporary facilities, buildings, machineries, tools, equipment, etc., without being liable before the contractor or any third party for any damage or loss or being responsible to pay any costs related to such items. The administration further has the right to keep the aforementioned items even after the completion of the work so as to ensure its rights and is entitled to sell them without a shred of liability for such sale.

Article (49/3) of the CCAG in France stipulates that execution on the contractor's account shall be directly performed by the administration, by carrying out in person the administration of the public works. The same Article further stipulates that upon withdrawing the work from the contractor, that person shall bear the increase in expenses occurred from performing such works.

When the administration executes the works on the contractor's account, it is then an agent who must exercise due care under such agency as in its private works.[37]

3) Penalty for delay The fines for delay are the most pressurizing means used; the "penalty for delay" is of fundamental importance to the foreign contractors as it has a punitive nature in Arab doctrine and jurisprudence.

37 The Supreme Administrative Court on 11/12/1965, Year 11, 128; (39) Ga'far 2000: 143.

Chapter 8

Penalty for Delay[1]: Penalty Clauses and Liquidated Damages in Accordance with Arab Legislation and Court Decisions (An Analytical Perspective)

Introduction

The purpose of this chapter is to examine the legal nature of liquidated damages (penalty for delay) in international public works agreements, with special reference to the Egyptian State Council (*Conseil d'Etat*) decisions, in the light of the influence of globalization on these contracts.

This chapter describes the situation in Egyptian legislation (State Procurement Law and the Egyptian Civil Code). It is an analytical perspective on the Egyptian State Council decisions in comparison with the Egyptian Court of Cassation decisions, as the Court of Cassation directly applies civil law provisions.

The Egyptian State Council plays a significant role in establishing and codifying rules of administrative contracts (*Les Contrats Administratifs*) since administrative law is not codified in Egypt. The State Council is the founder of the Administrative Contracts Theory established in 1946. Since then, the courts, and the General Assembly for Legal Opinion (*Fatwa*) and Legislation, have set out the legal framework of the criteria for administrative contracts.[2]

The system employed by the State Council is to some extent similar to the system employed by courts applying the common law, since administrative law has not been codified by the Egyptian legislator. It is worth recalling that lower administrative courts (appeal or first instance administrative courts) are not obliged to follow decisions of the Supreme Administrative Court.

Nevertheless, lower courts are always influenced by the decisions of the Supreme Court. Where views differ, lower courts can deal with new perspectives and develop their own reasoning after deliberations and voting by the majority of judges.[3]

Globalization plays a fundamental role in enhancing and modifying traditional administrative contract theory as a result of the new stipulations imposed by foreign contractors entering into infrastructure agreements with public juristic entities. A new era for a new legal structure has begun, since it is acceptable under the Egyptian legal system to stipulate arbitration as the only mechanism for dispute settlement in infrastructure projects[4] where it has been agreed by the

---

1 © Informa UK Limited. This chapter first appeared in *The International Construction Law Review* [2009] 26, 4, ICLR, 506–18, , and is reproduced by kind permission of the publisher and editors.

2 Supreme Administrative Court: Decisions Nos. 1558, 7 March 1964, and 3128, 24 January 1995, see Egyptian *Conseil d'Etat* 1996: 98–9; General Assembly for Legal Opinion (*Fatwa*) and Legislation, No. 403, 11 April 1990, Session, 21 March 1990, file 7/2/139.

3 Deliberations are obligatory and confidential pursuant to Article (166) of the Egyptian Civil and Commercial Procedural Law (No. 13 of 1968), which applies to State Council courts.

4 Article (13) of the Egyptian Arbitration Act (No. 27 of 1994), stipulates that, in civil and commercial disputes, if there is an arbitration clause in the contract or arbitration agreement the courts are prohibited from hearing the case.

contracting parties.[5] Moreover, the Egyptian legal system began to recognize foreign laws as the substantive laws applicable to a dispute rather than Egyptian laws applicable in similar cases, especially in arbitration rather than litigation.

These are some enhancements of the administrative contracts theory which are considered to result from globalization and the integration of the Egyptian legal system (to some extent) with the global legal and economic concepts that influence legislative and court decisions in Egypt.

Liquidated Damages in Egyptian Legislation

Liquidated damages under Egyptian legislation are treated as a penalty applicable for delay in the execution of works. The penalty is dual in nature: it acts as a punitive clause and exercises pressure upon the contractor.

Article (23) of the State Procurement Law promulgated by Law No. 89 of 1998 stipulates that:

> If the contracting party delayed the work after the set completion date, the authority concerned, can, for public interest, grant the contractor an extension of time for total completion and it can impose a penalty (fine) pursuant to percentages and rules stipulated by executive regulations. The total (fine) shall not exceed 3% of the total contract value in purchasing immovables, receiving services, consultation studies and technical works, and shall not exceed 10% in public works and transportation.
>
> The administration (state) shall collect the penalty for delay (fine) '*ipso facto*' without warning or any preliminary (or judicial) procedures. The contracting party can be exempt from the penalty, after a legal opinion from the State Council, if the delay was out of the control thereof. The authority concerned accepts in this case, after consulting with the State Council, to exempt the contracting party from the fine, if the delay did not cause any damage.
>
> The penalty imposed and collected from the contracting party will not violate the right of the authority concerned to reclaim compensation from the contractor for delay in executing works.

Article (83) of the Executive Regulations stipulates that: "the contractor is obliged to complete works to be able to do preliminary completion at stipulated time."

If the contractor delays the completion of the work, the contracting authority can, in the public interest, grant an extension of time for total completion. The penalty (fine) shall be imposed from the beginning of this extension of time until the preliminary completion at a rate of 1 per cent for every week or part of a week. The total value of the penalty (fine) shall not exceed 10 per cent of the total value of the contract price. The penalty (fine) shall be calculated and deducted from the value of the total works (the takeover certificate shall be considered), if the authority concerned decided that the delayed part of works of the project will directly or indirectly prevent the state from the utilization thereof at the stipulated time. If the authority concerned decided that the delayed part of the works will not cause such prevention, the fine calculation will be pursuant to previous percentages and conditions from the value of the delayed part of the works only.

---

5 A crucial question remains unanswered: can the parties go to the national courts if the time bar in the agreement to start arbitration has passed (i.e., FIDIC forms of contract stipulate a time limit to start arbitration)? For more details from the perspective of civil law countries see: Ismail 2003b: 497–504.

The fine shall be immediately imposed upon occurrence of the delay without taking any other procedures (i.e., notification, or any judicial procedures).

It is appropriate to refer to the previous State Procurement Law promulgated by Law No. 9 of 1983 and the Executive Regulations thereof and abrogated by the current legislation (No. 89 of 1998). It was prohibited, until the new legislation was promulgated, to exempt the contractor from the penalty even if no damages occurred to the state. The situation of the previous legislation was therefore that the penalty was compulsory and obligatory even if there were no damages to the contracting public juristic entity.

The new trend with the 1998 legislation and its Executive Regulations is that a contractor may be exempt from the penalty if the Legal Opinion Department of the State Council approved the exemption. Otherwise the contractor is obliged to pay the fine up to the cap (ceiling) stipulated under Article (23) of the 1998 legislation, and Article (83) of the Executive Regulations (10 per cent of the total value of the contract price) even if there is no loss or damage to the state! If there is a delay, the penalty should be paid "ipso facto," regardless of the fact that no damage or loss was suffered by the state.

Despite the fact that there are some enhancements in the new trend adopted by the current legislation, the fine still has its punitive and exorbitant nature. The penalty is due, in any circumstances, when there is a delay even in light of the stipulations of the current legislation. The penalty is an extravagant and exorbitant clause in the agreement in light of the State Procurement Law.

Public juristic entities (i.e., ministries, governorates, the cabinet, etc.) in Egypt still accept this and applies these stipulations by State Procurement Laws (No. 9 of 1983 and No. 89 of 1998) without considering the harmful effect on the contractor by calculating this punitive penalty (10 per cent of the total value of the contract price) and setting-off this amount from the payments, especially the final certificate. The contractor has to reclaim this amount through either State Council courts or arbitration. This chapter will examine the decisions of the Supreme Administrative Court of the Egyptian State Council and the Legal Opinion Department (*Fatwa*) from a comparative perspective with the civil law and Egyptian Court of Cassation (Civil and Commercial Circuits).

The Penalty Under the State Procurement Law of 1998 and Pre-estimated Compensation under the Egyptian Civil Code

Article (224) of the Egyptian Civil Code stipulates that:

1. The agreed compensation is not due if the debtor proved that the creditor did not suffer any damages (loss).

2. A judge (or arbitrator) can reduce the amount of compensation if the debtor proved that there is an exaggeration in that amount to a great extent or that the original obligation was partially executed.

3. Any agreement contrary to the above-mentioned provisions 224 (1) and 224 (2) is null and void.

Pursuant to Article (225), if "the damages exceeded the agreed compensation value, the creditor cannot claim more than the stipulated amount unless the debtor is accused of committing fraud or a fundamental mistake."

Egyptian doctrine[6] explains this agreed compensation as a pre-estimated compensation agreed between the contracting parties. This compensation is, however, not due, in the absence of loss or damages, to the creditor. The court or arbitral tribunal may reduce the compensation if it is not appropriate to the damages suffered, or "the contractor executed the contract partially" to create a contractual balance between the due compensation amount and the damages. This dimension in the Egyptian Civil Code (which is based on Napoleonic codes) is to maintain the fairness and balance of the contractual relationship.

These rules are mandatory pursuant to the Egyptian Civil Code. There is a need, therefore, to compare the nature of the pre-estimated and agreed compensation, on the one hand, and the penalties stipulated under the Egyptian State Procurement Law of 1998 on the other.

According to the nature of the penalties (fines) under Article (23) of Law No. 89 of 1998, these penalties resemble a fine on the contractor in public works agreements (domestic and international) up to 10 per cent of the total value of the contract price, even if no damages occurred to the state contracting entity.[7]

This is a mandatory rule in the Egyptian legal system under an administrative contract. Consequently, the state must take this action of a punitive nature pursuant to the law, and insert exorbitant clauses in an administrative contract in the light of this legislation without the need for any judicial action.

Conversely, the agreed compensation (liquidated damages) in the Egyptian Civil Code applies to civil and commercial contracts which are governed by private law. First, the compensation aims to compensate the creditor in case of damages only. Second, this compensation should be fair and adequate to the actual loss. Third, the national court or arbitral tribunal can exercise its power to review the amount of compensation to assure that it is fair and adequate. These rules are mandatory in the domain of civil and commercial agreements. International construction contracts fall under the scope of this article. Meanwhile, administrative contracts for public works, whether domestic or international, fall under the scope of Article (23) of the State Procurement Law and the Executive Regulations thereof fall under Article (83), unless there are different stipulations by the contractor.

Egyptian law thus recognizes rules the application of which can be avoided by the agreement of the contracting parties; they cannot avoid the application of any mandatory rules by their mutual consent as it is a matter of public policy. Thus, parties to any agreement cannot violate any valid mandatory rule in any circumstances under the Egyptian legal system.

Penalty Clauses or Liquidated Damages in Accordance with the Decisions of the Egyptian Courts

Egyptian State Council: Court Decisions

As the State Council has been codifying principles of administrative contracts since 1946, the Supreme Administrative Court has distinguished between penalties in administrative contracts and

---

6 Yehia, Abdel Wadood 1987: 52–55; Egyptian Court of Cassation, Decision No. 227, Civil Circuit, Judicial Year 19, Session, 25 December 1968.

7 It is worth mentioning that the parties to the contract can stipulate a different percentage or cap and this can supersede the cap or percentages stipulated by law (this very rarely happens), see: Opinion from General Assembly for legal Opinion and Legislation, No. 800, 13 December 1999, Session, 20 October 1999, file No. 54/1/358.

liquidated damages which were pre-estimated and agreed upon in civil and commercial transactions (private law contracts). The court confirmed that:

> Penalties in administrative contracts differ in nature from pre-estimated compensation in civil and commercial contracts. The latter is a pre-estimated compensation agreed upon between the parties and payable upon breach of contract by any of the contracting parties. This compensation is conditioned to be paid in all stipulations of the Egyptian law for compensation in general, such as the necessity of damages to the other contractor, notification to the party who caused the breach and a court judgment which can reduce compensation if one of the parties proved that compensation exceeds damages or loss.
>
> Meanwhile, the justification of penalties in administrative contracts is to guarantee the execution of these contracts at the stipulated time. The fundamental principle in administrative law of 'running the public utilities in discipline and regularity' is the main justification for and reason behind codifying these penalties in administrative contracts. These penalties (fines) are imposed by the administration (state) as an administrative procedure without court judgment or arbitral award, once a breach by the contractor occurs, the state can calculate the fine and settle the account of the contractor by setting-off the amount of fine from the payments made thereby pursuant to the contract without any necessity or need to prove damages.
>
> It is not acceptable for the contractor to prove that no damages occurred, as the administration (state) has stipulated, under the contract, a certain time for completion of works, taking into consideration the essential need for public utility to execute works at the stipulated time without delay.[8] Damages are always presumed.

The Supreme Court held in this leading case that

> the penalty (fine) is applicable in case of delay without a need to notify the contractor or to prove that damages occurred. If the appeal administrative court stipulated that there must be damages to the state to apply the penalty, this judgment by the appeal court should be annulled.

The court stated, in addition to the above-mentioned principles, that the administration (state) can reconsider the surrounding circumstances of the contract and exempt the contractor from the penalty (fine) if it assumed that there is no harm to the public interest caused by the delay, or that the final completion of works at the stipulated time is not necessary in this particular case. This is an implied exemption for the contractor from the penalty (fine).[9]

The Supreme Administrative Court exempts the contractor on some occasions from the penalty (fine) despite the fact that it has confirmed the punitive nature of the penalty as a penalty clause in the public works agreement imposed by the state upon the contractor without a need to prove that damages occurred to the state. In this case, there is a presumption that damages exist immediately when there is a delay.

8 Supreme Administrative Court–Egyptian State Council, *Principles of Supreme Administrative Court and the General Assembly for Legal Opinion (Fatwa) and Legislation in Administrative Contracts in Forty Years*, Decision 612, 21 September, 1960, 420.

9 Ibid.

In the past, the administration could not exempt the contractor from the penalty, as it needed a court decision or a legal opinion from the department concerned (*Fatwa* department) at the State Council pursuant to the current legislation No. 89 of 1998. This is the only difference between the old and new legislation, as the new legislation facilitated the process for the state to exempt the contractor from the penalty by only a legal opinion from the *Fatwa* department rather than a court judgment, which may take many years. If the contractor failed to obtain a legal opinion in his favour, he had to start arbitration or litigation, which would last for some time, during which the value of the currency might depreciate, causing the inflation rate to increase in Third World countries in particular.

The contractor can only reclaim the fine deducted from the payments, plus a simple interest rate of 5 per cent from the date of reclaiming the amount until the actual payment by the state, through either an enforceable court judgment (appeal court judgment at least) or an arbitral award pursuant to the Egyptian Arbitration Act No. 27 of 1994 and the amendments thereof (Law No. 9 of 1997) confirming the application of this act to administrative contracts, whether national or international.

Moreover, it is very difficult to deny the loss to a contractor and in addition the consequential loss that could not be recovered even by a court judgment in most cases. At that stage, the significance of arbitration appears, as it is in most cases, prompt and adequate to the loss because of the vast authority entrusted to arbitrators and the flexibility to apply different rules of law in various cases. The parties can achieve a rapid resolution through a final and binding award.

The Supreme Administrative Court in recent decisions[10] confirmed an extravagant and exorbitant fines clause as a penalty for delay despite the fact that in certain cases the contractor may be exempt.

It is fundamental to refer, at this stage, to the fact that the Supreme Administrative Court, in one of the most recent decisions, held that:

> at the scope of application of the previous Law No. 9 of 1983, the administration can impose a fine of 1% of the contract value in the first week of delay or part of it, 1.5% of the contract value in the second week of delay or part of it, 2% of the contract value in the third week of delay or part of it, 2.5% of the contract value in the fourth week of delay or part of it and 4% of the contact value for every month of delay or part of it. The total amount shall not exceed 15% of the total contract price according to the final certificate.

A new approach was adopted by the court confirming a new perspective in interpreting law No. 9 of 1983. The court confirmed that these rates shall not be calculated together, which means that in the fourth week of delay the court shall apply a fine of only 2.5 per cent rather than the old practice by courts, which used to add the fine of the four weeks together to be 7 per cent of the total value of the contract price (1% + 1.5% + 2% + 2.5% = 7%). The court confirmed that there is no addition to these percentages by calculating them together. Moreover, the court added another new approach that, in certain contracts, where the administration can get benefit from *part* of the completed works by the contractor, the stipulated percentage of 2.5 per cent at the fourth week, pursuant to the new interpretation, shall be calculated at the price of the other part of the contract that has not been completed. The price of the delayed part (in Egyptian pounds) = EGP107355.5 x 2.5% = EGP2684. This amount shall be deducted from the final certificate by set-off.[11]

---

10 Supreme Administrative Court, Decisions in Case No. 10834, Judicial Year 47, 30 May 2006, Third Circuit; and Case No. 11986, Judicial Year 48, 16 January 2007, Third Circuit (both unpublished).

11 Supreme Administrative Court, Case No. 11874, Judicial Year 49, Session, 10/3/2009.

This new approach reflects the extent to which globalization affects the application and interpretation of legislative clauses, even if they are punitive and extravagant. It is clear to what extent judges are trying to achieve fairness in the contractual relationship between state and contractor. They are obliged to apply the legislation as stipulated by the legislator. It is clear that there is an essential need by the Egyptian legislator to adopt new concepts which do not exist even in the new legislation, No. 89 of 1989.

*The General Assembly for Legal Opinion (*Fatwa*) and Legislation*

In 1956 the General Assembly for Legal Opinion (*Fatwa*) and Legislation pointed out that:

> The nature of administrative contracts is different from the nature of civil contracts as administrative contracts are made by and between a public juristic entity and a private entity in order to achieve public interest. The contracting parties in administrative contracts, entered into by the state, are not in equal bargaining power. The target of these contracts is to value public interest over the interest of the contractor. This target must appear in the provisions of the contract, the contractual relationship and, in particular, the application and interpretation of the contract.
>
> The administration (state) shall consider the punitive clauses stipulated under the contract and which are suitable to the nature, value and time considerations thereof in order to achieve final completion in a certain method so as to maintain regularity of public utilities … In case of delay in execution by the contractor, there is a fundamental presumption that damages exist regardless of the practical reality. Any delay by the contractor is considered an act of violation and disorganization employed by the administration in managing the institutions thereof. There is no doubt that this delay interferes with public interest which is the main concern in administrative contracts.[12]

In another decision, the General Assembly confirmed the views of the decisions of the Supreme Court that:

> The penalty for delay must be calculated and deducted from the payments made by the contractor by set-off. The contractor cannot be exempt from this penalty if the administration was ready to accept works upon final completion. The contractor can only be exempt if the state delayed accepting works past the stipulated time. The existing case was that the administration was ready for inspecting, commissioning and accepting works meanwhile the contractor delayed. The General Assembly applied the penalty for delay clauses.[13]

A leading principle confirms that a pre-exemption from the penalty for delay in a contract is illegal. The power to exempt a contractor shall be exercised only if it is necessary and in light of legislative and contractual stipulations (set out by the Egyptian legislator and Egyptian State Council).[14] In one of the recent decisions, which falls within the scope of application of the State Procurement Law of 1998, the General Assembly decided that the

12 General Assembly for Legal Opinion and Legislation, Case No. 637, 26 October 1956, Session, 13 June 1956, file No. 78/1/7.

13 General Assembly for Legal Opinion and Legislation, Case No. 1012, 14 November 1991, Session, 20 October 1991, file No. 47/1/138.

14 General Assembly for Legal Opinion and Legislation, Case No. 106, 22 January 1992, Session, 19 January 1992, file No. 54/1/291.

> penalty for delay in public works agreements is obligatory. There is an obligation upon the contractor to achieve final completion at stipulated time in the contract. If the contractor delayed in the execution of works as a result of default by the administration to execute its obligations, this obligation by the administration is fundamental to the contractor to carry out his obligations. The mutual consent of the contracting parties to modify the contract and add a clause for the extension of time, impliedly means an exemption from the penalty for delay at the stipulated extension of time period added to the contract by the parties.[15]

The General Assembly has affirmed on many occasions that civil and administrative contracts must be executed according to the principle of good faith (bona fide). The penalty for delay is stipulated for the specific purpose of regularly maintaining the attainment of public utility at the stipulated time. Damages are presumed. The contractor cannot be exempt unless there is force majeure or default by the administration. The administration has to exercise its power in imposing a penalty on the contractor or exempting him therefrom. If the administration, prima facie, exempts the contractor for particular reasons, it is legal that the administration can legally reimpose a penalty for delay if there are numerous considerations.[16]

Decisions of the Egyptian Court of Cassation (Civil and Commercial Circuits)

The Court of Cassation directly applied the stipulations of Article (224) of the Civil Code. The court held in some of the leading cases that, in the light of Article (224) of the Egyptian Civil Code, "if there is a penalty clause in the contract, damages are presumed unless the debtor proved the opposite or that stipulated compensation in the contract exceeded the actual loss."[17] The court held in recent cases that "the contracting parties can fix a pre-estimated compensation for damages as a result of non-performance of any of the stipulated obligations … If the debtor proved that the pre-estimated compensation exceeded the actual loss or that he performed some of his obligations, court shall reduce compensation to be adequate to actual loss."[18]

The same principles are still adopted by the court at present.

Conclusion

The judicial review of the State Council courts and General Assembly for Legal Opinion *(Fatwa)* and Legislation can, at its most optimistic scenario, exempt the contractor in certain cases stipulated by Egyptian State Council practice. The contractor may be exempt from the penalty for delay in case of force majeure or fundamental default by the state which exempts the contractor from his or her obligations and, consequently, from the penalty for delay. This is not contrary to the punitive nature of the penalty for delay clause as this clause is always a penalty clause. Egyptian administrative courts recognize penalty clauses in administrative contracts, whether national or international, and consider them to be legal.

15 General Assembly for Legal Opinion and Legislation, Case No. 364, 25 May 2003, Session, 16 April 2003, file No. 54/1/403.

16 Case No. 668, 25 August 2004, Session, 21 April 2004, file No. 47/2/449.

17 Egyptian Cassation Court, Case No. 415, Judicial Year 46, 13 February 1980; and Case No. 26, Judicial Year 28, 18 December 1973.

18 Egyptian Cassation Court, Cases Nos. 1859, 2444, 2447, Judicial Year 70, 12 June 2001.

If there are no damages, there is, consequently, no loss to the state. The contractor can only be exempt from the pre-estimated sum stipulated by the Procurement Law of 1998 or the contract, in the case of a legal opinion from the State Council.

These changes in the last decade are the direct result of globalization. Transfer of the legal culture of common law countries is of great importance, as administrative contract theory needs more modifications and enhancements.

Globalization plays a significant role in changing some of the main features of this theory through the use of international public works agreements with foreign contractors. It is a new trend in civil law legal culture.

Legislative reform of Article (23) of the State Procurement Law (No. 89 of 1998) is strongly recommended as there is an essential need to reduce the cap of the fine to be less than 10 per cent of the total value of the contract price.

It is also fundamental that the penalty shall be calculated according to the actual loss and that no pre-estimated and fixed sum by legislation and regulations shall be applied where it exceeds the actual loss. The penalty may even reflect the substantial loss to the state public utility and be calculated pursuant to this loss, which may be less than the actual loss in many cases.

Among other difficulties which need to be considered is that, in accordance with the principles of the administrative courts of the State Council,[19] a contractor, in certain cases, cannot suspend or terminate works if the administration terminates its payments. The contractor cannot claim to stop execution until its payments are receives from the state. In that case, the administration applies Article (23), on the penalty for delay, if the contractor does not achieve final completion at the stipulated date despite the fact that payments have not been made by the administration.

This critical situation also needs a legislative reform of the State Procurement Law (No. 89 of 1998), as termination of payments is an example of a fundamental default (breach of contract) by the state, pursuant to the Egyptian Civil Code. Some exceptions to this principle of Egyptian State Council courts are required as a direct result of globalization.

Contrary to this concept, in civil and commercial transactions, pursuant to Article (161) of the Egyptian Civil Code, if one party to a contract fails to fulfil their obligations, the other party can suspend or terminate performance.

Moreover, the proposed legislative reform must consider the dynamic relationship in international public works agreements, which differs from the static relationships in other transactions. This dynamic relationship is related to many factors such as contract price, total sum stipulated as a penalty, the extent to which it is adequate to the loss, currency depreciation, inflation rate, contractual relations with lending banks, insurance institutions and the change in raw materials prices in developing countries, which may change contract price under different circumstances.

---

19 The contractor cannot stop or suspend performance of the works in any circumstances even if the state fails to make payments; in that case the penalty for delay is applicable: Supreme Administrative Court, Case No. 5959, Judicial Year 44, 26 January 2001. On very rare occasions the court allowed the contractor to stop performance if the state delayed its payments (Case No. 4483, Judicial Year 41, Session, 6 May 1997). In some other (rare) cases the contractor stipulates at the time of contract that the period of late payments shall be added to the completion date. This clause is valid as it is not contrary to the mandatory rules of the State Procurement Law. An old legal opinion confirms that in some cases the contract provisions can supersede the Procurement Law: General Assembly for Legal Opinion and Legislation, Opinion No. 100, Session, 20 March 1985, file 47/2/350.

In conclusion, the penal nature of the penalty for delay clauses in the State Procurement Law (No. 89 of 1998) and the Executive Regulations under it, need legislative reform of the fine stipulated by the state as well as a reconsideration of many other aspects.

Globalization is playing a significant role as a tool to implement these legal views and facts to encourage private foreign entities entering into infrastructure agreements with states as well as financial institutions.

Modifications and enhancements to the legal regime governing international public works agreements will increase Inward Foreign Direct Investments (IFDI) in the construction sector and infrastructure projects.[20] Civil law concepts and mechanisms in the administrative contract need complete revision and the judicial review by the State Council courts will advance as a result of the legislative reform.

Finally, such legislative reform should assist arbitral processes in international construction contracts between developing countries and foreign contractors. The arbitral tribunal in applying substantive law to facts has to determine, first, if the contract is an administrative contract, and the fixed sum is a penalty and applicable regardless of any existing loss, or, secondly, if it is a commercial contract and, consequently, whether the pre-estimated compensation is, subject to the view of the arbitral tribunal, adequate for the actual loss. This is the current situation in the Egyptian legal system where a legislative reform should establish new concepts to be applied in both arbitration and litigation.

---

20 See: Ismail 2010c; Ismail 2010d: 175–85; Hamilton 2009; Ragab 2007. See also: http://www.conseil-etat-fr/jurispd/index-ac.1d0442shtml.

Chapter 9
Obstruction Encountering Performance

Introduction: Impediments to the Performance of International Public Works Agreements

A breach of mutual contractual obligations committed by the foreign contracting party or the owner is an impediment to the performance of a contract, which may disrupt the functioning of the public utility. However, some impediments not in the form of contractual breach may result in the absolute impossibility of performing the contractual obligations; some others may lead to the destabilizing of the contract's financial equilibrium and to complications in the fulfilment by the contracting party of its obligations.

This chapter explores the impediments to the performance of International Public Works Agreements and the reasons behind the impossibility of executing the contractual obligations. Force majeure and its effect upon exemption from liability will be examined. The chapter scrutinizes the foundations of the Prince Theory in terms of the contract's financial equilibrium, accidental circumstances and unforeseen physical difficulties. It examines the effect of the new conditions introduced into International Public Works Agreements on maintaining the contract's financial equilibrium and on the role of such jurisprudential theories, the administrative judge, and the international arbitrator, in restoring the contract's financial equilibrium under the aforementioned conditions and factors.

The Impossibility of Executing the Contractual Obligations

Force Majeure and Its Effect on Exemption from Liability in International Public Works Agreements

A fundamental concept of contract liability is the existence of a contractual breach and damage and the causal link between them. In addition, if the debtor pursuant to a contractual obligation has to fulfil a certain obligation, but fails to do so, the rule in Civil Code is that he or she must pay compensation unless the failure is due to an external cause beyond that person's control.

The impossible execution of an obligation can be factual or legal. Factually impossible execution is clearly related to real facts, and if owed to an external cause, the obligation to execute either in kind or by way of compensation is lifted. An external cause is a hardship, force majeure, the debtor's breach, or a third party's tort. The force majeure or the accidental event must be impossible to prevent, such as an earthquake, a flood, a volcanic eruption or an outbreak of war, all of which make the execution of the project impossible.

The force majeure must be warranted by two conditions: The first condition is that the event is accidental; the second condition is that the event cannot be prevented.

The external cause eliminates the causal link (*lien de causalité*) between the breach and the damage and can be a force majeure, an accidental event, a breach by the debtor or an act by a third party.[1]

Force majeure is a purely legal concept forged by the lawmaker as a preventive measure against any matter that may cause a breach of contractual obligations where it becomes impossible to perform them.[2]

Article (165) of the Egyptian Civil Code stipulates that:

> If a person proves that the damage has occurred due to an external cause beyond his control, such as an accidental event, a force majeure, or a tort by a third party, he is not obligated to compensate for such damage unless otherwise specified in a text or an agreement.

Syrian civil code stipulates the same. In accordance with the above Article, the external cause can be:

A force majeure or an accidental event A force majeure or an accidental event must be unpreventable and unforeseeable.

The Court of Cassation ruled that a force majeure must be unforeseeable and unpreventable. These two conditions are drawn from precedents exclusively examined by the courts; the cassation courts of all Arab countries concluded the same vision.[3]

The unforeseeable nature of the event is the first condition that must be established in this respect; a person is deemed negligent if he or she could foresee the event and did not take the necessary precautions to avoid the consequential effects. The criteria of unforeseeable must be an objective one, where the event cannot be foreseen by even the most prudent person, which makes it absolutely – and therefore not relatively – impossible.[4]

The second condition to be established is related to the unpreventable nature of the event. *Impossible* means absolute impossibility, whereupon there is an absolute impossibility of performing the obligation.

If both conditions are established, the debtor is exempted from the contractual liability, and the causality link (*lien de causalité*) between the breach and damage is then ruled out; hence, there is no ground for compensation in either case.[5]

Force majeure in comparative jurisprudence The concept of force majeure has great significance in all legal systems. In the English system, force majeure is dealt with "frustration of contract."[6] In

1 See: Yehia 1989: 256; Treitel 2004, Chapter 5: 191; Beale 2008, Vol. 1: 1479. McKendrick 1995a: 3–19; McKendrick 1995b: 21–31; Duncan Wallace 1995: 655. On public works agreements in Arab jurisprudence, see: El Hassan 1997: 89; Metawe 1998: 526. In force majeure in international public works agreements in French doctrine and jurisprudence, see: Kadiki 1979. In public works agreements, see: El Attar 1955: 291. In administrative contracts, see: Richer 1995: 214; De Laubadère, Moderne et Delvolvé 1983–1984, Tome II: 727. In building contracts in comparative jurisprudence and international customs, see: Thomas 1995); Bruner 1995: 274; Jones 1995: 295; Jeremiah 1995: Chen 1995: 328.

2 Wiwatpattarakul n.d. *ICLR* 1.

3 Egyptian Cassation Court, Civil Circuit, Session of 27/3/1980, Case No. 979 of 47, *The Collection of the Technical Bureau*, Judicial Year 31, Rule 183, 930.

4 Yehia 1989: 258.

5 Egyptian Cassation Court, Civil Circuit, session of 29/1/1976, *The Collection of the Technical Bureau*, Judicial Year 46, Rule 243, 27.

6 Beale 2008: 1479; Treitel 2004; McKendrick 1995a.

legal systems where laws are codified, such as German law and some Asian legal systems like Thai law, the concept of force majeure is under the impossible performance of the obligation.[7]

In the Thai legal system, a force majeure is deemed an event which cannot be prevented unless the claiming person has exercised due and reasonable diligence and care as may be expected from a prudent person when confronting a similar situation.

It is accepted to warrant force majeure in this legal system as a legitimate reason, so long as no breach has been committed by the claiming person.

Under such a legal system, construction contracts are commutative contracts so as to exempt the party from its obligations, if it is impossible for the other party to perform its obligations.

The Thai system differs in that the force majeure has a subjective criterion, which is the level of effort exerted by a prudent person to prevent such force majeure. In comparison, the Egyptian judiciary has an objective criterion whereupon it is absolutely impossible to perform the obligations, and the force majeure or the accidental event is unpreventable, which makes such performance absolutely impossible, not only to the debtor but also to any other person in the same position as the debtor.[8]

In Japanese law, the rules seem to be more objective; a force majeure is an event (such as a natural disaster) that is unforeseeable or unpreventable. In March 1980, the respondent, in a case heard before the Japanese courts, built for the claimant a wooden house on a small island. One year after, an extremely strong tornado – the strongest in the history of Japan – hit the island and the house. The court judgment stated that it was an extraordinarily mighty and destructive event, and on no account could the respondent prevent it, which meant that it was a force majeure.[9]

Prior to World War II, a public works agreement in Japan included a text providing that the contractor should bear all losses, despite that person's request to the government to amend such provision; however, this was not achieved until the outbreak of World War II.

With the promulgation of the Construction Law of 1949, it was necessary to include a clause on force majeure in agreements concluded between the contractors and the owners and to specify the compensation related thereto (C/19 of the Construction Law).

In 1950 and 1951, models of International Public Works Agreements and private construction contracts were issued, and, for the first time, they included a clause on force majeure.

In Japanese public works agreements, the contractor must advise the owner without delay if there were losses incurred by the former during execution of the work, in the preliminary stage of work or on site, with regard to raw materials or construction equipment, as a result of tornados, torrents, floods, earthquakes or any other natural or man-made disaster unrelated to either the contractor or the owner.

Prior to receiving the contractor's report, the owner must take stock of the losses incurred. Upon establishing such, the contractor can request a modification of the contract price or compensation for the damage sustained.[10]

Force majeure in the comparative judiciary In the French State Council judiciary, the Council expanded the concept of administrative force majeure whereupon the contracting party might

7 The Thai Civil and Commercial Code, Articles (216), (218), (217), (205), (370), (371) and (372). See: Wiwatpattarakul n.d.: 174.

8 The Supreme Administrative Court, Judgment No. 689 – 4, 12/12/1969, 5/15/106, see: Egyptian Conseil d'Etat 1996: 473.

9 Niwa n.d.: 179.

10 Niwa n.d.: 179.

request to terminate the contract with appropriate compensation, if any. According to this theory, the contracting party is entitled to withdraw from the contract where it is impossible to perform the obligation placed upon it.[11]

Within the scope of administrative force majeure, the contract is terminated under the continuity of an accidental circumstance or difficulties faced by the contracting party where it is impossible to carry out execution, or when the contract's financial equilibrium is destabilized beyond the reasonable level estimated by both parties during the drafting of the contract. It is then an area between the force majeure and its conventional concept and the theory of accidental circumstances.[12]

This was determined following the Council's recognition that a force majeure was not a reason to exempt the contractor from contractual obligations or from delaying performance, unless otherwise specified in the contract. The matter remained as such until 1858, where the jurisprudence construed that the opinion of the French State Council was under the influence of the principle of *Pacta Sunt Servanda*.[13]

Force majeure in the Egyptian Conseil d'Etat The Egyptian judiciary confirmed the established approaches adopted by Egyptian jurisprudence with regard to force majeure. The Supreme Administrative Court decided that where the impossibility to perform an obligation was attributed to an external cause, "the obligation to perform is then lifted, whether performance in kind or by way of compensation." An external cause is an accidental event, force majeure, debtor's breach or a third party's tort. A force majeure or an accidental event must be unforeseeable and unpreventable; if these two provisions exist, such event is then unpredictable and beyond the control of not only the debtor but also the most prudent person. The criterion is objective and not subject to the ordinary individual; nevertheless, it requires absolute impossibility. The force majeure or accidental event must be unpreventable; thus, if it is preventable, though unforeseeable, it is not a force majeure or accidental event. It must also render the execution absolutely impossible, not only for the debtor but also for any person who is in the position of the debtor. This point makes the distinct difference between a force majeure and an accidental event and the accidental events that render the execution cumbersome but not impossible. The effect of a force majeure or an accidental event varies according to the circumstances; if it was the sole cause for the damage that occurred, the causal link is then ruled out, which, in turn, provides an exemption from responsibility. The consequence can be the suspension of the execution and not the exemption from performing the obligation, until such event has ended. Both parties may modify their agreement in accordance with the effect of the force majeure or accidental event; for example, they may agree that the debtor shall not be exempted from the obligation and shall be responsible for the consequence of any external cause. Hence, although it is impossible to perform the obligation due to an external cause, such performance is not lifted but is replaced by compensation, where the debtor is like an insurance entity, and the creditor is the insurer against any event attributed to a force majeure. The aforementioned principles were codified by the Egyptian lawmakers in the Civil Code. While these principles are applied within the context of relationships under private law, the administrative judiciary has consistently taken them into consideration as a general principle to be applied in determining the administrative relations under public law, as long as it is in

11 See: Richer 1995: 214–15; Kadiki 1979: 239–45.

12 Said Amin 1991: 295–6; Richer 1995: 214–15.

13 El Hassan 1997: 90–91.

conformity with the functioning of the public utility and ensures the reconcilement of this latter with the individual interests.[14]

The Supreme Court also held that where an event was foreseeable though unpreventable, or vice versa, it was not deemed a force majeure and did not give rise to an exemption from responsibility. The Supreme Court also mentioned in its judgment that the intervention made by the Supreme Council of Antiquities was foreseeable and cannot be deemed an external cause or a force majeure, since it was expected – when concluding a contract – to suspend the work when there were archaeological finds on site.[15]

The Supreme Court added that the contracting parties might not modify their agreement to change the effect of force majeure, for example, by agreeing that the debtor would bear the consequential effect.[16]

Force Majeure and international arbitral awards The concept of force majeure has been applied in several international arbitral awards.

A dispute was related to a contract concluded between a Turkish company (B) and the Libyan authorities for the construction of an airport in Tripoli, Libya (main contract). On 8 March 1973, (B) subcontracted a Belgian company (A) on the basis of the FIDIC contract form under the Libyan law. An explosion in the airport during execution of the work gave rise to execution and payment problems of the subcontract. Both parties suspended the contract performance claiming that the other party had committed a breach of the contract (by virtue of a letter dated 11 April 1974 from (B), and a letter dated 21 May 1974 from (A)).

In March 1975, (A) initiated the arbitration procedures before the International Chamber of Commerce (ICC) in Paris, pursuant to the arbitration clause set forth in the contract, with a claim for payment of the work's value by virtue of the subcontract and compensation for a breach of contractual obligations committed by (B). Nevertheless, (B) commenced a counterclaim for a breach of contractual obligations committed by the subcontractor (A).

The tribunal ruled to have jurisdiction to settle the dispute arising from the subcontract and the individual contracts between (A) and (B) for the execution of the remaining works.

The tribunal ruled that the subcontract breach committed by (B) was not a consequence of the breach committed by (A), which must be compensated, and that the counterclaim filed by (B) was not acceptable as it was based upon the same grounds and facts.

In its justification of exempting (A) from any responsibility, the tribunal stated that the explosives were a force majeure, and (A) could not be held accountable for any serious breach in performing the contractual obligation. However, since the explosives were planted in airport ground – a target of recurrent artillery shelling during the war – this was a predictable situation; nevertheless, the significance and quantity of the explosives were far beyond the parties' estimate. This was evidenced by the mutual correspondence between the parties: the owner (the Libyan government), their representatives and the consultant as they indicated on several occasions the force majeure aspect with regard to the existing explosives.

14 The Supreme Administrative Court, Judgment No. 689 – 4 (12/12/1969, 5/15/106), see: Egyptian Conseil d'Etat 1996: 473.

15 The Supreme Administrative Court, Judgments No. 1320 and 1340 – 12 (15/2/1969, 14/48/373), see: Egyptian Conseil d'Etat 1996: 474.

16 The Supreme Administrative Court, Judgments No. 1320 and 1340 – 12 (15/2/1969, 14/48/373), see: Egyptian Conseil d'Etat 1996: 474.

On the other hand, in order to resolve the problem between the parties regarding the removal of the explosives, (A) confirmed that it had acted with due diligence and observed the instructions given by the consultant, which allowed for the timely removal of these explosives. On that basis, the tribunal concluded that no breach could be attributed to (A).[17]

In another dispute,[18] the respondent was performing a turnkey contract for the construction of a factory when a war broke out in the region, and the relationship between the countries of which the parties were nationals was compromised. The claimant in the dispute was a government-run company, and the respondent was entrusted to supply and operate the industrial equipment.

The initial effect of the outbreak of war was to repatriate the respondent's personnel who were of the same nationality. The second effect was that the respondent's government stated that the credit facility previously provided had been withdrawn.

By the end of the war, the claimant requested the respondent to complete the work to be executed under the contract; the latter refused such a request since it was impossible for the contract's personnel to return to work in that country, nor to be insured, in addition to the fact that the financial facility that had been provided by their government had been withdrawn.

In an interim award regarding whether there was a case of force majeure, the tribunal decided that such force was existent until the ceasefire. The arbitration tribunal judged that the respondent had reasons not to perform the contractual obligation by virtue of the claimant's law and Article (6/2) of the contract.

In addition to the risks posed by the war, which had forced the respondent not to perform the obligation, the agency letter sent by the respondent's government had requested that person to continue providing the necessary services and production by virtue of the letter of credit, since it was impossible to secure visas for the personnel to return to the claimant's country.

The claimant's defence stated that had the respondent sent a notice to the claimant, pursuant to Article (6/2), explaining the complications caused by the government and those related to the visa acquisition, the claimant would have empowered the respondent to perform the contract, given the national importance of the project.

Hence, the respondent's government and the political situation in the country did not ultimately represent a risk of any sort that could have prevented the execution of the project. The tribunal did not find that the respondent had exerted any effort to obtain the entry visas. The respondent did not prove that he or she had notified the claimant, pursuant to Article (6/2) of the contract, of the intention to resume the performance of the contractual obligation, since the claimant had provided finance for the remaining works prescribed in the contract. On that basis, the tribunal ruled out a case of force majeure.

This award shows that there was no event that the parties could not prevent; rather, there was an omission by the respondent for delaying the application for entry visas. The respondent was partly held accountable for the non-performance of the contractual obligation; therefore, the arbitral tribunal overruled the claim of a force majeure for the lack of its necessary conditions.

Force majeure in the forms of international construction contracts It is recognizable that the famous forms for international construction agreements are those applied when drafting International Public Works Agreements, considering that they are one of the most important international standards. Such models are adapted to suit the complex nature of public works agreements, for example:

---

17 Award of June 25, 1980, Case No. 2763, Jarvin, and Derains 1990: 157.

18 Award made in Case No. 1703 in 1971, Jarvin and Derains 1990: 6.

In its fourth version of 1987, the FIDIC contract model – the most common and prevailing model required for all projects financed by the World Bank – addressed the issue of force majeure. This model was brought up in various articles on force majeure cases where it pointed out the following:

(a) the legal and natural impossible performance attributed to the owner (Article 13/1)
(b) the risk of non-performance due to external circumstances beyond the control of both parties to the contract, which is attributed to the owner (Article 66/1)

Such a model specified certain cases, as follows:

(a) Articles (20) and (21) specify the non-performance cases resulting in loss of work that are generally attributed to the contractor, with the exception of eight special risks stated in Article (20/4) that are explicitly attributed to the owner:

i. wars (declared and undeclared, occupation or any hostile foreign acts);
ii. mutiny, revolutions, insurrection, military coups or civil war;
iii. ionizing radiation or the resulting pollution or nuclear waste, radiating activity caused by nuclear fuel or nuclear fuel burning, nuclear toxic active explosions or nuclear components;
iv. wave pressures caused by airplanes or other aerial devices moving at sonic or supersonic speeds;
v. political turmoil or disorder, unless resulting from the personnel of the contractor or subcontractors or from organization of the work;
vi. loss or damage caused by appropriation by the contractor to any part of the permanent work, except for those specified in the contract;
vii. loss or damage attributed to the work's design, except for any part of the design provided by the contractor or those in charge of the contractor;
viii. any act of nature that an experienced contractor cannot logically avoid by taking the necessary precautions.

The deposit required from the contractor whereby that person and the owner, as co-insurers, may exclude covering losses that might occur by the events mentioned in Article (20/4) and (i) through (iv) above.

(b) Delays attributed to the contractor (Articles 41–48), with the exception of delays resulting from a mandate given by the owner for additional work, where the unfavourable climatic conditions are excluded, any other reasons for such delays (mentioned in this model) or any other special conditions (Article 44/1).
(c) Failure to perform due to "special risks" (Article 65) that are generally attributed to the owner, including those special risks set forth in Article (20/4): destruction or losses caused by explosions (Article 65/4), outbreak of war in any parts of the world that may generally affect the work's execution (Article 65/5), risks related to successive legislation (Article 70), currency restrictions (Article 71/1) and depreciation of currency value (Article 72/1). If any of these risks takes place 28 days prior or subsequent to the tender offering to the contractor, it is then the owner's risk.

Article (19) of the new version of 1999 also addressed the same matter, and after having described the concept of force majeure, it indicated some cases although not covering them all.

The FIDIC form deals with events that may be "outside the control" of the parties to the contract, without the need to be "unforeseeable." They let the contract determine whether such events are foreseeable and preventable by the parties or not.[19]

Difficulty of Performing the Obligation

The concept of the contract's financial equilibrium[20] is one of the most important foundations in this area, which ensures the contract performance without encumbering any of the parties with changes effected during the execution of the contract.

In order to address the effect of the new legal nature of International Public Works Agreements upon these ideas, it is worth analyzing the effect of this new nature upon those ideas and its role in maintaining the contract's financial equilibrium by including to these agreements new provisions and mechanisms and to clarify their role in restoring the contract's financial equilibrium.

The Prince Theory ("Le Fait du Prince") in Public Works Agreements

While the administration in an administrative contract has the right to modify the obligations of the contracting party with direct decisions, whether by deducting or adding, such right is met with a corresponding right: to ensure the contract's financial equilibrium.[21]

The jurisprudence and judiciary recognize the right of the administration to modify the contracts, based on realizing the public interest. To apply such theory, several conditions must be fulfilled as follows:

Conditions for the application of the theory Doctrine and jurisprudence define the application of the Prince Theory as a special procedure whereby the contract's clauses can be directly modified, having an effect upon the execution conditions and imposing upon the contracting party new unexpected burdens.

The French judiciary provided the example of police procedures that led to an increase of the contracting party's obligations, such as the decision issued by the administration – the police in this case – requesting the contracting party to relocate the electric wires for public safety reasons,[22] as well as the decision issued by the administrative authority to the contracting party, upon which new burdens were imposed, by virtue of its power of supervision and direction. Another example was public works or physical works carried out by the administration causing injuries to the contracting party with regard to contract performance or increasing contractual obligations.[23]

Jurisprudence also considers that the promulgation of laws or regulations would increase the contracting party's obligations toward the administration, as a general procedure, according to the Prince Theory in administrative contracts. The French State Council was of the opinion

19 To assess force majeure in various standard forms of contracts see: Bruner 1995: 274.

20 For elaboration on this concept, see: El Tamawy 1991: 61.

21 El Tamawy 1991: 631. In French doctrine, see: De Laubadère, Moderne et Delvolvé 1983–1984, Tome 2: 515 *et seq*. Badawi 1954. In Arab doctrine, see: Abdel Azim 1989; Ga'far 2000: 170.

22 Badawi 1954: 104 *et seq*.

23 Kadiki 1979, Tome 1: 266.

that the general procedure that was not directly addressed to the contracting party would not be compensated, except in two cases: first, where the contract explicitly stated such clause and second, where such procedure was unexpected; hence, the Prince Theory was not applied, but rather the theory of accidental circumstances.

Where the general procedure results in a direct modification of the contract terms, whether by stopping their implementation, or by modifying them or by prematurely terminating the contract, the contracting party must be compensated on the basis of the Prince Theory, regardless of the legitimacy of these laws.[24]

The general procedure must also modify the external conditions for the execution, which would be more difficult for the contracting party to carry out. According to the French State Council, the rule is that the contracting party may not be indemnified for the damage sustained in such circumstances, except for extremely particular cases; as such, it can be said that the rule is to rule out the compensation, and the exception is to rule for it.[25, 26]

The Egyptian judiciary adopted the same approach. In its judgment issued on 16 June 1953, the Administrative Court ruled out the compensation of a company claiming for injuries sustained due to having been levied with a council tax for electricity although it was not a burden added to the company's obligations or destabilizing the contract's financial equilibrium. On 28 October 1964, the General Assembly of the Legal Opinion and Legislation ruled out the compensation of the Technical Company for Public Works for price differences for the supply of materials due to the 1956 war, a commission for Misr Company for Foreign Trade, an export bonus, a logistic duty and a maritime duty. The grounds for such ruling were that these sums of money were not in direct connection with the contracting administrative authority, where there must have been a special or general procedure issued by the administration to apply the Prince Theory, leading to a special injury incurred upon the contracting party, where he or she was the sole injured party by such general decision.[27]

The administrative judiciary in Egypt summarized the provisions for the application of the Prince Theory in administrative contracts as follows:[28]

1. that there is an administrative contract
2. that the injury is committed by the contracting authority
3. that the injury affects the contracting party regardless of how grave the injury is
4. that it is assumed that the contracting authority was not wrongful when taking such a harmful decision since it has a contractual obligation without a breach
5. that the procedure taken by the authority is not expected
6. that the contracting party has sustained a personal injury where he or she is the sole injured party by such general decision

---

24 Judgment of the French State Council issued on 23 March 1994 in the case of *Ste Energie électrique de la Basse – Loire*. The Council ruled out the compensation in certain cases for different reasons. See: the thesis of Badawi 1954: 167 *et seq.*

25 See: the thesis of Badawi (1954: 207 *et seq.*) and the judgment of the French State Council issued in January 1945 in the case of *Ste anonyme motobloc*, where it ruled out the compensation on the basis of the Prince Theory in the area of taxes and duties that rendered the execution difficult.

26 The Administrative Court – 16/6/1953, see: Egyptian Conseil d'Etat 1996, Judicial Year 7, 1578.

27 Legal opinions issued by the General Assembly of the Counsel Department, Judicial Year 19, 51.

28 The Supreme Administrative Court – Judgment No. 56 – 12 (20/5/1961, 6/141/1133) – Damascus; see: Egyptian Conseil d'Etat 1996, 42.

The harmful act is committed by the contracting authority The act must be committed by the contracting authority and not by any juristic entity other than the entity that concluded the contract; otherwise the condition of the Prince Theory is not fulfilled,[29] and we may apply the theory of accidental circumstances where appropriate.

The injury sustained by the contracting party is a personal unexpected injury The General Assembly of the Legal Opinion and Legislation confirmed that it was necessary to have this condition, that the injury sustained by the contracting party was a personal injury where no third party was affected by the general decision. The claim of the contracting companies for price increases to the contracts concluded with the Ministry of Housing before applying Law No. 63 of 1964 of Social Security had no legal grounds. The said law obligated all companies and not only the contracting companies to increase their social security contributions for seasonal labourers; hence, the Prince Theory could not be applied as the promulgation of such law was an expected procedure. The lawmaker declared in Law No. 92 of 1959 that the plan was to extend the social insurance benefits to cover all labourers, which rebuts that such increases were not expected.[30]

The procedure is issued by the contracting administrative authority The Supreme Administrative Court confirmed that the intervention of the Administrative Courts to realize the administrative contract's financial equilibrium, in application of the Prince Theory, would be possible when its conditions were fulfilled, including the condition that the harmful act was committed by the contracting administrative authority. In case such act was taken by a juristic entity that did not conclude the contract, one of the conditions of the Prince Theory was not then fulfilled and thus the theory could not be applied. However, this did not stop the application of the theory of accidental events where appropriate.[31]

The General Assembly of the Legal Opinion and Legislation concluded that the contract between the Ministry of Irrigation and a number of contractors for the execution of certain works in the Ministry's departments and inspection offices during the financial year 1969/1970 did not grant those contractors any rights to address the Ministry with a claim for price differences, as a result of an increase of the price tariffs of steel and cement or due to receiving quantities of imported steel in lieu of local steel, whether such price increases took place subsequent to concluding the contract or during the contract performance. These procedures were taken by an authority other than the contracting authority (Ministry of Irrigation), which meant that a fundamental condition for the application of the Prince Theory was not fulfilled.[32]

The effect of fixing the tender prices upon the application of the Prince Theory The administrative judiciary decided to fix the tender prices of the agreement concluded between the supplier and the administration as from the date of submitting the tender until the handover of the work, subject to the contract. These prices were not subject to any changes that might occur during the contract term, whether the reasons for such changes were related to foreign currency fluctuation, price increases or change in import, production or any other duties. The contracting party might not refer

29 The Supreme Administrative Court – Judgment No. 1562 – 10 and 67 – 11 (11/5/1968, 13/117/874), see: Egyptian Conseil d'Etat 1996: 424.

30 Legal Opinion No. 297 on 11/3/1965, session (24/2/1965 19/88/309), see: Egyptian Conseil d'Etat 1996: 426.

31 Case No. 562 of Year 10Q – session 11/5/1968.

32 File No. 78/1/46 – session 11/7/1971. *Modern Administrative Encyclopedia*, 1st edition, Vol. 18: 873.

to the Prince Theory or the theory of accidental circumstances to rest the claim for damages for injuries sustained due to any of the aforementioned changes.[33]

The consequences of applying the Prince Theory Upon the fulfilment of the theory's conditions and as a consequence of the act committed by the public authorities, the injured party was granted full compensation, in addition to possible exemption of delay fines, if it was established that such act made it difficult for the party to execute the work on time; it might even exempt the contracting party from the execution of the contract if the Prince Theory resulted in the impossible execution.

The contracting party had the right to terminate the contract in case the Prince Theory resulted in an excessive increase of that person's obligations.[34]

Jurisprudence had divergent opinions in establishing a compensation for the contracting party in the case of fulfilling the Prince Theory's conditions.

A group of jurists were of the opinion that the contract's financial equilibrium was the grounds for entitlement for compensation. The administration must restore such equilibrium every time it was destabilized, as a result of an act committed by the authority. The Egyptian State Council supported this opinion.[35]

Some jurists established the notion of financial equilibrium as a general rule, which was to obligate the administration to ensure the contract's financial equilibrium every time it was destabilized, whether it was the result of an act committed by the contracting authority or caused by an external factor beyond its control.[36]

It has been suggested that notion is as dangerous and inexact, as it is generalized, giving rise to compensation to the contracting party even if the financial equilibrium is not caused by the administration.[37]

However, it is not a correct notion as the compensation ruled for the contracting party, due to a breach committed by the authority to the contract's economies, does not always correspond with the contract's financial equilibrium that was taken into consideration when the contract was concluded. Arab doctrine provides two examples for such case: The contracting party may wrongly accept unfavourable prices when concluding the contract. If the authority intervenes in the contract performance afterwards, the court shall rule for full compensation, not based on the price accepted by the party at the time of concluding the contract but based on the real price at the time of the authority's intervention in the contract performance. This theory also applies in the case of price increases subsequent to concluding the contract, as the judge, when issuing a judgment, takes account of the new prices for compensation and not those specified at the time of concluding the contract.

The second example is the case of terminating the contract by the administration without any breach committed. The notion of financial equilibrium cannot warrant the compensation ruled by

33 The General Assembly of Legal Opinion and Legislation, File 78/1/29, session 28/10/1964, *Modern Administrative Encyclopedia*, 1st edition, Vol. 18: 882.

34 El Tamawy 1991: 653. For the effect of the Prince Theory and the Theory of Unforeseen Physical Circumstances in restoring the financial equilibrium of the administrative contract under unforeseen circumstances, see: Said Amin 1991: 302 *et seq.*; De Cayper 1993: 959.

35 The Supreme Administrative Court, Case No. 1562 of year 10Q, 67 of year 11Q, session 11/5/1968.

36 See: those who represent this approach, De Soto, a comment published in the Laws Journal in 1950, 455; an explanation of this notion in the Egyptian judiciary, a judgment issued by the administrative court on 30 June 1957.

37 Ismail 2003b; Badawi 1994.

the Administrative Court, as the financial equilibrium cannot be hypothetically discussed for a non-existing contract.[38]

Another jurisprudential opinion was that the second rule for compensation was the authority's contractual responsibilities. Those who did not recognize the notion of the contract's financial equilibrium called for this rule. As such, the administration had a contractual responsibility without a breach as the Prince Theory assumed that the authority was not wrongful when committing such act; however, the responsibility had different grounds.

It is clear that the notion of a contract's financial equilibrium complements the administration's contractual responsibility without a breach, but it is a responsibility to maintain the contract's financial equilibrium.

Professor De Laubadère was of the opinion that there was no difference between both notions, as according to the Prince Theory it was a contractual responsibility based upon the contract's financial equilibrium.[39]

This construes the condition currently imposed by the French State Council: that the Prince Theory is applied when the act is committed by the administration, and the compensation is denied where the act is performed by a public authority other than the contracting authority, which distinguishes between responsibility in the case of applying the Prince Theory to accidental circumstances and the unforeseen physical difficulties. This conciliatory solution is in line with sound legal logic as the contractual liability is due to the application of the Prince Theory that causes an injury to the contracting party and destabilizes the contract's financial equilibrium, although such injury is not grave.

The contracting party in International Public Works Agreements submits the tender taking into account certain prices and circumstances at the time of concluding the contract. If during the contract performance, the authority commits an act that requires the application of the Prince Theory, it has a contractual liability based upon the need to restore the contract's financial equilibrium.

The Prince Theory ("Le Fait du Prince") *in International Public Works Agreements*

Given the complex nature of the International Public Works Agreements, as they include terms that have changed the conventional nature of administrative contracts, we must study how these new contracts correspond with the Prince Theory.

The Prince Theory first requires the existence of an administrative contract. The international public works agreement, although complex in its nature, still contains some of the characteristics of the administrative contract, including provisions and exceptional rules sometimes contravening the general rule.[40]

The General Assembly of the Legal Opinion and Legislation of the State Council concluded that the agreement between the supplier and contracting authority to fix the prices included in the tender as from the date of submitting the tender and until the handover of the job, subject to the contract, implied that these prices were not subject to any changes that might occur during the contract term. This was concluded whether the reason for such changes were related to foreign currency fluctuation, price increases, change in import, production or any other duties.

The rationale behind this is that the contracting party may not hold the contracting authority responsible for any increase that may occur to these prices. This may not be claimed whether such

38 Badawi 1994.

39 De Laubadère, Moderne et Delvolvé 1983–1984, Tome II.

40 See: Chapter 3 of this book.

increase was due to foreign currency fluctuation or to any other circumstances, or it was an increase in import, production or any other duties, unless otherwise explicitly specified, as is the case of the contracting authority's right to modify the work subject of the contract, with some auxiliary works, based upon the power granted to the authority in this regard.

In such a case, the contracting party undertakes to maintain the prices submitted. However, fixing the tender prices, as from the date of submitting the tender and until the handover of the work subject of the contract, implies a corresponding right to the contracting party. This right is that these prices are not subject to changes that may affect their stability, such as change in import, product or any other duties.

The facts in the present dispute are, however, contrary to the above case. The contracting company undertook not to claim for any price increases, whether it was due to foreign currency fluctuation, price increases or changes in import, production or any other duties, unless otherwise set forth in the contract, as was the case with the rights of the contracting authority to modify the work subject of the contract. The contract specified that the contracting authority was exempt from responsibility to restore the contract's financial equilibrium.

It is evident that this reduces the role of the administrative judge or the international arbitrator when the International Public Works Agreements set forth such provisions ensuring the stability of duties and taxes and consequently protecting the foreign contracting party by guaranteeing that the contracting authority will not commit an act that would cause any injury to the contracting party.

Theory of Accidental Circumstances

Introduction

The theory of accidental circumstances was established within the provisions of the Civil Code, considering that the change in circumstances – during the contract performance – is the most important cause for the contract's financial equilibrium, which requires restoring the contract's economies.

Since this theory is founded within the provisions of the Civil Code, it is appropriate to refer to the general literature related to the Civil Code construing this theory.[41]

The basis of this theory was founded in the administrative contracts in the French State Council where it was set forth to address the accidental economic circumstances during World War I and recognized the right of the contracting party to compensation in case of those accidental circumstances. The purpose of this compensation was to sustain the functioning of the public utilities that provided citizens with services.[42]

The French State Council stipulated that in order to fulfil the condition of compensation entitlement, an accidental circumstance must be unexpected;[43] however, it ruled out the claim for compensation if the price increases were expected, which did not destabilize so much the contract's economies.[44]

---

41 See Arab jurisprudence: Ga'far 2000: 163; Abdel Azim 1990; Yehia 1989. More specifically, see: Metawe 1998: 531. In French jurisprudence, see: De Laubadère, Moderne et Delvolvé,1983–1984, Tome 2: 559; Clément et Richer 1989: 208 *et seq.*; Richer 1995: 210.

42 Clément et Richer 1989: 208.

43 C.E., 30 mai 1916, *Compagnie générale d'éclairage de Bordeaux*, leb., 125.

44 C.E., 7 juillet 1976, *Société démongeot, inedit,* Clément et Richer 1989: 208; C.E., 17 juin 1981, *Commune de Papeete*, Clément et Richer 1989: 208.

The Theory of Accidental Circumstances in Arab Jurisprudence

The Egyptian State Council established the foundations for the application of the theory of accidental circumstances in general, following the model of the French administrative judiciary, which was the founder of this theory.

The Supreme Administrative Court confirmed in an established judgment that the application of the theory of accidental circumstances in jurisprudence and administrative judiciary was subject to the occurrence of incidents or circumstances, be it natural or economic, during the contract performance or an act committed by a third party other than the contracting authority. The court stipulated that the contracting party could neither expect nor prevent these circumstances when concluding the contract and that they caused that individual serious injuries giving rise to grave destabilization of the contract's economies. The rationale behind the application of such theory, after fulfilling its conditions, was to obligate the authority to bear jointly the loss occurred during such accidental circumstances, so as to ensure the contract performance and the sustainability of the public utility. The role of the administrative judge was limited to rule for a suitable compensation without modifying the contractual obligations.[45]

The Supreme Court confirmed in another judgment that in order to apply the theory of accidental circumstances, the contract's economies must be gravely destabilized as this theory was based upon the concept of absolute justice – a mainstay of the administrative law. In addition, the purpose of this theory is to realize the public interest by ensuring the systematic and consistent functioning of the public utility and prompt services delivered to the public. The contracting party's intent was to help realize the public interest by fulfilling the obligation in an honest and adequate manner in consideration of a profit and fair return. This required understanding and collaboration in order to overcome the difficulties and impediments to perform the contract.

The court explained in this judgment the theory's purpose and essence and confirmed that the occurrence of accidental circumstances did not render the execution impossible, but cumbersome to carry out, destabilizing the contract's economies and causing losses to the contracting party exceeding the normal losses that any contracting party might have sustained.

In this regard, the court held that the purport of the theory of accidental circumstances is that, where circumstances or events take place during the administrative contract performance and are not expected when concluding the contract, by which the contract's economies are destabilized, and where such circumstances or events do not render the contract performance impossible but rather more cumbersome and more costly than reasonably estimated by both parties, and where the loss resulting therefrom is grave, exceptional and unexpected, exceeding the normal loss that any contracting party may sustain, the injured party has the right to request the other party to bear jointly the loss by partly compensating therein. As such, a new obligation is added to the contracting party's obligations that were not included in the contract, which means imposing an obligation upon the debtor in the administrative contract to pay the creditor a compensation to ensure the proper execution of the contract, so long as these unforeseen circumstances or events cause a loss to the debtor, which can be deemed as destabilizing the contract's economies.

It is evident that the Supreme Administrative Court imposed an obligation upon the administration to pay compensation to ensure the proper execution of the contract so long as

45 The Supreme Administrative Court, Judgment No. 1562 – 10, 67 – 11(11/5/1968), 13/117/874, see: Egyptian Conseil d'Etat 1996: 440. This theory was established by virtue of a judgment issued by the French State Council on 30 March 1916 – C.E., 20 mars 1916, *Compagnie générale d'éclairage de Bordeaux*, Leb, 125.

these unforeseen circumstances or events caused a loss to the debtor, which could be deemed as destabilizing the contract's economies. Nevertheless, the court asserted that the compensation paid by the creditor must be a part of the compensation for the loss sustained by the debtor who was not entitled to claim for compensation on the basis of loss of profits or unrealized gains.

The Court added that in order to estimate the destabilization of the contract's economies, considering its occurrence, all losses affecting the contract's economies must be taken into account. The contract must be considered as a whole, not as individual elements as some elements could be compensated, thereby offsetting other elements that caused a loss. As such, the destabilization of the contract's economies' could not be noticed or ascertained unless all the work related to the contract was completed.[46]

The Supreme Court held that the application of the theory of accidental circumstances in administrative contracts, and other matters related to the public law, was subject to the occurrence of such accidental circumstances during the contract performance and not after the contract completion.[47]

The Supreme Court distinguished between the accidental event and force majeure, describing that the unexpected price increases during the execution of administrative contracts, which gave rise to an increase of the contracting party's burdens by the grave losses that individual would sustain to the extent of gravely destabilizing the contract's economies, was an accidental circumstance and not a force majeure.[48]

Two important points are worth mentioning in order to consider them accidental circumstances in International Public Works Agreements, namely: the effect of successive legislation and foreign currency change upon the contract performance and the effect of the legislative stability clauses on resolving this problem:

The impact of successive legislation and the exchange rate of the foreign currency upon the contract performance The General Assembly of the Legal Opinion and Legislation issued an opinion that the application of a new legislation, such as the Law of General Tax on Sale promulgated under Law No. 11 of 1991, affected the sales prices set forth in contracts concluded before the enforcement of the said law, as the contracting companies agreed in the contracts with the pharmaceutical company that the value of the contracting work was total and final. As such, pursuant to the Civil Code provisions, the company might not claim for price increases resulting from the application of the Law of General Tax on the basis that it would have rendered the contract performance difficult. It was not apparent from the documents that the application of the said law would affect only the contracting company by sustaining grave loss, destabilizing the contract's economies; thus, one of the conditions of the theory of accidental circumstances was not fulfilled, and the General Assembly ruled against compensation on this basis.[49] In such a case, the General Assembly restricted the application of the theory and did not consider the successive tax legislation as causing financial burdens on the party or grounds for

46 The Supreme Administrative Court, Judgment No. 46 – 14(17/6/1972), 17/83/576, see: Egyptian Conseil d'Etat 1996: 442; The Supreme Administrative Court, Judgment Nos. 1223 and 1224, see: 27 (18/12/1984), 30/45/250, see: Egyptian Conseil d'Etat 1996: 446.

47 The Supreme Administrative Court, Judgment Nos. 843 & 922 – 26 (20/11/1982), 28/18/86, see: Egyptian Conseil d'Etat 1996: 458–9.

48 Administrative Court, Judgment No. 2150 – 6(9/6/1962), 7/96/1024, see: Egyptian Conseil d'Etat 1996: 458.

49 The General Assembly's legal opinion No. 328 on 24/4/1993, session (28/3/1993)47, Opinion No. 127 on 31/1/1993 – Session (31/1/1993) 47, see: Egyptian Conseil d'Etat 1996: 461–2.

compensation on the basis of the theory of accidental circumstances since it did not give rise to grave losses.

In another opinion, the General Assembly concluded that the Prime Minister's decree to devalue the Egyptian pound against the US dollar was a general exceptional event, pursuant to Article (147/2) of the Civil Code, where both parties could not expect it when concluding the contract. For the sake of argument, assuming that the party should have expected that the government might seek to devalue the Egyptian currency, the contracting party could not predict how far this devaluation would be; thus, the results and effect of this procedure upon the contract's financial equilibrium must exceed what the party would have expected when concluding the contract. In both cases, if the loss sustained by the party with the obligation to perform the contract rendered the fulfilment of the obligation cumbersome and gave rise to serious loss, the other party should jointly bear such loss, so as to make it reasonably bearable for that party. This means that the expected loss should be borne by the party with the obligation to perform the contract, whereas the unexpected loss should be jointly borne by both parties, in order to mitigate its gravity.[50]

In another opinion, the General Assembly concluded that the tender's general conditions, according to Article (20), stipulated that the tenders must be submitted for the supply of goods based upon the tax rate, production duties and any other duties applicable at the time. In case these rates and duties changed in the period between submitting the tender and the deadline for the supply of goods, and the supply took place within the specified period, the difference should be settled accordingly, on condition that the contractor had proofs of paying the duties on the supplied goods based upon the modified increased rates. If the modification required reducing the rates, the difference should be deducted from the contract's value unless the contractor had proofs that he or she paid the duties based on the original rates before the modification. Article (62) of the general conditions stated that "the final statement shall apply the rates included in the price tables, regardless of any price changes or currencies fluctuation." It also stated that "the contractor shall bear all price increases for the materials, freight, shipping, all types of insurance, and labour costs during the period of the work, and may not request any increase or change the prices he accepted."

By specifying these provisions, the court judgment varies according to the accidental reason affecting the tender's value. If the reason is attributed to market volatility and currency fluctuation, the contractor must bear the consequences, whether it is an increase or decrease in prices; if the reason is attributed to modification in taxes and duties, the ministry must bear the consequences as provided in Article (20), whether the reason affecting the tender's value has taken place before or after the contract conclusion.[51]

This shows that the State Council was hesitant to consider the market volatility and currency fluctuation as accidental circumstances, as the General Assembly had – in its opinion – considered it to be accidental circumstances on one occasion, and the Supreme Administrative Court denied such consideration on another.

The effect of the legislative stability clauses The same applies to the tax and customs legislation. In a judgment issued by the Supreme Administrative Court in the 1960s,[52] the court considered the modification of taxes and customs duties as accidental circumstances, which would not be

50 Legal Opinion No. 360 of 17/7/1954, *Modern Administrative Encyclopedia*, 1st edition, Vol. 18 (1986/1987), 796, Rule No. 568.

51 The Supreme Administrative Court – Case No. 1186 of year 10Q – session of 25/11/1967. *Modern Administrative Encyclopedia*, Vol. 18, 797–898, Rule No. 570.

52 Ibid.

valid without legislation. In the 1990s,[53] the General Assembly refused to consider the Law of General Tax on Sale as accidental circumstances unless – as expressed by the court – it rendered the contract performance difficult.

The above-mentioned principles were well established, decades ago, in Arab doctrine and jurisprudence.

The Theory of Unforeseen Physical Difficulties in International Public Works Agreements

Where there is a physical impediment to the performance of the contract, such as a rocky layer during the excavation process, rendering the fulfilment of the contractual obligations difficult and extremely cumbersome for the contracting party, this is considered a physical difficulty that was not taken into account when concluding the contract and setting up the prices.

In such a case, will the contracting party refuse to execute the obligations with the consequential damage that may occur to the public utility, subject of the administrative contract which was concluded for the developing, regulating or operating of such public utility?

The Establishment of the Theory in the French and Egyptian State Councils

This theory was established under the provisions of the French State Council, and the first judgment thereby issued was *Duche* on 24 June 1864. The State Council ruled in its judgment for compensation to the contracting party for any unforeseen physical difficulties that individual had encountered during the contract execution.[54]

The State Council granted the contractor the right to compensation for the unforeseen physical difficulties encountered during the contract execution, where they were not attributed to the contractor or to the administration.[55]

The theory was applied by the Egyptian State Council and consequently Arab doctrine, in the first judgment issued by the Administrative Court on 5 May 1953. However, the jurisprudence was of the opinion that the judgment had confused the theory of physical difficulties with that of accidental circumstances, as the former required full compensation while the latter required partial compensation to the extent that it would restore the contract's equilibrium and reinstitute its economies.

The administrative judiciary in Arab countries developed the theory of unforeseen physical difficulties based upon the judgments issued by the Supreme Administrative Court and the established opinion issued by the General Assembly of the Legal Opinion and Legislation in Egypt. In its old opinion issued in 1964, the General Assembly defined the theory of unforeseen physical difficulties, whereby the company could claim more payments than what was agreed upon, as follows:

> If the contracting party encounters, during the performance of his obligations, purely unexceptional physical difficulties that cannot absolutely be foreseen at the time of concluding the contract, and

53 The General Assembly's legal opinion No. 328 on 24/4/1993, session (28/3/1993)47, Opinion No. 127 on 31/1/1993 – Session (31/1/1993)47, see: Egyptian Conseil d'Etat 1996: 461–2.

54 Ga'far 2000: 183; Ga'far 1995: 186. See also: the Arab doctrine regarding the same notion: Abdel Azim 1990; Metawe 1998: 537; Raslan 1980: 825 *et seq*. See also: French doctrine: Richer 1995: 208; Chabanal et Jouquelet 1994: 159 *et seq*.; De Laubadère, Moderne et Delvolvé 1983–1984, Tome 2 : 499 *et seq*.

55 Ga'far 2000: 187.

> that make the contract performance a cumbersome mission, he has the right to full compensation for the injuries caused by such difficulties.

The compensation must fully cover all injuries by paying an extra amount added to the agreed upon prices.

The General Assembly specified the conditions for compensation according to this theory, which are summarized as follows:

1. These difficulties are physical, extraordinary, and exceptional.
2. These difficulties are physical and unforeseen, or it was not possible to foresee them at the time of concluding the contract.
3. The execution requires costs exceeding the prices agreed upon in the contract, and increases the burdens borne by the contracting party.[56]

Within these boundaries and controls, the contractor has the right to claim compensation; however, if one of the above conditions is not fulfilled, the theory cannot be applied, and the contractor has no right to any compensation.[57, 58]

These are the main principles for the theory of unforeseen physical difficulties as established by the Egyptian State Council, which is based upon the consideration of justice and the special nature of administrative contracts.[59]

56 Judgment No. 800 of 34 (19/5/1992) – Egyptian Ministry of Finance 2009: 464–76 – Rule No. 267.

57 Legal Opinion No. 95 of 4/2/1964, session (29/1/1964) 18-69-186, see: Egyptian Conseil d'Etat 1996: 463–4.

58 The General Assembly's legal opinion No. 95 on 4/2/1964, session (2/1/1964) 18-69-186, see: Egyptian Conseil d'Etat 1996: 466–8 – rule No. 268.

59 Ga'far 2000: 209.

Chapter 10
Alternative Dispute Resolution (ADR)

A Comparative Study in Anglo-American Doctrine

The New Legal Nature for International Public Works Agreements and its Impact on Dispute Resolution Mechanisms

As was concluded earlier, a new legal nature exists for International Public Works Agreements pursuant to new clauses in these agreements that were not recognized in state contracts in civil law jurisdictions. The direct impact of the new legal nature is the use of Alternative Dispute Resolution (ADR) mechanisms such as negotiation, mediation and arbitration.

Various civil law jurisdictions, particularly in Arab Middle Eastern countries, recognize arbitration as a fast and effective mechanism for dispute resolution, as it leads to a final, binding and enforceable award.

In most developed legal systems, negotiation and mediation play a significant role that may avoid arbitration, which is a costly process, particularly with the growth in cross-border transactions where the potential for dispute is high.[1]

New mechanisms are the trend in developing states in the last decade as the International Public Works Agreement differs from the domestic Public Works Agreement. The new trend was imposed by modifications and developments to the Public Economic Law and State Procurement Law in civil law jurisdictions in Arab Middle Eastern States. Privatization of public sector utilities, developments in the infrastructure sector and the promulgation of investment legislation in recent decades influenced, to a great extent, the legal culture in developing countries. The increase in Inward Foreign Direct Investments (IFDI) requires new mechanisms for settling disputes other than ordinary litigation.

The philosophy of ADR is that in the adversarial system, parties are using each piece of evidence or argument against each other to prove their case before a judge who imposes a decision that usually leads to a win/lose situation. The mental approach remains the same while the dispute lasts.[2] Meanwhile, ADR theory and practice, particularly in negotiation and mediation processes, are trying to achieve a win/win situation that will not violate any of the disputing parties' expectations to a great extent. Despite the fact that negotiation and mediation have narrow applications in Middle Eastern Arab countries, this same concept is significant.

At the beginning of the 1990s in the United States, the focus of statutes and commentary seemed to shift from experimentation to institutionalization. Congress imposed a requirement on every federal district court to convene a group to consider the increased use of dispute resolution procedures. International business transactions required the use of ADR mechanisms as a necessity.[3]

---

1 Mackie, Miles and Marsh 1995.

2 Bevan 1992: 1.

3 Goldberg, Sander and Rogers 1995: 9.

"*Le Contrat Administratif*" as a fundamental concept in civil law legal systems has drastically changed. It is appropriate at this stage to refer to the role of negotiation and mediation.

Historical Background

Centuries ago, before litigation was known as the state judicial power for dispute settlement,[4] disputes were generally settled by village priests and family friends. During the past three decades, the increase in negotiation and mediation and related processes in developed states was often called the Alternative Dispute Resolution (ADR) movement. Arbitration has been used in most American jurisdictions for more than 75 years and its use was favoured by law.[5]

Negotiation was one of the most important tools for dispute settlement in the pre-contractual steps until the dispute reached the national courts. Pre-trial adjudication played a significant role in dispute settlements, in place of national courts, especially in the United States. Mediation started in the United States with very limited scope compared to arbitration. Arbitration, a long time ago, was the main mechanism for dispute resolution. In the middle of the twentieth century, the role of mediation increased because the courts encouraged the process; the term used was *conciliation*, particularly in family law disputes. The increase in the use of ADR mechanisms became significant in the 1970s, especially when judges and lawyers referred to the delay and increase of costs in the litigation process.[6] ADR started to appear as an effective mechanism in place of normal litigation.

The main advantages of these mechanisms[7] are that they are low cost, fast, and maintain confidentiality for huge multinational companies; moreover, disputing parties can choose a specialized negotiator or mediator. The latter mechanisms are not only used for amicable settlement but also for preventing further disputes in the future.[8]

As the International Public Works Agreement is a complex longterm agreement, disputes may last for a few years. As a result, parties claim sums that may be subject to currency depreciation after a long time to achieve a final arbitral award.

Thus, the feasibility of ADR mechanisms has considerable impact on the contractual equilibrium of the contract as the target of the ADR to achieve a prompt resolution agreed by the disputing parties.

Negotiation The most common form of dispute resolution is negotiation. Negotiation has the advantage of allowing the parties themselves to control the process and, to some extent, the solution. It is a communication for the purpose of persuasion.

The parties refer the dispute to a third party, still having some control over the process but not necessarily over the solution.[9]

Negotiation is a preliminary step in dispute resolution as it may lead to a mutual agreement between the disputing parties;[10] hence, it could avoid the disputing parties' commencing arbitral proceedings, as they may have achieved mutual consent to their claims. Negotiating is a skill

4 Goldberg, Sander and Rogers 1995: 3, 6.

5 Goldberg, Sander and Rogers 1995: 6.

6 Goldberg, Sander and Rogers 1995: 7.

7 For ADR advantages, see: Mackie, Miles and Marsh 1995.

8 Sarie El Din 1996: 202.

9 See: Goldberg, Sander and Rogers 1995.

10 In negotiations generally, see: Bevan 1992: 3; Mackie, Miles and Marsh 1995: 20; Murray, Rau and Sherman 1989: 74.

lawyers may have a natural talent for, but unless a lawyer studies the process theory and practices the correct methods, he or she will be unable to use negotiating ability to the best effect.[11]

Negotiations play a significant role in the pre-contractual process,[12] generally in international business transactions and in International Public Works Agreements in particular.[13] There are two principal theories that attempt to explain the negotiation process: the competitive and the problemsolving. Both are integral to the process and contain elements essential to a full understanding of negotiation.[14]

Negotiations are mechanisms for competitive debate by which negotiating parties aim to achieve mutual consent through persuasion. In theory and in practice, it is a fundamental tool in pre-contractual steps and during the drafting of the agreement.[15] When a dispute arises, negotiation is a tool that has considerable weight in order to avoid arbitration costs, as arbitration leads to a binding and final award that may violate one of the disputing parties' expectations.

Negotiations have their unique tactics, such as how to arrange to negotiate in your own offices and to insist on this issue. The other party will be at a psychological disadvantage because he or she has to come to you. It is recommended to outnumber the other side or to do your best to ensure that your side is represented by at least the same number of persons. It is essential to time the negotiations to your advantage because if one side wants to get the discussion over with quickly, it usually loses. It is advantageous to begin one of your demands with a "precondition;" if the "precondition" is met, you start with a psychological advantage, a substantive gain and fewer items that are subject to compromise in the discussion that follows. It is better to make the other side tender the best offer and to make your first demand very high, to the extent that it makes a subsequent demand that is almost as high, but appearing to be a more reasonable compromise. You have to make your adversary believe you are serious. It is more appropriate to place your major demand at the beginning of the agenda and to make the other side make the first compromise. You can use two or more negotiators who play various roles. Demands and claims have to be raised as the negotiations progress.[16]

The art and science of negotiation are considered some of the main features and dimensions of the academic study of International Public Works Agreements and dispute resolutions of such agreements. The process of negotiation includes, pursuant to scholarly opinions, "eight distinct but often overlapping phases." They are:

Phase one:	the search for an arena
Phase two:	agenda and definition
Phase three:	exploring the field (emphasis on differences)
Phase four:	narrowing the differences
Phase five:	preliminaries to final bargain
Phase six:	final bargain
Phase seven:	ritualizing the outcome
Phase eight:	execution of outcome[17]

11 Murray, Rau and Sherman 1989: 74.

12 Loncle and Trochon 1997: 3.

13 Sarie El Din 1996: 203.

14 Murray, Rau and Sherman 1989: 75.

15 Ismail 2003b: 318–19.

16 Goldberg, Sander and Rogers 1995: 18–22; Mackie, Miles and Marsh 1995: 20–32.

17 Claims and Dispute Resolution, see: Gould and Russell 2007: 441.

The theoretical baseline of negotiation science is to assist academics as well as practitioners to understand the nature of negotiating activities and select the strategies and styles that enable them to achieve the desired results. Many academics and practitioners confuse the terms *theory*, *strategy* and *style*, often using them interchangeably. However, there are differences among the three concepts. *Theory* explains the system of assumptions, accepted principles and rules of procedures with which to analyze, predict and understand the nature of a certain situation. It clarifies what is happening but does not tell the negotiator how to respond to it. *Strategy* directs the negotiator to the specific goals to be achieved and the pattern of conduct that improves the chances of achieving these goals. *Style* is a more personal pattern that refers to the personal behavior the negotiator uses in carrying out the strategies he or she has chosen.[18]

Negotiators use the terms *competitive*, *problem solving*, *principled* or *cooperative* interchangeably and/or confusingly. A highly competitive negotiator can use a style that is friendly, relaxed and pleasing while still seizing every advantage to "win" for the client and/or to achieve a "win/win" situation. Problemsolving theory recognizes negotiations and other processes as the preferred means for resolving disputes. A problemsolver will tend to avoid confrontational strategies because of the likelihood of ending in a deadlock. Conversely, pursuant to competitive theory, a standoff in negotiations is a natural part of the dispute resolution.[19]

Finally, settlement may not be achievable, and in most jurisdictions the usual progression from a failed negotiation is either to litigation or arbitration. As Abraham Lincoln pointed out, "discourage litigation; persuade your neighbor to compromise whenever you can. Point out to them how the nominal winner is often a loser in fees, expenses and cost of time;" thus, and in the light of the latter concept, it is appropriate before scrutinizing arbitration in International Public Works Agreements, to refer to mediation as one of the dispute settlement mechanisms that has significantly increased in recent decades in developed jurisdictions, although it has not clearly appeared in Arab Middle Eastern jurisdictions. It is fundamental for developing states to learn from developed jurisdiction experience regarding the mediation process.

Mediation Mediation is the central most frequently adopted ADR technique around the globe.[20] It is "the use of a third party to help those in conflicts to do things and breach agreements which, unaided, they may never do, or may do so much later in the conflict that each side will have suffered further harm."[21] The concept is to open doors to assist disputing parties to achieve a satisfactory approach in a rational and problemsolving way, to clarify issues and to help negotiations by bringing objectivity to a dispute. Generally, mediation aims to put back into the hands of the parties the responsibility for the outcome. Unlike arbitration or litigation, there are no unpredictable findings. Disputing parties share the responsibility to achieve satisfactory results from their perspective. Each party wishes to achieve a "win" situation for himself or herself and a "lose" situation for his or her opponent. In fact, if a mediation agreement is achievable, it is by the consent of both parties who are trying to reach a "win/win" situation. Conversely, if either party fails to achieve a "win/win" situation and agrees to any other scenario, this implies that he or she accepts this approach to avoid serious unpredictability by a binding, final and enforceable arbitral award. Legal interpretation differs from other sciences, such as engineering. A single issue is controversial in

18 Murray, Rau and Sherman 1989: 75.
19 Murray, Rau and Sherman 1989: 88.
20 Mackie, Miles and Marsh 1995: 41.
21 Bevan 1992: 18.

terms of legal interpretation due to the controversy among various jurisdictions and legal cultures; thus a single issue for consideration and determination may have different interpretations in civil law jurisdictions to those of common law jurisdictions. In contrast, dimensions of a dam, a bridge, or a building are the same, if measured by different consultancy engineering firms from different countries.

Some scholars use the terms *mediation* and *conciliation* interchangeably. Sometimes the term *conciliation* is used to denote less formal procedures than *mediation*; moreover, it is argued that a conciliator is less active than a mediator. However, most often the terms *conciliation* and *mediation*, which are not accurately defined, are used interchangeably.[22]

The process works easily, as all parties to a dispute agree to mediate, then a location and time are arranged and a mediator is selected. The mediation begins with a joint session and everyone present. The mediator makes an opening statement explaining the process and his or her role as a mediator and asks each side in turn to make a presentation of its case and its position. Opening statements, which may be in writing, should last no more than ten to fifteen minutes, after which there is an opportunity to ask questions, both of the mediator and the other side. A mediator will have the opportunity to see each side in a private session.[23]

Mediators' strategies vary widely. Some mediators focus negotiations on satisfying the vital interests of each party, whereas others focus on legal rights. The process experienced mediators use is simple, even in complex disputes. Mediators traditionally enter disputes with little authority; their ability to help bring about settlements depends, partially, upon the willingness of the parties to accept the mediator. When trust has been established, parties can be expected to co-operate with the mediator, disclose their real interest and value the mediator's reaction.[24]

The mediator summarizes areas of agreement to motivate the parties toward a final settlement. If the parties move to mutual consent and common position upon disputing issues, the mediator starts drafting the agreement. It is preferred that the mediation agreement be in writing. There may be an enforcement clause that provides for monitoring by the mediator or another party and specifies what the parties will do if they believe the agreement has been violated.[25]

Mediation is a voluntary process, which means that the parties can leave when they wish. It is a non-binding process by which a mediator cannot impose a decision.[26] Moreover, it is a confidential process. A mediator may attempt to encourage exchange of information, provide new information, help the parties to understand each other's views, promote a productive level of emotional expression, encourage flexibility, let the parties know that their concerns are understood, stimulate the parties to suggest creative settlement and invent solutions that meet the fundamental interests of all parties.[27]

Unlike in arbitration, a conciliation or mediation clause is simply a declaration of intent that does not oblige the parties to refer a dispute to a mediator. Mediation is an informal process that may or may not result in an agreement between the parties on the disputed matters. Proposals

---

22 For the purpose of this study, both terms will be treated as synonyms. For the same approach see: Sarie El Din 1996: 205; and in Arab doctrine see: Ismail 2003b: 321–4.

23 Bevan 1992; Bunni 2005, 3rd edition: 425; Fouchard, Gaillard, Goldman 1996: 16 *et seq.*; Mackie, Miles and Marsh 1995: 76–9.

24 Goldberg, Sander and Rogers 1995: 105–6.

25 For a mediation agreement, for example, see: Mackie, Miles and Marsh 1995: 201; for more elaboration and explanation of the process, see: Goldberg, Sander and Rogers 1995: 110. In Arab doctrine, see: Ismail 2003b: 322–4.

26 Bevan 1992: 18–19.

27 Goldberg, Sander and Rogers 1995: 103.

made by the mediator are not final or binding upon the parties, who are free to accept or reject the expert's recommendations. As the mediator's recommendations and suggestions are not an arbitral award, they are not covered by the 1958 New York Convention on the Recognition and Enforcement of Foreign Arbitral Awards.[28]

A mediator should be a neutral and experienced advisor. Procedures should maintain simplicity, minimum delay, confidentiality and a short period for the conduct of mediation itself. International arbitral institutions such as the International Chamber of Commerce (ICC), American Arbitration Association (AAA), Cairo Regional Centre for International Commercial Arbitration (CRCICA) and the United Nations Commission on International Trade Law (UNCITRAL) provide mediation rules. The fundamental principles of ADR (i.e., non-binding nature, flexibility, party autonomy, volitional and confidentiality) are the foundations of the mediation and conciliation rules adopted by these organizations.[29]

If parties fail to achieve mutually agreed resolution through mediation and if there is an arbitration clause in the International Public Works Agreement, either party can start arbitral proceedings. A crucial question arises when the agreement stipulates that amicable settlement through mediation is a preliminary step before starting arbitral proceedings. If a party fails to start mediation and directly starts arbitral proceedings, can the other party allege that mediation is a condition precedent to start arbitral proceedings? In another words, either party cannot start arbitral proceedings without trying mediation as a preliminary step before arbitration and a condition precedent to start arbitral proceedings.

If either party fails to try mediation as an amicable settlement before starting arbitration, it will not deprive that individual of his or her substantial right to start arbitral proceedings pursuant to procedural rules and to claim his or her substantive rights. The concept of prescription in civil law jurisdiction is not applicable. This concept is a legislative mechanism by which a party cannot claim a substantive right after a certain period of time, which is 15 years in the Egyptian Civil Code Article (374) and Article (372) of the Syrian Civil code. The same legislative stipulation exists in all Arab civil codes.

Conclusion

Today, ADR mechanisms are a range of procedures that serve as alternatives to litigation and arbitration for the resolution of disputes that generally, but not necessarily, involve the intervention and assistance of a neutral third party who helps to facilitate the resolution. Despite the fact that these procedures are well known and advancing in developed countries, considerable efforts are still needed in Arab Middle Eastern and North African developing states to enhance investment atmosphere in the infrastructure sector to accept mediation and negotiations. As is pointed out above, it is unlikely that mediation violates parties' economic and contractual expectations. Among many other ADR mechanisms, mediation is of vital significance and needs to be considered by developing states. In light of the simplicity, rapidity, confidentiality, non-binding nature and various advantages of ADR, it is strongly recommended to adopt ADR mechanisms in standard forms of contracts that ought to be prepared by most developing states for infrastructure projects to avoid arbitration and litigation as exhausting resolutions to states and foreign investors in terms of expenses, fees and time. Further, encouraging ADR

28 Sarie El Din 1996: 205.

29 Sarie El Din 1996: 205–6.

mechanisms will increase Inward Foreign Direct Investment (IFDI) in developing states in the infrastructure sector, as the legal systems in Arab Middle Eastern developing states will maintain for foreign investors prompt and fair mechanisms for dispute settlement.

Chapter 11
Application of Alternative Dispute Resolution (ADR)

Mediation in Common Law Jurisdictions

Mediation in common law jurisdictions plays a significant role in dispute settlements in international business transactions. Not only mediation but also other methods of ADR, which are amicable techniques, are adopted in the context of International Public Works Agreements. Mediation has been institutionalized and developed through the ICC, the AAA, UNCITRAL and the CRCICA. Today, mediation is a well-known technique of vital importance as a dispute settlement mechanism in common law jurisdictions.[1]

Unlike common law jurisdictions, Arab Middle Eastern countries still lack a wide application of mediation practices. Most Arab Middle Eastern jurisdictions prefer arbitration as a dispute settlement mechanism leading to a binding, final and enforceable award. It is strongly recommended that Arab Middle Eastern jurisdictions strengthen the scope of application of mediation as a feasible technique that meets disputing parties' expectations. Further, it avoids parties' fees, expenses and cost of the time spent in arbitration. Simplicity of mediation, which may lead to an agreement and has its significance as a mechanism, needs to be considered by many jurisdictions. In the coming years it is expected, in the light of the globalization of law and the flow of Anglo-American culture to the Middle East region, that the codified and institutionalized rules will have a wide scope of application in civil law Arab Middle Eastern jurisdictions and in North African states. Foreign private entities from common law jurisdictions, particularly the United States and the United Kingdom, involved in various infrastructure projects in Arab Middle Eastern countries and in Latin American states, insist upon the application of ADR techniques as a safeguard to Foreign Direct Investments (FDI) allocated to these projects. The flow of capital invested in infrastructure projects requires a protection mechanism in case disputes arise. Infrastructure and public utility projects of various types, through traditional public works agreements, BOOT techniques or PPPs, encourage amicable settlement clauses in the agreements, as well as arbitration clauses.[2] One of the main factors considered by international financial institutions, when ranking developing states in terms of Inward Foreign Direct Investments (IFDI), is the effectiveness of the dispute settlement mechanisms in international business transactions with foreign private entities and the enforceability of the ADR resolutions within developing states' jurisdictions.[3]

It is clear that the FIDIC forms of contract, widely applied in the Middle East, adopted ADR in its recent edition.

1 Murray, Rau and Sherman 1989: 74; Goldberg, Sanders and Rogers 1995: 4; Bevan 1992: 27; Sarie El Din 1996: 202.

2 Ismail 2003b.

3 Ismail 2010d.

ADR in FIDIC Forms of Contracts

Article (67) of the *Fédération Internationale des Ingenieurs-Conseils* (FIDIC) form of contract, 4th edition, 1987, under "General Conditions," stipulates that:

> If a dispute of any kind whatsoever arises between the employer and the contractor in connection with, or arising out of, the contract or the execution of works whether during the execution of the works or after their completion and whether before or after repudiation or other termination of the contract, including any dispute as to any opinion, instruction, determination, certificate or valuation of the engineer, the matter in dispute shall in the first place, be referred in writing to the engineer with a copy to the other party. Such reference shall state that it is made pursuant to this clause. No later than the eighty-fourth day after the day on which he received such reference the engineer shall give notice of his decision to the employer and the contractor. Such decision shall state that it is made pursuant to this clause. ... If either the employer or the contractor is dissatisfied with any decision of the engineer, or if the engineer fails to give notice of his decision on or before the eighty-fourth day after the day on which he received the reference, than either the employer or the contractor may, on or before the seventieth day after the day on which he received notice of such decision, or on or before the seventieth day after the day on which the set period of eighty four days expired, as the case may be, give notice to the other party, with a copy for information to the engineer, of his intention to commence arbitration, as hereinafter provided as to the matter in dispute. Such notice shall establish the entitlement of the party giving the same to commence arbitration, as herein after provided, as to such dispute and subject to sub-clause 67.4, no arbitration in respect thereof may be commenced unless such notice is given. ...
>
> 67.2 Where notice of intention to commence arbitration as to a dispute has been given in accordance with sub-clause 67.1, the parties shall attempt to settle such dispute amicably before the commencement of arbitration. Provided that, unless the parties otherwise agree, arbitration may be commenced on or after the fifty-sixth day after the day on which notice of intention to commence arbitration of such dispute was given, even if no attempt at amicable settlement thereof has been made.

Clause (67.3(b)) stipulates that any dispute in respect of which amicable settlement has not been reached within the period stated in sub-clause (67.2), shall be finally settled, unless otherwise specified in the contract, under the rules of conciliation and arbitration of the ICC. It is clear that the FIDIC form of contract stipulates an amicable settlement before starting arbitral proceedings. Clause (67) did not specify which amicable settlement technique is applicable to this scenario, but generally ADR techniques are applicable. Clause (67), which had a wide scope of application worldwide, had some alterations and modifications to create a new mechanism, namely, the Dispute Adjudication Board.

New FIDIC General Conditions (1999)

Clause (20.5), Amicable Settlement, stipulates that if either party is not satisfied with the Dispute Adjudication Board's decision (Clause (20.4)), parties shall settle their dispute amicably before starting arbitral proceedings. If the parties have not reached such a settlement, arbitration must start before or by the 56th day from the date of the dissatisfaction of the DAB decision, even if there is no amicable settlement.

The drafting of the latter clause is clear, in that amicable settlement in this regard is not a condition precedent to begin arbitration. Either party can start arbitration, despite the fact that amicable settlement techniques have not been tried.

Role of ADR in France

Disputes which arise during the performance or after the performance of an administrative contract are subject to the agreement dispute settlement mechanisms. Parties can stipulate various contractual mechanisms for dispute settlements. *Les Modes Alternatifs de Règlement des Litiges* (Alternative Dispute Resolution) is a mechanism for dispute settlements if the litigation system in administrative contracts is unsatisfactory. The phenomenon is clear in contractual disputes, particularly taking into consideration the complexity of Public Works disputes. The administration can violate administrative contracts through *La Résiliation Administrative*, which can justify, from its perspective, that it is protecting public interests, and the contractor can start litigation procedures in administrative tribunals that deal with disputes that are considerably delayed. Furthermore, the administration will not pay compensation at the time of *La Résiliation Administrative*. However, delay caused by the national litigation system will cost the administration more in compensation and compounded interest. Today, non-judicial mechanisms are developing to a greater extent. The French *Conseil d'Etat*, in its famous report of 1993, "*Régler Autrement des Conflits*,"[4] pointed out various procedures such as the preliminary recourse to the administration – mediation-conciliation, *La Transaction* and arbitration. The French *Conseil d'Etat* stated that all these procedures are applicable to administrative contracts. Party autonomy is respected by the contracting parties; thus, if they referred to an alternative method, it must be considered by the administration. Conversely, if the dispute does not arise out of the contract but because of the decennial liability,[5] which has a legislative origin, either party may start litigation. However, parties can use alternative techniques if they agree and the dispute arises out of the contractual relationship, even after the contract is rescinded, according to *La Résiliation Administrative.*[6]

ADR in the Regulatory Framework in Civil Law Legal Systems

The General Administrative Conditions for public works agreements (*Cahier des Clauses Administratives Générales*), the CCAG, is a very important instrument in France, as the leading civil law jurisdiction, Article (50) of the CCAG, as amended in 2009, stipulates that[7] the administration's representative and the contractor shall endeavour to do their best for an amicable dispute settlement for the interpretation of the contract stipulations and performance.

4 *Régler Autrement des Conflits*: *Conciliation, Transaction, arbitrage en matière administrative, Conseil d'Etat, Section du Rapport et des Etudes* (1993).

5 Decennial liability in civil law legal systems is a stipulation in Civil Code by which the contractor and the engineer are liable for works for 10 years after the final completion (e.g., Article (651) of the Egyptian Civil Code; Syrian Civil Code, Article (617)).

6 Richer 1995: 241–2.

7 "*Le représentant du pouvoir adjudicateur et le titulaire s'efforceront de régler à l'amiable tout différend éventuel relatif à l'interprétation des stipulations du marché ou à l'exécution des prestations objet du marché.*"

Article (50.1.1) explained the *Mémoire en Réclamation*, or Memorandum of Claim, procedures. If a dispute arises between the contractor and the representative of the administration, the contractor must express the reasons for the conflict and the amount of claim, if any, and supply the necessary justifications. The contractor must pass the memorandum to the representative of the administration and provide a copy to the employer. If the complaint concerns *Le décompte général du marché* (the financial budget of the works), this report will be passed before the deadline of 45 days as from the announcement of the *Le décompte général* (the financial budget)

Article (50.1.2) pointed out that after consulting the employer, the administration's representative shall notify the contractor with a reasoned decision within 45 days from receiving the memorandum of claim. Article (50.1.3) stipulates that if there is an absence of announcement of a decision during the above-mentioned deadline, it is considered to be a refusal of the claim. Furthermore, Article (50.2) states that if no amicable settlement is achieved pursuant to Articles (50.1.1) and (50.1.2), then Articles (50.3) to (50.6) shall apply. The scope of the claim before the court is determined in Article (50.3.1) if the contractor has resorted to the administrative court, for the same reasons as expressed in the Memorandum of Claim. Article (50.3.2) stipulates that the contractor has a deadline of six months from the announcement of the decision taken by the representative of the administration to carry a claim before the competent administrative court. If this deadline expires, the decision shall be deemed as accepted and any complaint made thereafter would be void.

Legal Effect of ADR in International Public Works Agreements

Does ADR affect prescription and substantial rights in civil law legal systems? Prescription is a fundamental concept in civil law legal systems by which a claimant cannot claim substantial rights after a certain period of time.[8] This period is 15 years in Egypt (Article (374) of the Civil Code) and most Arab jurisdictions (Article (372) of the Syrian Civil Code). Article (383) of the Egyptian Civil Code stipulates that prescription can be terminated by recourse to litigation or starting any kind of litigation process before the courts. The claimant retains substantial rights and continues litigation proceedings.

In Middle Eastern civil law jurisdictions, the ADR mechanism does not terminate prescription unless arbitration or litigation procedures have begun. In other words, unlike arbitration, negotiations and mediation do not terminate prescription and start a new prescription period. If either party claims substantial rights through mediation and the prescription duration has started, that party has to claim substantial rights through arbitration or litigation. The reason is that legislation in civil law jurisdictions such as the Egyptian Arbitration Act and the Kuwaiti Civil and Commercial Procedural Law stated that arbitration as well as court procedures are a means of claiming substantive rights.

Despite the fact that other ADR mechanisms are institutionalized in arbitral institution rules, such as the CRCICA, national legislation has not yet codified those mechanisms.

It is controversial among commentators whether or not prescription can be terminated by the agreement of the parties. Some suggest that it is possible, as the prescription duration is not a matter of public policy;[9] others believe it is not possible.[10]

8 In Arab Civil Law Doctrine, see: El Sanhoury 1984: 1162; Yehia 1987: 370.

9 Abdel Latif 1996: 149.

10 Waly 1986: 40; El Sharkawy 1950: para. 464, 633.

Prescription can only be terminated by legislation as this supersedes agreements made by the contracting parties.

It is strongly recommended that Middle Eastern jurisdictions must codify negotiation and mediation as effective means of dispute settlements and that they should be an integral part of the judicial process, as well as arbitration. Furthermore, civil law legal systems in the above-mentioned countries will recognize the legal effect regarding prescription and all other concepts relating to civil law legal culture principles. Until legislation in Arab developing states recognizes ADR mechanisms, courts must consider the legal effect of these mechanisms and apply the party autonomy principle stipulated by the contracting parties.

ADR legislative and regulatory framework in the Egyptian Conseil d'Etat *and Arab Jurisdictions*

Article (28) of the Egyptian *Conseil d'Etat* Law No. 47 of 1972 stipulates that the *Commissaire d'Etat* shall find a mechanism for amicable settlement for the disputes between the parties. Despite the fact that this Article was promulgated in 1972, few applications have been issued to date. Furthermore, the president of the Egyptian *Conseil d'Etat* issued an administrative decree (which has a regulatory nature) to regulate procedures relating to the real implementation of Article (28) of the Egyptian *Conseil d'Etat* legislation. Decision No. 35 of 2003 dated 1 February 2003 stated in detail procedures for amicable settlements in the light of the Supreme Administrative Court Principles in Egypt, as this court is head of the judicial power in the Egyptian court hierarchy. The decree stipulates that if the *Commissaire d'Etat* suggests an approach for an amicable settlement for the substantive rights and either party, whether the state or the private entity, without justifiable reason, rejects the settlement, then the latter party may pay a fine pursuant to the *Commissaire d'Etat* decision. To date, the Egyptian *Conseil d'Etat* has not exercised amicable settlement in a wide scope.[11]

Conclusion

ADR techniques, other than arbitration, have not yet transferred from Anglo-American jurisdictions to civil law in developing countries, particularly Arab Middle Eastern and North African countries. The above-mentioned mechanisms have not transferred from civil law legal systems such as France to Arab civil law jurisdictions, despite the fact that both Arab developing states and France, as a developed jurisdiction, are sharing the same legal culture. Legal globalization, in this respect, has not influenced the ADR mechanisms to be applicable in a wider scope. It is recommended that legislatures in Arab states codify ADR mechanisms to be exercised by the disputing parties, as arbitration was codified years ago; they must be effective mechanisms, and a wide effect to party autonomy should be given in terms of ADR techniques.

11 Badran n.d; announcement by the President of the *Conseil d'Etat*, in *El Ahram* daily newspaper, 21 February 2003: 13. For further suggestions see: Ismail 2001: 32.

Chapter 12
Definition of Arbitration in International Public Works Agreements

Introduction

Arbitration is deemed the alternative means for the settlement of administrative contract disputes, especially under International Public Works Agreements; it plays a vital role in the resolution of disputes. With the availability of other various alternatives, arbitration receives significant preference from local, as well as international dispute arenas. Thus, parties to a dispute are provided with a judicial mechanism that they may voluntarily resort to for the settlement[1] of any existing or potential conflict that may arise between them.

Given the fact that disputing parties are the reason for the establishment of an arbitration tribunal, and that its legal personality is derived from their own will that it should exist, decisions issued by the tribunal are considered binding upon all parties concerned. However, a party may challenge an award issued by an arbitral tribunal in the event that a legal condition set by law to challenge such an award has been satisfied. Further, if an award has considerably prejudiced the interests of a party to an extent necessitating an appeal to be filed against it before a competent national court, this acts as ground to challenge the award.

Arbitration in developing countries is surrounded by special circumstances. As a means of resolving disputes, arbitration is distinguished from other means of dispute resolution by pertinent characteristics that have mustered the support of some and the opposition of others.

Furthermore, defining characteristics are attached to arbitration in International Public Works Agreements. Problems posed under these types of agreements are of a special technical nature. The intricate legal relations involved in International Public Works Agreements require their arbitrators to possess specific characteristic traits as well as expertise; this may not necessarily be the case with arbitrators in various other types of contracts. Arbitration may be classified into domestic arbitration and international arbitration, where each may further be sub-classified into institutional or *ad hoc*. To resolve such issues, a clear definition must first be given to the term *arbitration*. Reflection must also be made upon its characteristics, merits and demerits.

Due to the special problems posed during its practical application, it is also of paramount importance to tackle multiparty arbitration in these types of contracts, as well as the means of settling disputes arising in some types of International Public Works Agreements. Practical application will be based on FIDIC contracts as they are the most common standard form of contracts in use.

Definition of Arbitration

Due to the imprecise nature of arbitration, the term carries many different definitions under various fields of jurisprudence and legislation. The importance attached to the arbitrational

1 Lew, Mistelis and Kröll 2003: 1.

mechanism gives rise to a jurisprudential need for legal systems to set one comprehensive definition that can reflect characteristics unique to arbitration and exclusive from those of any other mechanism.

In this context, a reflection will first be given on the jurisprudential attempts to define arbitration. Reference will be made to the Egyptian Law on Arbitration in Civil and Commercial Matters promulgated by Law No. 27 of 1994, as well as the Arab Middle Eastern countries' jurisdiction and definition to the judicial definition of arbitration.

Jurisprudential Attempts to Define Arbitration

Jurisprudential attempts to define arbitration have varied. Under French jurisprudence, Bertrand Moreau and Jean Robert regard arbitration as "an independent system of justice that frees disputes from the grip of the public law to place them in the hands of individuals vested with the judicial mandate of resolving them."[2] This definition holds a number of fundamental characteristics of the concept of arbitration. First, it deals with the existence of a conflict and then it starts to resolve such conflict by means of individuals holding experience, capacity and expertise, apart from the state judiciary system.[3] Eventually, Bertrand Moreau and Jean Robert found themselves compelled to give arbitration the same definition found in other, prior books.[4]

Meanwhile, René David regards arbitration as "a means to resolving a situation that has developed between individuals by one or more person(s) known as arbitrator(s), where authority is vested in them by virtue of a special agreement giving them the power to judge without having to be mandated by the state."[5]

David has used the term *technique* (means) rather than *institution* (organization), thus giving a wider scope to the meaning of arbitration. With this lexical choice of words, David's definition of arbitration has become somewhat similar to the general definition of the term used in everyday common language, rather than to the legal definition being referred to in this text. On the other hand, Jarrosson has avoided the use of the word *technique* (means) in the definition he has provided because arbitration, from his perspective, bears more than one means to resolving disputes; to him, arbitration is an *institution* (organization), in the best sense of the word.[6]

The common denominator linking the definitions provided by Jean Robert and René David is that both render a presentation of the fundamental characteristics defining arbitration as well as a presentation of the nature of the arbitral process.

With respect to English jurisprudence, defining arbitration was not of great significance as much as it was significant to study all its practical aspects through extensive research and study. Accordingly, some books have come to reflect the concept of arbitration and define it as:

> the practice of arbitration, therefore, comes, so to speak, naturally to primitive bodies of law; and after courts have been established by the state and recourse to them has become the natural method

2 "*L'institution d'une justice privée grâce à laquelle les litiges sont soustraits aux juridictions de droit commun, pour être résolus par des individus revêtus pour la circonstance, de la mission de les juger.*" For the definition of arbitration under the Egyptian Doctrine, see: Abdel Kader 1996: 24; Al-Tihyewi,1994: 18; Metawe 1998: 19; Barakat 1996: 9.

3 Jarrosson 1987: 369.

4 Robert et Moreau 1967.

5 David 1982: 9.

6 Jarrosson 1987: 372.

> of settling disputes, the practice continues because the parties to a dispute want to settle them with less formality and expenses than is involved in a recourse to the courts.[7]

The above definition is more of a historical narrative than it is a comprehensive definition of arbitration. Sufficient proof of the fact that English jurisprudence has not taken particular interest in this theoretical aspect of arbitration is that many reference books did not render a definition of the term.[8]

Another opinion, in Arab doctrine, considers arbitration to be

> an agreement between parties to a specific legal relationship, contractual or otherwise, restricting settlement of a dispute that has risen, or will potentially rise, between them to individuals entrusted as arbitrators. Parties to a dispute shall choose their arbitrators or shall, at least, agree on a means of selecting their arbitrators. Parties may also entrust an authority or a permanent arbitration centre with organizing the arbitration process in accordance with the bylaws and regulations thereof.[9]

The previously rendered definitions provide description of the concept of arbitration, as well as its selective and judicial nature; nevertheless, they lack precision in their drafting and carry unnecessary redundancy.

Further, some people regard arbitration as "a binding means to the settlement of disputes arising between parties. In other words, it is a consensual agreement by virtue of which a person or persons not belonging to the judicial system is entrusted with the task of resolving the disputes."[10]

The obvious shortcoming of the previous definition is the fact that it is not a must for the arbitrator not to belong to the judicial system; as a matter of fact, the person acting as an arbitrator is a judge. Moreover, the definition does not reflect the judicial nature distinguishing arbitration from all other means of dispute settlement, including negotiation and mediation.

Definition of Arbitration Under Various State Legislation

Article (1442) of the new French Code of Civil Procedures as amended on 13 January 2011 deemed arbitration to be "an agreement whereby parties to a contract commit themselves to submit to arbitration disputes that may potentially arise between them."

From the drafting of this definition it is clear that such is not the case with current disputes. Although the French legislator accentuated the optional nature of arbitration, he failed to deliver accuracy in describing disputes as being probable cases in addition to being potential.

Some commentators[11] consider Article (10) of the Law on Arbitration in Civil and Commercial Matters, promulgated by Law No. 27 of 1994, to have indirectly alluded to the definition of arbitration while referring to the arbitration agreement. Article (10) states:

> 1) The arbitral agreement is an agreement by which the parties agree to resort to arbitration as a means of resolving all or some of the disputes which arose or which may arise between them in connection with a specific legal relationship, contractual or non contractual.

---

7 Holdsworth: 1964: 187.

8 For instance, there was no mention of the definition of the term *arbitration* in: Redfern and Hunter 1991; 1999. Craig, Park and Paulsson 1985.

9 Beriry 1995: 5.

10 Abdel Kader 1996: 25.

11 Al-Tihyewi 1994: 26.

2) The arbitral agreement may precede the occurrence of the dispute, whether such agreement exists independently or as a clause on a given contract in connection with all or some of the disputes which may arise between the parties. In such case, the subject matter of the dispute must be determined in the statement of claims referred to in paragraph (1) of article (30) hereof.

   The arbitral agreement may also be concluded after the occurrence of a dispute, even when such dispute is the subject of a court case; in such event, the agreement must determine the matters included in the arbitration, otherwise the arbitration shall be null and void.

3) Any Reference in the contract to a document containing an arbitration clause is deemed to be an arbitration agreement if the reference expressly provides that such clause is an integral part of the contract and is drafted in accordance with Article (13) of the present Law.

It is evident that the rendered definition is not in any way similar to the definition stated under French legislation, and that, at the same time, it provides a high degree of accuracy while being free of ambiguity. Article (10) deals with arbitration agreements and their definition, rather than defining arbitration as a mechanism for the resolution of disputes – current and potential – arising as a result of legal relationships.

Under Egyptian doctrine, there was an opinion[12] that arbitration has been defined under Article (1) of the new Egyptian Arbitration Act as arbitration between public law and private law entities, whatever the nature of the legal relationship around which the dispute revolves, when such arbitrations are conducted in Egypt or when the parties to an international commercial arbitration conducted abroad agree to subject it to the provisions of the present law.

Paragraph (1) of Article (4) of the general provisions of the same law further clarifies the matter by stating that: "the term *arbitration* as used in the present Law denotes the arbitration agreed upon by the parties to a dispute with their own free will, whether the body to which the arbitral mission is entrusted, by virtue of an arbitral agreement, is an institution or permanent arbitration centre or not."

From the preceding two articles, it is evident that the definitions have reflected the optional nature of resorting to arbitration. Further, paragraph (1) of the Article (4) has also stated that arbitration may be of an *ad hoc* nature; nevertheless, the definition fails to verify the judicial nature of arbitration.

Definition

Upon reflection of the various jurisprudential as well as legislative attempts to define arbitration, it is evident that they have all failed to provide an appropriate definition, with the exception of a few definitions provided by some legislation.

It is suggested that arbitration is "an agreement between parties to reach a final binding and enforceable quasi-judicial settlement of a current or potential dispute."

The latter definition is inclusive of the characteristics and elements of arbitration. It further provides a reflection of the judicial nature of arbitration and differentiates it from all other ADR means that are not judicially binding and enforceable in nature.

12 Abdel Kader 1996: 168.

Definition of International Commercial Arbitration

International commercial arbitration is a mechanism for disputes resolution that leads to a final, binding and enforceable award.[13] It is currently a principal method in developing states to resolve disputes between states and private foreign entities. The arbitral process concerns a settlement of a question by one or more arbitrators who derive their power from a private agreement, not from the authorities of a state.[14]

Arbitration, in short, "is a specially established mechanism for the final and binding determination of disputes, concerning a contractual or other relationship with an international element, by independent arbitrators, in accordance with procedures, structure and substantive legal or non-legal standards chosen directly or indirectly by the parties."[15] It is a process whereby parties in a dispute agree through an arbitration agreement to submit the matter in dispute to the decision of a person or persons and undertake to abide by the resulting decision.[16] In the last decades, developing states have modified and liberalized their legislation to adopt arbitration as a dispute mechanism particularly in disputes between states and foreign investors.[17]

The UNCITRAL Model Law[18] referred to the:

> 1) Arbitration agreement [as] an agreement by the parties to submit to arbitration all or certain disputes which have arisen or which may arise between them in respect of a defined legal relationship, whether contractual or not. An arbitration agreement may be in the form of an arbitration clause in a contract or in the form of a separate agreement.
>
> 2) The arbitration agreement shall be in writing.[19]

"An arbitration agreement must be in writing; otherwise it shall be null and void."[20]

---

13 Lew, Mistelis and Kröll 2003: 1; and, generally, see, Ismail 2003a.

14 In Arab arbitration legislation, generally, see: Egyptian Arbitration Act, Article (1); United Arab Emirates, Code of Civil Procedures, Article (203); Saudi Arbitration Act, Article (1); Qatar Code of Civil and Commercial Procedures, Article (190); Kuwaiti Code of Civil and Commercial Procedure 38 of 1980, Article (173); Kuwaiti Judicial Arbitration Act, Article (2); Omani Arbitration Act, Article (1); Libyan Code of Civil and Commercial Procedures, Article (739); Tunisian Arbitration Act, Article (1); Syrian Code of Civil Procedures, Article (506); Lebanese Code of Civil Procedures, Article (762) and (809); Jordanian Arbitration Act of 2001, Article (3) and Iraqi Code of Civil Procedures, Article (251). Lebanese, Egyptian and Jordanian acts have a liberal perspective in terms of express permission to arbitration in state disputes with foreign private entities.

15 Lew, Mistelis and Kröll 2003: 1.

16 Bunni 2005: 393.

17 Egyptian Arbitration Act, Article (1), Jordanian Arbitration Act of 2001, Article (3), Lebanese Code of Civil Procedures, Article (809).

18 Article (7), as adopted by the commission at its 39th session in 2006.

19 Egyptian Arbitration Act, Article (10).

20 Egyptian Arbitration Act, Article (10); in Arab Middle Eastern countries, see: Syrian Code of Civil Procedures, Article (509); Lebanese Code of Civil Procedures, Article (763); Jordanian Arbitration Act of 2001, Article (10); Emirates Code of Civil Procedures, Article (203), Qatar Code of Civil and Commercial Procedures, Article (190); Kuwaiti Code of Civil and Commercial Procedures, Article (173); Omani Arbitration Act, Article (12); Libyan Code of Civil and Commercial Procedures, Article (742) and Tunisian Arbitration Act, Article (6).

Arbitration is a private mechanism for dispute resolution selected and controlled by the parties and an alternative to national courts. Conversely, to national courts procedurals, the arbitral process has its private rules chosen by the parties whether it is *ad hoc* or institutional arbitration on one hand and it leads to an enforceable award on the other hand, which differs from mediation.[21]

Today, economic growth in developing states has parallel enhancements in terms of international business transactions between states and foreign private entities. These transactions not only include infrastructure projects but also energy projects for electricity stations, gas pipelines and liquefied natural gas (LNG). The latter projects include a set of complex contractual arrangements. Among these transactions is the Engineering, Procurement and Construction Site agreement (EPC), which has a special significance in the domain of International Public Works Agreements.

Foreign private entities insist upon the arbitration clause as one of the guarantees and incentives by which foreign entities protect their investments and substantive rights in the agreements through a fair and prompt mechanism that leads to a final, binding and enforceable arbitral award. Generally, states may prefer arbitration in order not to refer the dispute to the national courts of any other jurisdiction; meanwhile, foreign private entities may prefer arbitration to avoid the national courts of the hosting state. Foreign entities also prefer arbitration because they might think that there is an influence from governments of the hosting states on the national courts, which is not true in most cases.[22]

Developing states in past decades rejected arbitration as it had a past history of various problems related to losing arbitrations, in particular in the international arbitral institutions.

National and International Sources of Arbitration Law

The national sources of arbitration law in most Arab Middle Eastern jurisdictions generally derive from particular sources in Arab civil law jurisdictions such as the state constitution, which is always a written constitution in civil law Arab jurisdictions;[23] legislation such as either arbitration acts currently codified by states or Codes of Civil and Commercial Procedures, including certain rules and stipulations applicable to arbitration;[24] State Procurement laws;[25] regulations in countries where it already exists; and customs of the construction industry in the light of State Procurement laws and state contracts.[26]

The sources for international arbitration[27] consist of international rules, conventions and treaties. The most important sources in practice and for academia are the UNCITRAL Model Law (the Model Law) adopted by the United Nations Commission on International Trade Law in June 1985 and amendments as adopted in 2006, and the UNCITRAL arbitration rules (the UNCITRAL

21 Lew, Mistelis and Kröll 2003; Redfern and Hunter 2009.

22 Craig, Park and Paulsson 1985: 661.

23 For Arab written constitutions, generally, see: the Egyptian Constitution of 1971 as amended in 2007, the Constitution of Libya, the Constitution of Lebanon, the Constitution of Kuwait, the Constitution of Jordan, the Constitution of Oman, the Constitution of Syria, the Constitution of Morocco.

24 Arbitration Act currently codified such as: the Egyptian Act of 1994; the Omani Arbitration Act of 1997; the Jordanian Arbitration Act of 2001; the Saudi Arbitration Act of 1982 and the Tunisian Arbitration Act of 1992; the Code of Civil Procedures of the United Arab Emirates, Qatar, Kuwait, Libya, Algeria, Morocco, Iraq, Lebanon, Syria and the Sudan.

25 Egyptian State Procurement Law promulgated by Law No. 89 of 1998.

26 Bunni 2005: 396.

27 For instance see: http://www.uncitral.org; and http://www.icsid.org.

Rules) adopted by resolution of the General Assembly of the United Nations in December 1976 and amended in August 2010; the Washington Convention of 1965 on the Settlement of Investment Disputes between States and National or Other States; the Rules of Procedures for Arbitration Proceedings (Arbitration Rules) of the International Centre of Settlement of International Dispute (ICSID). It is appropriate to refer to the New York Convention of 1958 on the Recognition and Enforcement of Foreign Arbitral Awards as the pillar for successful enforcement of international arbitration awards worldwide.

The UNCITRAL Model Law was the main factor behind the development of modern arbitration laws in many jurisdictions, particularly in Middle Eastern Arab countries. The concepts of party autonomy and the supportive rule of courts to the arbitration process are the basis of the Model Law. The Model Law plays a significant role of modernization and liberalization of the arbitral process in most jurisdictions, in theory and in practice, in Arab states that promulgated arbitration legislation. In addition, UNCITRAL Rules, New York Convention and Washington Convention of 1965 as well as ICSID Arbitration Rules are the key features of a step forward toward a fully liberalized arbitral process in the Middle East as a direct result of legal globalization and to maintain protection of fair mechanism for dispute settlement to foreign investment.

The party autonomy principle, which is the arbitration agreement, is the source of law to the arbitral process.

Arbitration in State Contracts in Developing Countries

Perhaps the latest strides in economic growth within Third World countries may help pave the way for relevant agreements between states and private foreign entities to prevail and flourish.

Economic growth projects are not only restricted to infrastructure, but they also include energy projects for power stations and gas projects for liquefied natural gas (LNG).[28] Such nature-specific projects involve an intricate and complex series of international agreements pertinent not only to them but also to other projects, including the utilization of natural resources, like oil and gas used in many industries: LNG, petrochemicals and others.

States usually decide on arbitration to avoid resorting to courts of other states. On the other hand, a private foreign entity resorts to arbitration out of fear that governments of project-owning states may exercise pressure on their national courts, or it fears that failure to resort to arbitration may force a situation of state sovereignty to prevail.[29]

Developing countries were especially sensitive to arbitration as the historical background and problematic nature of arbitration in these countries were key players in its rejection. Third World countries became vulnerable to any means of settling contract disputes arising with private foreign parties other than resorting to competent national judiciaries.

28 Liquefied Natural Gas (LNG) projects involve the processing and liquefaction of gas, where it is then most likely to be exported by the gas-producing countries. There are only a handful of LNG projects running worldwide, and it was a great honor that I represented the Egyptian government as the Legal Negotiator and Senior Legal Official of the first nature-specific LNG project in Egypt. The aim of the project was to build a large LNG plant in Idco – Behira governorate for the liquefaction and export of gas. The project involved the conclusion of a number of interrelated international contracts for which I was responsible for carrying out relevant negotiations on the part of the Egyptian government from 2000 to mid-2002.

29 Craig, Park and Paulsson 1985: 661.

Statistics show[30] that the 11-year period from 1989 to 1999 involved 11,143 disputing parties in arbitration cases before the International Chamber of Commerce (ICC) in Paris. Out of these, 2,531 – approximately 23 per cent – were from developing countries, of which 1,073 – i.e., 42 per cent – were claimants. These figures strongly refute the claim that Third World countries may have fallen victim to arbitration. It is also worth noting that the presidency of the Court of Arbitration has gone to many non-Westerners. Out of 873 arbitrators with African, Asian, Latin American and Middle Eastern nationalities at the ICC in Paris, 20 per cent were appointed by the ICC and not by disputing parties. The same applies to the seat of arbitration. During the period from 1989 to 1999, roughly 323 arbitration cases took place in no fewer than 40 of the Third World countries within Africa, Asia, Latin America and the Middle East (60 in Singapore, 27 in Mexico, 13 in Egypt and nine in Tunisia).

It has become a top priority for the International Chamber of Commerce in Paris that developing countries, for whatever significant and effective role they have come to play, continually participate in its activities.[31]

State Sovereignty and International Arbitration

At times, states tend to invoke immunity against international commercial arbitration; nevertheless, the existence of an arbitration clause under a contract can usually mean that a country has waived such immunity. In other words, if a country consents to arbitration by signing an arbitration clause and later recants its consent, arbitration still prevails.

In the case of *Liamco v. Libya*, the US oil company tried to execute an arbitration award against the Libyan government after the latter had nationalized the company's rights stated under an oil concession agreement. With the refusal of Libya to take part in the relevant proceedings, an award was issued in Geneva in 1977 granting US$8 million in favour of the company. Liamco tried to have the arbitration award recognized in the state of Colombia; nevertheless, although the Colombian judge admitted competence to take cognizance of the dispute, he refused to exercise his competence for a law issued in a contracting state applying the concept of nationalization. For the judge to avoid having to contend the said arbitration award, he referred in his judgment to Article (5/2/a) of the New York Convention stating that "recognition and enforcement of an arbitral award may also be refused if the competent authority in the country where recognition and enforcement is sought finds that the subject matter of the difference is not capable of settlement by arbitration under the law of that country." Accordingly, with respect to the opinion of the judge, the action taken by the country was not grounds for arbitration.

Despite waiving state sovereignty, it was apparent that Liamco, in the event the act of breach on the part of the country was a direct result of a legislation issued therein, was going to deny arbitration concerning the claims stated under contract.

Liamco attempted attachment against Libyan assets in France, Sweden and Switzerland. In France, attachment was recognized by the French government, and Liamco attached some 29 Libyan assets. The French courts granted Liamco the right to ascertain that none of the assets were exempt from state immunity.

30 Craig, Park and Paulsson 1985: 662.

31 Craig, Park and Paulsson 1985: 662–3.

In Sweden, the Court of Appeal decided that the Libyan government had waived the right to invoke immunity by having accepted the arbitration clause. By doing so, the court made no distinction between immunities against jurisdiction and immunities against execution.

In Switzerland, the Federal Court annulled the judgment of the Court of Zurich to attach Libyan assets in six Swiss banks. The Federal Court did not reject the judgment but rather found that the Court of Zurich had no jurisdiction to attach Libyan assets on the grounds of absence of a "sufficient domestic relationship," which must be proved by the existence of some activities reflecting Swiss jurisdiction.[32]

To that extent, Liamco was nothing short of being the paramount cause behind the 1998 changes to the US legislation. The Foreign Sovereign Immunities Act (FSIA) was amended to allow the execution of arbitration awards against commercial properties and assets owned by foreign countries. Whether or not such assets were grounds for arbitration was not a matter of concern.[33]

The core importance attached to this case gave effect to many legislative amendments in numerous countries all around the world. Application and execution of arbitral awards, as well as attachment of foreign country assets, have become increasingly recognized through time.

Generally, there is a distinction between acts of private nature, whether civil or commercial, on the one hand and state activities, which are public, on the other. States are expected to be immune from legal proceeding in a foreign court in relation to their sovereign activities, while no immunity exists for activities of a purely commercial or private nature.[34]

State immunity can be from jurisdiction or execution. It has been settled in international doctrine that the existence of a valid arbitration agreement prevents reliance on sovereign immunity by the state.[35] The arbitration agreement is generally considered to be an implied waiver of immunity in relation to the arbitral tribunal itself. If the state agrees to arbitration, it cannot at a later stage resist the jurisdiction of the tribunal and thereby defeat the agreement it entered. However, in some Middle Eastern jurisdictions,[36] the administration's consent is compulsory to start arbitration proceedings against the government. The concerned minister's consent is obligatory for foreign or domestic investors to start arbitration.

Arbitration Agreement and State Sovereignty

A fundamental question arises as to the binding effect of an arbitration agreement signed by a public juristic entity and its contradictions sometimes with state immunity. Is a provision for arbitration necessary for a contracting country to be obliged to abide by it?

Conceptually, contracting parties come to an agreement with respect to international arbitration so that it eventually becomes a part of the contract between them, either in the form of an arbitration clause or an arbitration agreement. However, in the event parties fail to agree to resort to arbitration, can the contracting country be pressured into doing so?

There has certainly been a rising trend to grant a foreign party the right to resort to international arbitration against a contracting country even if that country has not signed an arbitration agreement.

---

32 Craig, Park and Paulsson 1985: 672–3.

33 For details, see: Lew, Mistelis and Kröll 2003: 759; *Libyan American Oil Company (LIAMCO) v. Socialist People's Libyan Arab Jamahiriya, 482, F Supp 1175 (DDC 1980).*

34 Lew, Mistelis and Kröll 2003: 744–5.

35 For an overview, see: Lew, Mistelis and Kröll 2003: 746; Redfern and Hunter 1991; 1999; see also: Redfern and Hunter 2009; Fouchard, Gaillard et Goldman 1999.

36 Egyptian Arbitration Act, 1994, S.1 as amended by Law No. 9 of 1997.

In the *Pyramids* case,[37] the claimant built his argument on a provision stated under the Egyptian Investment Law of 1974 stating that investment disputes may be resolved by virtue of the Convention on the Settlement of International Disputes between States and Nationals of Other States (Washington Convention), which Egypt ratified under Law No. 90 of 1971.

The government of the Arab Republic of Egypt made a defence, claiming that the provision does not suffice to establish jurisdiction of the arbitral tribunal. The defence was based on the fact that the provision includes two sentences that state "within the framework of the convention" and "where it applies," where each necessitates the acquisition of a special approval to resort to the International Centre for the Settlement of Investment Disputes (ICSID) in order to settle a dispute through arbitration. The arbitral tribunal denied all pretexts invoked by the Egyptian government.

In the *Pyramids* case the ICC arbitral tribunal rendered an award in favour of SPP, a Hong Kong based company, against Egyptian General Organization for Tourism and Hotels (EGOTH), an Egyptian public juristic entity, considering the words of the Minister of Tourism, "approved, agreed and ratified" after the cancellation of the project unilaterally by the Egyptian government. The arbitrators assumed jurisdiction and found that the government was a party to the arbitration agreement and consequently bound by the agreement. Egypt applied to the French courts for annulment of the award.[38] The *Cour D'Appel de Paris* vacated the award and upon appeal by SPP, the *Cour de Cassation* upheld the decision. The words "agreed, approved and ratified" must be interpreted in light of the Egyptian legal system and the contracting parties' declaration. The ratification was not a justification to the minister to become a party to the joint venture agreement.

In the *Westland* case, a joint venture between the English company Westland Helicopters and the Arab Organization for Industrialization (AOI), an international organization set up in 1975 by the Arab republic of Egypt, the Kingdom of Saudi Arabia, the United Arab Emirates and Qatar, AOI was dissolved by three member states for political reasons. Westland started arbitral proceedings against AOI and all four states based on the arbitration clause that was included in the shareholders' agreements concluded between AOI and Westland for setting up a joint venture company. Egypt denied being bound by the arbitration agreement, and all three Arab states did not participate in arbitration proceedings. The arbitral tribunal rendered an award on jurisdiction and held that:

> The tribunal had to examine the founding documents of the AOI which does not exclude liability of the state. If there are any national rules excluding liability, it is not applicable regarding the transnational nature of AOI. The tribunal decided that states were bound by the arbitration agreement entered into by AOI.

Egypt applied to the Swiss courts, and the *Tribunal Fédéral* annulled the award in relation to Egypt for lack of jurisdiction. The Swiss court held that an arbitration clause cannot be opposed by a party that did not sign it unless this party is bound by the signature of an entity or a third party empowered to act on behalf of the first party, on the basis of an act granting to that entity or third party the power to refer a dispute to arbitration. The court elaborated that AOI's autonomy rules out the possibility that its contracts with third parties, and more particularly the arbitration clause signed by it, may be considered as contracts concluded by a representative or any agency.

37 *Southern Pacific Properties v. Arab Republic of Egypt*, referred to in Craig, Park and Paulsson 1985: 664–5.

38 See: Redfern and Hunter 1991. See also: Redfern and Hunter 2009; Lew, Mistelis and Kröll 2003: 740–41.

The predominant roles played by these states in AOI and the AOI's highest authority, a committee consisting of ministers, cannot affect AOI's independence and legal personality, nor can it lead to the conclusion that AOI bound the founding states when dealing with third parties.[39] Moreover, the Geneva court of appeal and the *Tribunal Fédéral* also rejected the equity argument as equity cannot apply to this case. The court stated that there is no denial of justice as Westland can start litigation proceedings against Egypt in the Egyptian courts.

In another dispute between Manufacturers Hanover Trust Company and the Arab Republic of Egypt (General Authority for Investment and Free Zones – GAFI), the claimant company built its defence on the fact that the Egyptian government has shown legislative consent to the jurisdiction of the ICSID; however, the dispute was resolved before an arbitration award on jurisdiction was issued.[40]

The same rules apply if the question arises in the enforcement stage.[41] Enforcement of awards against Arab Middle Eastern states can face some difficulties regarding attaching stateowned property to a public juristic entity, with a separate legal personality, through national courts.

The above-mentioned perspectives are well illustrated by the United States courts in *S&Davis International Inc. v. The Republic of Yemen*.[42] United States courts held that ministerial intervention was the reason behind enforcement of the award against a public juristic entity owned by the state (property of a state-owned entity).

In conclusion, accession of countries to international treaties or conventions involving their legislative consent to arbitration only obliges them to accept such arbitration. International conventions function as domestic legislation in some countries whereas in others they transcend it. Accordingly, accession of a country to a convention necessitates its comprehensive abidance by its provisions. If a contracting country breaches its legislative obligations and chooses to deny arbitration, this acts as grounds for application of the fundamental rule stating that recanting a consented action is grounds for invalidation of the abjuration.

Great importance is undoubtedly attached to the application of Bilateral Investment Treaties (BITs).[43] In the France/Paraguay BIT of 1978, Article (8) states that an investor may resort to the ICSID for arbitration. Further, Article (10) of the agreement concluded by and between France and Yugoslavia in 1990 states that an investor may, in accordance with the UNCITRAL rules, resort to the ICSID or to arbitration if the state party to the dispute is not a member of the World Bank-affiliated ICSID. The 1989 BIT between France and Poland states under Article (8) that in expropriation disputes, an investor is entitled to resort to *ad hoc* arbitration in the event that no satisfactory response is received within a six-month period from the date of filing a complaint.

In this context, reference should also be made to the Franco-Moroccan agreement concluded in 1975 that states under Article (10) that an investor may seek ICSID arbitration under the proviso that the subject matter of the dispute is related to productive investment matters, having been approved by the host state and guaranteed by the state of the investor, and that the matter is of a legal nature and has not been dealt with satisfactorily by internal recourse within a two-year period.

---

39 For an analytical perspective, see: Lew, Mistelis and Kröll 2003: 741–43; Redfern and Hunter 1991; 1999. See also: Redfern and Hunter 2009: 465; Fouchard, Gaillard et Goldman 1999.

40 *Manufacturers Hanover Trust Company v. Arab Republic of Egypt and General Authority for Investment and Free Zones*, ICSID Cases, 31 March 1994, 27.

41 Lew, Mistelis and Kröll 2003: 743.

42 218 F 3d 1292, XXVI YBCA 978 (2001) 980 (11 Cir, 2000). For details, see: Lew, Mistelis and Kröll 2003: 743.

43 Craig, Park and Paulsson 1985: 665; also arbitration award issued by ICSID, concerning *Asian Agricultural Products LTD v. Republic of Sri Lanka.*

These international agreements furnish investors with an opportunity to resort to arbitration for the resolution of their disputes. Accordingly, the provision of an arbitration clause or an arbitration agreement is not necessarily elemental in this case; instead, the accession of a state to such a treaty will suffice. Once a contracting state has acceded to and ratified an international treaty, it has implicitly consented to the arbitrational jurisdiction of the ICSID or any other arbitration mechanism provided under the treaty. In this event, the arbitration clause or arbitration agreement stipulated under each individual contract will not need to provide reference to arbitration; rather, the general rule concerning a contracting state resorting to arbitration would already have been laid. The rule allows the state to be subject to arbitration, with a view to warding off any breach of international obligations and to divesting any *mala fides* (bad faith). As such, there is no room for breach of obligations when a state feels an urge to reject the arbitration clause; it automatically becomes liable to the previously mentioned rule stating that recantation of a consented action is grounds for invalidation of the abjuration.

Perhaps multilateral treaties assume a vital role in approving arbitration as a mechanism for the settlement of disputes, which can never be denied by a host country. A significant example of this is the North American Free Trade Agreement (NAFTA), in which the contracting states have agreed to arbitration as a mechanism for settling disputes.

Harmonizing International Public Works Agreements Arbitration and *Le Contrat Administratif* Constraints

Background

Arbitration in International Public Works Agreements was generally rejected in the past decades by the *Conseil d'Etat* in Egypt. Except for two legal opinions that were given by the General Assembly for Legal Opinion and Legislation in 1989 and 1993, confirming that arbitration is permitted in state contracts, the Supreme Administrative Court rejected arbitration in administrative contracts. This was before the promulgation of the Arbitration Act in Egypt in 1994. After the promulgation of the Arbitration Act in 1994 and until early 1997, it was controversial in Egypt whether arbitration was permitted in state contracts or not. A famous legal opinion was issued by the General Assembly for Legal Opinion and Legislation on 18 December 1996 rejecting arbitration in International Public Works Agreements. The opinion was based on the legal nature and the substance of *Le Contrat Administratif*, which, in the view of the General Assembly, reject arbitration in these contracts. Moreover, the General Assembly interpreted that Article (1) of the Arbitration Act in Egypt was general, and the rules of interpretation in Egyptian law stipulate that general clauses are not confirmed as long as they are not specific and addressed to a particular case objectively. The General Assembly concluded that in the light of the latter findings, it is not certain that arbitration is permitted in administrative contracts and particularly in the International Public Works Agreements.[44]

The Egyptian Parliament reacted positively and rapidly as it promulgated Law No. 9 of 1997 in early 1997, permitting arbitration in administrative contracts in particular. This legislation was one of the investment incentives guaranteed in Egypt, and it was one of the main factors in increasing the IFDI in the following decade before the economic crises of 2008.

44 The Egyptian General Assembly for Legal Opinion and Legislation, Legal Opinion No. 160, dated 22/2/1997, session 18/12/1996, file No. 54/1/339.

Law No. 9 of 1997 and the Egyptian Approach

The Egyptian legislature promulgated Law No. 9 of 1997 that amended Article (1) of Law No. 27 of 1994 and made arbitration in state administrative contracts affirmative. The amendment stipulates the consent of the minister concerned to the arbitration clause and/or arbitration agreement. This power cannot be delegated by the minister. It is true that a considerable criticism was addressed to the stipulation requiring the consent of the minister concerned to the arbitration agreement/clause as it is an exorbitant legislative clause.

Decisions of the Conseil d'Etat *Courts*

Courts decisions are still rare in the domain of the administrative arbitral process, and the role of the judicial power to assist arbitration decisions is also limited. The State Council was obliged to apply the Arbitration Act, which was not sufficiently influenced by cultural globalization movements and the flow of the Anglo-American legal culture to Egypt as a civil law country, despite the fact that it allowed arbitration in state contracts. The Egyptian legal culture was influenced by the flow of cultural globalization in many areas in the legal domain, yet this stipulation is still one of the rare rigid rules in the Arbitration Act.

It is appropriate at this stage to refer to the famous decision of the Administrative Appeal Court on 19 February 2006 in the *Malicorp Ltd.* case.[45] Malicorp Ltd., the respondent in this case, entered into a tender with a civil aviation corporation for the construction of the Ras Sedr airport. The civil aviation corporation was allowed an international tender to build, operate and manage the airport for a certain period of time and then transfer the airport to the state after the stipulated period.

The respondent, Malicorp, entered into a concession agreement with the claimant, the Minister of Civil Aviation, on 4 November 2000. The contract included an arbitration clause stating that any dispute that cannot be amicably settled shall finally be settled through an international commercial arbitration held in the Cairo Regional Centre for International Commercial Arbitration (CRCICA) pursuant to its valid rules at the concession agreement date. On 17 January 2001, Malicorp applied to establish a joint stock company pursuant to Egyptian laws. The aim of the company was to build, operate and manage the airport. Egyptian security authorities pointed out that Malicorp resorted to fraud in its deal with the Civil Aviation Authority concerning its creditworthiness because the capital of the company was only £2 sterling. There were also major contractual mistakes during the contractual process. The Public Funds Prosecution (*L'Avocat Générale*) started its proceedings by investigating the criminal case. The administration forfeited the performance bond and rescinded the contract (*La Résiliation Administrative*).

Malicorp started an arbitration proceeding (No. 382 of 2004) against the Egyptian government (Civil Aviation Authority) at the Cairo Regional Centre for International Commercial Arbitration (CRCICA). Malicorp was seeking US$508 million as compensation for damages. The Minister of Civil Aviation pointed out that the arbitration clause in the concession agreement signed by and between the defendant and the claimant was null and void, as the minister concerned did not ratify the arbitration clause as stipulated pursuant to Article (1) of Law No. 27 of 1994, which was amended by Law No. 9 of 1997. The claimant pointed out that if the arbitration clause is null and void, then dispute falls within the jurisdiction of the national courts (*Conseil d'Etat* courts). The court stated that the question is whether an arbitration agreement is valid and existent or not.

---

45 Case No. 18628, session 19/2/2006, Judicial Year 59, unpublished.

The court held that the administrative judge should not deny the jurisdiction granted to him pursuant to the constitution and legislation. Hence, the arbitral tribunal must dismiss the case unless there is a valid arbitration agreement/clause. If the arbitration agreement/clause is null and void, the national court must restore its jurisdiction.[46] The court cannot consider such a clause unless there is a ministerial consent to proceed on arbitration.

The court elaborated that Article (22) of the Arbitration Act that established the wellknown principle of *competence/competence* in the Egyptian legal system must not deprive national courts of their jurisdiction if the arbitration agreement/clause is null and void.

The court concluded that adopting any other views is a violation of the judicial authority role, the constitutional right to litigate and the supremacy of law principle. The mere fact is that the minister concerned has not approved the arbitration clause in the contract at this dispute. The arbitration agreement is null and void, and the Administrative Appeal Court restores its jurisdiction as it is the competent court in administrative contract disputes pursuant to the Egyptian Constitution (Article 172) and the *Conseil d'Etat* legislation (Article 10). Furthermore, the court terminated the arbitral proceedings in the abovementioned arbitration case in CRCICA.[47]

In a parallel arbitral award, the arbitral tribunal pointed out that the legislature required that the arbitration process in administrative contracts must have the consent of the minister or authority concerned for public juristic entities and prohibited delegation of power by the minister or authority concerned. Moreover, the Egyptian legislature entrusted the arbitral tribunal authority with deciding its jurisdiction.

The arbitral tribunal affirmed a vision that is contrary to that adopted in the Malicorp case by the *Conseil d'Etat* courts. It was held by this leading arbitral tribunal that the public juristic entity is responsible for contracting proceedings. Among these legal and administrative procedures is obtaining ministerial approval and consent to enter into agreements and their clauses (arbitration clauses). The sole responsibility lies with the public juristic entity to obtain ministerial consent on the arbitration clause/agreement. If the public entity fails in such procedure, either deliberately or by default, the liability of such failure will fall solely thereon. No contractor may fulfil these procedures as they are to be fulfilled by the public entity.

The justification of this conclusion relies on the fact that the relationship between the public entity and the contractor is a contractual one. This implies certain duties upon the administration, in particular, protecting the other contracting party to maintaining confidence and transparency in the administration's transactions. Since the process of obtaining the ministerial consent is basically the role of the administration, it is therefore impossible for the contractor (as a private juristic entity) to do so.

The provision of Article (1) of the Arbitration Act stipulating the necessity to obtain the consent of the minister concerned on the arbitration clause agreement is directed to administrative authorities not to private entities entering into contracts with the administration. The role of the administration is thus fundamental in controlling the contractual process and its management (from the time of the tender announcement until the final completion) in all legal and administrative aspects. If the legal effect of the failure of the administration to obtain ministerial consent on the arbitration clause is the nullification of the present clause, unpredictability and uncertainty will prevail as the administration can benefit from its default! The principles of legal logic, equality

46 The court adopted the same vision of the Supreme Administrative Court in one of its previous decisions: Case No 6268, session 31/5/2005, Judicial Year 46.

47 The Supreme Administrative Court affirmed this judgment and the same reasoning in Case No. 17254, session 19/3/2007, Judicial Year 52.

and fairness cannot accept this result. Moreover, to conclude that a contractual clause is null and void in the Egyptian legal system is conditional upon the existence of a legislative provision stipulating this vision, which, in this case, is absent. The Egyptian legislature did not stipulate that the arbitration contractual clause should be considered null and void in the event of failure to obtain ministerial consent.

The only legal consequence is the undertaking of administrative investigations against administrative employees for their default to obtain ministerial consent prior to the start of arbitration.

The arbitral tribunal found the arbitral process and arbitration clause valid and confirmed its jurisdiction to continue with the process pursuant to Article (22) of the Arbitration Act and to the *competence/competence* principle.

ICSID Convention

The ICSID Convention stipulates that a state party can only rely on sovereign immunity against execution under Article 55. Arbitration agreement is a mechanism for a waiver of immunity for actions to recognize the award and have it declared enforceable.[48] Article 54 from the ICSID Convention provides that the state has to honor the award. Further, it is an undertaking upon the contracting state as it has entered into an arbitration agreement. Despite the fact that it is respecting states undertaking to honor the award, the ICSID Convention allows immunity from execution (Article 55).

There are views that the waiver of immunity from jurisdiction implies a waiver of immunity from execution in France and Switzerland.[49] It is true that "purpose exception," which is the commercial activity purpose, is more important than waiver exception. This can be found in instruments in commercial arbitration in the international sphere.[50]

Advantages and Disadvantages of Arbitration

As a means of dispute settlement, arbitration is generally surrounded by advocacies and controversies. Although it is characterized by numerous advantages, opponents in some Arab jurisdictions see some disadvantages to it as well.[51]

On the one hand, unlike the judiciary, arbitration furnishes a degree of confidentiality to disputing parties;[52] it further allows them to select their arbitrators based on experience, expertise and outstanding skill in dealing with International Public Works Agreements and in resolving various special nature and, at times, very intricate related problems. To this end, arbitration is

48 Lew, Mistelis and Kröll 2003: 749–50; Redfern and Hunter, 1991 and 1991. See also: Redfern and Hunter 2009: 465.

49 Lew, Mistelis and Kröll 2003: 752.

50 Lew, Mistelis and Kröll 2003: 754–5; Redfern and Hunter, 1991 and 1991. See also: Redfern and Hunter 2009: 465.

51 Yahiel and Cranston 1985: 164; Kerr 1980.

52 As is the case with some "special nature" disputes, like those arising in cases involving technology transfer and intellectual property rights. See: "Confidentiality as an Advantage of Arbitration," in Abdel Kader 1996: 65.

considered time-saving, economic and very effective in resolving disputes in a practical, realistic and lawful manner. It leads to an enforceable resolution.

On the other hand, technically, arbitration allows the arbitral tribunal to take cognizance of a conflict from its onset up to its demise, in contrast to the judicial system that, in some countries, allows more than one judicial structure to take cognizance of the case with every judicial year. In other words, if a case lasts for more than one year, it consequently falls under more than one court; accordingly, it may receive a judgment from one jurisdiction that differs from the court that started scrutinizing the case at an earlier stage.

Generally, arbitration is considered more flexible and rapid when compared to other basic forms of litigation. In many cases, litigation proceedings tend to be very sluggish, especially when numerous phases of litigation and appeal are involved. Moreover, the optional nature attached to arbitration reveals a mere will of the parties involved to resolve the matter.[53]

What is mostly held against the arbitration system, especially in developing countries, is the fact that it allows the global capitalist system to take dominance over developing countries, as well as ensuring their constant economic dependence on it. That the arbitrator is not obliged to enforce a specific law makes dominance and dependence much more inviting. Parties to a dispute are free to choose the law they desire the arbitrator to apply; furthermore, the arbitrator is free to choose the law to be applied, should the parties not have already done so. It is, therefore, most likely that domestic laws applied in developing countries, whose poor economic conditions almost always make them the vulnerable party in a legal relationship, will not be favoured for enforcement.[54] Vulnerability may also emanate from detriment that will be caused as a result of enforcement of laws other than domestic ones. If the traditional approach had been adopted, the outcomes of such enforcement may very well have been unexpected to such an extent that their redress may, in many cases, fail. International Public Works Agreements are considered a fertile environment for such a problem.

Nevertheless, arbitration may be lauded for the opportunity it furnishes to the parties involved to empanel arbitrators experienced in the subject matter of the dispute. In other words, if a dispute revolving around a Public Works Agreement erupts, arbitrators with extensive experience and expertise in public works and administrative contracts, especially international administrative contracts, may be nominated to resolve the dispute in a manner that meets the convenience of the parties.

The same applies to all other forms of disputes, for example, disputes arising regarding matters related to banks, technology, shipping and others, which may necessitate the services of a qualified person to resolve them.[55]

Some commentators argue[56] that arbitration, resorted to as an alternative to the competent national judiciary, does not come cheap. Arbitral fees and administrative expenses are born by the

53 See: Beriry 1995: 8.

54 See: Beriry 1995: 12, 13. The Law on Arbitration in Civil and Commercial Matters, Explanatory Notes and all Relevant Preparatory Work, Publication of the Department of Legislation, Ministry of Justice, 1995. Discussions in the People's Assembly concerning the report issued by the committee established jointly between the Committee on Legislative and Constitutional Affairs and the office of the Committee on Economic Affairs concerning a draft law on international commercial arbitration. More precisely, the opinion of Parliament Member Diaa Ed-Din Dawood in his opposition to the Draft Law on International Commercial Arbitration promulgated by Law No. 27 of 1994. Dawood, as a socialist leader, linked arbitration with the concept of foreign concessions enforced during prior eras (83).

55 Abdel Kader 1996: 66.

56 Redfern and Hunter 1991: 24; Redfern and Hunter 1999: 24–25.

disputants sometimes as a percentage of the overall value of the dispute (*ad valerum* method). At times, such expenses and fees may well stretch across the exorbitant zone.[57]

Nevertheless, the greatest point of weakness of the arbitral system lies in the ineffective powers conferred episodically upon the arbitral tribunal. From time to time, the powers granted to the tribunal are no match for the gravity and nature of the matter under dispute. For instance, the arbitral tribunal cannot impose fines upon witnesses for failing to appear before it.

Absence of such powers may, in many cases, deter the arbitral tribunal from settling the dispute in a convenient manner.[58]

Finally, contrary to ordinary courts, a single arbitral tribunal lacks the ability easily to take cognizance of multiparty disputes,[59] another shortcoming of the arbitral system. A clear example can be seen in International Public Works Agreements when an employer enters into a contract with a main contractor and, in turn, the main contractor enters into contract with subcontractors and/or suppliers. If the employer chooses to resort to arbitration with a complaint against the main contractor, the contractor will refer to the subcontractors or suppliers, who will naturally inquire about the nature of the problem. To do so will require separate arbitrations,[60] which may lead to inconsistent findings.

In the ordinary litigation system, all parties to a single case will be brought together before a single court to take cognizance of all aspects of the dispute, and thus a single award will be issued after the procedures are consolidated.

Advantages of Arbitration in International Public Works Agreements

Arbitration as a process has various advantages. The process is, in most cases, expeditious and costeffective. It is a flexible process, adaptable to a particular dispute and more compatible with construction disputes, particularly in International Public Works Agreement disputes. These disputes have a particular type of complexity when there is multiparty arbitration. The arbitral tribunal in complex Public Works Agreement disputes may issue an interim or partial award. In complex Public Works Agreement disputes, there is an interim award in which liability is determined, followed by a decision on quantum. Parties will often make real attempts to settle the case between them to avoid further time and cost in arbitration.[61] These flexible mechanisms do not exist in litigation. Further, arbitration can take place in any country, in any language, and the appointed arbitrators can be from any nationality. The whole process is subject to the party autonomy principle, which relies on the consent of the parties.

Arbitration maintains confidentiality, as some Arab arbitration acts stipulate that the arbitral award is confidential unless otherwise agreed by the parties.[62] Thus, it is a private process that avoids disclosure of commercially sensitive data and trade secrets.

In public works disputes and in infrastructure projects generally, the process allows the parties the choice of a specialized arbitrator who is experienced and familiar with the nature of the dispute, whether legal or commercial. State procurement law and engineering dimensions have their significance in the process and qualifications required in the arbitrator. As international public

57 For details of the advantages and disadvantages of arbitration, see: Abdel Kader 1996: 65.

58 Redfern and Hunter 1991: 24; Redfern and Hunter 1999: 25.

59 Redfern and Hunter 1991: 25; Redfern and Hunter 1999: 25.

60 For disadvantages of the arbitral system, see: Issa n.d.; See also: David 1982: 103.

61 Bunni 2005: 389.

62 Egyptian Arbitration Act, Article (44); in Arab Arbitration Acts, Jordanian Arbitration Act, Article (42); Omani Arbitration Act, Article (44).

works disputes are often complex construction disputes in state contracts, and in many cases, they have multiparty characteristics, it is suggested that an arbitrator in such disputes should be a specialized arbitrator. International commercial arbitration can be tailored to the particular needs of the International Public Works Agreement disputes, their characteristics and their special nature in the international sphere. Unlike procedures in litigation, pleadings are submitted at or close to the appointment of arbitrators, which enables the arbitral tribunal to start with the case and to be in close touch with both sides, allowing the tribunal to be acquainted with the parties from different cultures, languages and backgrounds. It is possible, for instance, to arrange for the arbitral tribunal to inspect the site.[63]

Moreover, if the parties choose litigation instead of arbitration, the courts of at least two different jurisdictions may have overlapping roles with consequential difficulties in the enforcement of foreign judgments. International public works arbitration will avoid various problems that litigation may have such as the recognition and enforcement of foreign awards. The arbitral award will be enforceable in the light of the 1958 New York Convention, which has been ratified by more than 100 countries. An international treaty that has been ratified by parliaments of Arab Middle Eastern countries is a part of the legal system, as it becomes a valid legislation after ratification.[64] The New York Convention has been described as the single most important pillar of the recognition and enforcement of arbitral awards worldwide. It is reported that an estimated 98 per cent of awards in international arbitration generally are successfully enforced.[65]

As the award is final, binding and enforceable, and this is the main characteristic of arbitration that distinguishes the arbitral process from other ADR mechanisms, this final award is not subject to appeal in most Arab jurisdictions. In exhaustive lists, stipulated in national arbitration legislation, the arbitral award can be challenged on the grounds of misconduct by the arbitrators or error in law.[66] These exhaustive lists are not subject to analogy as the parties cannot add additional cases to challenge arbitral awards. The latter trend confirms the finality of the award. In international public works disputes, the arbitral tribunal has wider powers than the national courts in litigation to review the engineer's decision.

In many countries, resolution of cases brought before national courts may take years to resolve, costing litigants far more than what arbitration expenses and arbitrator fees put together would have cost; this refutes the opinion argued by some that arbitration costs exceed judiciary ones. Moreover, delayed resolution jeopardizes the rights of litigants, especially if such resolution comes long after anticipated, when economic changes have struck, and depreciation of the currency has occurred.

Regarding the argument that arbitration is a mechanism for capitalist systems to seize control over developing countries and to secure their dependence by enforcing laws other than those of the developing country, relevant reactions may be taken to counter such actions. High-calibre legal servants – magistrates or lawyers – can be highly trained and well educated about arbitration with all its relevant dimensions and implications; they may further be taught all relevant languages,

---

63 Bunni 2005: 388.

64 The Egyptian Constitution, Article (151). All Arab constitutions have the same provision; see: the Constitution of Libya; the Constitution of Syria; the Constitution of Oman; the Constitution of Kuwait.

65 Bunni 2005: 388–9; Lew, Mistelis and Kröll 2003; Redfern and Hunter 1991; 2009; Fouchard, Gaillard et Goldman 1999.

66 Egyptian Arbitration Act, Article (53); Jordanian Arbitration Act 2001, Articles (49–51); Lebanese Code of Civil Procedures, Articles (816–19); Omani Arbitration Act, Articles (53–54); Kuwaiti Code of Civil Procedures, Article (187); Emirates Code of Civil Procedures, Article (216); Tunisian Act, Article (78) and Morocco Code of Civil Procedures, Article (326).

thus warding off any malicious attempts. The presence of an experienced Arab arbitrator, well acquainted with the arbitral spectrum and steered away from its disadvantages, will lead to the pooling of long-awaited national interests.

Powers restricting arbitral tribunals during the course of exercising their duties in settling international contract disputes can be obviated by issuing national legislation regulating the process of arbitration and its proceedings. The legislation may allow the national judiciary to intervene in strict circumstances outlined to regulate the arbitration process and its relevant proceedings.[67]

Finally, the problem of multiparty disputes may be solved by consolidation of procedures to achieve a single award. Multiparty arbitration came into being for this reason.

Developing countries need to stay up to par with developed countries in their pursuit to conceptualize, understand and deal with the arbitration system, as well as to integrate it into their legislation. Besides, if a developing country enters into a dispute under any of its international contracts, arbitration will be the means to protect its rights and interests.

Characteristics of Arbitration

Scholarly opinions suggest that arbitration has a *mixed* or *hybrid* nature. The arbitrators' task is to resolve a dispute. Scholars suggest that arbitration is a contractual process, and it has a judicial nature regarding the final award that is binding and enforceable on both parties.[68]

There are various theories related to the legal nature of arbitration. They refer to the juridical nature of arbitration, the jurisdictional theory; the contractual theory and the mixed or hybrid theory.[69] Doctrine refers to the academic dimension of those theories. However, it is recommended that the legal nature of arbitration has an impact upon the arbitral process and international commercial arbitration practice.[70] It has both academic and practical dimensions.

The contractual theory is based on the perspective that consent to arbitration assumes consent of disputing parties to resolve a dispute amicably; moreover, it assumes that all parties have a common intention to comply with a legal rule contrary to one that solely protects the interest of the other party. It is mainly based on party autonomy.

Discrepancy between arbitration and the judiciary becomes very evident in the objectives sought by each. The judiciary aims at achieving overall welfare, whereas arbitration aims at achieving specific parties' interests.

Most important, when parties agree to seek arbitration, they implicitly agree to drop any lawsuits and to vest the arbitrator with an authority emanating from their own free will. In this case, the authority is not a judicial one; rather, it is based on the desire of the relevant parties.[71]

67 For instance, the arbitral tribunal may refer a no-show witness to the competent national court to be fined, should the latter, in accordance with the recommendations of the tribunal, see such action as relevant.

68 Lew, Mistelis and Kröll 2003; Redfern and Hunter 1991: 8; Redfern and Hunter 1999: 4; Jarrosson 1987: 39; Goldberg, Sander and Rogers 1995: 223; Robert et Moreau 1967: 260, 493. In Arab Middle Eastern doctrine, see: Shafick 1973–1974: 10, 73; Rashed 1984: 70–71; Radwan 1981: 20; Hashem 1990: 216.

69 For an analytical perspective, see: Lew, Mistelis and Kröll 2003: 71–83; Redfern and Hunter 1991: 8; Fouchard, Gaillard et Goldman 1999: 12.

70 Lew, Mistelis and Kröll 2003: 73.

71 See details of the following: Waly 1986: 39, 40. See details of the judicial nature of arbitration: Al-Tihyewi 1994: 52; Abdel Kader 1996: 52; Rashed 1984: 75; Lew 1978: 51; Redfern and Hunter 1991: 8; Redfern and Hunter 1999: 4; Jarrosson 1987: 39.

It has been argued that mixed arbitration and hybrid arbitration[72] are considered a compromise to the resolution of the problem.

Advocates of this philosophy consider arbitration to be contractual in that it is willingly agreed upon by the relevant parties; meanwhile, they consider it to be judicial in that its award is deemed binding upon parties. Accordingly, arbitration is considered in Arab Middle Eastern countries to be of a mixed nature based on the fact that both the contractual and judicial theories each have an aspect of validity to them. To that extent, it was wiser to integrate both theories and to consider arbitration doublenatured: contractual and judicial.[73]

It is clear that under Egyptian and Arab jurisprudence, arbitration is considered more judicial. In addition to the state judiciary, arbitration is considered another form of judiciary; it is no different from the foreign judiciary recognized by domestic laws or the judiciary assumed by religious, rather than state, authorities, just as is the case with denominational boards in Egypt.[74]

Arbitration is an optional process that parties can refer to by their consent. Moreover, it has the judicial nature. In Arab Middle Eastern doctrine, there were controversial views regarding the contractual or judicial nature. The contractual nature implies that both parties agreed to a particular dispute settlement mechanism and their mutual consent to apply a specific rule of law. The main feature of arbitration is that parties agree that they will not have recourse to the judicial system, and they will refer the dispute to an arbitrator.[75]

In addition, the jurisdictional theory refers to the state power to control the arbitral process that takes place within its jurisdiction. The "judicialization" of the arbitral process has been addressed in many commentators' writings as they refer to the judicial character of arbitration.[76] "The jurisdictional theory is based on the quasi-judicial role of the arbitrator, as an alternative to the local judge."[77] The arbitrators resolve a dispute by a final and binding award. The substance of the jurisdictional theory is that:

> It follows that the arbitrator, like the judge, draws his power and authority from the local law; hence the arbitrator is considered to closely resemble a judge … the only difference between judge and arbitrator is that the former derives his nomination and authority directly from the sovereign, whilst the latter derives his authority from the sovereign but his nomination is a matter of the parties.[78]

---

72 Redfern and Hunter 1991: 8; Redfern and Hunter 1999: 4; Jarrosson 1987: 39; Goldberg, Sander and Rogers 1995: 223; Robert et Moreau 1967: 493, 260. In Arab jurisprudence: Shafik 1973–1974: 10, 73. Shafik states that "arbitration in reality does not simply involve a mere process of seeking agreement or judiciary, rather, it is a system that involves a number of phases, in which each phase has its own traits and characteristics. The initial phase is agreement, the middle phase is proceedings and the final phase is an award; bearing in mind the variation in these phases with the variation of the applicable law;" Rashed 1984: 70–71; Radwan 1981: 20; Hashem 1990: 216.

73 Al-Tihyewi 1994: 171.

74 See arguments advocating the judicial nature of arbitration: Waly 1986: 40 *et seq.*; El Sanhoury 1989, Vol. 2: 650; El Sharkawy and Abdel Moneim 1950: 33; El Wafa 1965.

75 Lew, *supra*, note 71, 51; Redfern and Hunter: 1991: 8 and Redfern and Hunter 1999: 4; Jarrosson 1987: 39. In Arab Middle Eastern jurisdictions, see: Fathy, *supra*, note 71, 39–40; Rashed 1984: 75; Abdel Kader 1996: 52.

76 Fouchard, Gaillard et Goldman 1999: 12–13; Redfern and Hunter 1991: 8; Lew, Mistelis and Kröll 2003: 75.

77 Lew, Mistelis and Kröll 2003: 75.

78 Lew 1978: para. 66; Lew, Mistelis and Kröll 2003: 75.

The judicial character of arbitration that leads to a final, binding and enforceable award distinguishes the arbitral process from other ADR mechanisms, such as mediation and expert proceedings.

The contractual theory relies on the concept of party autonomy as arbitration has a contractual nature. It has its origins, existence and continuity from the parties' agreement. It is argued that arbitration was created by the will and consent of the parties. Further, this theory denies the control of the state over the arbitral process.[79] The origin of every arbitration is the arbitration agreement. The whole process relies on the parties' consent starting from the constitution of the arbitral tribunal until the final award, which is binding. The parties choose the arbitrators, the rules for procedures, the procedural law and the substantive law.[80] Moreover, they choose the seat and the language of arbitration. The whole process relies on the parties' agreement. The party autonomy is the governing factor of the whole process, and it is the baseline for the arbitrators who can exercise their power pursuant to it. It is true that the process depends mainly on the parties' intention, and it is suggested that the judicial nature of international arbitration in no way weakens the equally firm principle of the party autonomy. It is argued that the party autonomy principle has diminished in practice, as international commercial arbitration owes its success to the role of permanent arbitral institution. This is the phenomenon of the institutionalization of international arbitration.[81] However, it is recommended that the role of international and regional arbitral institutions should be seen as positive, as it increases the efficiency of the arbitral proceedings. It brings the process closer to a private court, which increases the credibility of the process and decreases the uncertainty and unpredictability. The institutionalization of the process maintains an ideal constitution of the arbitral tribunal in most cases, whether selected by the parties or by the institution as an appointing authority. It also maintains effective procedures in deciding challenges of arbitrators. Moreover, it procures harmonization and systematic regulatory framework of proceedings within the institutional context. This trend of institutionalization of the arbitral process is strongly recommended in international public works arbitration for complex disputes. It is strongly recommended for multi-party arbitration disputes that are common in infrastructure arbitration.

Further, it is suggested by some scholarly opinions that, nowadays, arbitration can be practised without contractual relationships. This can be illustrated in the unilateral commencement of arbitral proceedings that appears clearly in the 1965 ICSID Convention, Bilateral Investment Treaties (BITs), the 1992 North American Free Trade Agreement (NAFTA) and the Energy Charter Treaty signed in Lisbon on 17 December 1994.[82]

The mixed or hybrid theory aims to reconcile the jurisdictional and contractual theories. The compromise between the contractual and jurisdictional elements of arbitration is the core of the

79 Lew, Mistelis and Kröll 2003: 77.

80 The French New Code of Civil Procedure Article (1494), stating the possibility of applying the law chosen by the parties to arbitration proceedings and Article (1496) leaves open the possibility to choose the law applying to the merits of the case. In Switzerland, the Federal Private International Law enacted in 1987, which includes liberal provisions, is favourable to the theory. In Egyptian Law, see: Article (39); see also: Omani Arbitration Act, Article (39); Jordanian Arbitration Act of 2001, Article (36).

81 Fouchard, Gaillard et Goldman 1999: 31. And in examining the phenomenon of the institutionalization of international arbitration, see: 1999: 33–5, where it is pointed out that the Iran–United States Claims Tribunal, which was established by the Algiers Accords of 19 January 1981, is created by an international treaty, and its jurisdiction is compulsory for disputes between parties from Iran and the United States. It is argued that this mechanism weakens the contractual theory of arbitration.

82 Lew, Mistelis and Kröll 2003: 78; Redfern and Hunter 2009: 467–9; Fouchard, Gaillard et Goldman 1999: 29–35.

mixed theory. The arbitrators are exercising a quasi-judicial function without being members of the judicial power of the state or sitting at the state national courts as the state judge. Their function is equivalent to the state judge. Further, the whole process depends mainly upon the party autonomy and the parties' agreement to select arbitrators constituting the arbitral tribunal and all the following proceedings until the final award. The hybrid or mixed theory became the most recognized worldwide theory as the elements of the jurisdictional and contractual theory in international commercial arbitration academic life and practice. This private justice institution represented by the arbitral tribunal selected by the parties or the appointing authority, chosen by the parties, has its basis in the contractual arrangements. It leads at the end to an award similar to judicial awards that are final, binding and enforceable. This hybrid or mixed nature exists *de facto*.[83] The harmonization is clear between the contractual approach that respects to a great extent the party autonomy, as in French law, on the one hand and the jurisdictional approach, as in international instruments such as the New York Convention, on the other. In Arab Middle Eastern jurisdictions, the Egyptian Arbitration Act emphasizes that party autonomy is a fundamental principle of the arbitral process.[84] The same situation exists in Arab arbitration acts.[85] The Arab legal systems rely upon the national judicial system to control and regulate the arbitral process that takes place within its jurisdictions. This is clear in most arbitration legislation in Arab Middle Eastern and North African jurisdictions.[86] This is within the limits of party autonomy. It is certain that the Arab arbitration acts, whether separate arbitration acts or articles in Codes of Civil and Commercial Procedural laws, are much influenced by the UNCITRAL Model Law.

The parallel role of the national courts and judicial establishments in developing countries supporting the arbitral process is highly favoured in the international sphere and international organizations, as it is seen as a safeguard for Foreign Direct Investments (FDI) to developing states and encourages the increase of the Inward Foreign Direct Investments (IFDI).[87]

The hybrid or mixed nature arbitral process is recommended as an alternative to the state courts and leads to a final, binding and enforceable award. Arbitration is a mechanism of private justice similar to state courts. In Most Arab jurisdictions, it is final, which means that there is no appeal mechanism from the arbitration award.[88] Arbitration, *inter alia*, is controlled in certain

83 Lew, Mistelis and Kröll 2003: 80.

84 Egyptian Arbitration Act, Article (10).

85 Omani Arbitration Act Article (10); Jordanian Arbitration Act 2001, Article (9); and Syrian Code of Civil Procedures, Article (506). The same provisions exist in the Kuwaiti Code of Civil Procedures, the Moroccan Arbitration Act, the Saudi Arbitration Act, the Emirates Code of Civil Procedures, the Lebanese Code of Civil Procedures and the Tunisian Arbitration Act.

86 For instance, to enforce an arbitral award in the Tunisian Arbitration Act, Article (19) by the competent court and to challenge an arbitrator, Article (20), enforcement and challenging of arbitral award, Articles (78/1), (80–82); Article (43) of the Jordanian Arbitration Act to grant the competent national court and authority in case of a forged document, challenging an arbitral award, Articles (49–51), arbitral award enforcement, Article (54); Omani Arbitration Act, Article (37) granted the commercial national court authority to impose penalties (fines) upon witnesses who do not comply with tribunal orders, challenging an arbitral award, Article (54); Saudi Arbitration Act, Article (23) granting the competent court the authority to determine arbitrators' fees in case of lack of parties' agreement.

87 Bunni 2005: 389.

88 The situation varies from one jurisdiction to another. Some countries' legislation stipulates that there is no appeal mechanism from the arbitration award, such as the Egyptian Act, Article (48); the Omani Act, Article (52); the Emirates Code of Civil Procedures, Article (217); the Kuwaiti Code of Civil Procedures, Article (186); and the Tunisian Act, Article (78). On the other hand, in very few countries,

cases by state national courts. This is due to its judicial nature. The source of the national courts' role in assisting and controlling the arbitral process is the constitution of most Arab states and arbitration acts of these countries.[89] It is appropriate to refer to many conferences that were held at the Cairo Regional Centre (CRCICA) in the last decades concerning the role of the national courts in assisting the arbitral process in Arab Middle Eastern jurisdictions.[90] Nevertheless, by agreeing to start arbitration as an alternative to litigation, parties waive their constitutional rights to have their dispute heard by national courts. The right of litigation is a constitutional right in most Arab jurisdictions.[91] Most Arab countries' arbitration acts include the right of the national court to reject any dispute if there is an arbitration clause and/or agreement.[92] Finally, the hybrid or mixed nature of arbitration is a refined mixed theory that is formed of a mixture of legal ideologies to enable the arbitral process to meet parties' expectations.

International Commercial Arbitration and Domestic (National) Arbitration

The meaning of international commercial arbitration differs from one jurisdiction to another. The term *international* or *transnational* has various meanings in various jurisdictions and legal systems. *International* is used to draw the line between arbitrations that are domestic and those that in some way have international elements. In an international arbitration, the parties usually have no connection with the seat of arbitration. Furthermore, monetary awards in international arbitration are greater than sums in domestic arbitrations. In some states, it is permitted for states or state entities to enter into international arbitrations and not only into domestic arbitration. The UNCITRAL Model Law defined an arbitration as an international arbitration if:

a) The parties to an arbitration agreement have, at the time of the conclusion of that agreement their places of business in different states; or

b) one of the following places is situated outside the state in which the parties have their places of business:

   i) the place of arbitration if determined in, or pursuant to the arbitration agreement

---

arbitral awards are subject to appeal: the Libyan Code of Civil Procedures, Article (767); the Syrian Code of Civil Procedures, Article (532); and the Qatar Code of Civil Procedures, Article (205). This right of appeal is applicable unless the parties waived the right and agreed that the arbitral award is final and binding.

89 See: UNCITRAL Model Law, Article (1(3)).

90 Many conferences have been held at CRCICA in the last two decades concerning the judiciary's parallel role in Arab Middle Eastern jurisdictions to assist arbitral process in cooperation with the Egyptian Ministry of Justice and the Judiciary of Arab countries.

91 Article (68) of the Egyptian Constitution. The same provision exists in the Syrian Constitution, the Libyan Constitution, the Emirates Constitution, the Saudi Constitution, the Lebanese Constitution, the Omani Constitution, the Kuwaiti Constitution and the Jordanian Constitution.

92 For instance, the Egyptian Act, Article (13); the Jordanian Act of 2001, Article (12); the Omani Act, Article (13); the Emirates Code of Civil Procedures, Article (203); and the Kuwaiti Code of Civil Procedures, Article (173). The latter legislation is modernized a further step, as the national court is prohibited from hearing the case ipso facto in case there is an arbitration clause and/or agreement, without a need to be raised by either party as stipulated in the former countries' legislation.

ii) any place where a substantial part of the obligations of the commercial relationship is to be performed or the place with which the subject-matter of the dispute is most closely connected; or

c) the parties have expressly agreed that the subject matter of the arbitration agreement relates to more than one party.[93]

The definition pointed to two criteria: The first relates to parties who have places of business in different states, and this is a clear example of internationality when it is related to the parties. The second criterion is the internationality of the dispute itself, when, for instance, the place with which the subject matter of the dispute is most closely connected may be foreign to the parties. Further, the parties may choose a foreign place of arbitration, or they may have expressly agreed that the subject matter of the arbitration is related to more than one country, meaning that this subject matter has an international character.[94]

The French Code of Civil Procedures, as amended in January 2011, provides that "arbitration is international when it involves the interests of international trade."[95] This wide interpretation is able to include various transactions in the future. This is a favourable legislative policy adopted by the French legislature to include such transactions that have an international element.

The Egyptian Arbitration Act 1994 pointed out the same elements as the UNCITRAL Model Law; the Egyptian legislature added the case if the parties to an arbitration agreed to refer the dispute to a permanent arbitral institution or arbitration centre that is either inside the Arab Republic of Egypt or outside.[96]

It is recommended that the definition to the arbitration process should be international if it includes an international element, which reflects the transnational character of the dispute.

The meaning of *commercial* usually refers to a subject matter of a commercial character. In civil law jurisdictions, trade legislation enumerated commercial transactions that have such a nature and made a distinction between the latter transactions and civil transactions.[97] The significance of this distinction is that commercial transactions are subject to simple rules in evidence law and in prescription as a wellknown concept related to the expiry of substantial rights after a certain period of time.

The Model Law states:

> The term 'Commercial' should be given a wide interpretation so as to cover matters arising from all relationships of a commercial nature, whether contractual or not. Relationships of a commercial nature include, but are not limited to, the following transactions: any trade transaction for the supply or exchange of goods or services; distribution agreement; commercial representation or agency; factoring; leasing; construction of works; consulting; engineering; licensing; investment; financing; banking; insurance; exploitation agreement or concession; joint venture and other forms of industrial or business co-operation; carriage of goods or passengers by air, sea, rail or road.[98]

---

93 UNCITRAL Model Law, Article (1(3)).

94 Redfern and Hunter 2009: 12.

95 Article 1492 of the French Code of Civil Procedure as amended by Article (1504) on 13 January 2001. See also: Redfern and Hunter 2009: 10; Fouchard, Gaillard et Goldman 1999.

96 Egyptian Arbitration Act, Article (3).

97 Egyptian Trade Law No. 17 of 1999.

98 UNCITRAL Model Law, footnote to Article (1(1)).

The Egyptian Arbitration Act stipulates that:

> an arbitration is commercial if the dispute concerns a contractual legal relation which has an economic dimension whether contractual or not. This includes, but is not limited to, the supply of goods or services, commercial agencies, construction agreements, engineering or technical agreements, granting industrial or tourism or other licensing, transfer of technology, investment, development agreement, banking, insurance, transportation, exploration and exploitation of natural resources, energy supply, oil and gas pipelines agreements, highway and tunnels agreements, reclamation of agriculture lands, environment protection and nuclear reactor installation.[99]

The Egyptian and Omani legislators are more or less adopting the UNCITRAL approach with some modifications and alterations that are relevant to international business transactions, particularly international infrastructure agreements. International public works arbitration in Egypt falls within the definition of Articles (2) and (3) of the Egyptian Arbitration Act. The legislative policy behind this trend is to maintain a better atmosphere in the arbitral process that procures the increase of IFDI. After the promulgation of the Egyptian Arbitration Act of 1994, Egypt became the centre of international commercial arbitration of the Middle East under the auspices of CRCICA.

It is clear that the above- list is not exhaustive. Practice may add to this list various transactions such as PPPs and other transactions of a business or commercial nature.

Ad Hoc or Institutionalization of International Arbitration

Arbitration can be institutional or *ad hoc*; it is essential for the parties to determine which type is relevant for each case. *Ad hoc* arbitration is the form where the parties establish the arbitral process and all its determinants in the particular dispute. Conversely, if the parties have chosen a particular institution to govern the arbitration, the arbitration can take place at this institution pursuant to its rules. There are various reputable arbitral institutions worldwide such as the ICSID, ICC, LCIA, AAA, CRCICA and others. Each institution has its rules concerning procedures such as nomination and appointment of arbitrators, the degree of independence and impartiality of arbitrators and procedures of the arbitral tribunal during the hearings including, inter alia, the power of the tribunal to make orders concerning interim relief and how the arbitrators' fees are calculated. An ad hoc arbitration can be organized by the parties where they can select their own rules or refer to a particular set of institutional rules within their control. In fact, the latter process is to avoid the institution's cost. In case of absence of any agreement on the rules, arbitrators will refer to the *lex arbitri*. This technique can be adopted in small arbitrations; meanwhile, in huge monetary infrastructure arbitrations or even medium-sized claims, it is preferable that parties use a certain institution to govern the whole arbitral process in the light of its rules. To a great extent, this is a safeguard to promote a specific methodology that the parties agreed to in advance in their arbitration agreement, such as all the procedural rules of the said institution. Those procedures include various procedural matters such as the constitution of the arbitral tribunal and all the following procedures.[100]

---

99 Egyptian Arbitration Act, Article (2); for the same methodology, see: the Omani Arbitration Act, Article (2).

100 Lew, Mistelis and Kröll 2003: 31–40; Redfern and Hunter 1991; 2009; Fouchard, Gaillard et Goldman 1999; and in Arab doctrine, see: Ismail 2003a; Beriry 1995.

International Public Works Agreements states tend to select the institutional route as it is more convenient in Public Works Agreements, particularly if there is a possibility of a multiparty arbitration where the institution can be the appointing authority of the arbitral tribunal. Such mechanism is very well known in Public Works Agreements in state contracts as well as in construction contracts in private and commercial relations between private entities. The multilateral relations in a Public Works Agreement, for instance, between sovereign state and the contractor on the one hand and contractor and subcontractor on the other imply the necessity of the institutionalization of the arbitral process. In this context, the current trend is that all mediumsized and huge infrastructure projects where states or any of their public juristic entities are parties to the arbitration agreement stipulate that arbitration shall be held under the auspices of a particular institution. One may refer to the pivotal role of CRCICA as a reputable centre in the Middle East that has hosted thousands of arbitrations for three decades.

The International Chamber of Commerce (ICC) in Paris plays a significant role in arbitrations where Arab Middle Eastern states are involved with private foreign entities. When there is a dispute between different parties from different cultures, legal backgrounds, languages and different characteristics, the institutional rules of the ICC maintain good practice of the arbitral process despite the controversies between the disputing parties. As the ICC is a respected and reputable institution, it offers assistance to the process through the secretariat of the organization and the welldrafted set of arbitration rules by the most eminent experts in the field worldwide. Further, the unique function of the ICC court in its scrutiny of awards is a safeguard to a proper enforcement. Moreover, it procures consistency of the structure of the awards, which brings an element of certainty to the proceedings. The ICC respects to a great extent the autonomy principle as it allows the parties to choose the arbitrators, seat of arbitration, language, procedural and substantive laws. In addition, the ICC is located in France where the French Code of Civil Procedure, the new French Arbitration Act of 2011 and the French legal system emphasize the party autonomy principle. This is a fundamental principle in French law governing international business transactions and parties' choice to most issues of the arbitral process.[101] As a leading institution, the ICC has its regular publications and reports in the domain of international commercial arbitration. They periodically support the ICC rules as drafted by the most eminent practitioners and academics worldwide in the field.

Despite the above-mentioned advantages, some criticism is addressed to the ICC arbitration practice. It is argued that the administrative fees charged by the ICC are costly. They are collected in advance, and the interest accrued is not credited to the parties. The answer is that the fees are charged against an excellent and worthwhile service by a leading arbitral institution. Services provided by the ICC are the safeguard to the success of the arbitral process.

The Cairo Regional Centre for International Commercial Arbitration (CRCICA) plays a considerable role in supporting the arbitral process whether in international infrastructure disputes where states are involved or in various types of international commercial arbitration. CRCICA nowadays has a leading role in the region as the leading arbitral institution for the past three decades. It attracts disputing parties from all surrounding Arab countries. Most of the Egyptian government arbitrations were held under the auspices of the Cairo Centre, particularly state contracts with private foreign entities. The Centre now has credibility among foreign investors in Egypt in their disputes with the Egyptian government as it is an international organization with an international character and completely independent from any governmental influence. Further, the Centre played a significant role in codifying the Egyptian Arbitration Act in 1994, as it provided

101 Bunni 2005: 422–3.

the Egyptian legislature with eminent expertise in the field in the Middle East and provided the parliament with the appropriate approach as a result of long practice. It has its institutional rules that are unique in the Middle East and well respected by foreign investors as it fundamentally respects the party autonomy principle and allows, to some extent, the supportive and parallel role of the national courts to assist the arbitral process. The latter trend is exercised to the extent that is not violating the parties' choice to various elements of the process. It is of fundamental importance to highlight the fact that the Egyptian, Jordanian and Omani Arbitration Acts, as well as much other Arab legislation, were influenced, to a great extent, by the UNCITRAL Model Law. This is the sign of modernization and liberalization of the arbitration process in Arab Middle Eastern jurisdictions.

International Public Works Agreements in Standard Forms of Contracts

Various forms of construction contracts can be used in state infrastructure projects in developing Arab Middle Eastern countries. The most common in use in International Public Works Agreements and huge infrastructure projects are the FIDIC forms of contracts. The latter forms of contracts include special clauses for arbitration.

The FIDIC Form of Contracts Fourth Edition 1987 included arbitration as disputes settlement mechanism in clause 67.3. The 1999 Red Book, Yellow Book and Silver Book are the main instruments in the field, whether in practice or in academic research.[102]

The 1999 Red Book edition included in sub-clause 20.6 arbitration as a mechanism of disputes settlement in case of failure of amicable settlement by the parties. The 1999 Yellow Book included in sub-clause 20.2 details of disputes and arbitration; meanwhile, the 1999 Silver Book included in sub-clause 25.2.9 stipulations related to disputes and arbitration.

102 See, generally: Bunni 2005.

Chapter 13
Characteristics of International Public Works Disputes and Arbitrators

Given their special nature, International Public Works contracts require an arbitrator with specific qualifications. This chapter addresses the sole arbitrator system and the method whereby arbitrators are appointed.

Characteristics of Disputes Related to International Public Works Agreements

Disputes related to International Public Works Agreements are of a special nature, especially in light of the features that distinguish them from other contracts. Therefore, these features and characteristics should be reviewed to clarify them and to highlight the specifications required to be covered by the arbitrator in charge of settling disputes emanating from such contracts.

The special characteristics can be summed up as follows:[1]

1. International Public Works Agreements require numerous and different inputs to be delivered by suppliers and specialized entities that supply the project with various contracts, a matter which entails a series of sub-contractual arrangements, pertaining to the main project.
2. The contractor is required to coordinate with the various entities and the employer, together with the latter's employees, personnel and representatives; the engineer, architects and the employees thereof.
3. International Public Works Agreements contracts usually last for a long period of time. Starting with planning, placement of tender, through to the finalization of implementation, an International Public Works Agreements contract might last for several years, during which relations between the parties are scarcely calm or peaceful. This eventually gives rise to disputes during the implementation of the project between the parties to the main contract, or between the contractor and the subcontractors, or to a multilateral dispute between the contractor, the employer and one or more subcontractor(s).
4. An International Public Works Agreement should be completely finalized, even if a dispute arises during execution. This seems to be a recognized general rule in international public works contracts. This opinion finds ground in certain major contracts that provide for the impermissibility of initiating arbitration proceedings until after the completion of the contract.
5. The foregoing is duly provided for in the first and second editions of the FIDIC contracts. The third edition of the FIDIC 1977 provides that arbitration may only be initiated before the completion of execution. The FIDIC edition provides that arbitration proceedings may be initiated after the completion of performance of the contract in specific cases.[2]

---

1 Schneider 1984: 317.

2 Schneider 1984: 317.

6. A party to International Public Works Agreements is the state or a public juristic entity, the latter entity is almost always subject to certain rules and regulations promulgated by the state for the public persons thereof. The acts performed by the state, and the legislation promulgated thereby, represent an event of force majeure in certain contracts. No doubt the impact of such acts and how binding they are on other public law persons in the state and the contracts to which it is party have considerable significance, as this is a point that is usually raised in disputes related to International Public Works Agreements.
7. On the other hand, state agencies are mostly bureaucratic and sluggish in performance, especially when it comes to performance of payments due to the contractor so that the contractor can continue the works regularly. This represents one of the most significant roots of contention giving rise to arbitration in administrative contracts to which the state is party.
8. Disputes related to International Public Works Agreements initially focus on defective works, delay in execution and consequently liquidated damages, which are the points of importance for the state. The contractor, on the other hand, usually complains about the delays or insufficiency of payments, which find grounds in the agreement, or may claim additional payment in consideration of additional work performed or in consideration of a change of conditions that might cause economic imbalance in the contract.[3]
9. International Public Works Agreements are based on mutual contractual obligations between the contractor and the employer, whereby the former provides work in consideration of payments to be made by the latter in consideration of the work. On the other hand, such contracts have their special character in relation to the execution of the obligations contained therein, which are sometimes almost harmonized.

Execution of this kind of contract requires considerable co-operation between the employer and the contractor. The contractor should satisfy a number of elements that serve as grounds for the timing of completion and quality of works.

Accordingly, disputes are usually attributed to defective work or delayed execution, on the part of the employer or the contractor.

The essence of the contractual system in an international public works contract is based, to a great extent, on the idea of trust, where the contractor executes the contracted work and receives payment in consideration of the work performed and the satisfaction of the employer or the engineer in charge.

One of the key roots of contention in this kind of contract is the claim by the contractor for additional payments, either on grounds of the extension of execution, or additional work as a result of the foregoing, or for any other reasons. This can be due to change of circumstances during performance, which exhaust the contractor and negatively affect financial equilibrium or give rise to unforeseeable material difficulties that might lead to the aforementioned contractual imbalance.

Arbitral Tribunal in International Public Works Agreements

The arbitral tribunal constitutes either three arbitrators or a sole arbitrator. The sole arbitrator system, the earliest system, was provided for in Article (5) of the English Arbitration Act promulgated in 1950.

3 Schneider 1984: 317.

The foregoing suggests that the English legislature developed a general rule with the purpose that a sole arbitrator should be appointed or named to settle disputes

The English Arbitration Act 1996 stipulates in Article (15) that party autonomy is respected in terms of the freedom of the parties to agree on the number of arbitrators. In the case of the parties' failing to agree to the number of arbitrators, the tribunal shall consist of a sole arbitrator.

The French Code of Civil Procedures as amended on 13 January 2011 provides in Articles (1450) and (1451) that an arbitral tribunal may be constituted of a sole arbitrator or an odd number of arbitrators.

The UNCITRAL Arbitration Rules 1976 provide in Article (5) for the following: "If the parties have not previously agreed on the number of arbitrators (i.e. one or three), and if within fifteen days after the receipt by the respondent of the notice of arbitration the parties have not agreed that there shall be only one arbitrator, three arbitrators shall be appointed." The UNCITRAL Rules, as amended in 2010, stipulate: "If the parties have not previously agreed on the number of arbitrators, and if within 30 days after the receipt by the respondent of the notice of arbitration the parties have not agreed that there shall be only one arbitrator, three arbitrators shall be appointed."

Article (3) of the The London Court of International Commercial Arbitration (LCIA) rules preceding the latest rules enforced starting January 1998 provide that the expression "'court' includes the single arbitrator or all arbitrators in case more than one arbitrator are appointed."

The new ICC rules of 2008 stipulate in Article (2(i)) that "'Arbitral Tribunal' includes one or more arbitrators." The Egyptian Arbitration Act 27/1994 provides in Article (15) for the following: "The arbitral tribunal is composed, by agreement between the parties, of one arbitrator or more. In default of agreement on the number of arbitrators, the tribunal shall be composed of three arbitrators."

Egyptian legislation prefers three arbitrators in case the parties fail to agree. This could be attributed to the fact that the Egyptian legislation was recently promulgated, and thus it provides for this clause to accommodate recent intricate disputes – especially international public works contracts and related disputes of complicated character that require a tripartite arbitral tribunal of special expertise and skills.

The Three Arbitrator System

Most legislative systems provide that an arbitral tribunal should be composed of three arbitrators. Article (15) of the Egyptian Arbitration Law provides that in case the parties fail to agree on the number of arbitrators, the number of arbitrators shall be three.

Nevertheless, many laws require the number of arbitrators to be odd without specifying the exact number, thus leaving it to the consent of the parties, as is the case in new amendments to the French Civil Procedures Law in January 2011.

Article (15/2) of the Egyptian Arbitration Law provides the following: "If there is more than one arbitrator, the tribunal must, on pain of nullity, be composed of an odd number."

It is manifest from the foregoing that the Egyptian legislature takes as a general rule, in case the parties fail to agree, that the tribunal should be composed of three arbitrators. In all events, in case of more than one arbitrator, the number should be odd.

The Egyptian legislature provides that in case the number of arbitrators is not odd, the arbitration shall be null and void. Following are the various methods of appointment of arbitrators. Other Arab legislation, particularly Omani and Jordanian legislation, includes the same stipulations.

Methods of Appointing Arbitrators

There are various ways to appoint an arbitral tribunal. Arbitrators are in most cases selected, either upon the agreement of the parties concerned, or by a commercial association, professional organizations, arbitration organizations or the selected arbitrators. Finally, arbitrators may be appointed by national courts. Following is a review of the various ways whereby arbitrators are appointed.[4]

Appointment of Arbitrators by Agreement of the Parties

Appointment of arbitrators by the parties concerned is a common method, as it guarantees that parties select arbitrators upon their consent without intervention by third parties in the process of selection.

The parties' intention is clear in this method, as the essence of the arbitral process lies in the party autonomy. Since the arbitral tribunal derives its authority from the parties' consent, the best way is to have the arbitral tribunal directly appointed by those parties with no mediation.

It is preferable that in the case that the arbitrator is appointed upon agreement of the parties, such agreement should be reached after the dispute arises. The process of selection should be subject to negotiation among the parties and their legal representatives. Each party selects three or four nominees, viewed as appropriate to assume the role of arbitrator by referring to the expertise and qualifications of each, and names are exchanged for carrying out the selection process.

Another problem is that any of the arbitrators appointed as arbitrator may refuse to agree to a third arbitrator. This case is addressed by providing for a condition in the arbitral clause that stipulates that a third arbitrator should be appointed by an arbitration organization such as the ICC in Paris, or the President of the Cairo Regional Centre for International Commercial Arbitration (CRCICA), or the organization where the arbitration is seated as per the rules thereof, and this organization shall be agreed to in the arbitration clause.

In ad hoc arbitration, the *lex arbitri* (the seat of arbitration) that regulates the appointment process often provides that the appointment process should be undertaken by national courts. Nevertheless, appointment by national courts could result in the delay of the process due to the fact that national courts are overly occupied for deciding on several cases.

Appointment by Trade Associations and Professional Institutions[5]

Sometimes, the arbitral clause might provide for the appointment of arbitrator(s) by a trade association. This might take place at the request of the individual parties after the dispute arises. Professional institutions play a key role in this regard, as they have a roster of those viewed as appropriate to be nominated as arbitrators. A sole arbitrator or the third arbitrator is usually selected through any of these associations or institutions.

Arbitration Organizations

Each arbitral organization has its own rules, and when any organization appoints an arbitrator, it undertakes the appointment according to such special rules.

4 Redfern and Hunter1999, 3rd edition: 195.

5 Redfern and Hunter 1999, 3rd edition: 198.

For instance, the ICC Rules 2008 provide that in case there is a sole arbitrator, and the parties fail to appoint him or her within 30 days following the date of commencement of the claim for arbitration by the other party, the ICC shall appoint the arbitrator. These rules also provide that in case there is an arbitral tribunal made up of three arbitrators, the third arbitrator shall be appointed by the ICC, unless the parties appoint that person within the set time frame[6] (Article 8(3)(4)).

On the other hand, the ICSID rules provide that the Secretary General of the Centre is the authority who appoints arbitrators in ad hoc arbitrations that do not fall within the scope of the ICSID treaty, in case a party to the dispute is a governmental party.

Appointment of arbitrators by arbitration organizations has many advantages because of the fact that since such organizations work on a continual basis in international arbitration, they are fully knowledgeable about all the requirements and qualifications of the arbitrator to be appointed. These organizations usually have the names and qualifications of arbitrators in the various fields; thus they are highly ready to provide the service in relation to these fields.

Appointment by the Arbitrators Selected by the Parties

Appointment in this case is undertaken by the arbitrators already selected, where the two arbitrators appoint the third arbitrator who is the presiding arbitrator. This is an adopted rule per the rules of the UNCITRAL, the ICC and the LCIA.

For instance, Article (7(3)) of the UNCITRAL Rules 1976 provides for the following: "If within thirty days after the appointment of the second arbitrator the two arbitrators have not agreed on the choice of the presiding arbitrator, the presiding arbitrator shall be appointed by an appointing authority in the same way as a sole arbitrator would be appointed under Article 6."

The new 2010 version of the Rules stipulates in Article (9(3)) a similar provision to the above-mentioned clause. Article (9) referred to Article (8), which stipulated certain steps to be followed.

This is the most common method in operation, as it secures fair selection of the presiding arbitrator, given the fact that the presiding arbitrator is selected by the two arbitrators who were previously selected by the parties.

It is presumed that this is the right solution for settling the issue of selecting the third arbitrator, as both arbitrators select him. In case they fail within the period of time specified, starting from the date of appointing the second arbitrator, an arbitration organization shall select the third arbitrator within the period to be specified, either in the arbitration clause or the arbitration agreement.

Appointment by National Courts[7]

National courts shall appoint arbitrators, in case they have the jurisdiction and power of appointment. In case national courts satisfy these two elements, the approval by the parties may not be necessary.

National courts shall have jurisdiction in the case that the arbitration is conducted on their territory. Accordingly, in the case that the seat of arbitration is provided for in the arbitration clause or the arbitration agreement, no problem would arise, as the party who wishes to commence the arbitration proceedings shall resort to the competent national court for appointment.

As for the other assumption pertinent to the absence of provision for the seat of arbitration in the arbitration clause or agreement, the party who wishes to resort to arbitration may claim jurisdiction.

---

6 ICC Rules, 2/3 and 2/4.

7 Redfern and Hunter 1999, 3rd edition: 200.

In case the contractor wishes to sue the employer (the state), the contractor shall attempt to claim that national courts have jurisdiction on the ground that the governing law is the law enforceable in the respondent state on the territory in which the dispute is seated.

The contractor may also claim that the courts of the respondent state, being the home courts of the respondent, are the courts having jurisdiction of appointment.

Both arguments are acceptable in the counter-assumption, in the case that the state wishes to resort to arbitration versus the contractor; it may resort to the state courts having the governing law of the subject matter of the dispute for appointment. Such a state could be the contractor's country or any other country. In most cases, the state requests to have its courts as the courts having jurisdiction to undertake the appointment, as the state usually wants to have its law as the governing law of the subject matter of the dispute, and this usually agrees with the essence of the idea of the administrative contract,[8] which does not accommodate a law other than its national law to govern the dispute.

Appointment of Arbitrators in Arab Legislation

Article (17) of the Egyptian Arbitration Act provides that the parties to arbitration may agree on the selection of arbitrators and on the manner and time of their selection. In default of such agreement, the legislature differentiates between two assumptions:

1. If the arbitral tribunal is composed of a sole arbitrator, the court referred to in Article (9) of this law (Cairo Court of Appeals or any other court of appeals) shall select that person on the basis of a request by one of the parties.

2. If the arbitral tribunal is composed of three arbitrators, each of the parties shall select one arbitrator and the two appointed arbitrators thus shall select a third. If either party fails to appoint his arbitrator within 30 days from being requested to do so by the other party, or if the two arbitrators fail to select a third arbitrator within the 30 days following the appointment of the more recently appointed one, the court referred to in Article (9) shall undertake to make such selection on the basis of a request by one of the parties. The arbitrator selected by the two arbitrators appointed as aforesaid or by the court shall preside over the arbitral tribunal. These provisions shall apply to cases where the arbitral tribunal is composed of more than three arbitrators.

   The court shall, upon selecting the arbitrator, observe the requirements of this law. The law requires that the court rapidly passes its decision, and that such decision of appointment is incontestable in any way of appeal whatsoever. The foregoing shall be observed without prejudice to the revocation and removal cases set out in Articles (18) and (19).

   The Administrative Court shall have jurisdiction regarding the foregoing in case same is required by the nature of the dispute in question.

On the other hand, the power for appointment usually raises no issues when it comes to practical application; so long as the jurisdiction is satisfied, appointment is easily carried out.

8 See: the opinion of the General Assembly of the Egyptian State Council of 1989 and 1993, whereby arbitration may be conducted on administrative contracts within the framework of the meritorious regulations of the theory of administrative contract.

The Jordanian Arbitration Act of 2001 stipulates in Article (14) that the arbitral tribunal is composed by the agreement of the parties from one or more arbitrators. If the parties have not agreed to the number, arbitrators shall be three. If there is more than one arbitrator, the tribunal shall consist of an odd number; otherwise the arbitration shall be null and void.

The 1997 Omani Arbitration Act stipulates in Article (15) that the arbitral tribunal is composed according to the parties' agreement for one arbitrator or more. If there is no agreement by the parties to the number of arbitrators, the tribunal shall consist of three arbitrators. If there is more than one arbitrator, the number of arbitrators must be an odd number; otherwise, the arbitration shall be null and void.

The Tunisian Arbitration Act, Article (18) stipulates that the arbitral tribunal must consist of an odd number. Some other countries' legislations stipulate that if there is more than one arbitrator, the tribunal must consist of an odd number of arbitrators (Syrian Code of Civil Procedures, Article (511) and Libyan Code of Civil Procedure, Article (744)).

In Algerian law, the legislature stipulates that the arbitration agreement must determine the substance of disputes and the arbitrator's name; otherwise it shall be null and void. Meanwhile, the Lebanese Arbitration Act referred in Article (810) completely to the arbitration agreement to determine the methodology of constituting the arbitral tribunal.

It is clear that all Arab legislation supersedes party autonomy in constituting the arbitral tribunal. In all cases, the tribunal must consist of an odd number; otherwise the arbitration shall be null and void.

Qualifications of Arbitrators in International Public Works Agreements

Disputes related to international public works contracts are characterized by specific features. Therefore, the qualifications required to be satisfied by the arbitrator deciding on disputes of the kind should be in tandem with such features. Arbitrators in international works contracts should be specially qualified, so as to manage at the end to perform their mission by passing a ruling that realizes the justice aspired to by the parties to the dispute.

Based on the foregoing, in modern Arab arbitration practice an arbitrator could be a legal arbitrator or otherwise. It might be required to have an engineer act as arbitrator in works contracts. The dispute may require a person versed in certain aspects of technical engineering that are not satisfied by others to decide thereupon.

In addition to the foregoing, in order for a legal arbitrator to be qualified to decide on a dispute arising from international works contracts, the arbitrator should be knowledgeable about international arbitration either through studying or practice. The arbitrator should also be versed in the general rules of private international law, as this will be of great help in specifying the law governing the subject matter of the contract and the law governing the arbitration proceedings.

Further, the arbitrator in the capacity of a de facto or a de jure judge is required to be versed in the theory, fundamentals and legal bases of contracts, together with the laws of evidence and the general theories thereof in order to base a conviction on the evidence produced by the parties.[9]

Deciding upon international contracts-related disputes requires the arbitrator to be highly informed and versed in other languages;[10] it is preferable that an arbitrator in this kind of contract

9 Stephenson 1993: 28.

10 Redfern and Hunter 1999: 206.

be conversant with the arbitration language. This is so that the arbitrator is able to review any documents relating to the dispute, submissions from the parties and the relevant references in a language other than his or her mother tongue. Finally, the foregoing is crucial for the arbitrator to be able to write the arbitral award should it need to be written in the arbitration language agreed by the parties.

An arbitrator in International Public Works Agreements should be knowledgeable about the related aspects of international and economic trade and well-versed in the legal system that the parties wish to apply to the subject matter of the contract. The arbitrator also needs to know whether it belongs to the civil law system or the common law system, in order to apply the legal rules to the facts of the dispute in a manner that realizes justice between the parties to the dispute.

The arbitrator must also not be party to the dispute under consideration, or to have any personal interested in it,[11] or have previously exercised an option on the contract.[12]

Similarly, the engineer who supervises the process or who prepared for performance may not serve as arbitrator in a dispute arising between the employer and the contractor who performs the said process, as the engineer, as such, would have supervised the performance of the contractor, which would render the engineer party to the tabled dispute.

Challenging Arbitrators

An arbitrator is practically a judge, satisfying the conditions of impartiality and independence required by a judge. The arbitrator, upon appointment, should be independent of the parties to the dispute and should not receive any instructions from them.

The Arbitrators' Impartiality and Independence in Various Jurisdictions

Independence, as defined by Redfern and Hunter, means the absence of any financial relationship or any other relationship between the arbitrator and any of the parties. Partiality, on the other hand, means the existence of a relationship between one arbitrator and either party to the dispute.

It is deemed necessary by some that no relationship or interest whatsoever should exist between any arbitrator and any of the parties to the dispute; the arbitrator, thus, should not be a friend or relative of any of the parties. The arbitrator should not have any previous relationship or acquaintance with the merits of dispute,[13] or any financial interest whatsoever related to the subject matter of the dispute or any of the parties thereto.

The rule of impartiality and independence of arbitrators resonates in the rules of the UNICTRAL, ICC, LCIA and all Arab legislation.

UNCITRAL Rules[14] provide that any arbitrator may be challenged if circumstances exist that give rise to justifiable doubts as to the arbitrator's impartiality or independence. The ICC rules[15] provide that every arbitrator must be and remain independent of the parties involved in the

---

11 Al-Tihyewi 1994: 631; El Wafa 1988: 158.

12 See: the ruling of the Administrative Appeal Court – Contracts Circuit, Appeal No. 4860/49, unpublished.

13 Stephenson 1993: 27–8.

14 Article (10) of the UNCITRAL Rules 1976 and Articles (11–13) of the UNCITRAL Rules as amended in 2010.

15 Article (11) of the 2008 ICC Rules.

arbitration. They also provide for the possibility of challenging the arbitrator if he or she loses any independence from the parties to the dispute, as well as in other cases.

The LCIA Rules[16] provide that all members of the arbitral tribunal should be impartial and independent, and they are not required to be attorneys acting for the parties.

French law requires that arbitrators should satisfy the conditions of impartiality and independence, as the French Code of Civil Procedures provides in that in the case that an arbitrator is not impartial, this might serve as grounds for setting aside the arbitral award, should such an award be passed in France. The same situation exists in the new amended French legislation of 13 January 2011.

The aforementioned legislation has made considerable strides in international arbitration and has required a high degree of impartiality and independence on the part of the arbitrators.

The English Arbitration Act promulgated in 1950 provides in Article (23) that an arbitrator is revoked in the case of misconduct during proceedings, thus implying lack of impartiality and independence *vis-à-vis* the parties to the dispute.[17]

The new English Arbitration Act promulgated in 1996 provides in Article (24(1)(a)) for the same. In Egypt, Article (18) of the Egyptian Arbitration Law 27/1994 provides for the following:

1. An arbitrator may only be revoked if serious circumstances casting doubts on his impartiality and independence are established.

2. Neither party to the arbitration may revoke the arbitrator that such party appoints or takes part in the appointment thereof except for a reason that becomes unveiled after such appointment takes place.

The purport of the foregoing is that an arbitrator may only be revoked if that person's impartiality or independence is proved to be absent. Further, the parties to the arbitration may not, jointly or severally, revoke the arbitrator unless the reason for such revocation takes place after the appointment is made.

It is manifest that all Arab legislation adopted the same legislative policy as that adopted by the UNCITRAL Rules, which require, in turn, as an imperative procedure that serious doubts should be established regarding the arbitrator's impartiality and independence. It is appropriate to refer to the Omani Act, Articles (18), (19); the Jordanian Act of 2001, Articles (17), (18); the Tunisian Act, Articles (21), (22); the Kuwaiti Code of Civil Procedures, Article (178); the Lebanese Code of Civil Procedures, Article (770); the Libyan Code, Article (748); the Syrian Code, Articles (515), (516).

Upon reviewing the comparative legislation and the most operative rules in international arbitration, it becomes obvious that arbitration in international works contracts, representing a significant part of international arbitration, requires a high degree of impartiality and independence. An arbitrator should be impartial *vis-à-vis* the parties to the dispute; and upon the appointment, that person is supposed to be independent thereof, as he or she is similar to a judge who does not represent either litigant. Rather, the arbitrator becomes part of the impartial independent arbitral tribunal, which continues to consider the dispute in the light of the documents that furnish the facts of the dispute, in order to reach a binding award that realizes the justice aspired to.

16 Article (3) of the LCIA old rules, and Articles (5/3) and (10) of the new rules of 1998.

17 Mustill and Boyd 1989: 247–57.

Procedures of Challenging – the Policy Adopted by the Egyptian Legislature

An arbitrator's impartiality and independence are among the most significant pillars of the arbitration process, including arbitration in international public works contracts. Thus, the revocation procedures in international arbitration are the same procedures adopted in international public works contracts arbitration.

These procedures are usually mainstreamed in the legal system of the given country, seat of arbitration, or in the arbitration rules selected by the individuals. In this regard, reference will be made to the revocation and removal procedures in comparative legislation; then to international practice and usage; and, finally, the Egyptian legislation in the light of the Arbitration Law. The English Arbitration Act of 1996 addresses the same issue in Article (24) thereof.

Arab Arbitration Acts, particularly by the Egyptian legislature, provide in the new Arbitration Law, Article (19), for the following:

1. A motion for revocation shall be submitted to the arbitral tribunal in writing stating the reasons for revocation within fifteen days as of the date of the applicant's knowledge of the constitution of this tribunal or of the conditions justifying revocation. In case the arbitrator requested to be revoked does not step aside, the arbitral tribunal shall decide upon the application for revocation.

2. Revocation requested by a party who previously applied for the revocation of the same arbitrator in the same arbitration shall be dismissed.

3. The applicant of revocation may appeal against the decision dismissing the application thereof within thirty days as of the date of being informed of dismissal before the court referred to in Article (9) hereof. The decision passed by the said court shall be incontestable.

4. Application for revocation or appeal against the arbitral award dismissing same shall not give rise to suspension of arbitration proceedings. In case an arbitrator is decided to be revoked, either by the arbitral tribunal or the court upon considering the appeal, this will eventually render the arbitral procedures taken, including the arbitrators' award, as null and void.

This Article regulates the revocation and removal procedures and provides that the award whereby the arbitrator is revoked issued by either the arbitral tribunal or the court upon considering the appeal shall render the arbitral proceedings taken thus far as null and void including the arbitrator's award. Meanwhile, it does not provide for the suspension of the arbitral proceedings upon the application for revocation or the appeal against the arbitral award dismissing revocation.

UNCITRAL and ICC Rules

The UNCITRAL Model Law, on the other hand, provides in Article (13) that the parties are free to agree on a procedure for challenging an arbitrator, subject to the provisions of paragraph (3) of this Article.

Failing such agreement, a party who intends to challenge an arbitrator shall, within 15 days after becoming aware of the constitution of the arbitral tribunal or after becoming aware of any circumstance referred to in Article (12(2)), send a written statement of the reasons for the challenge to the arbitral tribunal. Unless the challenged arbitrator withdraws from office or the other party agrees to the challenge, the arbitral tribunal shall decide on the challenge. Sub-clause (3) of the same Article provides that if a challenge under any procedure agreed upon by the parties or under the procedure of paragraph (2) of this Article is not successful, the challenging party may request, within 30 days after having received notice of the decision rejecting the challenge, the court or other authority specified in Article (6) to decide on the challenge, which decision shall be subject to no appeal; while such a request is pending, the arbitral tribunal, including the challenged arbitrator, may continue the arbitral proceedings and make an award. After the issuance of this award, the arbitral tribunal shall resume the arbitral proceedings.

The superseded ICC Rules provide in Article (2(8)) that a challenge of an arbitrator, whether for an alleged lack of independence or otherwise, is made by submitting to the Secretary General of the court a written statement specifying the facts and circumstances on which the challenge is based. The same is stated in the amended version of the ICC Rules as of 2008, Article (11).

In order for the application for revocation to be acceptable, it should be sent by the applicant for revocation within 30 days as from receipt by the same party of the appointment of the arbitrator requested to be revoked officially by the court or within 30 days as of the date of knowledge by the applicant for revocation of the circumstances and conditions giving rise to revocation.

The foregoing shows that the revocation of an arbitrator, due to lack of independence of the parties to the dispute, or lack of impartiality, has gained the attention of arbitration rules in major arbitration organizations regarding revocation procedures, periods and the authorities entrusted with deciding upon the matter in case the arbitral tribunal fails to decide thereupon.

The foregoing applies to International Public Works Agreements. The Arab judiciary requires a high degree of impartiality to be satisfied by the arbitrator in such contracts. These contracts constitute a significant part of the state's plan for development, and many such contracts are related to infrastructure. This consequently impacts the economic and social infrastructure of the state. It requires the arbitrator in any dispute arising from any of these contracts to be absolutely impartial and independent.

Arab legislation provides in the Arbitration Acts for revocation and removal procedures that are applied by the Egyptian judiciary in its latest judgments, which imply the requirement thereby of a high degree of impartiality and independence to be satisfied by the arbitrator, especially in public works contracts. Therefore, it can be concluded that the arbitrator is a judge in the true sense of the word.

Chapter 14
Multiparty Arbitration in International Public Works Agreements

Multiparty arbitration gives rise to many issues related to practical application in these contracts. Such issues often arise from international public works contracts that require special skill, starting with agreement on the wording of the contract and the arbitration clause, and ending with the issuing of an award that realises the justice to which the parties to the dispute aspire.

This chapter deals with the definition of multiparty arbitration in international public works contracts and its significance. It scrutinizes the issues raised by multiparty arbitration in international works contracts, with special focus on the issue of appointment of arbitrators and the constitution of the arbitral tribunal in cases where the number of arbitrators exceeds one. In the course of studying this issue, the Dutco case is duly analyzed, including the solution proposed by the ICC in Paris and the author's opinion regarding the foregoing.

Definition of Multiparty Arbitration in International Public Works Agreements

Multiparty arbitration means that arbitration in a particular case involves more than two parties. This is manifest in International Public Works Agreements. When the state sues the contractor, the latter, in turn, has recourse to the sub-contractors and suppliers, thus highlighting the significance of multiparty arbitration.

In cases where the state sues the main contractor, that person, in turn, sues the sub-contractors and suppliers through other separate *ad hoc* arbitrations. Nevertheless, it is better to decide upon such disputes and sub-disputes by way of a single arbitral tribunal. First, multiparty arbitration can avoid inconsistent findings that might overcomplicate the process, particularly in terms of enforcement. Furthermore, deciding on all these disputes via one arbitral tribunal saves time, effort and expenses that could have been expended in several separate *ad hoc* arbitrations.

This has eventually given rise to the significance of multiparty arbitration, which addresses the attempt at compromising inconsistent findings that are unenforceable and that may overcomplicate the process instead of settling it. The English judiciary stressed, not very long ago, the significance of avoiding the issuance of contradictory awards in separate *ad hoc* arbitrations.[1] This is illustrated by many examples; some of them are explained below.

The ADGAS Arbitration[2]

The facts of this case could be summed up as follows: the ADGAS Company filed arbitration against the main contractor (a US contracting company) regarding a public works contract in Abu

1 *Abu Dhabi Gas Liquefaction co. Ltd. v. Eastern Bechtel Corporation* (1982), 2 Lloyd's Rep. 425, 427.

2 Referred to in Redfern and Hunter 1999, 3rd edition: 177–8.

Dhabi on the basis that the tanks built to keep gas were defective. However, the US contractor denied ADGAS's claim, indicating that if there were error in this concern, it should be attributed to the Japanese sub-contractor who supplied and installed the tanks.

The ADGAS Company, owner of the gas factory, filed an *ad hoc* arbitration in London before a sole arbitrator against the main contractor of the US company, which, in turn, filed a separate arbitration against the Japanese sub-contractor, regarding the sub-contract also made between it and the latter in London.

The employer refused to involve the sub-contractor in the joint arbitration; the same refusal was made by the Japanese sub-contractor.

The Court of Appeals in the United Kingdom decided that if there are three parties to a dispute brought before the English court, it is inevitable that all three parties appear before the court in the same dispute and proceedings. However, if the dispute is to be settled by way of arbitration, arbitration procedures may not be consolidated in one dispute to be considered together, without the consent of the parties, which is one of the key elements for the arbitral process.

Nevertheless, the US contractor filed an application to the court for the appointment of a sole arbitrator to decide on both disputes in one award. The court concluded that it is preferable to settle the matter by a single arbitration that leads to one award on both, to avoid inconsistent findings that might arise in case the matter is settled by way of two separate arbitrations.[3]

Given the foregoing, it becomes obvious that a multiparty arbitration is of paramount importance to reach a solution for settling separate disputes among more than two parties. This is often the case in international public works contracts, which are usually complicated and interrelated among more than two parties. Therefore, settling the matter in a single arbitration seems convenient and avoids inconsistent findings, a matter that gives rise to numerous complications in the actual enforcement of these awards.

Multiparty Arbitration for Parties to International Public Works Agreements[4]

The mechanism of a multiparty arbitration can best be construed by considering the position of the employer, the main contractor and the sub-contractor in an attempt to learn the perspective of each to this kind of arbitration and jurisprudence of this kind of contract.

The importance attached by the employer to multiparty arbitration is not in any sense less than that attached by the main contractor and sub-contractor. All that is sought by the employer is to prove the liability by the main contractor *vis-à-vis* the claims attributed to the former. Nevertheless, the employer may not be able to prove the main contractor liable for all the omissions committed by the sub-contractors.[5]

Therefore, in case the work is not satisfactory to the employer, it will be imperative to commence arbitration proceedings against the main contractor, whereas the latter would have thus digressed from the subject matter of the contract.

If the main contractor argues that the matter does not fall within the scope of his responsibility, and that it is the responsibility of a sub-contractor, it shall be eventually and imperatively incumbent

3 It seems to me highly desirable that this should be done so as to avoid inconsistent findings. Lord Denning, *Abu Dhabi Gas Liquefaction Co. Ltd. v. Eastern Bechtel Corporation* (1982), Lloyd's Rep. 425, 427.

4 Lloyd 1991: 61.

5 Lloyd 1991: 61, 64.

on the employer to take procedures against the sub-contractor due to the breach by the latter of the contract between same and the employer.

The main contractor has positive interest in a single tribunal hearing and deciding upon the dispute involving him- or herself, the employer and the sub-contractor, especially if he wishes to prove the error of the sub-contractors to avoid liability for omission attributed thereto. However, this position on the part of the main contractor might change if such arbitration adversely affects the main contractor by proving his or her omission *vis-à-vis* the employer on the grounds that the main contractor should have furnished the sub-contractor with instructions or directives to accomplish the job as desired, yet failed to do so. This eventually renders the main contractor liable for all works *vis-à-vis* the employer.[6]

The sub-contractor might be interested in a single tribunal that always depends on the right of the sub-contractor to receive amounts due.[7] In case this right to receive payments due is conditional upon the receipt by the main contractor of the amounts due, the former shall certainly be interested in securing a procedural method whereby the main contractor is involved in his or her claim versus the employer, which shall include the sub-contractor's claim.

In case the sub-contractor's claim is dependent on success in proving that the main contractor is the serious guarantor of payment by the employer, sub-contractors shall have their claims:

1. Against the main contractor, who will be liable either with or without having recourse on the employer: An example of this is illustrated when it is claimed that the work due by the sub-contractor is delayed, which depends on the proof by the main contractor that the reason for delay is something attributed to the employer, to which the former could be held liable.

2. Against the main contractor when the sub-contractor is either:

    a) not liable *vis-à-vis* the employer because the main contractor will not sustain any damages except for the amount that he or she might pay to the sub-contractor; or
    b) responsible for the remaining liability only because the main contractor's loss represents a minimal portion of the sub-contractor's loss.[8]

The agreement made with the sub-contractor may contain provisions whereby the sub-contractor selects three types of procedure:

1. Direct arbitration against the main contractor regarding matters where the main contractor is exclusively liable *vis-à-vis* the sub-contractor.
2. A claim against the main contractor, or that the dispute should be brought before the competent arbitrator to decide upon the main contract disputes due to the existence of a relationship between this dispute, the main contract, and the arbitration related to the latter.
3. A direct claim against the employer but through the main contractor when the sub-contractor is entitled to use the name of the main contractor to motion the main contractor's arbitration against the employer and take the appropriate procedures for him- or herself.[9]

---

6 Lloyd 1991: 61, 64.
7 Lloyd 1991:.61, 65.
8 Lloyd 1991: 61, 65.
9 Lloyd 1991: 61, 65.

In addition to the foregoing, the contract between the main contractor and the sub-contractor may provide for the sub-contractor's right to employ the same rights and benefits enjoyed by the main contractor *vis-à-vis* the employer.

The model of the sub-contractor's contract regarding the civil engineering work[10] includes similar provisions, yet simpler. The significance of this model lies in the intense use thereof at the international level, especially if the main contract is a FIDIC contract, which is accompanied by the said model in the majority of cases.

Issues Raised by Multiparty Arbitration in International Public Works Agreements

The constitution of the arbitral tribunal in multiparty arbitration might cause complications in cases of tripartite courts. In ordinary arbitration, each party to the dispute selects an arbitrator, and then both arbitrators choose a presiding arbitrator (third arbitrator). However it is totally different in multiparty arbitration. In FIDIC contracts, a dispute might arise between the employer and the main contractor, who in turn refers to the sub-contractor; thus there are three parties to the dispute.

How is a Tripartite Arbitral Tribunal Selected?

Would the employer select an arbitrator while the main contractor and the sub-contractor select another? Or will this option be unfair for both of them, in case of conflict of interests between them.

What is the criterion whereby each party shall be enabled to select an arbitrator? Is it the criterion of common interest of each party? If two parties have a common interest, they might, rather, appoint one arbitrator to represent their common interests.

However, the complication surfaces the most in consortium contracts,[11] where a project is usually executed by more than one company, and a dispute might arise between some of these companies or between the companies on the one hand and the employer and certain sub-contractors on the other. This gives rise to the same issue related to the method whereby the arbitral tribunal is to be chosen by all parties to the dispute in order to achieve equality, fairness and justice as much as possible among the litigants regarding the selection of arbitrators. To settle this issue, we selected a famous example which wrecked havoc in practical application, namely the Dutco case.

The *Dutco Case*[12]

The facts of this case could be summed up as follows: BKMI (a German company) entered into a consortium agreement with Siemens (a German company) and Dutco Company (a company incorporated and organized under the laws of Abu Dhabi) to execute the turnkey contract of a cement factory for the employer from the Sultanate of Oman.

The consortium agreement included an arbitration clause that provided that in the case that a dispute arises between the parties to the agreement which is not amicably settled, it shall be settled

10 The Federation of Civil Engineering Contractors (FCEC).

11 Sarie El Din 1996: 218; see also: Ismail 2003b: 474.

12 Sarie El Din 1996: 217.

by way of the rules of conciliation and arbitration of the ICC by three arbitrators, and Paris shall be the seat of arbitration.

A dispute indeed arose between Dutco and the other two companies. Dutco requested to resort to arbitration and appointed an arbitrator on its part. Nevertheless, BKMI and Siemens objected, requesting that Dutco file a separate *ad hoc* arbitration for each of them. The ICC asked both objecting companies to appoint one arbitrator for both of them; the two companies accepted together while preserving their rights.

The arbitral tribunal issued an interim award regarding jurisprudence where it clarified that the parties to the dispute have a common interest in settling the dispute by way of multiparty arbitration due to the character of the consortium agreement that involves the likelihood of a dispute arising in such a manner. Further, the arbitration clause referred to the ICC in general and was not singled out from multiparty arbitration. Therefore, the dispute was perceived to be settled by multiparty arbitration.

The arbitral tribunal also added that the phrase *each party* in Article (2(4)) of the ICC Rules involves reference to one or more claimant(s) and one or more respondent(s) and is to be construed according to the surrounding conditions as the right of each party to select an arbitrator is not absolute and may be waived.

In its ruling, the tribunal specified that compiling the fragments of the dispute in the procedures of one arbitration does not violate the rules of equity and equality among the parties to the dispute and does not involve any breach of internal French public policy or the rules of international public policy.

BKMI and Siemens resorted to the Paris Court of Appeals to revoke the preliminary award passed by the ICC and based on Article (1502(2)) and (1502(5)) of the French Civil Procedures Law on the grounds that the consortium agreement is totally free from any reference to multiparty arbitration. Moreover, BKMI and Siemens claimed that the rules of equality among individuals were violated per this ruling and consequently the international public policy rules, as both companies were deprived of the ability to appoint a special arbitrator, whereas Dutco managed to appoint an arbitrator.

The Paris Court of Appeals[13] passed a ruling on 5 May 1989 supporting the arbitral award issued by the ICC in Paris and rejecting the appeal filed by both companies and the two grounds thereof. Thus, it established the common intention of the parties to resort to multiparty arbitration using the arbitration clause included in the consortium agreement. The court also added that the constitution of the arbitral tribunal took place as per the ICC rules and decided that this constitution does not infringe the principle of equality among the parties in choosing their arbitrators although they appointed a common arbitrator for both of them.

The French Court of Cassation established in a leading ruling passed thereby[14] initially that the principle of equality among the parties to the dispute is a public order matter, and that this right to equality may not be waived prior to the dispute; it may only be waived after the dispute arises. The court concluded that the ruling of the Paris Court of Appeals involved a breach of the principle of equality that entails the revocation thereof.[15]

The track adopted by the ICC was similar to the direction adopted thereby previously for settling the same issue in similar cases.[16] The ICC issued a guide[17] at a date preceding the *Dutco*

---

13 Ruling of Paris Court of Appeal dated 5 May 1989.

14 Ruling of the French Court of Cassation dated 7 January 1992.

15 See the comment on this ruling: Delvolvé 1993:197; Sarie El Din 1996: 11; Schuartz,1993: 9; see also: Seppala 1993.

16 See: *Arab Republic of Egypt v. Westland Helicopters Ltd.* (Cour de Justice, Geneva, 26 November 1982, affirmed by the Tribunal fédéral Suisse, 16 May 1983).

17 Guide to Multi-Party Arbitration under the (4) Rules of the ICC Court of Arbitration, ICC publication No. 404.

case that included a solution for this issue. In this guide, the ICC stated that all arbitrators should be appointed by the International Court of Arbitration without any of the parties having the authority to appoint arbitrators, especially in international construction and works contracts and industrial establishment contracts.

In a report by the Paris ICC[18] on multiparty arbitration, the ICC stressed the same purport stated thereby in its previous report: as the ICC is responsible for appointing the court of arbitration in case the same cannot be achieved by the parties to the dispute.

It is recommended that this is the best approach that should be adopted. In consolidation of this view, all parties should, upon formulating the arbitration clause in any FIDIC contract, provide that in case of multiparty arbitration, there should be an appointing authority. For example, if the arbitration is conducted pursuant to the CRCICA, the CRCICA should appoint the arbitral tribunal whether constituted with a sole arbitrator or three arbitrators. This approach will save the parties to the dispute the issue of the method whereby the arbitral tribunal is constituted and the issues raised by this process when a dispute arises among more than two parties, which often happens in FIDIC contracts, especially considering that the Egyptian Arbitration Law is silent regarding multiparty arbitration.

Finally, it is suggested that multiparty arbitration should be multi-institutional. The organization under which the arbitration is conducted is usually the appointing authority.[19] This is to avoid issues that might arise regarding the appointing authority, so that the contract provides for the institution or the organization serving as the seat for arbitration as per the rules thereof.

18 Commission on International Arbitration (meeting of 28 April 1994). Final report on Multi-Party Arbitration. Report by the working group approved by the commission. Submitted to the 77th session of the executive board, Paris, 14 June 1994.

19 See: Ismail 1996; see also: Lloyd n.d.: 61.

Chapter 15
Mechanisms of Disputes Settlement in International Public Works Agreements

FIDIC Form of Contracts

This chapter discuss the methods of dispute settlement in international norms and practices. Toward this end, it is imperative to tackle certain contracts with special focus on FIDIC contracts due to the major significance attached to such contracts in practical application and the practical issues raised thereby that should be decisively settled at the local and international levels.

In an attempt to settle practical issues arising from FIDIC-related dispute settlement, it is appropriate to Clause 67 of these contracts, 4th edition, to explain the engineer's role and whether that person is an arbitrator or a quasi-arbitrator, together with the legal nature of the decisions passed thereby. The chapter deals with the time bar provided for in the 4th edition (1987) of Article (67) and Clause 20 of the new edition (1999), the legal nature of these time limits and the consequences of not following these time bars, together with the possibility of resorting to the national judiciary in case of missing the said limits.

The Engineer's Role under Clause 67 of the FIDIC Contract (4th Edition)

The FIDIC contract is one of the most common contracts in the field of International Public Works Agreements. It is a well-known fact that the engineer's role in this model is very wide in scope as the engineer is the contract administrator (project manager), and some take the view[1] that he or she might, in addition, be a quasi-arbitrator, notwithstanding that he or she acts on the employer's behalf.

In civil law, the contractual relationship is established between the engineer and the employer and not the contractor. Under the same system, the engineer often exercises broad powers. Accordingly, the engineer has broad powers under FIDIC contracts.

Under the international system[2] of international public works and civil engineering agreements, the role of the engineer differs widely, as that person acts to a great extent as the employer's representative and is vested with the contractual powers assigned to the employer by virtue of the contract.

The engineer's jobs under an International Public Works Agreement differ in most legal systems: That person is responsible for the preliminary works of planning for the project and the required feasibility studies and is thus the planner of the project. During the execution of the project, the engineer acts on behalf of the employer in the relationship with the contractor, as he or she may make decisions related to the project planning, change or add work, and in the meantime, acts as supervisor of the work being done.

1 Nicklisch 1990: 322; Bunni 1997: 155.

2 Nicklisch 1990: 324.

In this sense, the engineer is a representative of the employer.[3] Under the FIDIC agreements, the engineer assumes a third job and is the administrator of the contract. In this regard, the engineer should be impartial, independent and totally neutral when dealing with the parties to the contract. One of the most significant jobs of the engineer in this concern is to issue performance certificates,[4] on the basis of which receipts are cashed. The engineer also approves the additional payments that might be claimed by the contractor and the additional time of performance, together with the additional work, and determines whether there are impediments hindering the progress of work.

Furthermore, the engineer, under the FIDIC contract, must make decisions to settle disputes between the parties to the contract, pursuant to Article (67) of the FIDIC contract. In case neither party challenges such decisions by requesting to resort to arbitration, the engineer's decision shall subsequently be deemed final and binding.

Commentators view that the engineer's role in this sense is a quasi-arbitral function. Toward the end of achieving the job, the engineer should be impartial when deciding upon disputes arising from international construction and civil engineering works contracts between the contractual parties. In this capacity, the engineer does not represent his or her personal interest, or the employer's interest, or the contractor's interest. The engineer should be impartial and completely independent when performing these duties and act as an impartial authority for dispute settlement.

The powers vested in the engineer, in order to be impartial under the English system, find their ground in the urgent need for an authority to make impartial decisions during the actual execution of the project. Therefore, several systems under which construction contracts models are created took into consideration the need for creating a decision-making authority for dispute settlement during the actual performance of the contract.

Public works contracts are characterized by long-term agreements; they involve considerable complications that could give rise to a lot of issues during execution. These contracts need effective decision-making authority during the period of execution of the project. Is the engineer, while exercising these powers, an arbitrator or a quasi-arbitrator?[5]

A scholarly opinion believes that the engineer is not an arbitrator, and that the final and binding decision is not an arbitral award. Under the Egyptian Arbitration and Arab Middle Eastern States laws, an arbitrator is supposed to be a person who is totally far from the legal relationship that gave rise to the dispute between the individuals; that fact is not satisfied by the engineer because that person is indeed the employer's representative in the execution of the contract in Arab countries' legal systems.

Whereas the engineer acts in favour of one of the parties, the engineer is as such not impartial or neutral *vis-à-vis* the parties to the dispute, as he or she falls short on the condition of impartiality *vis-à-vis* those two parties.

Moreover, the engineer is not required to observe any procedural rules upon issuing a decision. In this regard, the decision-making process differs from arbitration, which is characterized by procedural rules that contradict an arbitrator's functions and duties. It is unviable for the engineer's final and binding decision to serve as an arbitral award as it can hardly be a res judicata ruling or self-executing.

Last but not least, if the engineer's decision is final and binding, it becomes contestable by way of arbitration under Article (67(4)), which provides for the possibility of resorting to arbitration together with reserving the right to resort to the competent national court.[6]

---

3 Bunni 1997: 163.

4 See: FIDIC, 4th edition, 1987: Clause 60.

5 Bunni 1997: 182–3.

6 El Geddawy 1996. See, on the engineer's role: El-Kholy 1993: 22–23.

It is true that the engineer is not an arbitrator under Egyptian law or any Arab arbitration acts, since the engineer, while exercising all his or her powers, is the employer's representative.[7] In the case that the engineer only performs material works, then that individual is acting as contractor, whereas if such material works are mixed up with legal acts, the contract is a mixture of contracting and agency. This eventually requires that the provisions of both contracting and agency would apply. However, the element of contractor is prevalent; in case of conflict between provisions, the contracting agreement provisions shall prevail. It is inconceivable in this regard that the engineer would be vested with arbitral or quasi-arbitral competence, as the Arab judiciary requires a high degree of impartiality; therefore in the case that any of the arbitrators previously expressed an opinion in regard to the execution of the project, that arbitrator would have lost the condition of impartiality.[8] Accordingly, the engineer is not perceived to act as either arbitrator or quasi-arbitrator.

Article (6) of the Egyptian Arbitration Law provides for the following: "If the parties to arbitration agree to subject the legal relationship between them to the provisions of a model contract, an international convention, or another document, then the provisions of such a document, including those related to arbitration, must be enforced." This is recognition of the provision of Article (67) of the FIDIC contract. Therefore, it definitely does not recognize any arbitral or quasi-arbitral powers for the engineer. Rather, it draws on the provision of this Article in relation to the regulatory provisions to regulate the dispute settlement procedures whereby the engineer is empowered to make decisions, as we view them as preliminary, unless either party upon its own discretion deems it necessary to resort to arbitration, as Article (67) does not lend any qualification to the engineer's decisions. Subsequently, it is suggested to adapt these decisions in tandem with our legal system, which never gives room to any arbitral or quasi-arbitral capacities for the engineer, considering that individual is the representative of the employer in such contracts. As for the time limit set out in Article (67), such time limits are of an organizational nature, as will be discussed.

The Necessity of a Decision-Making Authority in Disputes Arising from Major Public Works and Civil Engineering Contracts

The powers with which the engineer is vested under the English system and which empower him or her to act impartially find their ground in the need for a decision-making authority during the actual execution of the project. Further, the discrepancy between legal systems of states where the engineer is accepted to be a decision-maker during the performance of the project, whereas this is unacceptable in some other systems, requires that a decision-making authority be created within a framework acceptable by all legal systems.

International public works and civil engineering contracts – like all long-term complicated agreements – have their own special design and formulation that require a decision-making authority during the performance of the contract and dispute settlement, at least temporary disputes, notwithstanding the kinds of disputes[9] that are likely to arise between the parties to the contract. Meanwhile, there should be a contract manager to supervise and ensure that performance shall take place by professional experts in the field. In addition to this, this authority should be totally aware of the technical and contractual aspects, as well as the various aspects that might arise during the performance of the contract.

7 Al-Sanhoury 1989: Part VII, 'Work and Employment Contracts', Vol. 1: 236.

8 See: the ruling passed by the Appeal Administrative Court in Case 4860 of 49, unpublished.

9 Nicklisch 1990: 324.

The jurisprudence of international contracts does not provide any ground for such authority.[10] Furthermore, this international system of such contracts provides for the parties with the rights granted thereto, the obligations they have to observe and their mutual relationship. This system tries to cover all situations and positions that might arise in the course of the contract performance.

A defined authority vested with the power during the performance of this contract to make specific decisions to settle disputes and make compromises between the contractual parties that might change during the performance of the contract is not acknowledged by this system.

Defining this authority is left for the parties to the contract to provide for this authority either in writing in the contract or by undertaking any of the procedures that enable same to have this authority in place to perform the duties thereof.

An example to illustrate the foregoing is the appointment of a third party as arbitrator or quasi-arbitrator or technical expert, which eventually guarantees the impartiality and independence of the decision-making authority. Arbitration may be provided in the contract; thus, the preliminary procedures, especially preserving the evidence and preliminary judgments may be unfeasible in general. Complementary procedures may pave the way for the parties to benefit from such preliminary procedures to a specific degree.

When it comes to practical reality, these difficulties mean that the parties might try to resort to compromises satisfactory to all parties during the performance of the contract and to postpone litigation or arbitration until the end of the contract term or the completion of the project. The need for a well-informed expert, who is very well versed in the aspects of the project, to be involved in the actual performance of the project is a point of interest in the English system.[11]

Given the fact that the engineer performs the planning work of the project, in addition to other functions, that person is well informed about the project. Eventually, the engineer is always abreast of the nature of issues that might arise and require a decision to settle the dispute. In international practice, being in such a position, and as is believed by some, the engineer is thus vested with quasi-arbitral powers. Thus, the engineer should be impartial and independent.

In international construction and civil engineering works contracts, many intricate jobs are assigned to the engineer, starting with the inception of the project and continuing through its various phases. The engineer prepares for the tender with the documents required for contracting and supervises the performance of work on the employer's behalf. Therefore, suspicion that usually arises regarding the impartiality and independence of the engineer is usually justifiable.

The English system also stresses that the engineer is required to perform duties and issue decisions in this regard with impartiality and fairness.[12] That individual should perform these duties with impartiality, honesty and professional integrity *vis-à-vis* the parties to the contract.

The engineer is required to perform three duties: First, the engineer is the person in charge of the project planning; second, the engineer is the employer's agent and finally, the engineer is responsible for dispute settlement in the capacity as binding decision-making authority.

The engineer acts as an impartial authority; hence, that individual may make a decision that contradicts the employer's interest. Further, in case the issue in question involves errors in the planning phase, engineers make decisions against themselves.[13]

---

10 Nicklisch 1990: 324.

11 Nicklisch 1990: 324.

12 Nicklisch 1990: 325.

13 Nicklisch 1990: 325.

All parties to the contract should wait for the engineer's decision. They should also expect that the engineer does not receive any directives from the employer.[14] The ICC has created an agency to finalize the arbitral process conducted therein, namely the International Centre for Technical Expertise. The contractual parties are entitled to select the appropriate expert during the performance of the procedure of evidence preservation. At the level of practical application, it is manifest that the expert play an effective and significant role in the evidence preservation process during the execution of the contract, for the arbitration phase might require this process due to its paramount importance during the final phase.

Although the expert's opinion is not binding, his or her impartial opinion in this regard is often of considerable importance. The ICC established the ICC Pre-Arbitral Referee Procedure to be operated with the aforementioned expertise procedures duly stipulated in the ICC Rules. The pre-arbitral referee procedures go in tandem with the necessary pre-arbitral procedures to preserve the evidence and preliminary decisions required by the roots of contention. These rules entered into force as of 1 January 1990. They may extend independent and impartial authority that enables same to assume the engineer's function vested therewith under the English system.[15]

Nicklisch ultimately takes the view that international construction and civil engineering works contracts in the coming phase must provide that decision-making procedures should be adopted during the execution of the contract, and preliminary procedures should be taken to settle disputes side by side with the ICC rules. In addition to this, these rules should be included in the FIDIC contract; they replace the engineer's role wholly and partially, as the case may be, a matter that casts shadows of doubt and suspicion on that person's impartiality and independence.

It is true that Nicklisch's opinion is sound and commendable, especially in relation to the inclusion in the contract of a dispute settlement mechanism during the actual execution of the contract, which issues binding decisions, and the party rejecting such decisions should resort to arbitration.

Instead of providing for this dispute settlement mechanism in Article (67) of the FIDIC contract (4th edition) and vesting the engineer with this power, it is suggested that this authority should be assigned to an impartial committee. This committee should be constituted of a technical member (impartial technical expert selected by the ICC in Paris from the technical expertise centre affiliated thereto and definitely not from among the project engineers) or the CRCICA, a member with a legal background who has experience and knowledge about international construction and civil engineering works contracts, the requirements thereof and the nature of disputes arising therefrom, and a third casting member with an engineering or a legal background. This committee shall be entrusted with the powers of dispute settlement in relation to the contract, and it will issue its justified decision within a specific period of time. The individuals, thereafter, shall be entitled to challenge this decision by way of court or arbitration as the case may be within a specific period of time as well, a fact that maintains stability. However, the lapse of the said period of time shall not deprive the individuals from their right to resort to arbitration or court and shall not infringe on the material right in any way whatsoever. In this

14 See the engineer's liability *vis-à-vis* the contractor in the light of the FIDIC contract from the perspective of the English judiciary: *Pacific Associates v. Baxter* (1989) I W.L. R. 1550, 1172, 1190 and 1991; see also: Nicklisch 1990; Bunni 1997: 183; and All England Law Reports (Aller), 159, which said, "quasi arbitrator" in rejection of the work: "Mr Justice Purchas … I am quite unable to accept the proposition that the role played by the Engineer under GC 67 was anything other than a review of an earlier executive decision made in the course of its function as supervising engineer and subject to arbitration under the latter provisions of GC 67."

15 Nicklisch 1990: 340.

regard, it could be safely said that this committee is vested with quasi-arbitral powers, as it is totally impartial from the parties to the dispute, as they choose the members of the committee from the moment of signing the contract, and the committee commences its operations at that point in time and continues until the work is duly finalized.

Each party may select a member of the committee; one party chooses the technical member, another chooses the legal member and the third casting member is to be chosen by both parties, or appointed by the CRCICA in the Middle East region.

It is suggested that this is an impartial quasi-arbitral administrative standing committee, which starts with the inception of the project and the signing of the contract and then advances with the progress of the project, especially complex long-term contracts. It is also considered an impartial arbitral tribunal that swiftly makes decisions within a few days. Therefore, the individuals are entitled to appeal within a few days (30 days, for example). The decision is to be appealed by way of court or arbitration. Otherwise, the decision will be final.

Finally, this authority should be provided for in the public works contract form at the local level and in another international form of public works and civil engineering works contract. The necessity of drafting standard forms, whether local or international, is of fundamental importance to Arab Middle Eastern developing states. Therefore, the administrative body when concluding its local and domestic contracts would adopt this mechanism or method for dispute settlement early before resorting to arbitration. This might considerably save time and expenses that might be enormous, especially with infrastructure and mega construction contracts concluded by the country in this phase of economic growth.

FIDIC Amendment (4th Edition): Clause 67 on the Decision-Making Authority (Dispute Adjudication Board – DAB)

In application of the foregoing discretion,[16] Clause 67 of the FIDIC contract (Part I) was amended in relation to the general provisions of civil engineering works contracts, in case the parties decide to replace the decision-making engineer with a dispute settlement body.

The amendment of Clause 67(1) provides that in case a dispute, of any kind whatsoever, arises between the employer and the contractor in relation to the contract or execution of works, or either of them, and any dispute attributed to any opinion, instructions, definition, certificate or evaluation by the engineer, the dispute shall be referred in writing to the decision-making authority for its decision. This referral must be made as per this Article of the contract.

In case the parties fail to define the members of the DAB in the contract, the parties shall, within 28 days starting with the commencement of execution, appoint the members to the DAB together. The DAB members must be qualified to carry out their duty, and those members could be either one or three persons.

In case the DAB is constituted of three persons, each party should appoint one person; both parties then agree to appoint a third person who shall preside over the committee.

The members of the committee shall be appointed per the conditions of the FIDIC contract as perceived by the parties. And each member of the committee should be independent of the parties to the contract throughout his or her mandate and should act impartially.

16 For recent studies in English jurisprudence dealing with this issue, see: Bunni 1997: 437–8; Seppala 1997: 443.

The first clause of the amended Clause 67 defined the committee members' pay, the method of specifying same, the part due by each party and the method whereby the committee members are removed.

The second sub-clause of Clause 67 provides for the mechanism whereby the committee operates with an engineer (for knowledge) and requires that the parties should provide the committee with all necessary information and give their access to the site as required by the committee members.

The committee has full power to:

- set the applicable procedures to consider the dispute;
- define its jurisdiction and define the scope of any referred dispute;
- take the initiative by defining the facts and matters requiring the decision to be made;
- use the information of any of the experts therein, if any;
- define the system of interest payment as per the contract;
- specify appropriate procedures such as temporary or precautionary measures;
- consider and review any opinion, instructions, definition, certificate or evaluation.

The engineer is required to refer to the dispute in question. The committee shall issue its reasoned decision within 84 days as of the date of dispute referral thereto, provided the parties and the engineer are notified thereof.

This clause also regulates the mechanism of appeal against the committee's decision by way of arbitration in case the decision is unacceptable to either party. The committee also defines the period of time for appeal by way of arbitration as it provides that on, or prior to, the 28th day after receiving the committee's decision, the other party shall inform the engineer of dissatisfaction with this decision.

In case the committee fails to inform same of its decision during, or prior to, the 84th day following the referral of the dispute thereto, both parties shall on or prior to the 28th day after the end of the 84th day inform the other party, and the engineer of the dissatisfaction thereof.

In case the committee informed the employer or the contractor or the engineer of its decision in the dispute without objection on their part to this decision on or prior to the 28th day after the date of receipt by the parties of the committee's decision, the committee's decision shall be deemed final, and binding on the contractor and the employer.

Clause 67(3) provides for a mechanism for the amicable settlement of disputes in case of dissatisfaction with the committee's decision to avoid resorting to arbitration. In case the parties fail to agree otherwise, the arbitration shall commence – on or after – the 56th day following the date on which the parties report their dissatisfaction with the committee's decision, even if no attempt is made to amicably settle the dispute.

Clause 67(4) requires that the dispute be settled by way of arbitration pursuant to the ICC Rules, unless otherwise agreed by the parties.

Clause 67(5) provides for the necessity of resorting to arbitration in case either party fails to concede to the committee's decision in case the decision becomes final and irrevocable.

In case any member of the committee is removed, or if the mandate thereof expires, any dispute referred to under Clause 67(2) shall be finally settled by way of arbitration pursuant to the provision of Article 67(4) (Article 67(6)). It is true that this amendment coincides with our approach that a decision-making authority should be appointed in the course of execution of works, as set out herein.

It is suggested that public works and civil engineering forms of contracts, proposed at both local and international levels, should include a similar authority to settle and decide on disputes during execution, taking into consideration the different elements of its constitution whether it is local or international.

The Situation under the New Edition of FIDIC (1999)

Clause 20 of the new edition of the FIDIC model elaborates the dispute settlement mechanism used for disputes arising from this agreement.

At the outset of the Article, there is a clarification of the method to be adopted by the contractor to claim rights due thereto, such as extension of time or additional payments and notifying the engineer of the contractor's claims within 28 days from the time the incident triggering the claim comes to the contractor's knowledge.

Clause 20(2) provides for the appointment and operation of the Dispute Adjudication Board (DAB). The board is constituted of one or three qualified members; in case the parties fail to define the number, they shall be three.

If the DAB is made up of three members, every party shall appoint a member. The two members shall select the third one who shall preside over the DAB. The DAB regulates the provisions related to the selection of its members, the makeup of its members and its decisions.

Within 84 days as of the date of referring the dispute, the DAB issues its reasoned decision, issued according to the provision of Clause 20(4), knowing that this decision is binding on both parties, who shall immediately observe same, given the points which were not considered either amicably or by way of arbitration. The contractor shall continue to execute the work.

In case either party is not satisfied with the DAB's decision, it shall inform the other party of its dissatisfaction within 28 days. In case the DAB fails to issue its decision within 84 days, either party shall, within 28 days after the lapse of this period, send a notification to the other party of its dissatisfaction.

In all events, the said notice should include that it is served under Clause 20(4), and it should also contain the subject matter of the dispute and the reasons for dissatisfaction.

Notwithstanding the provision of Clause 20(7) (failure to agree with the DAB's decision) and Clause 20(8), neither party shall be able to initiate arbitration to settle the dispute, unless the aforementioned dissatisfaction is notified as per this sub-clause.

In case the DAB furnishes either party with its decision and neither of them reports dissatisfaction within 28 days as of the date of receiving the DAB's decision, such decision shall be deemed final and binding to both parties.

Clause 20(5) provides for the possibility for amicable settlement in case of notification of dissatisfaction with the DAB's decision prior to commencing the arbitration procedures. Accordingly, in case the parties agree otherwise, arbitration may start on or after the 56th day following the day of notice of dissatisfaction, even if there is no attempt at amicable settlement.

Clause 20(6) provides that arbitration is the last resort for dispute settlement. Clause 20(7) provides that in case of disagreement with the DAB's decision and in case neither party reports its dissatisfaction per the time set in Clause 20(4), the DAB's decision shall be final and binding. If the parties refuse to comply with the decision, one party shall refer the dispute to arbitration under the provision of Clause 20(6), and the provisions of Clause 20(4) and Clause 20(5) shall not apply.

The issue that arises in light of the foregoing is as follows: If the DAB's decision is final and binding, and the time bar for challenging same lapses per Clause 20(4), Clause 20(5) stated that the dispute may be referred to arbitration. Nevertheless, is the time bar provided for in these clauses organizational or a prescribed time that leads to the lapse of the substantive right? And what are the consequences thereof? In other words, do the parties still have the right to resort to the competent courts claiming substantive rights despite the fact they lost the opportunity to resort to arbitration because of the lapse of the time bar?

The Legal Nature of the Time Bar Provided for in the FIDIC Form of Contracts (4th Edition – 1987)

Clause 67 of the FIDIC (4th edition) provides that in case a dispute arises between the contractor and the employer, the injured party shall refer the dispute to the engineer to make a decision thereupon within 84 days. In case either party to the dispute is dissatisfied with the engineer's decision, or if the engineer fails to issue a decision within 84 days, either the contractor or the employer shall notify the other of his or her desire to initiate the arbitration procedures within 70 days.

If neither party notifies the other of a desire to initiate arbitration within the said period, arbitration may not start before 56 days to give the parties the opportunity to settle the dispute amicably. After 56 days, the arbitration may be initiated pursuant to the ICC Rules or any other rules to be agreed by the parties.

Clause 67(1) stated the penalty for breaching these dates; thus, it provides that the engineer's decision is final and binding on both the contractor and the employer. Clause 20(4) of the 1999 edition provides that in case either party is dissatisfied with the DAB's decision, such party shall, within 28 days of receiving such decision, notify the other party of the dissatisfaction. In case the DAB fails to issue its decision within 84 days (or if another time limit is provided) as of the date of receipt of this notification or payment, either party, within 28 days of the aforementioned period, shall notify the other of the dissatisfaction.

In these cases, a notice of dissatisfaction must specify, according to Clause 20(4), the grounds for dispute and the reasons for dissatisfaction.

Notwithstanding the aforementioned in Clause 20(7) (failure to comply with the DAB's decision) and Clause 20(8), no party may resort to arbitration unless same fails to report dissatisfaction pursuant to this Clause 20(4). The DAB's decision shall be final and binding in case either party fails to report its dissatisfaction within 28 days.

Clause 20(5) provides that in case of dissatisfaction and sending a notice thereof under Clause 20(4), the parties shall settle the dispute amicably prior to initiating arbitration. Accordingly, unless otherwise agreed by the parties, the arbitration shall start within or after 56 days from the day following the expression of dissatisfaction, even if no attempt is made toward amicable dispute settlement.

Pursuant to these provisions, if the time bar lapses, the dispute shall not be referred to arbitration.

Questions arise: Are the time bars provided in these Articles considered organizational or prescribed dates that cause the lapse of the substantive right? And what are the consequences?

An eminent commentator pointed out[17] that the 70-day period per the provision of Clause 67 of the FIDIC agreement is an organizational, procedural period for the following reasons:

1. The Egyptian Arbitration Act promulgated in 1994 provides in Article (13(1)) that "A court seized with a dispute in respect of which an arbitral agreement exists must rule the case non

17 El Geddawy 1996.

admissible if the respondent invokes a plea of non admissibility before raising any request or defense in the case."

2. It is incumbent that in case a dispute in respect of which an arbitral agreement exists is filed to a court, the court shall dismiss the case, such dismissal shall apply to the procedural formal aspects only without applying in any way whatsoever to the substantive right itself.
3. The dates provided for in the arbitration clause shall be binding for the arbitral tribunal, rather than the competent national court, especially if the arbitration starts after the lapse of these dates; the competent arbitral tribunal shall decide its non-jurisdiction without tackling the substantive right. The matter here is related to defence of procedural rather than substantive nature.
4. Prescription periods have a different nature under Egyptian law. The lapse of the period does not preclude the hearing of the case as per Article (374) to Article (388) of the Egyptian Civil Code. Prescription periods only impact the substantive right, whereby the person entitled to the right may not claim same by way of court. In other words, when the national court in Egypt decides not to hear a case because of the lapse of the period specified, it should initially verify that it has jurisdiction to consider the case. Prescription-based defence shall not influence the jurisdiction of a national court, because it is a defence related to the subject matter of the case that impacts the substantive right, and if it is adopted, the right shall lapse by way of a court ruling.
5. In consideration of the foregoing, in case the defence is based on a specific period for prescription under the governing law and before the arbitral tribunal, this defence shall not impact the jurisdiction of the arbitral tribunal. Indeed, a defence based on prescription of a case will only be decided after verifying the jurisdiction of the arbitral tribunal as this defence relates to the substance and not the procedural issues or jurisdiction.
6. The time bar provided for in Clause 67 is not of a prescription nature. Therefore, it does not contradict any provision based on prescription in the Arab legislation.
7. Further, the period provided for in Clause 67 relates to the right to resort to arbitration whereas the prescription period relates to the right to resort to litigation before national courts.
8. Dr El Geddawy quotes Dr Mahmoud Hashem's view in Arab doctrine, stating: "The right to resort to arbitration is a legal privilege in favor of the parties to the dispute," as they might have agreed to refer any dispute to arbitration instead of the national competent courts.
9. Eventually, the right to resort to arbitration differs from the right to resort to national courts. The latter right is a legal privilege for one person who claims entitlement to a right or a legal position. This privilege, when exercised, allows the plaintiff to obtain a ruling from the competent national court in the subject matter of the case.
10. Claims of rights or legal positions do not provide sufficient grounds for resorting to arbitration; this rather takes place in case both parties are satisfied with resorting to arbitration; i.e., they are satisfied to refer the dispute to a selected person instead of referring same to the national court.
11. In case either party fails to obtain the satisfaction of the other part to resort to arbitration, such party shall not be able, solely, to refer the dispute to arbitration. In case such party wishes to obtain his or her right, the court will be the only way to be adopted by following the procedures prescribed for a court case and verifying the conditions required for filing same.[18]

18 Hashem 1990: 58–9.

12. After the right to arbitration and the right to resort to national courts have been considered, it becomes manifest that the legal provisions of prescription in the Arab legislation only relate to the right to take judicial proceedings before the national court rather than arbitration.
13. On the other hand, the reference in "the lapse of the time limits" is to the period during which the national court is precluded from hearing the case, and the substantive right is protected by the judicial case. All legal provisions dealing with prescription are explicit in this regard.

Based on the foregoing, the right to resort to arbitration does not fall within the scope of these provisions as it is a right of a procedural nature that has been established by virtue of a joint agreement among the individuals.

The procedural nature of the right to resort to arbitration is not controversial. Indeed, the right, which was created by the consent of both parties, directly impacts the judicial case and the litigation procedures before the national court. Furthermore, this would preclude the national court from hearing the case, the subject of the arbitration agreement.

In summation, Dr El-Geddawy[19] is of the view that the prescription periods provided for in Egyptian and Arab laws relate to the right to resort to a judicial procedure and the impact of the lapse of the time bar on the substantive right, whereas the periods in Article (67) relate to the right to resort to arbitration and the impact of the lapse of the time bar thereupon without affecting the substantive right.

The question is: Does the lapse of the time bar provided for in Clause 67 cause the prescription of the right to resort to a competent national court? It is axiomatic that the lapse of this time bar would deprive the arbitral tribunal of its jurisdiction and the award thereof shall be vulnerable to challenge.

English commentators[20] analyzed the same issue in depth. The English doctrine also takes the view that the wording of Article (67) of the FIDIC agreements, using "final and binding" is decisive, and does not imply any doubt regarding the construction of solving the issue at stake to the support of the previous opinion.[21]

In Egyptian jurisprudence it is the view of some[22] that arbitration is the exception to the general rule as disputes are settled by national courts;[23] in case there is an arbitration agreement, that shall prevent national courts from considering the dispute so long as the said agreement continues to be in force. If, however, this agreement is revoked for any reason, jurisdiction shall be restored by the national courts (Article (13) of the new Arbitration Law). The right of litigation before the national courts is a constitutional right. The same vision applies to all Arab jurisdictions.[24]

It is true that if the time limits provided for in Clause 67 of the FIDIC agreement, relating to arbitration in construction contracts, lapse without arbitration taking place, they cause the prescription of the parties' right to take the dispute to arbitration. The provisions relating to prescription in the Egyptian Civil Code, however, deal with the substantive right, where the case serves as a method whereby the person entitled to the right protects his or her right; thus the right remains with no case to protect it.

---

19 El Geddawy 1996.

20 Duncan Wallace 1986a: 280.

21 Duncan Wallace 1986a: 280.

22 El Geddawy 1996.

23 Egyptian Court of Cassation, Case 1579 of 49, dated 10/2/1986.

24 The same concept applies to Arab jurisdictions as they are all civil law countries, and all Arab civil codes and arbitration acts were directly influenced by the Egyptian legal system.

It is noticeable that the end sought by the 84-day period specified for the engineer's decision and a period for the parties to resort to arbitration within 70 days is to settle the disputes arising from public works contracts rapidly. In case such periods lapse without resorting to arbitration, this sole channel for dispute settlement would be blocked. Nevertheless, this does not entail the lapse of the parties' right to resort to the national competent courts to claim their rights so long as the prescription period has not been duly exhausted.

In terms of Clause 20 of the FIDIC agreement (the new edition 1999), the same above-mentioned concept applies.

The right to litigation and to resort to the national courts is a constitutional right duly established by Article (68) of the Permanent Constitution of the Arab Republic of Egypt promulgated in 1971 and amended in 2007 and in all Arab constitutions.[25] Article (172) of the Egyptian Constitution entrusts the State Council with deciding on all other administrative disputes. Accordingly, the State Council has jurisdiction to decide on all administrative disputes; therefore, if the parties fail to resort to arbitration, it is incumbent on them to resort to their natural judge in operation of the two constitutional principles, namely that the right to litigation is secured for all, and that the State Council is the body having fundamental jurisdiction to decide on administrative disputes. This general fundamental principle is provided for by the Constitution and the State Council Law promulgated by virtue of Article (10) in Law 47/1972 that provides for the jurisdiction of the State Council to consider administrative contracts disputes. This fundamental principle renders the State Council the body having jurisdiction to consider disputes related to international public works contracts upon the lapse of the periods prescribed for arbitration, pursuant to Article (67) of the FIDIC agreement, 4th edition, and Article (20) thereof in the 1999 edition. This is the situation in Arab Middle Eastern jurisdictions.

Conclusions

The legal globalization phenomenon is a fundamental factor behind the flow of the Anglo-American jurisdictions to Arab civil law jurisdictions in terms of International Public Works Agreements. Its new legal nature due to the new contractual clauses, new types of agreements, new legislative steps to maintain financial equilibrium and new trends taken by the judiciary in Arab countries to protect foreign investors is a direct effect of legal globalization. The direct result is that disputes settlement in the domain of International Public Works Agreements and state contracts are considerably changed, regarding the fact that new mechanisms have appeared in the last two decades, particularly arbitration. Today, civil law legal systems and, in particular, Arab Middle Eastern countries began a new era in the field of states' infrastructure projects in the light of the new contractual mechanisms and disputes settlements in this context.

It is appropriate to refer to the following conclusions and recommendations achieved through this study:

1. The cultural and legal globalization phenomenon as a transnational socioeconomic phenomenon is a direct result of coordination cooperation and the transfer among various cultures, particularly the flow of the Anglo-American legal culture to civil law jurisdictions,

---

25 Ismail 2003a: 504; and Arab constitutions such as the Libyan Constitution, the Lebanese Constitution, the Jordanian Constitution, the Kuwaiti Constitution, the Omani Constitution, the Moroccan Constitution and the Syrian Constitution.

and the clash of civilizations theory is not applicable in the states' international business transactions context as proved in an earlier stage of this study.

2. The legal globalization phenomenon has considerable effects on International Public Works Agreements and infrastructure projects in Arab Middle Eastern countries. This is clear in the light of the new types of agreements that have appeared in the last decade, particularly BOT, BOOT and PPPs. New international instruments were recognized in practice and in academic studies. The latter instruments clearly represent new ideologies to be adopted in the field of liberalization and modernization of the concept of *Le Contrat Administratif*, especially the standard forms of contracts and the institutional arbitration rules of the regional and international arbitration institutions that are applicable by Arab countries at both levels. Further, the new legislation in the Arab world, particularly arbitration acts in the last 15 years, modifications and enhancements to states' procurements laws and legislation liberalizing public utilities concessions such as PPPs and BOOT in Egypt are of fundamental importance in this transition period. It is recommended that all Arab states should follow the Egyptian model in PPPs and public utilities in some sectors in Egypt. In arbitration, all Arab countries were influenced by the Egyptian experience of the Egyptian Arbitration Act of 1994. It is strongly recommended that the Egyptian parliament shall promulgate a new legislation for all BOT/BOOT transactions in the countries and not organize these transactions in specific sectors as is the case now. The Egyptian State Procurement Law has constructive modifications regarding contract price in the last few years due to the rapid change of cement and reinforcement iron prices as the Egyptian market is directly influenced by international market prices. The international demand for Egyptian cement plays a significant role in increasing cement prices in the domestic markets. It is recommended that all Arab states shall follow the same legislative methodology.
3. It is true that the latter modifications and liberalization to *Le Contrat Administratif* theory, the new legislative steps adopted by Arab states, particularly in disputes settlements, and the new contractual mechanisms appearing in infrastructure projects are a main factor in attracting FDI in the field of the infrastructure sector in the Middle East. Thus, it is recommended that all Arab countries must codify separate arbitration acts following Egypt, Oman, Tunisia and Jordan. Most Arab arbitration rules are incorporated in Codes of Civil Procedures. A fully liberalized arbitral process requires separate arbitration acts in all Arab countries despite the fact that the Emirates arbitration rules in Code of Civil Procedures are significantly advanced. The latter trend is an exception.
4. It is worth stating that all Arab arbitration legislation has been directly influenced by the Egyptian Arbitration Act of 1994. The Act was influenced to a great extent by the UNCITRAL Model Law. One may refer to the fact that Egyptian, Jordanian, Omani, Tunisian and Emirates legislation have achieved significant results toward the liberalization, modernization and internationalization of the arbitral process in the Middle East region.
5. It is of fundamental importance to refer to the fact that most Arab countries entered into Bilateral Investment Treaties (BITs). Consequently, those treaties offer protection to private foreign investors in infrastructure projects in Arab countries to start arbitral proceedings against states without the administration's consent in each particular case. This protection is consistent with the 1965 ICSID Convention. Moreover, BITs prohibit expropriation. In all Arab constitutions, BITs or any international treaties are integral parts of the legislation after ratification by the state's parliament.
6. The constitutional amendments in Egypt in 2007 are not adopting certain ideologies – whether socialist like the previous constitution (1971) or another ideology. However, the

constitution left the presidential and parliamentary elections to determine the political and economic ideology to be adopted for each period. One may refer to the French experience when President Valéry Giscard d'Estaing adopted free market economy policies, and after a certain period of time and due to some domestic changes, President François Mitterrand changed to socialist policies. It is also clear that the economic ideologies to be adopted before the economic crises in 2008 are completely different from those to be adopted after the crises. These polices directly affect international infrastructure agreements in developing states and mechanisms whether legislative or contractual. Further, it directly affects the IFDI to developing states and the new creative policies to be adopted in order not to lose FDI in the field of infrastructure sector. These new policies are to be adopted to facilitate investment procedures such as establishing companies in the host state in a short time with simple steps, the right for some projects for some exemptions from some taxes and customs duties plus other procedures.

7. States are still playing the role of employer, supervisor, legislator and regulator in the light of the increasing trend of liberalization of infrastructure and public utilities projects. In Arab countries, where culture is a dynamic value changing from one country to another and from time to time, governments represent the nation in managing and operating public utilities. Thus, despite the flow of the Anglo-American legal culture to Arab countries, states still maintain their national identity by keeping some of their sovereignty through the Administrative Contract Penalties that still exist, to some extent, despite the new legal nature of the International Public Works Agreements.
8. There is an essential need in Arab Middle Eastern states to raise the level of awareness among practitioners and academics in the field of international infrastructure projects and arbitration as well as expertise in negotiating and drafting international state transactions with private foreign entities. That expertise must be from the legal, economic, engineering and any other background needed for the process starting from preparing for tender until final completion. Disputes settlement mechanisms are of fundamental importance for developing nations as there is a long history with some developing states in international institutions such as ICSID and previously the ICC after the institutionalization of the arbitral process. The latter institutionalization is recommended because of the complex, and in many cases, multiparty arbitration disputes in International Public Works Agreements.
9. It is of fundamental importance that civil law Arab countries must change the punitive nature of the penalty for delay as the liquidated damages must be fair and equal to actual loss suffered by the administration and public utilities. Consequently, to achieve tangible increase in the IFDI in infrastructure projects, developing states must offer incentives to foreign investors instead of contractual clauses or legislative stipulations imposed in international agreements, which are of a punitive nature.
10. The principle of *Exception non Adimpleti Contractus* (exception of non-performed contract) must be applicable within the administrative contracts to achieve equal bargaining power between state and contractor. This will be a considerable factor in enhancing the FDI atmosphere in the construction industry in the field of state contracts. Legislative amendments are needed in most Arab states. It is true that this principle exists in Article (161) of the Egyptian Civil Code and in all Arab civil codes. However, the Egyptian *Conseil d'Etat* courts adopted a contrary view and rejected the application of the principle in administrative contracts since 1948 as explained before.

11. The leading Arab judiciary was influenced by the legal globalization to some extent. This clearly appears in the Egyptian *Conseil d'Etat* decisions in the penalty for delay and many other areas within International Public Works Agreements context as explained in this study.
12. There is an essential need for Arab developing states to tailor a standard form of contract for state International Public Works Agreements and another form for domestic agreements. This will be subject to amendments according to negotiations with foreign or domestic investors.
13. Arab arbitration legislation delegated to the judicial authority a constructive role in assisting the arbitral process. This has been scrutinized in this study from a comparative perspective in Arab legislation such as the Egyptian Arbitration Act, which refers cases of the challenging of arbitrators to the national courts; meanwhile, some Arab legislation stipulates that penalties (fines) be imposed by national courts on witnesses who do not comply with arbitral tribunal orders and directions.
14. The arbitral process needs further liberalizing steps, particularly if the consent of the administration is required to start arbitration. It is against fairness principles to sign an arbitration clause by and between a host state and a foreign investor and afterwards, when a dispute arises, the administration (the minister concerned) must grant consent. In some cases in practice, states tend to withhold the process. The situation will be difficult if the investor is not protected by a certain instrument such as a BIT. This study scrutinized carefully the above-mentioned scenario.
15. It is of great significance to developing states when promulgating PPP legislation to treat these transactions as private and commercial transactions. The French *Conseil d'Etat* trend considering PPPs as administrative contracts is applicable in the French legal system where the surrounding culture and atmosphere encourage IFDI even if there are penalties in the PPP agreements. When considering the same situation in developing countries, the analogy seems very difficult, particularly regarding states' unilateral powers upon exercising some exorbitant clauses such as *La Résiliation Administrative* to the contract by the state. These excessive powers exercised by developing states are dangerous to foreign investors, particularly when bureaucracy, corruption and, to some extent, bad faith by the host state exist when the state exercises its unilateral powers. Thus, it is recommended for developing countries when promulgating PPP legislation to liberalize the latter transactions from the *Le Contrat Administratif* stipulations and constraints as the French *Conseil d'Etat* trend may not be useful for developing states that are suffering from budget deficits and trying to increase IFDI in the field of public utilities.

It is clear that the above-mentioned results and recommendations are the beginning of a new era in Arab civil law countries in the Middle East. The Public Economic Law is a new branch of states' international transactions that is currently beginning to appear in a few academic studies in the Middle East. This is the deterioration of *Le Contrat Administratif* theory in the light of legal globalization in civil law legal systems.

Annex 1

UNCITRAL

United Nations Commission on International Trade Law

UNCITRAL Model Law on International Commercial Arbitration 1985

With amendments as adopted in 2006

Contents

Resolutions adopted by the General Assembly

40/72. Model Law on International Commercial Arbitration of the United Nations Commission on International Trade Law

The General Assembly,

Recognizing the value of arbitration as a method of settling disputes arising in international commercial relations,

Convinced that the establishment of a model law on arbitration that is acceptable to States with different legal, social and economic systems contributes to the development of harmonious international economic relations,

Noting that the Model Law on International Commercial Arbitration[1] was adopted by the United Nations Commission on International Trade Law at its eighteenth session, after due deliberation and extensive consultation with arbitral institutions and individual experts on international commercial arbitration,

Convinced that the Model Law, together with the Convention on the Recognition and Enforcement of Foreign Arbitral Awards[2] and the Arbitration Rules of the United Nations Commission on International Trade Law[3] recommended by the General Assembly in its resolution 31/98 of 15 December 1976, significantly contributes to the establishment of a unified legal framework for the fair and efficient settlement of disputes arising in international commercial relations,

1. *Requests* the Secretary-General to transmit the text of the Model Law on International Commercial Arbitration of the United Nations Commission on International Trade Law, together with the *travaux préparatoires* from the eighteenth session of the Commission, to Governments and to arbitral institutions and other interested bodies, such as chambers of commerce;

2. *Recommends* that all States give due consideration to the Model Law on International Commercial Arbitration, in view of the desirability of uniformity of the law of arbitral procedures and the specific needs of international commercial arbitration practice.

112th plenary meeting
11 December 1985

1 Official Records of the. General Assembly, Fortieth Session, Supplement No. 17 (A/40/17), annex I.
2 United Nations, Treaty Series, vol. 330, No. 4739, p. 38.
3 United Nations publication, Sales No, E.77.V.6.

Resolutions adopted by the General Assembly

[*on the report of the Sixth Committee (A/61/453)*]

61/33. Revised articles of the Model Law on International Commercial Arbitration of the United Nations Commission on International Trade Law, and the recommendation regarding the interpretation of article II, paragraph 2, and article VII, paragraph I, of the Convention on the Recognition and Enforcement of Foreign Arbitral Awards, done at New York, 10 June 1958.

The General Assembly,

Recognizing the value of arbitration as a method of settling disputes arising in the context of international commercial relations,

Recalling its resolution 40/72 of 11 December 1985 regarding the Model Law on International Commercial Arbitration,[4]

Recognizing the need for provisions in the Model Law to conform to current practices in international trade and modern means of contracting with regard to the form of the arbitration agreement and the granting of interim measures,

Believing that revised articles of the Model Law on the form of the arbitration agreement and interim measures reflecting those current practices will significantly enhance the operation of the Model Law,

Noting that the preparation of the revised articles of the Model Law on the form of the arbitration agreement and interim measures was the subject of due deliberation and extensive consultations with Governments and interested circles and would contribute significantly to the establishment of a harmonized legal framework for a fair and efficient settlement of international commercial disputes,

Believing that, in connection with the modernization of articles of the Model Law, the promotion of a uniform interpretation and application of the Convention on the Recognition and Enforcement of Foreign Arbitral Awards, done at New York, 10 June 1958,[5] is particularly timely,

1. *Expresses* its appreciation to the United Nations Commission on International Trade Law for formulating and adopting the revised articles of its Model Law on International Commercial Arbitration on the form of the arbitration agreement and interim measures, the text of which is contained in annex I to the report of the United Nations Commission on International Trade Law on the work of its thirty-ninth session,[6] and recommends that all States give favourable consideration lo the enactment of the revised articles of the Model Law, or the revised Model Law on International

---

4 Official Records of the General Assembly, Fortieth Session, Supplement No. 17 (A/40/17), annex 1.

5 United Nations, Treaty Series, vol. 330, No. 4739.

6 Official Recants of the General Assembly, Sixty-first Session, Supplement No. 17 (A/61/17).

Commercial Arbitration of the United Nations Commission on International Trade Law, when they enact or revise their laws, in view of the desirability of uniformity of the law of arbitral procedures and the specific needs of international commercial arbitration practice;

2. *Also expresses its appreciation* to the United Nations Commission on International Trade Law for formulating and adopting the recommendation regarding the interpretation of article II, paragraph *2,* and article VII, paragraph 1, of the Convention on the Recognition and Enforcement of Foreign Arbitral Awards, done at New York, 10 June 1958, the text of which is contained in annex II to the report of the United Nations Commission on International Trade Law on the work of its thirty-ninth session;

3. *Requests* the Secretary-General to make all efforts to ensure that the revised articles of the Model Law and the recommendation become generally known and available.

64th plenary meeting
4 December 2006

Part One

UNCITRAL Model Law on International Commercial Arbitration

(United Nations documents A/40/17, annex I and A/61/17, annex I)

(As adopted by the United Nations Commission on International Trade Law on 21 June 1985, and as amended by the United Nations Commission on International Trade Law on 7 July 2006)

CHAPTER I. GENERAL PROVISIONS

Article I, Scope of application[7]

(1) This Law applies to international commercial[8] arbitration, subject to any agreement in force between this State and any other State or States.
(2) The provisions of this Law, except articles 8, 9, 17 H, 17 I, 17 J, 35 and 36, apply only if the place of arbitration is in the territory of this State.

(Article 1(2) has been amended by the Commission at its thirty-ninth session, in 2006)

(3) An arbitration is international if:
(a) the parties to an arbitration agreement have, at the time of the conclusion of that agreement, their places of business in different States; or
(b) one of the following places is situated outside the State in which the parties have their places of business:
(i) the place of arbitration is determined in, or pursuant to, the arbitration agreement;
(ii) any place where a substantial part of the obligations of the commercial relationship is to be performed or the place with which the subject matter of the dispute is most closely connected; or
(c) the parties have expressly agreed that the subject matter of the arbitration agreement relates to more than one country.
(4) For the purposes of paragraph (3) of this article:
(a) if a party has more than one place of business, the place of business is that which has the closest relationship to the arbitration agreement;
(b) if a party does not have a place of business, reference is to be made to his habitual residence.

---

7 Article headings are for reference purposes only and are not to be used for purposes of interpretation.

8 The term "commercial" should be given a wide interpretation so as to cover matters arising from all relationships of a commercial nature, whether contractual or not. Relationships of a commercial nature include, but are not limited to, the following transactions: any trade transaction for the supply or exchange of goods or services: distribution agreement; commercial representation or agency; factoring; leasing: construction of works; consulting; engineering; licensing; investment; financing; banking; insurance; exploitation agreement or concession; joint venture and other forms of industrial or business cooperation; carriage of goods or passengers by air, sea, rail or road.

(5) This Law shall not affect any other law of this State by virtue of which certain disputes may not be submitted to arbitration or may be submitted to arbitration only according to provisions other than those of this Law.

Article 2. Definitions and rules of interpretation

For the purposes of this Law:
(a) "arbitration" means any arbitration whether or not administered by a permanent arbitral institution;
(b) "arbitral tribunal" means a sole arbitrator or a panel of arbitrators;
(c) "court" means a body or organ of the judicial system of a State;
(d) where a provision of this Law, except article 28, leaves the parties free to determine a certain issue, such freedom includes the right of the parties to authorize a third party, including an institution, to make that determination;
(e) where a provision of this Law refers to the fact that the parties have agreed or that they may agree or in any other way refers to an agreement of the parties, such agreement includes any arbitration rules referred to in that agreement;
(f) Where a provision of this Law, other than in articles 25*(a)* and 32(2) *(a),* refers to a claim, it also applies to a counter-claim, and where it refers to a defence, it also applies to a defence to such counter-claim.

Article 2 A. International origin and general principles

(As adopted by the Commission at its thirty-ninth session, in 2006)

(1) In the interpretation of this Law, regard is to be had to its international origin and to the need to promote uniformity in its application and the observance of good faith.
(2) Questions concerning matters governed by this Law which are not expressly settled in it are to be settled in conformity with the general principles on which this Law is based.

Article 3. Receipt of written communications

(1) Unless otherwise agreed by the parties:
(a) any written communication is deemed to have been received if it is delivered to the addressee personally or if it is delivered at his place of business, habitual residence or mailing address; if none of these can be found after making a reasonable inquiry, a written communication is deemed to have been received if it is sent to the addressee's last-known place of business, habitual residence or mailing address by registered fetter or any other means which provides a record of the attempt to deliver it;
(b) the communication is deemed to have been received on the day it is so delivered.
(2) The provisions of this article do not apply to communications in court proceedings.

Article 4. Waiver of right to object

A party who knows that any provision of this Law from which the parties may derogate or any requirement under the arbitration agreement has not been complied with and yet proceeds with the arbitration without stating his objection to such non-compliance without undue delay or, if a time-limit is provided therefor, within such period of time, shall be deemed to have waived his right to object.

Article 5. Extent of court intervention

In matters governed by this Law, no court shall intervene except where so provided in this Law.

Article 6. Court or other authority for certain functions of arbitration assistance and supervision

The functions referred to in articles 11 (3), 11(4), 13(3), 14.16 (3) and 34(2) shall be performed by . [Each state enacting this model law specifies the, courts or, where referred to therein, other authority competent to perform these functions[.

CHAPTER II. ARBITRATION AGREEMENT

Option I

Article 7. Definition and form of arbitration agreement

(As adopted by the Commission at its thirty-ninth session, in 2006)

(1) "Arbitration agreement" is an agreement by the parties to submit to arbitration all or certain disputes which have arisen or which may arise or which may arise between them in respect of a defined legal relationship. Whether contractual or not. An arbitration agreement may be in the form of an arbitration clause in a contract or in the form of a separate agreement.
(2) The arbitration agreement shall be in writing.
(3) An arbitration agreement is in writing if its content is recorded in any form, whether or not the arbitration agreement or contract has been concluded orally, by conduct, or by other means.
(4) The requirement that an arbitration agreement be in writing is met by an electronic communication if the information contained therein is accessible so as to be useable for subsequent reference; "electronic communication" means any communication that the parties make by means of data messages; "data message" means information generated, sent, received or stored by electronic, magnetic, optical or similar means, including, but not limited to, electronic data interchange (EDI), electronic mail, telegram, telex or telecopy.
(5) Furthermore, an arbitration agreement is in writing if it is contained in an exchange of statements of claim and defence in which the existence of an agreement is alleged by one party and not denied by the other.
(6) The reference in a contract to any document containing an arbitration clause constitutes an arbitration agreement in writing, provided that the reference is such as to make that clause part of the contract.

Option II

Article 7. Definition of arbitration agreement

(As adopted by the Commission at its thirty-ninth session, in 2006)

"Arbitration agreement" is an agreement by the parties to submit to arbitration all or certain disputes which have arisen or which may arise between them in respect of a defined legal relationship, whether contractual or not.

Article 8. Arbitration agreement and substantive claim before court

(1) A court before which an action is brought in a matter which is the subject of an arbitration agreement shall, if a party so requests not later than when submitting his first statement on the substance of the dispute, refer the parties to arbitration unless it finds that the agreement is null and void, inoperative or incapable of being performed.
(2) Where an action referred to in paragraph (1) of this article has been brought, arbitral proceedings may nevertheless be commenced or continued, and an award may be made, while the issue is pending before the court.

Article 9. Arbitration agreement and interim measures by court

It is not incompatible with an arbitration agreement for a party to request, before or during arbitral proceedings, from a court an interim measure of protection and for a court to grant such measure.

CHAPTER III. COMPOSITION OF ARBITRAL TRIBUNAL

Article 10. Number of arbitrators

(1) The parties are free to determine the number of arbitrators.
(2) Failing such determination, the number of arbitrators shall be three.

Article 11. Appointment of arbitrators

(1) No person shall be precluded by reason of his nationality from acting as an arbitrator, unless otherwise agreed by the parties.
(2) The parties are free to agree on a procedure of appointing the arbitrator or arbitrators, subject to the provisions of paragraphs (4) and (5) of this article.
(3) Failing such agreement,

(a) in an arbitration with three arbitrators, each party shall appoint one arbitrator, and the two arbitrators thus appointed shall appoint the third arbitrator; if a party fails to appoint the arbitrator within thirty days of receipt of a request to do so from the other party, or if the two arbitrators fail to agree on the third arbitrator within thirty days of their appointment, the

appointment shall be made, upon request of a party, by the court or other authority specified in article 6;

(b) in an arbitration with a sole arbitrator, if the parties are unable to agree on the arbitrator, he shall be appointed, upon request of a party, by the court or other authority specified in article 6.

(4) Where, under an appointment procedure agreed upon by the parties,

(a) a party fails to act as required under such procedure, or

(b) the parties, or two arbitrators, are unable to reach an agreement expected of them under such procedure, or

(c) a third party, including an institution, fails to perform any function entrusted to it under such procedure,

any party may request the court or other authority specified in article 6 to take the necessary measure, unless the agreement on the appointment procedure provides other means for securing the appointment,

(5) A decision on a matter entrusted by paragraph (3) or (4) of this article to the court or other authority specified in article 6 shall be subject to no appeal. The court or other authority, in appointing an arbitrator, shall have due regard to any qualifications required of the arbitrator by the agreement of the parties and to such considerations as are likely to secure the appointment of an independent and impartial arbitrator and, in the case of a sole or third arbitrator, shall take into account as well the advisability of appointing an arbitrator of a nationality other than those of the parties.

Article 12. Grounds for challenge

(1) When a person is approached in connection with his possible appointment as an arbitrator, he shall disclose any circumstances likely to give rise to justifiable doubts as to his impartiality or independence An arbitrator, from the time of his appointment and throughout the arbitral proceedings, shall without delay disclose any such circumstances to the parties unless they have already been informed of them by him.

(2) An arbitrator may be challenged only if circumstances exist that give rise to justifiable doubts as to his impartiality or independence, or if he does not possess qualifications agreed to by the parties. A party may challenge an arbitrator appointed by him, or in whose appointment he has participated, only for reasons of which he becomes aware after the appointment has been made.

Article 13. Challenge procedure

(1) The parties are free to agree on a procedure for challenging an arbitrator, subject to the provisions of paragraph (3) of this article.

(2) failing such agreement, a party who intends to challenge an arbitrator shall, within fifteen days after becoming aware of the constitution of the arbitral tribunal or after becoming aware of any circumstance referred to in article 12(2) send a written statement of the reasons for the challenge to the arbitral tribunal.

(3) If a challenge under any procedure agreed upon by the parties or under the procedure of paragraph (2) of this article is not successful, the challenging party may request, within thirty days after having received notice of the decision rejecting the challenge. The court or other authority

specified in article 6 to decide on the challenge, which decision shall be subject to no appeal; while such a request is pending, the arbitral tribunal, including the challenged arbitrator, may continue the arbitral proceedings and make an award.

Article 14. Failure or impossibility to act

(1) If an arbitrator becomes *de jure* or *de facto* unable to perform his functions or for other reasons fails to act without undue delay, his mandate terminates if he withdraws from his office or if the parties agree on the termination. Otherwise, if a controversy remains concerning any of these grounds, any party may request the court or other authority specified in article 6 to decide on the termination of the mandate, which decision shall be subject to no appeal.
(2) If, under this article or article 13(2), an arbitrator withdraws from his office or a party agrees to the termination of the mandate of an arbitrator, this does not imply acceptance of the validity of any ground referred to in this article or article 12(2).

Article 15. Appointment of substitute arbitrator

Where the mandate of an arbitrator terminates under article 13 or 14 or because of his withdrawal from office for any other reason or because of the revocation of his mandate by agreement of the parties or in any other case of termination of his mandate, a substitute arbitrator shall be appointed according to the rules that were applicable to the appointment of the arbitrator being replaced.

CHAPTER IV. JURISDICTION OF ARBITRAL TRIBUNAL

Article 16. Competence of arbitral tribunal to rule on its jurisdiction

(1) The arbitral tribunal may rule on its own jurisdiction, including any objections with respect to the existence or validity of the arbitration agreement. For that purpose, an arbitration clause which forms part of a contract shall be treated as an agreement independent of the other terms of the contract. A decision by the arbitral tribunal that the contract is null and void shall not entail *ipso jure* the invalidity of the arbitration clause.
(2) A plea that the arbitral tribunal does not have jurisdiction shall be raised not later than the submission of the statement of defence. A party is not precluded from raising such a plea by the fact that he has appointed, or participated in the appointment of, an arbitrator. A plea that the arbitral tribunal is exceeding the scope of its authority shall be raised as soon as the matter alleged to be beyond the scope of its authority is raised during the arbitral proceedings. The arbitral tribunal may, in either case, admit a later plea if it considers the delay justified.
(3) The arbitral tribunal may rule on a plea referred to in paragraph (2) of this article either as a preliminary question or in an award on the merits. If the arbitral tribunal rules as a preliminary question that it has jurisdiction, any party may request, within thirty days after having received notice of that ruling, the court specified in article 6 to decide the matter, which decision shall be subject to no appeal; while such a request is pending, the arbitral tribunal may continue the arbitral proceedings and make an award.

CHAPTER IV A. INTERIM MEASURES AND PRELIMINARY ORDERS

(As adopted by the Commission at its thirty-ninth session, in 2006)

Section 1. Interim measures

Article 17. Power of arbitral tribunal to order interim measures

(1) Unless otherwise agreed by the parties, the arbitral tribunal may, at the request of a party, grant interim measures.
(2) An interim measure is any temporary measure, whether in the form of an award or in another form, by which, at any time prior to the issuance of the award by which the dispute is finally decided, the arbitral tribunal orders a party to:

(a) Maintain or restore the status quo pending determination of the dispute;
(b) Take action that would prevent, or refrain from taking action that is likely to cause, current or imminent harm or prejudice to the arbitral process itself;
(c) Provide a means of preserving assets out of which a subsequent award may be satisfied; or
(d) Preserve evidence that may be relevant and material to the resolution of the dispute.

Article 17 A. Conditions for granting interim measures

(1) The party requesting an interim measure under article *1(2)(a), (b)* and *(c)* shall satisfy the arbitral tribunal that:

(a) Harm not adequately reparable by an award of damages is likely to result if the measure is not ordered, and such harm substantially outweighs the harm that is likely to result to the party against whom the measure is directed if the measure is granted; and
(b) There is a reasonable possibility that the requesting party will succeed on the merits of the claim. The determination on this possibility shall not affect the discretion of the arbitral tribunal in making any subsequent determination.

(2) With regard to a request for an interim measure under article *1(2)(d),* the requirements in paragraphs *(1)(a)* and *(b) of* this article shall apply only to the extent the arbitral tribunal considers appropriate.

Section 2. Preliminary orders

Article 17 B. Applications for preliminary orders and conditions for granting preliminary orders

(1) Unless otherwise agreed by the parties, a party may, without notice to any other party, make a request for an interim measure together with an application for a preliminary order directing a party not to frustrate the purpose of the interim measure requested.
(2) The arbitral tribunal may grant a preliminary order provided it considers that prior disclosure of the request for the interim measure to the party against whom it is directed risks frustrating the purpose of the measure.
(3) The conditions defined under article 17A apply to any preliminary order, provided that the harm to be assessed under article 17A(1)(a), is the harm likely to result from the order being granted or not.

Article 17 C. Specific regime for preliminary orders

(1) Immediately after the arbitral tribunal has made a determination in respect of an application for a preliminary order, the arbitral tribunal shall give notice to all parties of the request for the interim measure, the application for the preliminary order, the preliminary order, if any, and all other communications, including by indicating the content of any oral communication, between any party and the arbitral tribunal in relation thereto.
(2) At the same time, the arbitral tribunal shall give an opportunity to any party against whom a preliminary order is directed to present its case at the earliest practicable time.
(3) The arbitral tribunal shall decide promptly on any objection to the preliminary order.
(4) A preliminary order shall expire after twenty days from the date on which it was issued by the arbitral tribunal. However, the arbitral tribunal may issue an interim measure adopting or modifying the preliminary order, after the party against whom the preliminary order is directed has been given notice and an opportunity to present its case.
(5) A preliminary order shall be binding on the parties but shall not be subject to enforcement by a court. Such a preliminary order does not constitute an award.

Section 3. Provisions applicable to interim measures and preliminary orders

Article 17 D. Modification, suspension, termination

The arbitral tribunal may modify, suspend or terminate an interim measure or a preliminary order it has granted, upon application of any party or, in exceptional circumstances and upon prior notice to the parties, on the arbitral tribunal's own initiative.

Article 17 E. Provision of security

(1) The arbitral tribunal may require the party requesting an interim measure to provide appropriate security in connection with the measure.
(2) The arbitral tribunal shall require the party applying for a preliminary order to provide security in connection with the order unless the arbitral tribunal considers it inappropriate or unnecessary to do so.

Article 17 F. Disclosure

(1) The arbitral tribunal may require any party promptly to disclose any material change in the circumstances on the basis of which the measure was requested or granted.
(2) The party applying for a preliminary order shall disclose to the arbitral tribunal all circumstances that are likely to be relevant to the arbitral tribunal's determination whether to grant or maintain the order, and such obligation shall continue until the party against whom the order has been requested has had an opportunity to present its case. Thereafter, paragraph (1) of this article shall apply.

Article 17 G. Costs and damages

The party requesting an interim measure or applying for a preliminary order shall be liable for any costs and damages caused by the measure or the order to any party if the arbitral tribunal later determines that, in the circumstances, the measure or the order should not have been granted. The arbitral tribunal may award such costs and damages at any point during the proceedings.

Section 4. Recognition and enforcement of interim measures

Article 17 H. Recognition and enforcement

(1) An interim measure issued by an arbitral tribunal shall be recognized as binding and, unless otherwise provided by the arbitral tribunal, enforced upon application to the competent court, irrespective of the country in which it was issued, subject to the provisions of article 17 I.
(2) The party who is seeking or has obtained recognition or enforcement of an interim measure shall promptly inform the court of any termination, suspension or modification of that interim measure.
(3) The court of the State where recognition or enforcement is sought may, if it considers it proper, order the requesting party to provide appropriate security if the arbitral tribunal has not already made a determination with respect to security or where such a decision is necessary to protect the rights of third parties.

Article 17 I. Grounds for refusing recognition or enforcement[9]

(1) Recognition or enforcement of an interim measure may be refused only:
(a) At the request of the party against whom it is invoked if the court *is* satisfied that:
(i) Such refusal is warranted on the grounds set forth in article 36(1) (a)(1), (ii), (iii) or (iv): or
(ii) The arbitral tribunal's decision with respect to the provision of security in connection with the interim measure issued by the arbitral tribunal has not been complied with; or
(iii) The interim measure has been terminated or suspended by the arbitral tribunal or, where so empowered, by the court of the State in which the arbitration takes place or under the law of which that interim measure was granted; or
(b) If the court finds that:
(i) The interim measure is incompatible with the powers conferred upon the court unless the court decides to reformulate the interim measure to the extent necessary to adapt it to its own powers and procedures for the purposes of enforcing that interim measure and without modifying its substance; or
(ii) Any of the grounds set forth in article *36(1)(b)(i)* or (ii), apply to the recognition and enforcement of the interim measure.
(2) Any determination made by the court on any ground in paragraph (1) of this article shall be effective only for the purposes of the application to recognize and enforce the interim measure. The court where recognition or enforcement is sought shall not, in making that determination, undertake a review of the substance of the interim measure.

9 The conditions set forth in article 17 1 are intended to limit the number of circumstances in which the court may refuse to enforce an interim measure. It would not be contrary to the level of harmonization sought by these model provisions if a State were to adopt fewer circumstances in which enforcement may be refused.

Section 5. Court-ordered interim measures

Article 17 J. Court-ordered interim measures

A court shall have the same power of issuing an interim measure in relation to arbitration proceedings, irrespective of whether their place is in the territory of this State, as it has in relation to proceedings in courts. The court shall exercise such power in accordance with its own procedures in consideration of the specific features of international arbitration.

CHAPTER V. CONDUCT OF ARBITRAL PROCEEDINGS

Article 18. Equal treatment of parties

The parties shall be treated with equality and each party shall be given a full opportunity of presenting his case.

Article 19. Determination of rules of procedure

(1) Subject to the provisions of this Law, the parties are free to agree on the procedure to be followed by the arbitral tribunal in conducting the proceedings.
(2) Failing such agreement, the arbitral tribunal may, subject to the provisions of this Law, conduct the arbitration in such manner as it considers appropriate. The power conferred upon the arbitral tribunal includes the power to determine the admissibility, relevance, materiality and weight of any evidence.

Article 20. Place of arbitration

(1)The parties are free to agree on the place of arbitration. Failing such agreement, the place of arbitration shall be determined by the arbitral tribunal having regard to the circumstances of the case, including the convenience of the parties.
(2) Notwithstanding the provisions of paragraph (1) of this article, the arbitral tribunal may, unless otherwise agreed by the parties, meet at any place it considers appropriate for consultation among its members, for hearing witnesses, experts or the parties, or for inspection of goods, other property or documents.

Article 21. Commencement of arbitral proceedings

Unless otherwise agreed by the parties, the arbitral proceedings in respect of a particular dispute commence on the date on which a request for that dispute to be referred to arbitration is received by the respondent.

Article 22. Language

(1) The parties are free to agree on the language or languages to be used in the arbitral proceedings. Failing such agreement, the arbitral tribunal shall determine the language or languages to be used in the proceedings. This agreement or determination, unless otherwise specified therein, shall apply

to any written statement by a party, any hearing and any award, decision or other communication by the arbitral tribunal.
(2) The arbitral tribunal may order that any documentary evidence shall be accompanied by a translation into the language or languages agreed upon by the parties or determined by the arbitral tribunal.

Article 23. Statements of claim and defence

(1) Within the period of time agreed by the parties or determined by the arbitral tribunal, the claimant shall state the facts supporting his claim, the points at issue and the relief or remedy sought, and the respondent shall state his defence in respect of these particulars, unless the parties have otherwise agreed as to the required elements of such statements. The parties may submit with their statements all documents they consider to be relevant or may add a reference to the documents or other evidence they will submit.
(2) Unless otherwise agreed by the parties, either party may amend or supplement his claim or defence during the course of the arbitral proceedings, unless the arbitral tribunal considers it inappropriate to allow such amendment having regard to the delay in making it.

Article 24. Hearings and written proceedings

(1) Subject to any contrary agreement by the parties, the arbitral tribunal shall decide whether to hold oral hearings for the presentation of evidence or for oral argument, or whether the proceedings shall be conducted on the basis of documents and other materials. However, unless the parties have agreed that no hearings shall be held, the arbitral tribunal shall hold such hearings at an appropriate stage of the proceedings, if so requested by a party.
(2) The parties shall be given sufficient advance notice of any hearing and of any meeting of the arbitral tribunal for the purposes of inspection of goods, other property or documents.
(3) All statements, documents or other information supplied to the arbitral tribunal by one party shall be communicated to the other party. Also any expert report or evidentiary document on which the arbitral tribunal may rely in making its decision shall be communicated to the parties.

Article 25. Default of a party

Unless otherwise agreed by the parties, if, without showing sufficient cause,

(a) the claimant fails to communicate his statement of claim in accordance with article 23(1), the arbitral tribunal shall terminate the proceedings;
(b) the respondent fails to communicate his statement of defence in accordance with article 23(1), the arbitral tribunal shall continue the proceedings without treating such failure in itself as an admission of the claimant's allegations;
(c) any party fails to appear at a hearing or to produce documentary evidence, the arbitral tribunal may continue the proceedings and make the award on the evidence before it.

Article 26. Expert appointed by arbitral tribunal

(1) Unless otherwise agreed by the parties, the arbitral tribunal

(a) may appoint one or more experts to report to it on specific issues to be determined by the arbitral tribunal;

(b) may require a party to give the expert any relevant information or to produce, or to provide access to, any relevant documents, goods or other property for his inspection.
(2) Unless otherwise agreed by the parties, if a party so requests or if the arbitral tribunal considers it necessary, the expert shall, after delivery of his written or oral report, participate in a hearing where the parties have the opportunity to put questions to him and to present expert witnesses in order to testify on the points at issue.

Article 27. Court assistance in taking evidence

The arbitral tribunal or a party with the approval of the arbitral tribunal may request from a competent court of this State assistance in taking evidence.

The court may execute the request within its competence and according its rules on taking evidence.

CHAPTER VI. MAKING OF AWARD AND TERMINATION OF PROCEEDINGS

Article 28. Rules applicable to substance of dispute

(1) The arbitral tribunal shall decide the dispute in accordance with such rules of law as are chosen by the parties as applicable to the substance of the dispute. Any designation of the law or legal system of a given State shall be construed, unless otherwise expressed, as directly referring to the substantive law of that State and not to its conflict of laws rules,
(2) Failing any designation by the parties, the arbitral tribunal shall apply the law determined by the conflict of laws rules which it considers applicable,
(3) The arbitral tribunal shall decide *ex aequo et bono* or as *amiable compositeur* only if the parties have expressly authorized it to do so.
(4) In all cases, the arbitral tribunal shall decide in accordance with the terms of the contract and shall take into account the usages of the trade applicable to the transaction.

Article 29. Decision-making by panel of arbitrators

In arbitral proceedings with more than one arbitrator, any decision of the arbitral tribunal shall be made, unless otherwise agreed by the parties, by a majority of all its members. However, questions of procedure may be decided by a presiding arbitrator, if so authorized by the parties or all members of the arbitral tribunal.

Article 30. Settlement

(1) If, during arbitral proceedings, the parties settle the dispute, the arbitral tribunal shall terminate the proceedings and, if requested by the parties and not objected to by the arbitral tribunal, record the settlement in the form of an arbitral award on agreed terms.
(2) An award on agreed terms shall be made in accordance with the provisions of article 31 and shall state that it is an award. Such an award has the same status and effect as any other award on the merits of the case.

Article 31. Form and contents of award

(1) The award shall be made in writing and shall be signed by the arbitrator or arbitrators. In arbitral proceedings with more than one arbitrator, the signatures of the majority of all members of the arbitral tribunal shall suffice, provided that the reason for any omitted signature is stated.
(2) The award shall state the reasons upon which it is based, unless the parties have agreed that no reasons are to be given or the award is an award on agreed terms under article 30.
(3) The award shall state its date and the place of arbitration as determined in accordance with article 20(1). The award shall be deemed to have been made at that place.
(4) After the award is made, a copy signed by the arbitrators in accordance with paragraph (1) of this article shall be delivered to each party.

Article 32. Termination of proceedings

(1) The arbitral proceedings are terminated by the final award or by an order of the arbitral tribunal in accordance with paragraph (2) of this article.
(2) The arbitral tribunal shall issue an order for the termination of the arbitral proceedings when:
(a) the claimant withdraws his claim, unless the respondent objects thereto and the arbitral tribunal recognizes a legitimate interest on his part in obtaining a final settlement of the dispute;
(b) the parties agree on the termination of the proceedings;
(c) the arbitral tribunal finds that the continuation of the proceedings has for any other reason become unnecessary or impossible.
(3) The mandate of the arbitral tribunal terminates with the termination of the arbitral proceedings, subject to the provisions of articles 33 and 34(4).

Article 33. Correction and interpretation of award; additional award

(1) Within thirty days of receipt of the award, unless another period of time has been agreed upon by the parties:
(a) a party, with notice to the other party, may request the arbitral Tribunal to correct in the award any errors in computation, any clerical or typographical errors or any errors of similar nature;
(b) if so agreed by the parties, a party, with notice to the other party, may request the arbitral tribunal to give an interpretation of a specific point or part of the award.

If the arbitral tribunal considers the request to be justified, it shall make the correction or give the interpretation within thirty days of receipt of the request. The interpretation shall form part of the award.
(2) The arbitral tribunal may correct any error of the type referred to in paragraph *(1)(a)* of this article on its own initiative within thirty days of the date of the award.
(3) Unless otherwise agreed by the parties, a party, with notice to the other party, may request, within thirty days of receipt of the award, the arbitral tribunal to make an additional award as to claims presented in the arbitral proceedings but omitted from the award. If the arbitral tribunal considers the request to be justified, it shall make the additional award within sixty days.
(4) The arbitral tribunal may extend, if necessary, the period of time within which it shall make a correction, interpretation or an additional award under paragraph (1) or (3) of this article.

(5) The provisions of article 31 shall apply to a correction or interpretation of the award or to an additional award.

CHAPTER VII. RECOURSE AGAINST AWARD

Article 34. Application for setting aside as exclusive recourse against arbitral award

(1) Recourse to a court against an arbitral award may be made only by an application for setting aside in accordance with paragraphs (2) and (3) of this article.
(2) An arbitral award may be set aside by the court specified in article 6 only if:
(a) the party making the application furnishes proof that:
(i) a party to the arbitration agreement referred to in article 7 was under some incapacity; or the said agreement is not valid under the law to which the parties have subjected it or, failing any indication thereon, under the law of this State; or
(ii) the party making the application was not given proper notice of the appointment of an arbitrator or of the arbitral proceedings or was otherwise unable to present his case; or
(iii) the award deals with a dispute not contemplated by or not falling within the terms of the submission to arbitration, or contains decisions on matters beyond the scope of the submission to arbitration, provided that, if the decisions on matters submitted to arbitration can be separated from those not so submitted, only that part of the award which contains decisions on matters not submitted to arbitration may be set aside; or
(iv) the composition of the arbitral tribunal or the arbitral procedure was not in accordance with the agreement of the parties, unless such agreement was in conflict with a provision of this Law from which the parties cannot derogate, or, failing such agreement, was not in accordance with this Law; or
(b) the court finds that:
(i) the subject matter of the dispute is not capable of settlement by arbitration under the law of this State; or
(ii) the award is in conflict with the public policy of this State.
(3) An application for setting aside may not be made after three months have elapsed from the date on which the party making that application had received the award or, if a request had been made under article 33, from the date on which that request had been disposed of by the arbitral tribunal.
(4) The court, when asked to set aside an award, may, where appropriate and so requested by a party, suspend the setting aside proceedings for a period of time determined by it in order to give the arbitral tribunal an opportunity to resume the arbitral proceedings or to take such other action as in the arbitral tribunal's opinion will eliminate the grounds for setting aside.

CHAPTER VIII RECOGNITION AND ENFORCEMENT OF AWARDS

Article 35. Recognition and enforcement

(1) An arbitral award, irrespective of the country in which it was made, shall be recognized as binding and, upon application in writing to the competent court, shall be enforced subject to the provisions of this article and of article 36.

(2) The party relying on an award or applying for its enforcement shall supply the original award or a copy thereof. If the award is not made in an official language of this State, the court may request the party to supply a translation thereof into such language.[10]

(Article 35(2) has been amended by the commission at its thirty-ninth session, in 2006)

Article 36. Grounds for refusing recognition or enforcement

(1) Recognition or enforcement of an arbitral award, irrespective of the country in which it was made, may be refused only:

(a) at the request of the party against whom it is invoked, if that party furnishes to competent court where recognition or enforcement is sought proof that:

(i) a party lo the arbitration agreement referred to in article 7 was under some incapacity or the said agreement is not "valid under the law" to which the parties have subjected it or, failing any indication thereon, under the law of the country where the award was made; or

(ii) the party against which the award is invoked was not given proper notice of the appointment of an arbitrator or of the arbitral proceedings or was otherwise unable to present his case; or

(iii) the award deals with a dispute not contemplated by or not falling within the terms of the submission to arbitration, or it contains decisions on matters beyond the scope of the submission to arbitration, provided that, if the decisions on matters submitted to arbitration can be separated from those not so submitted, that part of the award which contains decisions on matters submitted to arbitration may be recognized and enforced; or

(iv) the composition of the arbitral tribunal or the arbitral procedure was not in accordance with the agreement of the parties failing such agreement, was not in accordance with the law of the country where the arbitration took place; or

(v) the award has not yet become binding on the parties or been set aside or suspended by a court of the country in which, or under the law of which, that award was made; or

(b) if the court finds that:

(i) the subject matter of the dispute is not capable of settlement by arbitration under the law of this State; or

(ii) the recognition or enforcement of the award would be contrary to the public policy of this State.

(2) If an application for setting aside or suspension of an award has been made to a court referred to in paragraph *(I)(a)(v)* of this article, the court where recognition or enforcement is sought may, if it considers it proper, adjourn its decision and may also, on the application of the party claiming recognition or enforcement of the award, order the other party to provide appropriate security.

10 The conditions set forth in this paragraph are intended to set maximum standards. It would, thus, not he contrary to the harmonization to be achieved by the model law if a State retained even less onerous conditions.

Annex 2

UNCITRAL ARBITRATION RULES

(As revised in 2010)

SECTION I. INTRODUCTORY RULES

Scope of application*

Article 1

1. Where parties have agreed that disputes between them in respect of a defined legal relationship, whether contractual or not, shall be referred to arbitration under the UNCITRAL Arbitration Rules, then such disputes shall be settled in accordance with these Rules subject to such modification as the parties may agree.
2. The parties to an arbitration agreement concluded after 15 august 2010 shall be presumed to have referred to the rules in effect on the date of commencement of the arbitration, unless the parties have agreed to apply a particular version of the rules.
That presumption does not apply where the arbitration agreement has been concluded by accepting after 15 August 2010 an offer made before that date.
3. These Rules shall govern the arbitration except that where any of these Rules is in conflict with a provision of the law applicable to the arbitration from which the parties cannot derogate, that provision shall prevail.

* A model arbitration clause for contracts can be found in the annex to the Rules.

Notice and calculation of periods of time

Article 2

1. A notice, including a notification, communication or proposal, may be transmitted by any means of communication that provides or allows for a record of its transmission.
2. If an address has been designated by a party specifically for this purpose or authorized by the arbitral tribunal, any notice shall be delivered to that party at that address, and if so delivered shall be deemed to have been received. Delivery by electronic means such as facsimile or email may only be made to an address so designated or authorized.
3. In the absence of such designation or authorization, a notice is:
   (a) received if it is physically delivered to the addressee; or
   (b) deemed to have been received if it is delivered at the place of business, habitual residence or mailing address, of the addressee.

4. If, after reasonable efforts, delivery cannot be effected in accordance with paragraphs 2 or 3, a notice is deemed to have been received if it is sent to the addressee's last-known place of business, habitual residence or mailing address by registered letter or any other means that provides a record of delivery or of attempted delivery.
5. A notice shall be deemed to have been received on the day it is delivered in accordance with paragraphs 2, 3 or 4, or attempted to be delivered in accordance with paragraph 4. A notice transmitted by electronic means is deemed to have been received on the day it is sent, except that a notice of arbitration so transmitted is only deemed to have been received on the day when it reaches the addressee's electronic address.
6. For the purpose of calculating a period of time under these Rules, such period shall begin to run on the day following the day when a notice is received. If the last day of such period is an official holiday or a non-business day at the residence or place of business of the addressee, the period is extended until the first business day which follows. Official holidays or non-business days occurring during the running of the period of time are included in calculating the period.

Notice of arbitration

Article 3

1. The party or parties initiating recourse to arbitration (hereinafter called the "claimant") shall communicate to the other party or parties (hereinafter called the "respondent") a notice of arbitration.
2. Arbitral proceedings shall be deemed to commence on the date on which the notice of arbitration is received by the respondent.
3. The notice of arbitration shall include the following:
   (a) A demand that the dispute be referred to arbitration;
   (b) The names and contact details of the parties;
   (c) Identification of the arbitration agreement that is invoked;
   (d) Identification of any contract or other legal instrument out of or in relation to which the dispute arises or, in the absence of such contract or instrument, a brief description of the relevant relationship;
   (e) A brief description of the claim and an indication of the amount involved, if any;
   (f) The relief or remedy sought;
   (g) A proposal as to the number of arbitrators, language and place of arbitration, if the parties have not previously agreed thereon.
4. The notice of arbitration may also include:
   (a) A proposal for the designation of an appointing authority referred to in article 6, paragraph 1;
   (b) A proposal for the appointment of a sole arbitrator referred to in article 8, paragraph 1;
   (c) Notification of the appointment of an arbitrator referred to in articles 9 or 10.
5. The constitution of the arbitral tribunal shall not be hindered by any controversy with respect to the sufficiency of the notice of arbitration, which shall be finally resolved by the arbitral tribunal.

Response to the notice of arbitration

Article 4

1. Within 30 days of the receipt of the notice of arbitration, the respondent shall communicate to the claimant a response to the notice of arbitration, which shall include:
   (a) The name and contact details of each respondent;
   (b) A response to the information set forth in the notice of arbitration, pursuant to article 3, paragraphs 3 (c) to (g).
2. The response to the notice of arbitration may also include:
   (a) Any plea that an arbitral tribunal to be constituted under these Rules lacks jurisdiction;
   (b) A proposal for the designation of an appointing authority referred to in article 6, paragraph 1;
   (c) A proposal for the appointment of a sole arbitrator referred to in article 8, paragraph 1;
   (d) Notification of the appointment of an arbitrator referred to in articles 9 or 10;
   (e) A brief description of counterclaims or claims for the purpose of a set-off, if any, including where relevant, an indication of the amounts involved, and the relief or remedy sought;
   (f) A notice of arbitration in accordance with article 3 in case the respondent formulates a claim against a party to the arbitration agreement other than the claimant.
3. The constitution of the arbitral tribunal shall not be hindered by any controversy with respect to the respondent's failure to communicate a response to the notice of arbitration, or an incomplete or late response to the notice of arbitration, which shall be finally resolved by the arbitral tribunal.

Representation and assistance

Article 5

Each party may be represented or assisted by persons chosen by it. The names and addresses of such persons must be communicated to all parties and to the arbitral tribunal. Such communication must specify whether the appointment is being made for purposes of representation or assistance. Where a person is to act as a representative of a party, the arbitral tribunal, on its own initiative or at the request of any party, may at any time require proof of authority granted to the representative in such a form as the arbitral tribunal may determine.

Designating and appointing authorities

Article 6

1. Unless the parties have already agreed on the choice of an appointing authority, a party may at any time propose the name or names of one or more institutions or persons, including the Secretary-General of the Permanent Court of Arbitration at The Hague (hereinafter called the "PCA"), one of whom would serve as appointing authority.
2. If all parties have not agreed on the choice of an appointing authority within 30 days after a proposal made in accordance with paragraph 1 has been received by all other parties, any party may request the Secretary-General of the PCA to designate the appointing authority.

3. Where these Rules provide for a period of time within which a party must refer a matter to an appointing authority and no appointing authority has been agreed on or designated, the period is suspended from the date on which a party initiates the procedure for agreeing on or designating an appointing authority until the date of such agreement or designation.
4. Except as referred to in article 41, paragraph 4, if the appointing authority refuses to act, or if it fails to appoint an arbitrator within 30 days after it receives a party's request to do so, fails to act within any other period provided by these Rules, or fails to decide on a challenge to an arbitrator within a reasonable time after receiving a party's request to do so, any party may request the Secretary-General of the PCA to designate a substitute appointing authority.
5. In exercising their functions under these Rules, the appointing authority and the Secretary-General of the PCA may require from any party and the arbitrators the information they deem necessary and they shall give the parties and, where appropriate, the arbitrators, an opportunity to present their views in any manner they consider appropriate. All such communications to and from the appointing authority and the Secretary-General of the PCA shall also be provided by the sender to all other parties.
6. When the appointing authority is requested to appoint an arbitrator pursuant to articles 8, 9, 10 or 14, the party making the request shall send to the appointing authority copies of the notice of arbitration and, if it exists, any response to the notice of arbitration.
7. The appointing authority shall have regard to such considerations as are likely to secure the appointment of an independent and impartial arbitrator and shall take into account the advisability of appointing an arbitrator of a nationality other than the nationalities of the parties.

SECTION II. COMPOSITION OF THE ARBITRAL TRIBUNAL

Number of arbitrators

Article 7

1. If the parties have not previously agreed on the number of arbitrators, and if within 30 days after the receipt by the respondent of the notice of arbitration the parties have not agreed that there shall be only one arbitrator, three arbitrators shall be appointed.
2. Notwithstanding paragraph 1, if no other parties have responded to a party's proposal to appoint a sole arbitrator within the time limit provided for in paragraph 1 and the party or parties concerned have failed to appoint a second arbitrator in accordance with articles 9 or 10, the appointing authority may, at the request of a party, appoint a sole arbitrator pursuant to the procedure provided for in article 8, paragraph 2, if it determines that, in view of the circumstances of the case, this is more appropriate.

Appointment of arbitrators (articles 8 to10)

Article 8

1. If the parties have agreed that a sole arbitrator is to be appointed and if within 30 days after receipt by all other parties of a proposal for the appointment of a sole arbitrator the parties have

not reached agreement thereon, a sole arbitrator shall, at the request of a party, be appointed by the appointing authority.
2. The appointing authority shall appoint the sole arbitrator as promptly as possible. In making the appointment, the appointing authority shall use the following list-procedure, unless the parties agree that the list-procedure should not be used or unless the appointing authority determines in its discretion that the use of the list-procedure is not appropriate for the case:

(a) The appointing authority shall communicate to each of the parties an identical list containing at least three names;

(b) Within 15 days after the receipt of this list, each party may return the list to the appointing authority after having deleted the name or names to which it objects and numbered the remaining names on the list in the order of its preference;

(c) After the expiration of the above period of time the appointing authority shall appoint the sole arbitrator from among the names approved on the lists returned to it and in accordance with the order of preference indicated by the parties;

(d) If for any reason the appointment cannot be made according to this procedure, the appointing authority may exercise its discretion in appointing the sole arbitrator.

Article 9

1. If three arbitrators are to be appointed, each party shall appoint one arbitrator. The two arbitrators thus appointed shall choose the third arbitrator who will act as the presiding arbitrator of the arbitral tribunal.
2. If within 30 days after the receipt of a party's notification of the appointment of an arbitrator the other party has not notified the first party of the arbitrator it has appointed, the first party may request the appointing authority to appoint the second arbitrator.
3. If within 30 days after the appointment of the second arbitrator the two arbitrators have not agreed on the choice of the presiding arbitrator, the presiding arbitrator shall be appointed by the appointing authority in the same way as a sole arbitrator would be appointed under article 8.

Article 10

1. For the purposes of article 9, paragraph 1, where three arbitrators are to be appointed and there are multiple parties as claimant or as respondent, unless the parties have agreed to another method of appointment of arbitrators, the multiple, parties jointly, whether as claimant or as respondent, shall appoint an arbitrator.
2. If the parties have agreed that the arbitral tribunal is to be composed of a number of arbitrators other than one or three, the arbitrators shall be appointed according to the method agreed upon by the parties.
3. In the event of any failure to constitute the arbitral tribunal under these Rules, the appointing authority shall, at the request of any party, constitute the arbitral tribunal and, in doing so, may revoke any appointment already made and appoint or reappoint each of the arbitrators and designate one of them as the presiding arbitrator.

Disclosures by and challenge of arbitrators ** (articles 11to 13)

Article 11

When a person is approached in connection with his or her possible appointment as an arbitrator, he or she shall disclose any circumstances likely to give rise to justifiable doubts as to his or her impartiality or independence. An arbitrator, from the time of his or her appointment and throughout the arbitral proceedings, shall without delay disclose any such circumstances to the parties and the other arbitrators unless they have already been informed by him or her of these circumstances.

** Model statements of independence pursuant to article 11 can be found in the annex to the Rules.

Article 12

1. Any arbitrator may be challenged if circumstances exist that give rise to justifiable doubts as to the arbitrator's impartiality or independence
2. A party may challenge the arbitrator appointed by it only for reasons of which it becomes aware after the appointment has been made.
3. In the event that an arbitrator fails to act or in the event of the *de jure* or *de facto* impossibility of his or her performing his or her functions, the procedure in respect of the challenge of an arbitrator as provided in article 13 shall apply.

Article 13

1. A party that intends to challenge an arbitrator shall send notice of its challenge within 15 days after it has been notified of the appointment of the challenged arbitrator, or within 15 days after the circumstances mentioned in articles 11 and 12 became known to that party.
2. The notice of challenge shall be communicated to all other parties, to the arbitrator who is challenged and to the other arbitrators. The notice of challenge shall state the reasons for the challenge.
3. When an arbitrator has been challenged by a party, all parties may agree to the challenge. The arbitrator may also, after the challenge, withdraw from his or her office. In neither case does this imply acceptance of the validity of the grounds for the challenge.
4. If, within 15 days from the date of the notice of challenge, all parties do not agree to the challenge or the challenged arbitrator does not withdraw, the party making the challenge may elect to pursue it. In that case, within 30 days from the date of the notice of challenge, it shall seek a decision on the challenge by the appointing authority.

Replacement of an arbitrator

Article 14

1. Subject to paragraph 2, in any event where an arbitrator has to be replaced during the course of the arbitral proceedings, a substitute arbitrator shall be appointed or chosen pursuant to the procedure provided for in articles 8 to 11 that was applicable to the appointment or choice of the arbitrator

being replaced. This procedure shall apply even if during the process of appointing the arbitrator to be replaced, a party had failed to exercise its right to appoint or to participate in the appointment.
2. If, at the request of a party, the appointing authority determines that, in view of the exceptional circumstances of the case, it would be justified for a party to be deprived of its right to appoint a substitute arbitrator, the appointing authority may, after giving an opportunity to the parties and the remaining arbitrators to express their views:
(a) appoint the substitute Arbitrator; or
(b) after the closure of the hearings, authorize the other arbitrators to proceed with the arbitration and make any decision or award.

Repetition of hearings in the event of the replacement of an arbitrator

Article 15

If an arbitrator is replaced, the proceedings shall resume at the stage where the arbitrator who was replaced ceased to perform his or her functions, unless the arbitral tribunal decides otherwise.

Exclusion of liability

Article 16

Save for intentional wrongdoing, the parties waive, to the fullest extent permitted under the applicable law, any claim against the arbitrators, the appointing authority and any person appointed by the arbitral tribunal based on any act or omission in connection with the arbitration.

SECTION III. ARBITRAL PROCEEDINGS

General provisions

Article 17

1. Subject to these Rules, the arbitral tribunal may conduct the arbitration in such manner as it considers appropriate, provided that the parties are treated with equality and that at an appropriate stage of the proceedings each party is given a reasonable opportunity of presenting its case. The arbitral tribunal, in exercising its discretion, shall conduct the proceedings so as to avoid unnecessary delay and expense and to provide a fair and efficient process for resolving the parties' dispute.
2. As soon as practicable after its constitution and after inviting the parties to express their views, the arbitral tribunal shall establish the provisional timetable of the arbitration. The arbitral tribunal may, at any time, after inviting the parties to express their views, extend or abridge any period of time prescribed under these Rules or agreed by the parties.
3. If at an appropriate stage of the proceedings any party so requests, the arbitral tribunal shall hold hearings for the presentation of evidence by witnesses, including expert witnesses, or for oral

argument. In the absence of such a request, the arbitral tribunal shall decide whether to hold such hearings or whether the proceedings shall be conducted on the basis of documents and other materials.
4. All communications to the arbitral tribunal by one party shall be communicated by that party to all other parties. Such communications shall be made at the same time, except as otherwise permitted by the arbitral tribunal if it may do so under applicable law.
5. The arbitral tribunal may, at the request of any party, allow one or more third persons to be joined in the arbitration as a party provided such person is a party to the arbitration agreement, unless the arbitral tribunal finds, after giving all parties, including the person or persons to be joined, the opportunity to be heard, that joinder should not be permitted because of prejudice to any of those parties. The arbitral tribunal may make a single award or several awards in respect of all parties so involved in the arbitration.

Place of arbitration

Article 18

1. If the parties have not previously agreed on the place of arbitration, the place of arbitration shall be determined by the arbitral tribunal having regard to the circumstances of the case.

• The award shall be deemed to have been made at the place of arbitration.

2. The arbitral tribunal may meet at any location it considers appropriate for .deliberations. Unless otherwise agreed by the parties, the arbitral tribunal may also meet at any location it considers appropriate for any other purpose, including hearings.

Language

Article 19

1. Subject to an agreement by the parties, the arbitral tribunal shall, promptly after its appointment, determine the language or languages to be used in the proceedings. This determination shall apply to the statement of claim, the statement of defence, and any further written statements and, if oral hearings take place, to the language or languages to be used in such hearings.
2. The arbitral tribunal may order that any documents annexed to the statement of claim or statement of defence, and any supplementary documents or exhibits submitted in the course of the proceedings, delivered in their original language, shall be accompanied by a translation into the language or languages agreed upon by the parties or determined by the arbitral tribunal.

Statement of claim

Article 20

1. The claimant shall communicate its statement of claim in writing to the respondent and to each of the arbitrators within a period of time to be determined by the arbitral tribunal. The claimant

may elect to treat its notice of arbitration referred to in article 3 as a statement of claim, provided that the notice of arbitration also complies with the requirements of paragraphs 2 to 4 of this article.
2. The statement of claim shall include the following particulars:
(a) The names and contact details of the parties;
(b) A statement of the facts supporting the claim;
(c) The points at issue;
(d) The relief or remedy sought;
(e) The legal grounds or arguments supporting the claim,
3. A copy of any contract or other legal instrument out of or in relation to which the dispute arises and of the arbitration agreement shall be annexed to the statement of claim.
4. The statement of claim should, as far as possible, be accompanied by all documents and other evidence relied upon by the claimant, or contain references to them.

Statement of defence

Article 21

1. The respondent shall communicate its statement of defence in writing to the claimant and to each of the arbitrators within a period of time to be determined by the arbitral tribunal. The respondent may elect to treat its response to the notice of arbitration referred to in article 4 as a statement of defence, provided that the response to the notice of arbitration also complies with the requirements of paragraph 2 of this article.
2. The statement of defence shall reply to the particulars (b) to (e) of the statement of claim (article 20, paragraph 2). The statement of defence should, as far as possible, be accompanied by all documents and other evidence relied upon by the respondent, or contain references to them,
3. In its statement of defence, or at a later stage in the arbitral proceedings if the arbitral tribunal decides that the delay was justified under the circumstances, the respondent may make a counterclaim or rely on a claim for the purpose of a set-off provided that the arbitral tribunal has jurisdiction over it.
4. The provisions of article 20, paragraphs 2 to 4, shall apply to a counterclaim, a claim under article 4, paragraph 2 (f), and a claim relied on for the purpose of a set-off.

Amendments to the claim or defence

Article 22

During the course of the arbitral proceedings, a party may amend or supplement its claim or defence, including a counterclaim or a claim for the purpose of a set-off, unless the arbitral tribunal considers it inappropriate to allow such amendment or supplement having regard to the delay in making it or prejudice to other parties or any other circumstances. However, a claim or defence, including a counterclaim or a claim for the purpose of a set-off, may not be amended or supplemented in such a manner that the amended or supplemented claim or defence falls outside the jurisdiction of the arbitral tribunal.

Pleas as to the jurisdiction of the arbitral tribunal

Article 23

1. The arbitral tribunal shall have the power to rule on its own jurisdiction; including any objections with respect to the existence or validity of the arbitration agreement. For that purpose, an arbitration clause that forms part of a contract shall be treated as an agreement independent of the other terms of the contract. A decision by the arbitral tribunal that the contract is null shall not entail automatically the invalidity of the arbitration clause.
2. A plea that the arbitral tribunal does not have jurisdiction shall be raised no later than in the statement of defence or, with respect to a counterclaim or a claim for the purpose of a set-off, in the reply to the counterclaim or to the claim for the purpose of a set-off. A party is not precluded from raising such a plea by the fact that it has appointed, or participated in the appointment of, an arbitrator. A plea that the arbitral tribunal is exceeding the scope of its authority shall be raised as soon as the matter alleged to be beyond the scope of its authority is raised during the arbitral proceedings. The arbitral tribunal may, in either case, admit a later plea if it considers the delay justified.
3. The arbitral tribunal may rule on a plea referred to in paragraph 2 either as a preliminary question or in an award on the merits. The arbitral tribunal may continue the arbitral proceedings and make an award, notwithstanding any pending challenge to its jurisdiction before a court.

Further written statements

Article 24

The arbitral tribunal shall decide which further written statements, in addition to the statement of claim and the statement of defence, shall be required from the parties or may be presented by them and shall fix the periods of time for communicating such statements.

Periods of time

Article 25

The periods of time fixed by the arbitral tribunal for the communication of written statements (including the statement of claim and statement of defence) should not exceed 45 days. However, the arbitral tribunal may extend the time limits if it concludes that an extension is justified.

Interim measures

Article 26

1. The arbitral tribunal may, at the request of a party, grant interim measures.
2. An interim measure is any temporary measure by which, at any time prior to the issuance of the award by which the dispute is finally decided, the arbitral tribunal orders a party, for example and without limitation, to:

(a) Maintain or restore the status quo pending determination of the dispute;

(b) Take action that would prevent, or refrain from taking action that is likely to cause, (i) current or imminent harm or (ii) prejudice to the arbitral process itself;

(c) Provide a means of preserving assets out of which a subsequent award may be satisfied; or

(d) Preserve evidence that may be relevant and material to the resolution of the dispute.

3. The party requesting an interim measure under paragraphs 2 (a) to (c) shall satisfy the arbitral tribunal that:

(a) Harm not adequately reparable by an award of damages is likely to result if the measure is not ordered, and such harm substantially outweighs the harm that is likely to result to the party against whom the measure is directed if the measure is granted; and

(b) There is a reasonable possibility that the requesting party will succeed on the merits of the claim. The determination on this possibility shall not affect the discretion of the arbitral tribunal in making any subsequent determination.

4. With regard to a request for an interim measure under paragraph 2 (d), the requirements in paragraphs 3 (a) and (b) shall apply only to the extent the arbitral tribunal considers appropriate.

5. The arbitral tribunal may modify, suspend or terminate an interim measure it has granted, upon application of any party or, in exceptional circumstances and upon prior notice to the parties, on the arbitral tribunal's own initiative.

6. The arbitral tribunal may require the party requesting an interim measure to provide appropriate security in connection with the measure.

7. The arbitral tribunal may require any party promptly to disclose any material change in the circumstances on the basis of which the interim measure was requested or granted.

8. The party requesting an interim measure may be liable for any costs and damages caused by the measure to any party if the arbitral tribunal later determines that, in the circumstances then prevailing, the measure should not have been granted. The arbitral tribunal may award such costs and damages at any point during the proceedings.

9. A request for interim measures addressed by any party to a judicial authority shall not be deemed incompatible with the agreement to arbitrate, or as a waiver of that agreement.

Evidence

Article 27

1. Each party shall have the burden of proving the facts relied on to support its claim or defence.

2. Witnesses, including expert witnesses, who are presented by the parties to testify to the arbitral tribunal on any issue of fact or expertise may be any individual, notwithstanding that the individual is a party to the arbitration or in any way related to a party. Unless otherwise directed by the arbitral tribunal, statements by witnesses, including expert witnesses, may be presented in writing and signed by them.

3. At any time during the arbitral proceedings the arbitral tribunal may require the parties to produce documents, exhibits or other evidence within such a period of time as the arbitral tribunal shall determine.

4. The arbitral tribunal shall determine the admissibility, relevance, materiality and weight of the evidence offered.

Hearings

Article 28

1. In the event of an oral hearing, the arbitral tribunal shall give the parties adequate advance notice of the date, time and place thereof.
2. Witnesses, including expert witnesses, may be heard under the conditions and examined in the manner set by the arbitral tribunal.
3. Hearings shall be held in camera unless the parties agree otherwise. The arbitral tribunal may require the retirement of any witness or witnesses, including expert witnesses, during the testimony of such other witnesses, except that a witness, including an expert witness, who is a party to the arbitration shall not, in principle, be asked to retire.
4. The arbitral tribunal may direct that witnesses, including expert witnesses, be examined through means of telecommunications that do not require their physical presence at the hearing (such as video conferencing).

Experts appointed by the arbitral tribunal

Article 29

1. After consultation with the parties, the arbitral tribunal may appoint one or more independent experts to report to it, in writing, on specific issues to be determined by the arbitral tribunal. A copy of the expert's terms of reference, established by the arbitral tribunal, shall be communicated to the parties.
2. The expert shall, in principle before accepting appointment, submit to the arbitral tribunal and to the parties a description of his or her qualifications and a statement of his or her impartiality and independence. Within the time ordered by the arbitral tribunal, the parties shall inform the arbitral tribunal whether they have any objections to the expert's qualifications, impartiality or independence. The arbitral tribunal shall decide promptly whether to accept any such objections. After an expert's appointment, a party may object to the expert's qualifications, impartiality or independence only if the objection is for reasons of which the party becomes aware after the appointment has been made. The arbitral tribunal shall decide promptly what, if any, action to take.
3. The parties shall give the expert any relevant information or produce for his or her inspection any relevant documents or goods that he or she may require of them. Any dispute between a party and such an expert as to the relevance of the required information or production shall be referred to the arbitral tribunal for decision.
4. Upon receipt of the expert's report, the arbitral tribunal shall communicate a copy of the report to the parties, which shall be given the opportunity to express, in writing, their opinion on the report. A party shall be entitled to examine any document on which the expert has relied in his or her report.
5. At the request of any party, the expert, after delivery of the report, may be heard at a hearing where the parties shall have the opportunity to be present and to interrogate the expert. At this

hearing, any party may present expert witnesses in order to testify on the points at issue. The provisions of article 28 shall be applicable to such proceedings.

Default

Article 30

1. If, within the period of time fixed by these Rules or the arbitral tribunal, without showing sufficient cause:
(a) The claimant has failed to communicate its statement of claim, the arbitral tribunal shall issue an order for the termination of the arbitral proceedings, unless there are remaining matters that may need to be decided and the arbitral tribunal considers it appropriate to do so;
(b) If the respondent has failed to communicate its response to the notice of arbitration or its statement of defence, the arbitral tribunal shall order that the proceedings continue, without treating such failure in itself as an admission of the claimant's allegations; the provisions of this sub-paragraph also apply to a claimant's failure to submit a defence to a counterclaim or to a claim for the purpose of a set-off.
2. If a party, duly notified under these Rules, fails to appear at a hearing, without showing sufficient cause for such failure, the arbitral tribunal may proceed with the arbitration.
3. If a party, duly invited by the arbitral tribunal to produce documents, exhibits or other evidence, fails to do so within the established period of time, without showing sufficient cause for such failure, the arbitral tribunal may make the award on the evidence before it.

Closure of hearings

Article 31

1. The arbitral tribunal may inquire of the parties if they have any further proof to offer or witnesses to be heard or submissions to make and, if there are none, it may declare the hearings closed.
2. The arbitral tribunal may, if it considers it necessary owing to exceptional circumstances, decide, on its own initiative or upon application of a party, to reopen the hearings at any time before the award is made.

Waiver of right to object

Article 32

A failure by any party to object promptly to any non-compliance with these Rules or with any requirement of the arbitration agreement shall be deemed to be a waiver of the right of such party to make such an objection, unless such party can show that, under the circumstances, its failure to object was justified.

SECTION IV. THE AWARD

Decisions

Article 33

1. When there is more than one arbitrator, any award or other decision of the arbitral tribunal shall be made by a majority of the arbitrators.
2. In the case of questions of procedure, when there is no majority or when the arbitral tribunal so authorizes, the presiding arbitrator may decide alone, subject to revision, if any, by the arbitral tribunal.

Form and effect of the award

Article 34

1. The arbitral tribunal may make separate awards on different issues at different times.
2. All awards shall be made in writing and shall be final and binding on the parties. The parties shall carry out all awards without delay.
3. The arbitral tribunal shall state the reasons upon which the award is based, unless the parties have agreed that no reasons are to be given.
4. An award shall be signed by the arbitrators and it shall contain the date on which the award was made and indicate the place of arbitration. Where there is more than one arbitrator and any of them fails to sign, the award shall state the reason for the absence of the signature.
5. An award may be made public with the consent of all parties or where and to the extent disclosure is required of a party by legal duty, to protect or pursue a legal right or in relation to legal proceedings before a court or other competent authority.
6. Copies of the award signed by the arbitrators shall be communicated to the parties by the arbitral tribunal.

Applicable Law, *amiable compositeur*

Article 35

1. The arbitral tribunal shall apply the rules of law designated by the parties as applicable to the substance of the dispute. Failing such designation by the parties, the arbitral tribunal shall apply the law which it determines to be appropriate.
2. The arbitral tribunal shall decide as *amiable compositeur* or *ex aequo et bono* only if the parties have expressly authorized the arbitral tribunal to do so.
3. In all cases, the arbitral tribunal shall decide in accordance with the terms of the contract, if any, and shall take into account any usage of trade applicable to the transaction.

Settlement or other grounds for termination

Article 36

1. If, before the award is made, the parties agree on a settlement of the dispute, the arbitral tribunal shall either issue an order for the termination of the arbitral proceedings or, if requested by the parties and accepted by the arbitral tribunal, record the settlement in the form of an arbitral award on agreed terms. The arbitral tribunal is not obliged to give reasons for such an award.
2. If, before the award is made, the continuation of the arbitral proceedings becomes unnecessary or impossible for any reason not mentioned in paragraph 1, the arbitral tribunal shall inform the parties of its intention to issue an order for the termination of the proceedings. The arbitral tribunal shall have the power to issue such an order unless there are remaining matters that may need to be decided and the arbitral tribunal considers it appropriate to do so.
3. Copies of the order for termination of the arbitral proceedings or of the arbitral award on agreed terms, signed by the arbitrators, shall be communicated by the arbitral tribunal to the parties. Where an arbitral award on agreed terms is made, the provisions of article 34, paragraphs 2, 4 and 5, shall apply.

Interpretation of the award

Article 37

1. Within 30 days after the receipt of the award, a party, with notice to the other parties, may request that the arbitral tribunal give an interpretation of the award.
2. The interpretation shall be given in writing within 45 days after the receipt of the request. The interpretation shall form part of the award and the provisions of article 34, paragraphs 2 to 6, shall apply.

Correction of the award

Article 38

1. Within 30 days after the receipt of the award, a party, with notice to the other parties, may request the arbitral tribunal to correct in the award any error in computation, any clerical or typographical error, or any error or omission of a similar nature. If the arbitral tribunal considers that the request is justified, it shall make the correction within 45 days of receipt of the request.
2. The arbitral tribunal may within 30 days after the communication of the award make such corrections on its own initiative.
3. Such corrections shall be in writing and shall form part of the award. The provisions of article 34, paragraphs 2 to 6, shall apply.

Additional award

Article 39

1. Within 30 days after the receipt of the termination order or the award, a party, with notice to the other parties, may request the arbitral tribunal to make an award or an additional award as to claims presented in the arbitral proceedings but not decided by the arbitral tribunal.
2. If the arbitral tribunal considers the request for an award or additional award to be justified, it shall render or complete its award within 60 days after the receipt of the request. The arbitral tribunal may extend, if necessary, the period of time within which it shall make the award.
3. When such an award or additional award is made, the provisions of article 34, paragraphs 2 to 6, shall apply.

Definition of costs

Article 40

1. The arbitral tribunal shall fix the costs of arbitration in the final award and, if it deems appropriate, in another decision.
2. The term "costs" includes only:
   (a) The fees of the arbitral tribunal to be stated separately as to each arbitrator and to be fixed by the tribunal itself in accordance with article 41;
   (b) The reasonable travel and other expenses incurred by the arbitrators;
   (c) The reasonable costs of expert advice and of other assistance required by the arbitral tribunal;
   (d) The reasonable travel and other expenses of witnesses to the extent such expenses are approved by the arbitral tribunal;
   (e) The legal and other costs incurred by the parties in relation to the arbitration to the extent that the arbitral tribunal determines that the amount of such costs is reasonable;
   (f) Any fees and expenses of the appointing authority as well as the fees and expenses of the Secretary-General of the PCA.
3. In relation to interpretation, correction or completion of any award under articles 37 to 39, the arbitral tribunal may charge the costs referred to in paragraphs 2 (b) to (f), but no additional fees.

Fees and expenses of arbitrators

Article 41

1. The fees and expenses of the arbitrators shall be reasonable in amount, taking into account the amount in dispute, the arbitrators and any other relevant circumstances of the case.

2. If there is an appointing authority and it applies or has stated that it will apply a schedule or particular method for determining the fees for arbitrators in international cases, the arbitral tribunal

in fixing its fees shall take that schedule or method into account to the extent that it considers appropriate in the circumstances of the case.

3. Promptly after its constitution, the arbitral tribunal shall inform the parties as to how it proposes to determine its fees and expenses, including any rates it intends to apply. Within 15 days of receiving that proposal, any party may refer the proposal to the appointing authority for review. If, within 45 days of receipt of such a referral, the appointing authority finds that the proposal of the arbitral tribunal is inconsistent with paragraph 1, it shall make any necessary adjustments thereto, which shall be binding upon the arbitral tribunal.

4. (a) When informing the parties of the arbitrators' fees and expenses that have been fixed pursuant to article 40, paragraphs 2 (a) and (b), the arbitral tribunal shall also explain the manner in which the corresponding amounts have been calculated.

   (b) Within 15 days of receiving the arbitral tribunal's determination of fees and expenses, any party may refer for review such determination to the appointing authority. If no appointing authority has been agreed upon or designated, or if the appointing authority fails to act within the time specified in these Rules, then the review shall be made by the Secretary-General of the PCA.

   (c) If the appointing authority or the Secretary-General of the PCA finds that the arbitral tribunal's determination is inconsistent with the arbitral tribunal's proposal (and any adjustment thereto) under paragraph 3 or is otherwise manifestly excessive, it shall, within 45 days of receiving such a referral, make any adjustments to the arbitral tribunal's determination that are necessary to satisfy the criteria in paragraph 1. Any such adjustments shall be binding upon the arbitral tribunal.

   (d) Any such adjustments shall either be included by the arbitral tribunal in its award or, if the award has already been issued, be implemented in a correction to the award, to which the procedure of article 38, paragraph 3, shall apply.

5. Throughout the procedure under paragraphs 3 and 4, the arbitral tribunal shall proceed with the arbitration, in accordance with article 17, paragraph 1.

6. A referral under paragraph 4 shall not affect any determination in the award other than the arbitral tribunal's fees and expenses; nor shall it delay the recognition and enforcement of all parts of the award other than those relating to the determination of the arbitral tribunal's fees and expenses.

Allocation of costs

Article 42

1. The costs of the arbitration shall in principle be borne by the unsuccessful party or parties. However, the arbitral tribunal may apportion each of such costs between the parties if it determines that apportionment is reasonable, taking into account the circumstances of the case.

2. The arbitral tribunal shall in the final award or, if it deems appropriate, in any other award, determine any amount that a party may have to pay to another party as a result of the decision on allocation of costs.

Deposit of costs

Article 43

1. The arbitral tribunal, on its establishment, may request the parties to deposit an equal amount as an advance for the costs referred to in article 40, paragraphs 2 (a) to (c).
2. During the course of the arbitral proceedings the arbitral tribunal may request a supplementary deposits from the parties.
3. If an appointing authority has been agreed upon or designated, and when a party so requests and the appointing authority consents to perform the function, the arbitral tribunal shall fix the amounts of any deposits or supplementary deposits only after consultation with the appointing authority, which may make any comments to the arbitral tribunal that it deems appropriate concerning the amount of such deposits and supplementary deposits.
4. If the required deposits are not paid in full within 30 days after the receipt of the request, the arbitral tribunal shall so inform the parties in order that one or more of them may make the required payment. If such payment is not made, the arbitral tribunal may order the suspension or termination of the arbitral proceedings.
5. After a termination order or final award has been made, the arbitral tribunal shall render an accounting to the parties of the deposits received and return any unexpended balance to the parties.

Annex

Model arbitration clause for contracts

Any dispute, controversy or claim arising out of or relating to this contract, or the breach, termination or invalidity thereof, shall be settled by arbitration in accordance with the UNCITRAL Arbitration Rules.

Note: parties should consider adding:
The appointing authority shall be ...(name of institution or person):
The number of arbitrators shall be... (one or three):
The place of arbitration shall be ... (town and country):
The language to be used in the arbitral proceedings shall be ...

• **Possible waiver statement**
Note – If the parties wish to exclude recourse against the arbitral award that may be available under the applicable law they may consider adding a provision to that effect as suggested below, considering, however, that the effectiveness and conditions of such an exclusion depend on the applicable law.

Waiver: The parties hereby waive their right to any form of recourse against an award to any court or other competent authority, insofar as such waiver can validly be made under the applicable law.

Model statements of independence pursuant to article 11 of the Rules
No circumstances to disclose:

I am impartial and independent of cash of the parties and intend to remain so. To the best of my knowledge, there are no circumstances, past or present, likely to give rise to justifiable doubts as to my impartiality or independence; I shall promptly notify the parties and the other arbitrators of any such circumstances that may subsequently come to my attention during this arbitration.

Circumstances to disclose:
I am impartial and independent of each of the parties and intend to remain so. Attached is a statement made pursuant to article 11 of the UNCITRAL Arbitration Rules of (a) my past professional, business and other relationships with the parties and (b) any other relevant circumstances. [Include statement] I confirm that those circumstances do not affect my independence and impartiality. I shall promptly notify the parties and the other arbitrators of any such further relationships or circumstances that may subsequently come to my attention during this arbitration.

Note – Any party may consider requesting from the arbitrator the following addition to the statement of independence:

I confirm, on the basis of the information presently available to me, that I can devote the time necessary to conduct this arbitration diligently, efficiently and in accordance with the time limits in the Rules.

Annex 3
CONVENTION ON THE SETTLEMENT OF INVESTMENT DISPUTES BETWEEN STATES AND NATIONALS OF OTHER STATES

Preamble

The Contracting States

Considering the need for international cooperation for economic development, and the role of private international investment therein;
Bearing in mind the possibility that from time to time disputes may arise in connection with such investment between Contracting States and nationals of other Contracting States;
Recognizing that while such disputes would usually be subject to national legal processes, international methods of settlement may be appropriate in certain cases;
Attaching particular importance to the availability of facilities for international conciliation or arbitration to which Contracting States and nationals of other Contracting States may submit such disputes if they so desire;
Desiring to establish such facilities under the auspices of the International
Bank for Reconstruction and Development;
Recognizing that mutual consent by the parties to submit such disputes to conciliation or to arbitration through such facilities constitutes a binding agreement which requires in particular that due consideration be given to any recommendation of conciliators, and that any arbitral award be complied with; and
Declaring that no Contracting State shall by the mere fact of its ratification, acceptance or approval of this Convention and without its consent be deemed to be under any obligation to submit any particular dispute to conciliation or arbitration,
Have agreed as follows:

Chapter I International Centre for Settlement of Investment Disputes

Section 1 Establishment and Organization

Article 1

(1) There is hereby established the International Centre for Settlement of Investment Disputes (hereinafter called the Centre).

(2) The purpose of the Centre shall be to provide facilities for conciliation and arbitration of investment disputes between Contracting States and nationals of other Contracting States in accordance with the provisions of this Convention.

Article 2

The seat of the Centre shall be at the principal office of the International Bank for Reconstruction and Development (hereinafter called the Bank). The seat may be moved to another place by decision of the Administrative Council adopted by a majority of two-thirds of its members.

Article 3

The Centre shall have an Administrative Council and a Secretariat and shall maintain a Panel of Conciliators and a Panel of Arbitrators.

Section 2 The Administrative Council

Article 4

(1) The Administrative Council shall be composed of one representative of each Contracting State. An alternate may act as representative in case of his principal's absence from a meeting or inability to act.
(2) In the absence of a contrary designation, each governor and alternate governor of the Bank appointed by a Contracting State shall be *ex officio* its representative and its alternate respectively.

Article 5

The President of the Bank shall be *ex officio* Chairman of the Administrative Council (hereinafter called the Chairman) but shall have no vote. During his absence or inability to act and during any vacancy in the office of President of the Bank, the person for the time being acting as President shall act as Chairman of the Administrative Council.

Article 6

(1) Without prejudice to the powers and functions vested in it by other provisions of this Convention, the Administrative Council shall:

(a) adopt the administrative and financial regulations of the Centre;
(b) adopt the rules of procedure for the institution of conciliation and arbitration proceedings;
(c) adopt the rules of procedure for conciliation and arbitration proceedings (hereinafter called the Conciliation Rules and the Arbitration Rules);
(d) approve arrangements with the Bank for the use of the Bank's administrative facilities and services;
(e) determine the conditions of service of the Secretary-General and of any Deputy Secretary-General;
(f) adopt the annual budget of revenues and expenditures of the Centre;

(g) approve the annual report on the operation of the Centre.

The decisions referred to in sub-paragraphs (a), (b), (c) and (f) above shall be adopted by a majority of two-thirds of the members of the Administrative Council.

(2) The Administrative Council may appoint such committees as it considers necessary.

(3) The Administrative Council shall also exercise such other powers and perform such other functions as it shall determine to be necessary for the implementation of the provisions of this Convention.

Article 7

(1) The Administrative Council shall hold an annual meeting and such other meetings as may be determined by the Council, or convened by the Chairman, or convened by the Secretary-General at the request of not less than five members of the Council.

(2) Each member of the Administrative Council shall have one vote and, except as otherwise herein provided, all matters before the Council shall be decided by a majority of the votes cast.

(3) A quorum for any meeting of the Administrative Council shall be a majority of its members.

(4) The Administrative Council may establish, by a majority of two-thirds of its members, a procedure whereby the Chairman may seek a vote of the Council without convening a meeting of the Council.

The vote shall be considered valid only if the majority of the members of the Council cast their votes within the time limit fixed by the said procedure.

Article 8

Members of the Administrative Council and the Chairman shall serve without remuneration from the Centre.

Section 3 The Secretariat

Article 9

The Secretariat shall consist of a Secretary-General, one or more Deputy Secretaries-General and staff.

Article 10

(1) The Secretary-General and any Deputy Secretary-General shall be elected by the Administrative Council by a majority of two-thirds of its members upon the nomination of the Chairman for a term of service not exceeding six years and shall be eligible for re-election. After consulting the members of the Administrative Council, the Chairman shall propose one or more candidates for each such office.

(2) The offices of Secretary-General and Deputy Secretary-General shall be incompatible with the exercise of any political function. Neither the Secretary-General nor any Deputy Secretary-General may hold any other employment or engage in any other occupation except with the approval of the Administrative Council.

(3) During the Secretary-General's absence or inability to act, and during any vacancy of the office of Secretary-General, the Deputy Secretary-General shall act as Secretary-General. If there shall be more than one Deputy Secretary-General, the Administrative Council shall determine in advance the order in which they shall act as Secretary- General.

Article 11

The Secretary-General shall be the legal representative and the principal officer of the Centre and shall be responsible for its administration, including the appointment of staff, in accordance with the provisions of this Convention and the rules adopted by the Administrative Council. He shall perform the function of registrar and shall have the power to authenticate arbitral awards rendered pursuant to this Convention, and to certify copies thereof.

Section 4 The Panels

Article 12

The Panel of Conciliators and the Panel of Arbitrators shall each consist of qualified persons, designated as hereinafter provided, who are willing to serve thereon.

Article 13

(1) Each Contracting State may designate to each Panel four persons who may but need not be its nationals.
(2) The Chairman may designate ten persons to each Panel. The persons so designated to a Panel shall each have a different nationality.

Article 14

(1) Persons designated to serve on the Panels shall be persons of high moral character and recognized competence in the fields of law, commerce, industry or finance, who may be relied upon to exercise independent judgment. Competence in the field of law shall be of particular importance in the case of persons on the Panel of Arbitrators.
(2) The Chairman, in designating persons to serve on the Panels, shall in addition pay due regard to the importance of assuring representation on the Panels of the principal legal systems of the world and of the main forms of economic activity.

Article 15

(1) Panel members shall serve for renewable periods of six years.
(2) In case of death or resignation of a member of a Panel, the authority which designated the member shall have the right to designate another person to serve for the remainder of that member's term.
(3) Panel members shall continue in office until their successors have been designated.

Article 16

(1) A person may serve on both Panels.
(2) If a person shall have been designated to serve on the same Panel by more than one Contracting State, or by one or more Contracting States and the Chairman, he shall be deemed to have been designated by the authority which first designated him or, if one such authority is the State of which he is a national, by that State.
(3) All designations shall be notified to the Secretary-General and shall take effect from the date on which the notification is received.

Section 5 Financing the Centre

Article 17

If the expenditure of the Centre cannot be met out of charges for the use of its facilities, or out of other receipts, the excess shall be borne by Contracting States which are members of the Bank in proportion to their respective subscriptions to the capital stock of the Bank, and by Contracting States which are not members of the Bank in accordance with rules adopted by the Administrative Council.

Section 6 Status, Immunities and Privileges

Article 18

The Centre shall have full international legal personality. The legal capacity of the Centre shall include the capacity:

(a) to contract;
(b) to acquire and dispose of movable and immovable property;
(c) to institute legal proceedings.

Article 19

To enable the Centre to fulfil its functions, it shall enjoy in the territories of each Contracting State the immunities and privileges set forth in this Section.

Article 20

The Centre, its property and assets shall enjoy immunity from all legal process, except when the Centre waives this immunity.

Article 21

The Chairman, the members of the Administrative Council, persons acting as conciliators or arbitrators or members of a Committee appointed pursuant to paragraph (3) of Article 52, and the officers an employees of the Secretariat

(a) shall enjoy immunity from legal process with respect to acts performed by them in the exercise of their functions, except when the Centre waives this immunity;
(b) not being local nationals, shall enjoy the same immunities from immigration restrictions, alien registration requirements and national service obligations, the same facilities as regards exchange restrictions and the same treatment in respect of travelling facilities as are accorded by Contracting States to the representatives, officials and employees of comparable rank of other Contracting States.

Article 22

The provisions of Article 21 shall apply to persons appearing in proceedings under this Convention as parties, agents, counsel, advocates, witnesses or experts; provided, however, that sub-paragraph (b) thereof shall apply only in connection with their travel to and from, and their stay at, the place where the proceedings are held.

Article 23

(1) The archives of the Centre shall be inviolable, wherever they may be.
(2) With regard to its official communications, the Centre shall be accorded by each Contracting State treatment not less favourable than that accorded to other international organizations.

Article 24

(1) The Centre, its assets, property and income, and its operations and transactions authorized by this Convention shall be exempt from all taxation and customs duties. The Centre shall also be exempt from liability for the collection or payment of any taxes or customs duties.
(2) Except in the case of local nationals, no tax shall be levied on or in respect of expense allowances paid by the Centre to the Chairman or members of the Administrative Council, or on or in respect of salaries, expense allowances or other emoluments paid by the Centre to officials or employees of the Secretariat.
(3) No tax shall be levied on or in respect of fees or expense allowances received by persons acting as conciliators, or arbitrators, or members of a Committee appointed pursuant to paragraph (3) of Article 52, in proceedings under this Convention, if the sole jurisdictional basis for such tax is the location of the Centre or the place where such proceedings are conducted or the place where such fees or allowances are paid.

Chapter II Jurisdiction of the Centre

Article 25

(1) The jurisdiction of the Centre shall extend to any legal dispute arising directly out of an investment, between a Contracting State (or any constituent subdivision or agency of a Contracting State designated to the Centre by that State) and a national of another Contracting State, which the parties to the dispute consent in writing to submit to the Centre. When the parties have given their consent, no party may withdraw its consent unilaterally.

(2) "National of another Contracting State" means:

(a) any natural person who had the nationality of a Contracting State other than the State party to the dispute on the date on which the parties consented to submit such dispute to conciliation or arbitration as well as on the date on which the request was registered pursuant to paragraph (3) of Article 28 or paragraph (3) of Article 36, but does not include any person who on either date also had the nationality of the Contracting State party to the dispute; and

(b) any juridical person which had the nationality of a Contracting State other than the State party to the dispute on the date on which the parties consented to submit such dispute to conciliation or arbitration and any juridical person which had the nationality of the Contracting State party to the dispute on that date and which, because of foreign control, the parties have agreed should be treated as a national of another Contracting State for the purposes of this Convention.

(3) Consent by a constituent subdivision or agency of a Contracting State shall require the approval of that State unless that State notifies the Centre that no such approval is required.

(4) Any Contracting State may, at the time of ratification, acceptance or approval of this Convention or at any time thereafter, notify the Centre of the class or classes of disputes which it would or would not consider submitting to the jurisdiction of the Centre. The Secretary-General shall forthwith transmit such notification to all Contracting States. Such notification shall not constitute the consent required by paragraph (1).

Article 26

Consent of the parties to arbitration under this Convention shall, unless otherwise stated, be deemed consent to such arbitration to the exclusion of any other remedy. A Contracting State may require the exhaustion of local administrative or judicial remedies as a condition of its consent to arbitration under this Convention.

Article 27

(1) No Contracting State shall give diplomatic protection, or bring an international claim, in respect of a dispute which one of its nationals and another Contracting State shall have consented to submit or shall have submitted to arbitration under this Convention, unless such other Contracting State shall have failed to abide by and comply with the award rendered in such dispute.

(2) Diplomatic protection, for the purposes of paragraph (1), shall not include informal diplomatic exchanges for the sole purpose of facilitating a settlement of the dispute.

Chapter III Conciliation

Section 1 Request for Conciliation

Article 28

(1) Any Contracting State or any national of a Contracting State wishing to institute conciliation proceedings shall address a request to that effect in writing to the Secretary-General who shall send a copy of the request to the other party.

(2) The request shall contain information concerning the issues in dispute, the identity of the parties and their consent to conciliation in accordance with the rules of procedure for the institution of conciliation and arbitration proceedings.
(3) The Secretary-General shall register the request unless he finds, on the basis of the information contained in the request, that the dispute is manifestly outside the jurisdiction of the Centre. He shall forthwith notify the parties of registration or refusal to register.

Section 2 Constitution of the Conciliation Commission

Article 29

(1) The Conciliation Commission (hereinafter called the Commission) shall be constituted as soon as possible after registration of request pursuant to Article 28.
(2) (a) The Commission shall consist of a sole conciliator or any uneven number of conciliators appointed as the parties shall agree.
(b) Where the parties do not agree upon the number of conciliators and the method of their appointment, the Commission shall consist of three conciliators, one conciliator appointed by each party and the third, who shall be the president of the Commission, appointed by agreement of the parties.

Article 30

If the Commission shall not have been constituted within 90 days after notice of registration of the request has been dispatched by the Secretary-General in accordance with paragraph (3) of Article 28, or such other period as the parties may agree, the Chairman shall, at the request of either party and after consulting both parties as far as possible, appoint the conciliator or conciliators not yet appointed.

Article 31

(1) Conciliators may be appointed from outside the Panel of Conciliators, except in the case of appointments by the Chairman pursuant to Article 30.
(2) Conciliators appointed from outside the Panel of Conciliators shall possess the qualities stated in paragraph (1) of Article 14.

Section 3 Conciliation Proceedings

Article 32

(1) The Commission shall be the judge of its own competence.
(2) Any objection by a party to the dispute that that dispute is not within the jurisdiction of the Centre, or for other reasons is not within the competence of the Commission, shall be considered by the Commission which shall determine whether to deal with it as a preliminary question or to join it to the merits of the dispute.

Article 33

Any conciliation proceeding shall be conducted in accordance with the provisions of this Section and, except as the parties otherwise agree, in accordance with the Conciliation Rules in effect on the date on which the parties consented to conciliation. If any question of procedure arises which is not covered by this Section or the Conciliation Rules or any rules agreed by the parties, the Commission shall decide the question.

Article 34

(1) It shall be the duty of the Commission to clarify the issues in dispute between the parties and to endeavour to bring about agreement between them upon mutually acceptable terms. To that end, the Commission may at any stage of the proceedings and from time to time recommend terms of settlement to the parties. The parties shall cooperate in good faith with the Commission in order to enable the Commission to carry out its functions, and shall give their most serious consideration to its recommendations.
(2) If the parties reach agreement, the Commission shall draw up a report noting the issues in dispute and recording that the parties have reached agreement. If, at any stage of the proceedings, it appears to the Commission that there is no likelihood of agreement between the parties, it shall close the proceedings and shall draw up a report noting the submission of the dispute and recording the failure of the parties to reach agreement. If one party fails to appear or participate in the proceedings, the Commission shall close the proceedings and shall draw up a report noting that party's failure to appear or participate.

Article 35

Except as the parties to the dispute shall otherwise agree, neither party to a conciliation proceeding shall be entitled in any other proceeding, whether before arbitrators or in a court of law or otherwise, to invoke or rely on any views expressed or statements or admissions or offers of settlement made by the other party in the conciliation proceedings, or the report or any recommendations made by the Commission.

Chapter IV Arbitration

Section 1 Request for Arbitration

Article 36

(1) Any Contracting State or any national of a Contracting State wishing to institute arbitration proceedings shall address a request to that effect in writing to the Secretary-General who shall send a copy of the request to the other party.
(2) The request shall contain information concerning the issues in dispute, the identity of the parties and their consent to arbitration in accordance with the rules of procedure for the institution of conciliation and arbitration proceedings.

(3) The Secretary-General shall register the request unless he finds, on the basis of the information contained in the request, that the dispute is manifestly outside the jurisdiction of the Centre. He shall forthwith notify the parties of registration or refusal to register.

Section 2 Constitution of the Tribunal

Article 37

(1) The Arbitral Tribunal (hereinafter called the Tribunal) shall be constituted as soon as possible after registration of a request pursuant to Article 36.
(2) (a) The Tribunal shall consist of a sole arbitrator or any uneven number of arbitrators appointed as the parties shall agree.
(b) Where the parties do not agree upon the number of arbitrators and the method of their appointment, the Tribunal shall consist of three arbitrators, one arbitrator appointed by each party and the third, who shall be the president of the Tribunal, appointed by agreement of the parties.

Article 38

If the Tribunal shall not have been constituted within 90 days after notice of registration of the request has been dispatched by the Secretary-General in accordance with paragraph (3) of Article 36, or such other period as the parties may agree, the Chairman shall, at the request of either party and after consulting both parties as far as possible, appoint the arbitrator or arbitrators not yet appointed. Arbitrators appointed by the Chairman pursuant to this Article shall not be nationals of the Contracting State party to the dispute or of the Contracting State whose national is a party to the dispute.

Article 39

The majority of the arbitrators shall be nationals of States other than the Contracting State party to the dispute and the Contracting State whose national is a party to the dispute; provided, however, that the foregoing provisions of this Article shall not apply if the sole arbitrator or each individual member of the Tribunal has been appointed by agreement of the parties.

Article 40

(1) Arbitrators may be appointed from outside the Panel of Arbitrators, except in the case of appointments by the Chairman pursuant to Article 38.
(2) Arbitrators appointed from outside the Panel of Arbitrators shall possess the qualities stated in paragraph (1) of Article 14.

Section 3 Powers and Functions of the Tribunal

Article 41

(1) The Tribunal shall be the judge of its own competence.
(2) Any objection by a party to the dispute that that dispute is not within the jurisdiction of the Centre, or for other reasons is not within the competence of the Tribunal, shall be considered by

the Tribunal which shall determine whether to deal with it as a preliminary question or to join it to the merits of the dispute.

Article 42

(1) The Tribunal shall decide a dispute in accordance with such rules of law as may be agreed by the parties. In the absence of such agreement, the Tribunal shall apply the law of the Contracting State party to the dispute (including its rules on the conflict of laws) and such rules of international law as may be applicable.
(2) The Tribunal may not bring in a finding of *non liquet* on the ground of silence or obscurity of the law.
(3) The provisions of paragraphs (1) and (2) shall not prejudice the power of the Tribunal to decide a dispute *ex aequo et bono* if the parties so agree.

Article 43

Except as the parties otherwise agree, the Tribunal may, if it deems it necessary at any stage of the proceedings,

(a) call upon the parties to produce documents or other evidence,
and
(b) visit the scene connected with the dispute, and conduct such inquiries there as it may deem appropriate.

Article 44

Any arbitration proceeding shall be conducted in accordance with the provisions of this Section and, except as the parties otherwise agree, in accordance with the Arbitration Rules in effect on the date on which the parties consented to arbitration. If any question of procedure arises which is not covered by this Section or the Arbitration Rules or any rules agreed by the parties, the Tribunal shall decide the question.

Article 45

(1) Failure of a party to appear or to present his case shall not be deemed an admission of the other party's assertions.
(2) If a party fails to appear or to present his case at any stage of the proceedings the other party may request the Tribunal to deal with the questions submitted to it and to render an award. Before rendering an award, the Tribunal shall notify, and grant a period of grace to, the party failing to appear or to present its case, unless it is satisfied that that party does not intend to do so.

Article 46

Except as the parties otherwise agree, the Tribunal shall, if requested by a party, determine any incidental or additional claims or counterclaims arising directly out of the subject-matter of the dispute provided that they are within the scope of the consent of the parties and are otherwise within the jurisdiction of the Centre.

Article 47

Except as the parties otherwise agree, the Tribunal may, if it considers that the circumstances so require, recommend any provisional measures which should be taken to preserve the respective rights of either party.

Section 4 The Award

Article 48

(1) The Tribunal shall decide questions by a majority of the votes of all its members.
(2) The award of the Tribunal shall be in writing and shall be signed by the members of the Tribunal who voted for it.
(3) The award shall deal with every question submitted to the Tribunal, and shall state the reasons upon which it is based.
(4) Any member of the Tribunal may attach his individual opinion to the award, whether he dissents from the majority or not, or a statement of his dissent.
(5) The Centre shall not publish the award without the consent of the parties.

Article 49

(1) The Secretary-General shall promptly dispatch certified copies of the award to the parties. The award shall be deemed to have been rendered on the date on which the certified copies were dispatched.
(2) The Tribunal upon the request of a party made within 45 days after the date on which the award was rendered may after notice to the other party decide any question which it had omitted to decide in the award, and shall rectify any clerical, arithmetical or similar error in the award. Its decision shall become part of the award and shall be notified to the parties in the same manner as the award. The periods of time provided for under paragraph (2) of Article 51 and paragraph (2) of Article 52 shall run from the date on which the decision was rendered.

Section 5 Interpretation, Revision and Annulment of the Award

Article 50

(1) If any dispute shall arise between the parties as to the meaning or scope of an award, either party may request interpretation of the award by an application in writing addressed to the Secretary-General.
(2) The request shall, if possible, be submitted to the Tribunal which rendered the award. If this shall not be possible, a new Tribunal shall be constituted in accordance with Section 2 of this Chapter. The Tribunal may, if it considers that the circumstances so require, stay enforcement of the award pending its decision.

Article 51

(1) Either party may request revision of the award by an application in writing addressed to the Secretary-General on the ground of discovery of some fact of such a nature as decisively to affect the award, provided that when the award was rendered that fact was unknown to the

Tribunal and to the applicant and that the applicant's ignorance of that fact was not due to negligence.
(2) The application shall be made within 90 days after the discovery of such fact and in any event within three years after the date on which the award was rendered.
(3) The request shall, if possible, be submitted to the Tribunal which rendered the award. If this shall not be possible, a new Tribunal shall be constituted in accordance with Section 2 of this Chapter.
(4) The Tribunal may, if it considers that the circumstances so require, stay enforcement of the award pending its decision. If the applicant requests a stay of enforcement of the award in his application, enforcement shall be stayed provisionally until the Tribunal rules on such request.

Article 52

(1) Either party may request annulment of the award by an application in writing addressed to the Secretary-General on one or more of the following grounds:
(a) that the Tribunal was not properly constituted;
(b) that the Tribunal has manifestly exceeded its powers;
(c) that there was corruption on the part of a member of the Tribunal;
(d) that there has been a serious departure from a fundamental rule of procedure; or
(e) that the award has failed to state the reasons on which it is based.
(2) The application shall be made within 120 days after the date on which the award was rendered except that when annulment is requested on the ground of corruption such application shall be made within 120 days after discovery of the corruption and in any event within three years after the date on which the award was rendered.
(3) On receipt of the request the Chairman shall forthwith appoint from the Panel of Arbitrators an *ad hoc* Committee of three persons. None of the members of the Committee shall have been a member of the Tribunal which rendered the award, shall be of the same nationality as any such member, shall be a national of the State party to the dispute or of the State whose national is a party to the dispute, shall have been designated to the Panel of Arbitrators by either of those States, or shall have acted as a conciliator in the same dispute. The Committee shall have the authority to annul the award or any part thereof on any of the grounds set forth in paragraph (1).
(4) The provisions of Articles 41–45, 48, 49, 53 and 54, and of Chapters VI and VII shall apply *mutatis mutandis* to proceedings before the Committee.
(5) The Committee may, if it considers that the circumstances so require, stay enforcement of the award pending its decision. If the applicant requests a stay of enforcement of the award in his application, enforcement shall be stayed provisionally until the Committee rules on such request.
(6) If the award is annulled the dispute shall, at the request of either party, be submitted to a new Tribunal constituted in accordance with Section 2 of this Chapter.

Section 6 Recognition and Enforcement of the Award

Article 53

(1) The award shall be binding on the parties and shall not be subject to any appeal or to any other remedy except those provided for in this Convention. Each party shall abide by and comply with

the terms of the award except to the extent that enforcement shall have been stayed pursuant to the relevant provisions of this Convention.
(2) For the purposes of this Section, "award" shall include any decision interpreting, revising or annulling such award pursuant to Articles 50, 51 or 52.

Article 54

(1) Each Contracting State shall recognize an award rendered pursuant to this Convention as binding and enforce the pecuniary obligations imposed by that award within its territories as if it were a final Judgment of a court in that State. A Contracting State with a federal constitution may enforce such an award in or through its federal courts and may provide that such courts shall treat the award as if it were a final judgment of the courts of a constituent state.
2) A party seeking recognition or enforcement in the territories of a Contracting State shall furnish to a competent court or other authority which such State shall have designated for this purpose a copy of the award certified by the Secretary-General. Each Contracting State shall notify the Secretary-General of the designation of the competent court or other authority for this purpose and of any subsequent change in such designation.
(3) Execution of the award shall be governed by the laws concerning the execution of judgments in force in the State in whose territories such execution is sought.

Article 55

Nothing in Article 54 shall be construed as derogating from the law in force in any Contracting State relating to immunity of that State or of any foreign State from execution.

Chapter V Replacement and Disqualification of Conciliators and Arbitrators

Article 56

(1) After a Commission or a Tribunal has been constituted and proceedings have begun, its composition shall remain unchanged; provided, however, that if a conciliator or an arbitrator should die, become incapacitated, or resign, the resulting vacancy shall be filled in accordance with the provisions of Section 2 of Chapter III or Section 2 of Chapter IV.
(2) A member of a Commission or Tribunal shall continue to serve in that capacity notwithstanding that he shall have ceased to be a member of the Panel.
(3) If a conciliator or arbitrator appointed by a party shall have resigned without the consent of the Commission or Tribunal of which he was a member, the Chairman shall appoint a person from the appropriate Panel to fill the resulting vacancy.

Article 57

A party may propose to a Commission or Tribunal the disqualification of any of its members on account of any fact indicating a manifest lack of the qualities required by paragraph (1) of Article 14. A party to arbitration proceedings may, in addition, propose the disqualification of an arbitrator on the ground that he was ineligible for appointment to the Tribunal under Section 2 of Chapter IV.

Article 58

The decision on any proposal to disqualify a conciliator or arbitrator shall be taken by the other members of the Commission or Tribunal as the case may be, provided that where those members are equally divided, or in the case of a proposal to disqualify a sole conciliator or arbitrator, or a majority of the conciliators or arbitrators, the Chairman shall take that decision. If it is decided that the proposal is well founded the conciliator or arbitrator to whom the decision relates shall be replaced in accordance with the provisions of Section 2 of **Chapter III** or ***Section 2*** of **Chapter IV**.

Chapter VI Cost of Proceedings

Article 59

The charges payable by the parties for the use of the facilities of the Centre shall be determined by the Secretary-General in accordance with the regulations adopted by the Administrative Council.

Article 60

(1) Each Commission and each Tribunal shall determine the fees and expenses of its members within limits established from time to time by the Administrative Council and after consultation with the Secretary-General.
(2) Nothing in paragraph (1) of this Article shall preclude the parties from agreeing in advance with the Commission or Tribunal concerned upon the fees and expenses of its members.

Article 61

(1) In the case of conciliation proceedings the fees and expenses of members of the Commission as well as the charges for the use of the facilities of the Centre, shall be borne equally by the parties. Each party shall bear any other expenses it incurs in connection with the proceedings.
(2) In the case of arbitration proceedings the Tribunal shall, except as the parties otherwise agree, assess the expenses incurred by the parties in connection with the proceedings, and shall decide how and by whom those expenses, the fees and expenses of the members of the Tribunal and the charges for the use of the facilities of the Centre shall be paid. Such decision shall form part of the award.

Chapter VII Place of Proceedings

Article 62

Conciliation and arbitration proceedings shall be held at the seat of the Centre except as hereinafter provided.

Article 63

Conciliation and arbitration proceedings may be held, if the parties so agree, (a) at the seat of the Permanent Court of Arbitration or of any other appropriate institution, whether private or public, with which the Centre may make arrangements for that purpose; or (b) at any other place approved by the Commission or Tribunal after consultation with the Secretary-General.

Chapter VIII Disputes between Contracting States

Article 64

Any dispute arising between Contracting States concerning the interpretation or application of this Convention which is not settled by negotiation shall be referred to the International Court of Justice by the application of any party to such dispute, unless the States concerned agree to another method of settlement.

Chapter IX Amendment

Article 65

Any Contracting State may propose amendment of this Convention. The text of a proposed amendment shall be communicated to the Secretary-General not less than 90 days prior to the meeting of the Administrative Council at which such amendment is to be considered and shall forthwith be transmitted by him to all the members of the Administrative Council.

Article 66

(1) If the Administrative Council shall so decide by a majority of two-thirds of its members, the proposed amendment shall be circulated to all Contracting States for ratification, acceptance or approval. Each amendment shall enter into force 30 days after dispatch by the depositary of this Convention of a notification to Contracting States that all Contracting States have ratified, accepted or approved the amendment.
(2) No amendment shall affect the rights and obligations under this Convention of any Contracting State or of any of its constituent subdivisions or agencies, or of any national of such State arising out of consent to the jurisdiction of the Centre given before the date of entry into force of the amendment.

Chapter X Final Provisions

Article 67

This Convention shall be open for signature on behalf of States members of the Bank. It shall also be open for signature on behalf of any other State which is a party to the Statute of the International

Court of Justice and which the Administrative Council, by a vote of two-thirds of its members, shall have invited to sign the Convention.

Article 68

(1) This Convention shall be subject to ratification, acceptance or approval by the signatory States in accordance with their respective constitutional procedures.
(2) This Convention shall enter into force 30 days after the date of deposit of the twentieth instrument of ratification, acceptance or approval. It shall enter into force for each State which subsequently deposits its instrument of ratification, acceptance or approval 30 days after the date of such deposit.

Article 69

Each Contracting State shall take such legislative or other measures as may be necessary for making the provisions of this Convention effective in its territories.

Article 70

This Convention shall apply to all territories for whose international relations a Contracting State is responsible, except those which are excluded by such State by written notice to the depositary of this Convention either at the time of ratification, acceptance or approval or subsequently.

Article 71

Any Contracting State may denounce this Convention by written notice to the depositary of this Convention. The denunciation shall take effect six months after receipt of such notice.

Article 72

Notice by a Contracting State pursuant to Articles 70 or 71 shall not affect the rights or obligations under this Convention of that State or of any of its constituent subdivisions or agencies or of any national of that State arising out of consent to the jurisdiction of the Centre given by one of them before such notice was received by the depositary.

Article 73

Instruments of ratification, acceptance or approval of this Convention and of amendments thereto shall be deposited with the Bank which shall act as the depositary of this Convention. The depositary shall transmit certified copies of this Convention to States members of the Bank and to any other State invited to sign the Convention.

Article 74

The depositary shall register this Convention with the Secretariat of the United Nations in accordance with Article 102 of the Charter of the United Nations and the Regulations thereunder adopted by the General Assembly.

Article 75

The depositary shall notify all signatory States of the following:

(a) signatures in accordance with Article 67;

(b) deposits of instruments of ratification, acceptance and approval in accordance with Article 73;

(c) the date on which this Convention enters into force in accordance with Article 68;

(d) exclusions from territorial application pursuant to Article 70;

(e) the date on which any amendment of this Convention enters into force in accordance with Article 66; and

(f) denunciations in accordance with Article 71.

DONE at Washington, in the English, French and Spanish languages, all three texts being equally authentic, in a single copy which shall remain deposited in the archives of the International Bank for Reconstruction and Development, which has indicated by its signature below its agreement to fulfil the functions with which it is charged under this Convention.

References

Abdel Azim, Dr Abdessalaam Hameed 1989. The Effect of the Prince Theory on the Performance of Administrative Contracts. N.p.

—, 1990. The Accidental Circumstances and Physical Difficulties on the Performance of Administrative Contracts. N.p.

Abdel Badie, Dr Mohamed Salah 1993. The Power of the Authority to Terminate Administrative Contract, PhD, Faculty of Law, Ain Shams University, Cairo.

Abdel Baki, Abdel Fatah, 1984. The Encyclopedia of Egyptian Civil Law, Contract and Unilateral Acts Theory, a Comparative Study with Islamic Doctrine. N.p.

Abdel Kader, Nariman 1996. Arbitration Agreement Pursuant to Arbitration Act No. 27 of 1994. Cairo: Dar El Nahda El Arabia.

Abdel Latif, Abla 1990. The Assignment Theory in Administrative Law. N.p.

—, 1996. Prescription, 2nd edition. N.p.

Abdel-Wahab, Mohamed Salah. 2006. Cultural Globalization and Public Policy: Exclusion of Foreign Law in the Global Village. Law and Sociology, 8. Ed. Michael Freeman. Oxford: Oxford University Press.

—, 2005. Globalization Influence upon Various Areas of Law, Cultural Globalization and Public Policy: Exclusion of Foreign Law in the Global Village. Law and Sociology, 8. Oxford: Oxford University Press.

A.D.V. de S. Indraratna, Athula Ranasinghe 2006. Public-Private Sector Partnership in Economic Development: A Case for Sri Lanka. Colombo: Sri Lanka Economic Association.

Akitoby, Bernardin, Hemming, Richard and Schwartz, Gerd 2007. Public Investment and Public-Private Partnerships. Washington, D.C.: International Monetary Fund.

Al-Tihyewi, Mahmoud 1994. Arbitration Agreement and its Stipulations in the Code of Civil Procedures and Arbitration Act. PhD thesis, Cairo University.

Amin, Mohamed Said see Said, Amin Mohamed.

APS Review Downstream Trends, 2010. Egypt, The Power Sector. LexisNexis (January).

Auby, Jean-Marie et Bon, Pierre 1995. Droit administratif des biens. 3ème édition. Paris: Dalloz.

Badawi, Sarwat. 1954. Le Fait du prince dans les contrats administratifs. Paris: L.G.D.J.

—, 1994. The General Theory of Administrative Law. 5th edition. Cairo: Dar El Nahda El Arabia.

—, 2007. Hierarchies of Administrative Decrees and the Illegality Principle. Cairo: Dar El Nahda El Arabia.

Badran, Mohamed n.d. ADR for Administrative Dispute in Egyptian Administrative Law. Unpublished paper.

Barakat, Aly 1996. Arbitration under the Egyptian and Comparative Laws. PhD thesis, Cairo University.

Barral, Welber and Haas, Adam 2007. Public–Private Partnership (PPP) in Brazil. The International Lawyer (Fall), 41; Int'l Law, 957.

Bateson, David 1997. New China BOOT Regulations. ICLR, 14, Part I.

Batiffol, Henri, 1968. Encyclopédie juridique Dalloz: répertoire de droit international. Tome 1: Contrats et conventions. Paris: Dalloz.

Beale, Hugh (ed.) 2008. Chitty on Contracts. 30th edition. London: Sweet and Maxwell.
Beriry, Mokhtar 1995. International Commercial Arbitration. Cairo: N.p.
Bevan, Alexander 1992. Alternative Dispute Resolution. London: Sweet and Maxwell.
Bird, Bella 2000. How to Promote and Strengthen Civil Society Partnerships in National Programs. OECD Report 11–12 December. Development Partnership Forum. Uganda: OECD Civil Society Unit.
Bovis, Christopher 2006. EC Public Procurement: Case Law and Regulation. Oxford: Oxford: University Press.
— 2010. Public Procurement, Public-Private Partnerships and Public Services in the EU. European Public Private Partnership Law Review, 2. Lexxion.
Brard, Yves, 1994 [1985]. Droit administratif des biens et de la fonction publique. Paris. Dalloz [1er édition: Unive].
Bruner, Phillipe Lane 1995. Force Majeure under International Law and International Construction Contract Model Forms. Vol. 12 (April). ICLR.
Bunni, Nael G. 1997. The FIDIC Forms of Contract. 2nd edition. Oxford: Blackwell.
— 2005. The FIDIC Forms of Contract. 3rd edition. Oxford: Blackwell.
Burdon, Tony 2000. How to Promote and Strengthen Civil Society Partnerships in National Programs. OECD Report 11–12 December. Development Partnership Forum 2000. Discussion paper presented by Tony Burdon. OECD.
Chabanol, Daniel et Jouquelet, Jean-Pierre 1994. 2ème édition. Marchés publics de travaux. Paris: Editions du Moniteur.
Chapus, René, 1995. Droit administrative général. 8éme édition. Tome 2. Paris: Montchrestien.
Chelbi, Afif 2010. Tunisia. APS Review Downstream Trends, April. Online. LexisNexis.
Chen, John C. 1995. Force Majeure in Construction Contracts, Taiwan. ICLR, Part 2 (April).
Clément, Jacques and Richer, Daniel 1989. Les Marchés publics de travaux des collectivités territoriales. 2nd edition. Paris: Economica.
— n.d. Syndicat intercommunal du bassin d'Arcachon. Inédit. 394.
Colaiuta, Virginie A. 2010. Acceleration of Works and Penalties for Delay in France in Construction Projects. ICLR, 27, Part III. July.
Cook, Jacques 2008. Contract Format and Contract Drafting/Financing. Modern Enhancements for PPP Concession Agreements. The Construction Lawyer, 24 (Fall).
Craig, Laurence, Park, William W. and Paulsson, Jan 1985. International Chamber of Commerce Arbitration. ICC Publishing.
David, René 1982. L'Arbitrage dans le commerce international. Paris: Economica.
De Cuyper, Jean-Quentin 1992. Le fait du prince libère-t-il une enterprise publique de ses obligations contractuelles ? Analyse de la pratique arbitrale. Revue de Droit des Affaires Internationales (R.D.A.I.), No. 2.
De Laubadère, André, Moderne, Franck and Delvolvé, Pierre, 1983–1984. Traité des contrats administratifs. 2 tomes. 2ème édition. Paris: L.G.D.J.
—, Venezia, Jean-Claude et Gaudement, Yves 1995. Traité de droit administratif. 10th edition. Paris: L.G.D.J.
Delvolvé, Jean Louis 1993. Multipartisme. The Dutco Decision of the French Cour de Cassation. International Arbitration.
Donnelly, Catherine 2007. Delegation of Governmental Power to Private Parties: A Comparative Perspective. Oxford: Oxford University Press.
Dufau, Jean 1988. Le Droit des travaux publics. Tome 1. Paris. Editions du Moniteur.
Duguit, Léon 1927. Traité de droit constitutionnel. 8 tomes Paris: Cujas.

Duncan Wallace, I.N. 1986. Construction Contracts, Principles and Policies in Tort and Contract. London: Sweet and Maxwell.
Duncan Wallace, I.N. 1986a. Construction Contracts, Principles and Policies in Tort and Contract. London: Sweet and Maxwell.
—, 1986b. Turnkey Contracts, The Liability of Contractors, ed. H.H. Humphrey Lloyd, QC, Centre for Commercial Law Studies, Queen Mary College, University of London.
—, 1995. Hudson's Building and Engineering Contracts.11th edition, Vol. I. London: Sweet and Maxwell.
Eberlei, Walter 2000. Civil Society Participation Within the Framework of the Poverty Eradication Action Plan (PEAP) of Uganda. Report of the Organization for Economic Co-operation and Development, December. Uganda: OECD.
Eggleston, Brian 1997. Liquidated Damages and Extension of Time in Construction Contract. Oxford: Blackwell Science.
Egyptian Conseil d'Etat 1996. Legal Principles in Administrative Contracts by the Egyptian State Council in 40 Years: Collection of Supreme Administrative Court Judgments and Legal opinions from the General Assembly for Legal Opinion (Fatwa) and Legislation.
Egyptian Ministry of Finance 2009. Update on the National Program for Public Private Partnership, PPP Central Unit, June: 6. See: http://www.mof.gov.eg (accessed 31 July 2010).
El Attar, F. 1955. Les Marchés de travaux publics. Thesis, Paris.
Elbana, Atef, 1984. Administrative Contracts. Cairo: n.p.
— 1992. El Wassit in Administrative Law. Cairo: n.p.
El Geddawy, Ahmed 1996. The Time Limit for Commencing Arbitration under FIDIC Rules Relating to Construction Contracts: Its Nature and Effect in Light of Egyptian Law. Paper presented in the International Commercial Arbitration Conference organized by CRCICA, Nile Hilton Hotel, Cairo. June.
El Hassan, Absy Abdelkader 1997. Obligations and Rights of the Parties in the Performance of a Public Works Contract, PhD Thesis, Cairo University.
El Howeidy, El Sallal Gom'a 1994. The Power of the Authority to Terminate Unilaterally the Administrative Contract. Masters thesis. Egypt: Tanta University.
El-Kholy, A. 1993. The Engineer's Unique Dual Role, Recent Development in Arab Law. Paper presented to the Conference on the Latest Developments in International Construction Contracts in Cairo. April. CRCICA.
El Sanhoury, Abdel Razek 1984. The General Theory of Obligations, Part 3: Expiry of Obligations. N.p.
—, 1989. El Wassit in Civil Law. 2nd edition. N.p.
El Sharkawi, Mahmoud S. 1992. International Commercial Contracts. A Special Study of the International Sale of Goods Contract. Cairo: Dar El-Nahda El Arabia.
El Sharkawy, Abdel Monem 1950. Civil and Commercial Procedures. N.p.
El Sharkawy, Soad, 1993. Constitution Liberalization and The Egyptian Constitution 1971. Cairo: Dar El Nahda El Arabia.
— 1995. The Administrative Contracts. Cairo: Dar El Nahda El Arabia.
— 2003. The Administrative Contracts. Cairo: Dar El Nahda El Arabia.
El Tamawy, Soliman 1966. The General Theory of Administrative Decrees. 3rd edition. N.p.
— 1991. The General Principles of Administrative Contracts. 5th edition. N.p.
El Wafa, Ahmed Abou 1965. The Theory of Sentences in the Code of Procedures. Cairo: n.p.
— 1988. Optional and Mandatory Arbitration. 5th edition. Cairo: n.p.
El Younsi, M. 1994. Les Règles matérielles du droit des contrats d'état. Tome II. Paris, thesis.

Fayyad, Abdel Meguid 1974. The Theory of Penalties in Administrative Contracts. Faculty of Law, Ain Shams University, Cairo.

Featherstone, M. (ed.) 1990. Global Culture: Nationalism, Globalisation and Modernity. London: Sage.

Fekry, Fathy 1994. Lectures in Administrative Contracts. N.p.

Ferrari, P. 1975. Essai sur la notion de co-auteurs d'un acte unilatéral en droit administrative français, en Recueil d'études en hommage à Charles Eisenmann. Paris: Cujas.

Fiszbein, Ariel and Lowden, Pamela 1999. Working Together for a Change, Government, Business, and Civic Partnerships for Poverty Reduction in Latin America and the Caribbean. Washington, D.C.: The World Bank.

Fouchard, Phillipe 1970. Quand un arbitrage est-il international? Revue de L'Arbitrage, 74.

Fouchard, Philippe, Gaillard, Emmanuel et Goldman, Berthold 1999. Traité de l'arbitrage commercial international. Paris. Litec.

Ga'far, Anas 1995. The Theory of Unforeseen Physical Difficulties in Civil Works Contracting, a Study of the Key Economic and Legal Aspects. Cairo. Shalakany Law Firm Publications.

— 2000. Administrative Contracts. Cairo: Dar El Nahda El Arabia.

Gad Nassar, Gaber 2002. BOOT Agreements and the Modernization of Concession Agreements, a Criticism to the Traditional Theory of Concession Agreements. Cairo: Dar El Nahda El Arabia.

Germain, Amber E. 2005. Civil Society Engagement in Poverty Reduction Strategies: The Ghana HIPC Watch Experience. Accra, Ghana: A2 Associates Ltd/Institute of Commonwealth Studies.

Goldberg, Stephen, Sander, Frank and Rogers, Nancy 1995. Dispute Resolution: Negotiation, Mediation and Other Processes. Law School Case Book Series, London: Butterworths.

Gould, Nicholas and Russell, Victoria 2007. Construction Law and Management, ed. Keith Pickavance. Informa. 2007: 441.

Hamilton, Geoffrey 2009. FDI, the Global Crisis and Sustainable Recovery. Working Paper for Public Private Partnerships and FDI as a Means of Securing a Sustainable Recovery. Paper submitted to the Fourth Columbia International Investment Conference, Vale Columbia Center, Columbia Law School, 5–6 November. New York: Columbia University.

Hanafi, Said and El Dardiry, Khaled 2010. PPPs in Egypt. ICLR, 27, Part 4 (October).

Harper, Malcolm 2000. Public Services Through Private Enterprise. London: Intermediate Technology Publications.

Hashem, Mahmoud 1990. The General Theory of Arbitration in Civil and Commercial Provisions, Part I: Arbitration Agreement, a Comparative Study Between Empirical Laws and Islamic Jurisprudence. Cairo: Dar Alfikir Alarabi.

Helmy Fahmy, Omar 1993. Effects of Administrative Contract. N.p.

— n.d. General Stipulations of Administrative Contracts. N.p.

Holdsworth, William Searle 1964. History of English Law. Vol. XIV. London: Sweet and Maxwell.

Hughes, G.A. and Barber, J.N. 1993. Building and Civil Engineering Claims in Perspective. 3rd Edition. Harlow, Essex, UK: Longman.

Huntington, Samuel P. 1996. The Clash of Civilizations and the Remaking of World Order. London: Simon & Schuster.

International Centre for Public Enterprises in Developing Countries 1981. Financing of Public Enterprises in Developing Countries, ed. Praxy Fernandes. Ljubljana, Yugoslavia.

Ismail, Mohamed A.M. 1996. Appointing the Arbitral Tribunal in Multi-Party Arbitration. Paper presented to the Conference on Arbitration in FIDIC Agreements held by CRCICA in May 1996 at Nile Hilton Hotel, Cairo.

— 2001. The Suggested Role of the Egyptian State Council. El Ahram Daily Newspaper, 31 July: 32.

— 2003a International Construction Contracts Arbitration. Beirut: El Halabi.
— 2003b. Arbitration in International Public Works Agreements. (In Arabic). Beirut: El Halabi.
— 2009. Globalization and Liquidated Damages on International Public Works Agreements in Egypt: An Analytical Perspective on the Penalty for Delay Clause in Infrastructure Agreements, The International Construction Law Review, 26, Part IV, October, Informa.
— 2010a. Globalization and Contract Price in International Public Works Agreements in the Egyptian State Procurement Law: New Trends. The International Construction Law Review, 27, Part 1, January, Informa.
— 2010b. Globalization and Contractual Regime in International Public Works Agreements in Egypt. ICLR, 27, Part III, July, Informa.
— 2010c. Legal Globalization and PPPs in Egypt: An Analytical and Comparative Perspective on the Current Legislative and Judicial Modifications to and Enhancements of the Administrative Contractual Regime on PPP Transactions. The European Public Private Partnership Law Review, 1 (March), Berlin, Lexxion.
— 2010d. Public Economic Law and the New International Administrative Contract. Beirut: El Halabi (in Arabic).
Issa, Hossam, n.d. Studies of the Legal Mechanisms of International Dependency, International Commercial Arbitration, a Critical Perspective. Cairo: N.p.
Jarrosson, Charles 1987. La Notion d'arbitrage. Paris: L.G.D.J.
Jarvin, Sigvard and Derains, Yves 1990. Collection of ICC Arbitral Awards, 1974–1985. London and The Netherlands: Kluwer Law International.
— and Arnaldez, Jean-Jacques. 1994. Collection of ICC Arbitral Awards 1986–1990. London and The Netherlands: Kluwer Law International.
Jones, Douglas 1995. Force Majeure in Australian Construction Law. ICLR. Part 2 (April).
Kadiki, Khaled 1979. Contrats internationaux de travaux publics et développement en Libye. Tome 1. Thesis, Dijon.
Kamel Leila, Mohamed 1969. Principles of Administrative Law. N.p.
Kassis, Antoine 1993. Le Nouveau droit Européen des contrats internationaux. Paris: L.G.D.J.
Kerr, Michael 1980. International Arbitration v. Litigation. Journal of Business Law 164.
Khoo, Salma Nasution, 2001. The Sustainable Penang Initiative: Creating State-Society Partnerships for Sustainable Development. International Institute for Environment and Development, December.
Lalive, J.F. 1983. Contrats entre états ou enterprises étatiques et personnes privées. Tome II. The Hague: Académie de Droit International.
Leboulonger, Philippe 1985. Les Contrats entre états et entreprises privées étrangers. Paris: Economica.
Lew, Julian D.M. 1978. Applicable Law in International Commercial Arbitration. London: Kluwer International.
— Mistelis, Loukas and Kröll, Stefan 2003. Comparative International Commercial Arbitration. London: Kluwer Law International.
Lloyd, Humphrey n.d. Multi-Party Arbitration, A National Experience. ICC Publications.
— 1991. Multi-Party Clauses and Agreements. Paper given in Stockholm. Revised version. ICC Publications.
Loncle, J.M. and Trochon, J.Y. 1997. The Negotiating Phase of International Contracts, International Business Law Journal, 1.
Loquin, Eric, 1977. Note sous arrêt des Courts d'Appel de pais, 13 décembre 1975, Clunet.

Mackie, Karl J., Miles, D. And Marsh W. 1995. The ADR Practice Guide: Commercial Dispute Resolution. 1st edition. London: Butterworths.
Maim Green, Guillermo and McGrath Beaumont, Meaghan 2006. Latin America. The International Lawyer (Summer) 40. Int'l Law, 581.
McKendrick, Ewan 1995a. Force Majeure and Frustration of Contract. 2nd edition. Informa.
— 1995b. Force Majeure in French Law, in McKendrick, Ewan, Force Majeure and Frustration of Contract. 2nd edition. Informa.
Metawe, Ahmad Hassaan 1998. Arbitration in International Construction Contracts, PhD thesis, Cairo University.
Meyer-Stamer, Jörg 1997. Technology, Competitiveness and Radical Policy Change. The Case of Brazil. London and Portland, OR: Frank Cass (in association with the German Development Institute, Berlin).
Moderne, F. 1975. Autour de la nature juridique des accords conclus entre l'administration et les organisation professionnelles en matière de prix. Dr. Soc.
Monteira de Barros, Cecilia Vidigal 2009. PPPs in Brazil. Informa: International Construction Law Review, 26, Part 2: 180–81.
Morduchowicz, Alejandro 2001. Private Education Funding and (de) Regulation in Argentina, National Center for the Study of Privatization in Education. Occasional Paper No. 36. Teachers College. New York: Columbia University.
Murdoch, John and Hughes, Will 2000. Construction Contracts, Law and Management. 3rd revised edition. London: Taylor & Francis (Spon Press).
Murray, John S., Rau, Alan Scott and Sherman, Edward S. 1989. Processes of Dispute Resolution: The Role of Lawyers, University Case Book Series. New York: The Foundation Press.
Mustill, Michael J. and Boyd, Stewart C. 1989. Commercial Arbitration, 2nd edition. LexisNexis.
Nicklisch, Fritz, 1990. The Role of the Engineer as a Contract Administrator and Quasi-Arbitrator in International Construction and Civil Engineering Projects, ICLR 322.
Niwa, Kazuhiko n.d. Force Majeure in Japan – Law and Practice. ICLR 1.
Peirano, Claudia and Vargas, Jaime 2005. Private Schools with Public Financing in Chile, in Private Education and Public Policy in Latin America, ed. Laurence Wolff, Juan Carlos Navarro and Pablo González. Washington D.C.: Preal.
Pickavance, Keith (ed.) 2007. Construction Law and Management. Informa. Contribution by Nick Carnell, pp. 269–91.
Radwan, Abou Zeid 1981. General Principles of International Commercial Arbitration. Cairo: Dar Alfikr Alarabi.
Ragab, Mahmoud 2007. PPP Agreements. Beirut: Dar El Nahda El Arabia.
Raslan, Anwar Ahmed, 1994. Administrative Law. N.p.
Rashed, Samia. 1984. Arbitration Agreement, Vol. 1. Cairo: N.p.
Raslan, Anwar 1980 [1948]. The Theory of Unforeseen Physical Difficulties. Journal of Law and Economy, 3 and 4 (1980).
— 1994. Administrative Law. N.p.
Redfern, Alan and Hunter, Martin 1991. International Commercial Arbitration. 2nd edition. London: Sweet and Maxwell.
— 1999. International Commercial Arbitration. 3rd edition. London: Sweet and Maxwell.
— 2009. International Commercial Arbitration. 5th edition. London: Sweet and Maxwell.
Reich, Arie, 1999. International Public Procurement Law. The Evolution of International Regimes on Public Purchasing. London: Kluwer Law International.
Riad, Rached, 1988. Conflict of Laws and Conflict of International Jurisprudence. N.p.

Richer, Laurent, 1995. Droit des contrats administratifs. Paris: L.G.D.J.
Robert, Jean et Moreau, Bertrand 1967. L'Arbitrage civil et commercial en droit interne et international privé. 4th edition. Paris: Dalloz.
Sabiani, François, 1995. Marchés publics de travaux et contrats voisins. 5th edition. Paris: Belfond.
Sachs, Jeffrey D. 2005. The End of Poverty. London: Penguin Books.
— 2008. Common Wealth. London: Penguin Books.
Said, Aly 2006. Principle of Not Executing Contract. N.p.
Said Amin, Mohamed 1991. General Principles for the Performance of Administrative Contracts. Cairo: N.p.
— 1992. A Study of Administrative Contracts and Concluding Stipulations. Cairo: Dar El Thakafa Elgameya.
Samuel, Geoffrey 2010. Law of Obligations. Cheltenham, UK: Edward Elgar.
Sarie El Din, Hani 1996. Consortia Agreements in the International Construction Industry. London: Kluwer Law International.
— 2001. Legal and Contractual Arrangements for Infrastructure Projects Financed by Private Sector. Cairo: Dar El Nahda El Arabia.
— 2002. Legal and Contractual Regime for BOOT, El Ahram El Eqtisadi Book, No. 177.
Sauvant, Karl P. 2008. The FDI Recession has Begun. Columbia FDI Perspectives, No. 1, 22 (November). Vale Columbia Center on Sustainable International Investment, Columbia University.
Schneider, Michael E. 1984. Arbitration of Construction Disputes. ICLR 317.
Schuartz, E. 1993. Multi-Party Arbitration and the ICC in the Wake of Dutco. Journal of International Arbitration.
Scriven, John and Pritchard, Nigel 1999. Construction Litigation Practice, A Contractual Guide to Major Construction Projects. London. Sweet and Maxwell.
Seppala, Christopher R. 1993. French Supreme Court Nullifies ICC Practice for Appointment of Arbitrators in Multi-Party Arbitration Cases, ICLR: 222–7.
— 1997. The New FIDIC Provisions for a Dispute Adjudication Board. ICLR 14.
Shafick, Mohsen. Turnkey Contracts, Cairo, Dar El Nahda El Arabia.
Shafick, Mohsen 1973–1974. International Commercial Arbitration. Lecture, Faculty of Law, Cairo University.
Snowdon, Brian 2007. Globalisation, Development and Transition. Conversations with Eminent Economists. Cheltenham, UK. Edward Elgar.
Southard, Katharine 2010. U.S. Electric Utilities: The First Public-Private Partnerships? Cont. L.J. 395 (Winter).
Stanley, Jeremiah, 1995. Insurability of Force Majeure Events in Construction Contracts, ICLR, Part 2 (April).
Stein, Stephen 1994. Build, Operate, Transfer (BOT) – A Re-Evaluation, ICLR 11, Part II.
Stephenson, Douglas A. 1993. Arbitration Practice in Construction Contracts. 3rd edition. London: Spon Press.
Stiglitz, Joseph E. 2004. Globalization and its Discontents. New York: W.W. Norton.
— 2007. Making Globalization Work. New York: W.W. Norton.
Thomas, Christopher S. 1995. Aspects of Building Contracts: A Comparative View of English and French Law in the Light of Potential Harmonization, PhD thesis, School of Law, Kings College London.
Treitel, G.H. 1988. Remedies for Breach of Contract: A Comparative Account. Oxford: Clarendon Press.

— 1994. Frustration and Force Majeure. London: Sweet and Maxwell.
Turner, Dennis F., 1994. Building Contracts, 5th edition. Harlow, Essex, UK: Longman Scientific and Technical.
Uff, John 2009. Construction Law. 10th edition. London: Sweet and Maxwell.
Verveniotis, George 1994. The Concession Agreement Legislation (BOT), Recent Developments. ICLR 11, Part I.
Villa, Leonardo and Duarte, Jesús 2005. Concessionary Public Schools in Bogotá: An Innovation in School Management in Colombia, Private Education and Public Policy in Latin America, ed. Laurence Wolff, Juan Carlos Navarro and Pablo González. Washington, D.C.: Preal.
Waly, Fathy 1986. El Wassit in Civil Law Procedures. Cairo: Dar El Nahda El Arabia.
Wolf, Laurence, 2005. Public Policy and Private Education: Where to Now?, in Private Education and Public Policy in Latin America, ed. Laurence Wolff, Juan Carlos Navarro and Pablo González. Washington D.C.: Preal.
Westring Arlandabonan, Gosta 1997. Swedish Experiment in Selecting a BOT Contractor Using Public Procedures, ICLR 14, Part I.
Wiwatpattarakul, Pronchai n.d. A Critical Examination of the Concept of Force Majeure at Thai Law and Its Impact in the Context of Construction Contracts, ICLR 1.
Yahiel, E. Brown and Cranston, R.M. 1985. Arbitration and Dispute Resolution in the International Construction Industry, ICLR, Vol. 2, Part 3.
Yehia, Abdel Wadood 1987. Obligation Stipulations at Egyptian Civil Law. Cairo: N.p.
— 1989. The General Theory of Obligations, Part I, Sources of Obligations. Cairo: N.p.
Zatezalo-Falator, Milica 2010. Public Private Partnerships in France, State Guarantees Support the Congested Pipeline. Columbia Journal of International Law (Spring). Available at: http://www.cjel.net/online/16_1-zatezalofalatar/ (accessed 31 July 2011). LexisNexis.

Index

For Product Safety Concerns and Information please contact our EU representative GPSR@taylorandfrancis.com Taylor & Francis Verlag GmbH, Kaufingerstraße 24, 80331 München, Germany

Batch number: 10726306

Printed by Printforce, the Netherlands